A Practical Introduction to Security and Risk Management

Bruce Newsome
University of California, Berkeley

Los Angeles | London | New Delhi
Singapore | Washington DC

Los Angeles | London | New Delhi
Singapore | Washington DC

FOR INFORMATION:

SAGE Publications, Inc.
2455 Teller Road
Thousand Oaks, California 91320
E-mail: order@sagepub.com

SAGE Publications Ltd.
1 Oliver's Yard
55 City Road
London EC1Y 1SP
United Kingdom

SAGE Publications India Pvt. Ltd.
B 1/I 1 Mohan Cooperative Industrial Area
Mathura Road, New Delhi 110 044
India

SAGE Publications Asia-Pacific Pte. Ltd.
3 Church Street
#10-04 Samsung Hub
Singapore 049483

Acquisitions Editor: Jerry Westby
Editorial Assistant: MaryAnn Vail
Production Editor: Brittany Bauhaus
Copy Editor: Lana Arndt
Typesetter: C&M Digitals (P) Ltd.
Proofreader: Theresa Kay
Indexer: Diggs Publication Services, Inc.
Cover Designer: Michael Dubowe
Marketing Manager: Terra Schultz

Printed in the United States of America

Library of Congress Cataloging-in-Publication Data

Newsome, Bruce.

A practical introduction to security and risk management : from the global to the personal / Bruce Newsome.

pages cm
Includes bibliographical references and index.

ISBN 978-1-4522-9027-0 (pbk. : alk. paper)
ISBN 978-1-4833-1340-5 (web pdf : alk. paper)
ISBN 978-1-4833-2485-2 (epub : alk. paper)

1. Risk management. 2. Risk assessment. 3. Security systems. I. Title.

HD61.N52 2013
658.4'7—dc23 2013031584

This book is printed on acid-free paper.

SFI label applies to text stock

13 14 15 16 17 10 9 8 7 6 5 4 3 2 1

Brief Contents

Detailed Contents

About the Author

Bruce Newsome, PhD, is Lecturer in International Relations at the University of California, Berkeley. Previously he consulted to governments on security and risk while employed by the RAND Corporation in Santa Monica, California. He earned his undergraduate degree with honors in War Studies from Kings College London, a master's degree in Political Science from the University of Pennsylvania, and a PhD in Strategic Studies from the University of Reading.

PART I

Analyzing and Assessing Security and Risks

The chapters in this part of the book will help you understand, analyze, and assess security and capacity (Chapter 2); risk (Chapter 3); hazards, threats (the sources of negative risks), and contributors (the sources of positive risks) (Chapter 4); target vulnerability and exposure (Chapter 5); probability and uncertainty (Chapter 6); and events and returns (Chapter 7).

In the process, readers will learn how different advocates and authorities contest the definitions, analysis, and assessments, how different activities, operations, and missions face imperfect trade-offs that are exacerbated by poor analysis and assessment, and how some simple rules and practical techniques dramatically improve understanding and functionality.

Introduction: Why Security and Risk Management Matters

What is this book about?

In this book, readers will learn how to understand, analyze, assess, control, and generally manage security and risks from the personal to the operational.

Security, as described in Chapter 2, is, essentially, freedom from negative risks. Risks, as described in Chapter 3, are the potential returns (consequences, effects, etc.) of an event. Risks are inherently uncertain, and many people are uncomfortable with uncertainty, but security and risk management is a practical skill set that anyone can access. Readers of this book do not need to learn theory or many facts but will be introduced to the processes by which security and risks can be managed and to the contexts of many real risks. Readers will be left informed enough to start managing security and risks for themselves or to further investigate the subject.

We all should care about better security and risk management because, if done well, we would live in a more secure and less risky world. Awareness of risk is entirely healthy, because everything we do is literally risky; by simply interacting socially or undertaking any enterprise, "everyone willingly takes risks" (Adams, 1995, p. 16).

Unfortunately, not all security and risk management is conscious or sensible. People tend to obsess about certain risks and ignore others or manage risks in distorted ways that discredit the whole practice of management. Unfortunately, in the past, security management and risk management were routinely separated, with all sorts of disciplinary and professional incompatibilities, but security and risk management are complementary and properly tackled together.

Public expectations for security continue to grow, but sensitivity to certain risks and dissatisfaction with their management also continue to grow. In the last two decades or so, official and private authorities—international institutions, governments, trade associations, general managers, employers, contractors, and employees—have formally required better management and specified how it should be delivered, stimulating more disputes about proper definitions and practices.

This book provides a new practical guide to the proper synthesis of security and risk management.

Private Requirements for Security and Risk Management

Outside of government, private citizens and managers of commercial activities want or are expected to take more responsibility for their own security. For instance, public authorities urge private citizens to prepare for emergencies at home, to consult official advisories before they travel, and to rely less on public protections. Commercial organizations reserve more internal resources or acquire their own protections after finding public protections or private insurers less reliable. Managers of projects, operations, information, acquisitions, and human resources now routinely include security or risk management within their responsibilities. According to Gary Heerkens, "Risk and uncertainty are unavoidable in project life and it's dangerous to ignore or deny their impact . . . Risk management is not just a process—it's a mindset" (2002, pp. 142, 151).

Public Attention to Risk

Security is a primary responsibility of government, which acquires militaries, police forces, coast guards, border protections, health authorities, and various regulators to ensure the security of their territory and citizens. By the 1970s, public authorities managed security and risks mostly in the sense that they managed public safety and controlled crime. For instance, in 1974 the British legislated in favor of a Health and Safety Executive, passed new legislation protecting employees, and increased public entitlements. However, these actions failed to control other risks, such as terrorism, and encouraged inflated views of some risks, such as workplace risks (which have declined), while neglecting other risks, such as sexual risks (which have increased). Even where risks have not increased in any real sense, societies have developed into *risk societies* that show increased sensitivity to risk in general, though they neglect or activate certain hazards, such as environmental hazards, due to misplaced attention to some risks over others (Beck, 1995; Beck, Ritter, & Lash, 1992; Wisner, Blaikie, Cannon, & Davis, 2004, pp. 16–18).

Requirements for Better Management

The increased salience of both security and risk is indicated by the shift in United Nations (UN) operational management from an official objective of *safety and security* to *security risk management* (since 2005), followed by the Humanitarian Practice Network's similar objective (2010). A publicly accessible online tool (http://books.google.com/ngrams) suggests that use in books of the terms *risk*, *security risk*, *international risk*, and *global risk* grew over the last three decades by several orders of magnitude each and peaked around 2006 (the data runs out in 2008).

Increased attention to security and risk does not always produce better management of security and risk. The requirement for wider security management is often met by narrower sets of skills. Requirers could outsource to specialist security or risk management contractors, but some of these providers have betrayed their clients with superficial skills and even ethical or legal violations. For instance, in February 2013, the U.S. Government unveiled a civil lawsuit, following similar suits by several states and the District of Columbia, alleging that a risk rating agency had defrauded investors by supplying ratings of the risks of financial products that were not as independent as the agency had claimed.

Organizations usually lack a manager trained to manage risks across all domains and levels, although general managers may have some training. Organizations often assign corporate responsibilities for risk management to their finance, information, or project managers, who should offer some generalizable skills in security management or risk management, although each domain has peculiar risks and a particular approach. Financial risk management and project risk management are not perfectly transferable and have suffered crises of credibility since the latest global financial crash (2007–2008).

Project risk management is tainted by repeated official and corporate failures to manage the largest acquisition projects. Information managers also often lead corporate risk management, but national governments continue to complain about growing information insecurity. Meanwhile, many corporations are in the habit of hiring former law enforcement or intelligence officials as security or risk managers, but their particular skills usually do not extend to generalizable skills in security and risk management.

Criminologists generally "maintain that security is a subject that has yet to be adequately covered by any specific discipline or in a satisfactory interdisciplinary fashion" (Van Brunschott & Kennedy, 2008, p. 18). Even in practices and professions of relevance (such as policing), security and risk management is not necessarily a focus, as noted in the following:

> The wide array of risk-related concepts shows how deeply embedded these ideas are in our thinking about crime. Yet, relatively little effort has been made to sort out the different meanings of risk and their importance for analyzing criminal events . . . It is also the case, as we will demonstrate, that criminologists have spoken about and understand risk as an element of crime. Interestingly enough, in their discussions of risk, these analysts have tended to treat risk lightly, rarely incorporating it explicitly into their studies of motivation, opportunity, or prevention (although, of course, a large part of the field is attuned to the ideas of risky lifestyles and rational choices based on risk). (Kennedy & Van Brunschot, 2009, pp. 10, 12)

Official Standardization

Some of the dissatisfaction with security and risk management has prompted more standardization, in the hope that the many competing and loosely defined ways in which people manage security and risk can be replaced by the best ways. Standardization is the process of defining standards for behavior and understanding. Standards describe how concepts should be understood and how activities should be performed. Standardization certainly helps interoperability and accountability and may replace inferior practices with superior practices.

Over the last few decades, more international authorities, national authorities, trade associations, and private corporations have developed standard practices for managing risk and security and for describing their management of security and risk to each other. From the late 1980s, after comparisons with the apparently superior performance of the private sector in delivering services or acquiring items as planned, democratic governments started to escalate the importance of risk management and standardized how their agents should manage risks, initially mostly in the context of the acquisition of capabilities. For instance, in 1989 the U.S. Defense Systems Management College issued guidance on risk management. In 1992, the British Ministry of Defense (MOD) started to issue *risk guidelines*. In both cases, the emphasis was on defense acquisitions.

In 1995, the Australian and New Zealand Governments issued their first binational risk management standard, which was adopted by or influenced many other governments, including the British, Canadian, and U.S. Governments. However, the latter three governments continue to negotiate between international standards and departmental standards, effectively negotiating between those who prescribe one standard and those who prefer decentralized choice. In a large government, specialized departments can justify different effective standards, but differences interfere with coordination, and some standards can be inferior, not just different. Some of the highest departments still contest basic concepts of security and risk, with consequences for assessments and treatments on the scale of billions of dollars. The United Kingdom, Canada, and the United States have dealt with enormous risks and intercepted some spectacular threats but continue to reveal inadequacies in their security and risk management, most observably during the management of defense, homeland security, information security, and diplomatic security.

All three governments are disproportionately involved in building the capacity of foreign governments, but most governments have effectively elevated the Australian/New Zealand standard for risk management to a common standard of which new versions were published in 1999, 2004, and November 2009, the last version endorsed by the International Organization for Standardization (ISO). In practice, subscribing departments often adapt the standard for their own purposes and have struggled with parts of the standard, but at least they have a common source.

In the United States, any of the Government Accountability Office (GAO), Department of Homeland Security (DHS), Department of Defense (DOD), or Department of Treasury could be the U.S. Government's center of excellence for security or risk management. Even the Congressional Research Service has taken a role in critiquing and thence developing how departments manage security and risk. The Federal Bureau of Investigations (FBI) and Central Intelligence Agency (CIA) and the rest of the *intelligence community* have plenty at stake in security, not to mention other authorities at state, city, and local levels. These departments and their agencies, bureaus, and offices tend to internal standardization but are often in dispute. Elected officials have led many investigations and reports on official security and risk management, often with very peculiar understandings of security and risk.

In the Canadian Government, the Department of National Defense and Public Safety Canada (since 2003) are the leading coordinators of military security and civilian risk management, respectively, although other departments lead the management of particular risks. Neither has a mandate to order other departments to manage security or risk in certain ways, although Public Safety Canada issues guidance and encouragement to other departments. Public Safety Canada tends to admit the ISO standard but has adapted parts and continues to adapt it, with primarily British and Dutch influence. The Canadian police forces have no national standard setting authority, although the national association—the Canadian Association of Police Boards—has developed risk policies, and the Canadian Police College teaches risk management to police executive and board members. The Royal Canadian Mounted Police (the federal police service) and the Ontario Provincial Police each has a risk management policy and a risk group. Municipal police forces are governed by provincial laws and overseen by police boards or commissions, none of which has standardized risk management, although some, such as those in Edmonton, Alberta, and Toronto, have formal risk management policies and practices.

In 1997, the British Treasury, under the direction of the Cabinet Office, published guidance that required the government to assess the risks of all project and program options and specifically warned against past overoptimism. Before the year was out, the Treasury required statements on Internal Financial Control (which official commissions had recommended to commercial companies in previous years) from all departments starting fiscal year 1998 to 1999 and issued guidance on controlling fraud. In February 2000, the Treasury first circulated guidance on the management of risk for use by all of government; in December, it required from all departments of government by the end of the

2002/2003 fiscal year "a fully embedded system of internal control" of risk (U.K. Treasury, 2004). In August 2000, the National Audit Office (NAO) issued best practices gathered from mostly the private sector; in November, the British Standards Institution (BSI) published its guidance on *corporate governance* and *internal control*. Also in 2000, the MOD mandated both a risk management plan and a risk management strategy to its own standards for all acquisitions projects. By the 2000s, official efforts refocused on increased hazards like weather storms, diseases, and terrorists. In July 2001, the British government established the Civil Contingencies Secretariat, responsible for business continuity across government and for policy for planning the response to national emergencies. The Prime Minister's Office (2002) published as policy a declaration that risk management is "central to the business of government." In 2004, the Treasury (p. 9) reminded government that "[r]isk is unavoidable, and every organization needs to take action to manage risk in a way which it can justify to a level which is tolerable." The Treasury reported that "government organizations now have basic risk management processes in place" (2004, p. 11) but stopped short of standardization across government. Even though the British executive formally advocated more international cooperation in the assessment and management of international risks (Strategy Unit, 2005, p. 15), it has not formally adopted international standardization. The British Standards Institution and private British organizations have published standards for simultaneous private and public use but generally conform with the ISO (see: Association of Insurance and Risk Managers, ALARM The National Forum for Risk Management in the Public Sector, & the Institute of Risk Management [AIRMIC, ALARM, and IRM], 2002, and BSI, 2000 and 2009), while the government has endorsed none for use government wide.

Benefits of Good Management

Security and risk management (at least when performed well) offers benefits: it improves security, strategy, resource allocation, planning, communications and transparency, and thereby confidence. The NAO sought to transfer commercial practices to government with the following promise:

> Risk management can help departments improve their performance in a number of ways. It can lead to better service delivery, more efficient use of resources, better project management, help minimize waste, fraud and poor value for money, and promote innovation. (2000, p. 4)

The Australian/New Zealand standard promised the following example benefits:

1. Increased likelihood of achieving objectives;
2. Proactive management;
3. Awareness of the need to identify and treat risk throughout the organization;
4. Improved identification of opportunities and threats;
5. Compatibility of practices;
6. Compliance with relevant legal and regulatory requirements and norms;
7. Improved financial reporting;
8. Improved governance;

9. Improved stakeholder confidence and trust;
10. Reliable base for decision making and planning;
11. Improved controls;
12. More effective allocation and use of resources for controlling risks;
13. Improved operational effectiveness and efficiency;
14. Enhanced health, safety, and environmental protection;
15. Improved management of incidents;
16. Reduced losses;
17. Improved organizational learning;
18. Improved organizational resilience. (2009, pp. iv–v)

One private study found that Fortune 1,000 companies with more advanced management of their property risks produced earnings that were 40% less volatile, while the other companies were 29 times more likely to lose property and suffered 7 times costlier losses due to natural causes (F.M. Global, 2010, p. 3).

This Book

The aim of this book is to give practical knowledge of and practical skills in the management of security and risk. The managerial skill set is practical, with analytical skills in understanding the sources of risk, some basic mathematical methods for calculating risk in different ways, and more artistic skills in making judgments and decisions about which risks to control and how to control them.

This book introduces the skills and gives the reader different tools and methods to choose from. These skills are multilevel and interdisciplinary. Readers are shown not only, for instance, how to defend themselves against terrorists but also how to identify strategies for terminating the causes of terrorism or to co-opt political spoilers as allies.

In this book, readers will learn how to

- understand, analyze, and assess security and risk;
- understand and analyze the sources of risk, including hazards, threats, and contributors;
- understand and analyze the potential targets by their exposure and vulnerability;
- understand and assess uncertainty and probability;
- understand and assess the potential returns of an event;
- develop an organization's culture, structure, and processes congruent with better security and risk management;
- establish risk sensitivity and tolerability and understand the difference between real risk and perceived risk;
- control risks and select different strategies for managing risks;

- record, communicate, review, and audit risk management; and
- improve security in primary domains, including
  - operations and logistics,
  - physical sites,
  - information, communications, and cyber space,
  - ground, air, and maritime transportation, and
  - personal security.

Part 1 describes how to analyze security and assess security and risks back to the causes and sources through the relevant concepts: security and incapacity (Chapter 2), risk (Chapter 3), hazards, threats, and contributors (Chapter 4), target exposure and vulnerability (Chapter 5), uncertainty and probability (Chapter 6), and returns (Chapter 7).

Part 2 describes how to manage security and risk, including the development of or choice between different cultures, structures, and processes (Chapter 8), establishing tolerability and sensitivity levels (Chapter 9), controlling and strategically responding to risks (Chapter 10), and recording, communicating, reviewing, assuring, and auditing risk and security (Chapter 11).

The third and final part introduces ways to improve security in the main domains: operational and logistical security (Chapter 12); physical (site) security (Chapter 13); information, communications, and cyber security (Chapter 14); transport security (Chapter 15); and personal security (Chapter 16).

Security and Capacity

This chapter's two main sections describe, respectively, security and capacity, which is often conflated with security but is not the same. Readers will learn how to define, analyze, and assess both concepts.

 Security

This section concerns security. The subsections below first define security, explain how security is described at different levels, describe the main academic and official domains of security (including national security, homeland security, international security, and human security), and describe how to assess security.

Defining Security

Security is the absence of risks. Thus, security can be conceptualized as the inverse of risk and any of its sources or associated causes, including threats, hazards, exposure, or vulnerability (all of which are defined in subsequent chapters).

Security as a term is often used in combination or interchangeably with safety, defense, protection, invulnerability, or capacity, but each is a separate concept, even though each has implications for the other. For instance, safety implies temporary sanctuary rather than real security, while defense implies resistance but does not guarantee security.

Pedagogy Box 2.1 Definitions of Security

Unofficial

According to semantic analysts, security is "the state of being or feeling secure," and being *secure* means that we are "certain to remain safe and unthreatened" (https://framenet.icsi.berkeley.edu). For criminologists, "[s]ecurity is the outcome of managing risk in the face of a variety of harms . . . [or] freedom from danger, fear, or anxiety" (Van Brunschot & Kennedy, 2008, p. 10). For the Humanitarian Practice Network (2010, p. xviii) *security* is "freedom from risk or harm resulting from violence or other intentional acts" while *safety* is "freedom from risk or harm as a result of unintentional acts (accidents, natural phenomenon, or illness)."

North Atlantic Treaty Organization (NATO)

Security is "the condition achieved when designated information, material, personnel, activities, and installations are protected against espionage, sabotage, subversion, and terrorism, as well as against loss or unauthorized disclosure." A *safe area* is "in peace support operations, a secure area in which NATO or NATO-led forces protect designated persons and/or property." The *defense area* is "the area extending from the forward edge of the battle area to its rear boundary. It is here that the decisive battle is fought" (NATO, 2008).

United States

For the Department of Defense, security is "measures taken by a military unit, activity, or installation to protect itself against all acts designed to, or which may, impair its effectiveness; a condition that results from the establishment and maintenance of protective measures that ensure a state of inviolability from hostile acts of influences." The DOD dictionary does not define *safety*, *public safety*, *defense*, or *defense area*. A *safe area* is "a designated area in hostile territory that offers the evader or escapee a reasonable chance of avoiding capture and of surviving until he or she can be evacuated." *Civil defense* is "all those activities and measures designed or undertaken to: minimize the effects upon the civilian population caused or which would be caused by an enemy attack on the United States; deal with the immediate emergency conditions that would be created by any such attack; and effectuate emergency repairs to, or the emergency restoration of, vital utilities and facilities destroyed or damaged by any such attack" (U.S. DOD, 2012b, pp. 39, 275).

Canada

The Canadian government has no official definition of *security* but the *Policy on Government Security* (effective July 2009) defines *government security* as "the assurance that information, assets and services are protected against compromise and individuals are protected against workplace violence. The extent to which government can ensure its own security directly affects its ability to ensure the continued delivery of services that contribute to the health, safety, economic well-being, and security of Canadians."

Public Safety Canada's internal *Security Policy* includes an effective operational definition of security: "Security implies a stable, relatively predictable environment in which an individual or group may pursue its objectives without disruption or harm, or without fear of disturbance or injury." Public Safety Canada defines *public safety* as "the protection of all citizens by implementing measures that safeguard national security, improve emergency management, combat crime, and promote community safety" (Public Safety Canada, 2012, p. 76).

The Canadian Army's glossary defines *defense* as "the operations undertaken to prevent the enemy from seizing terrain or breaking through into a defended area."

Britain

The UK MOD (November 2009, p. 6) uses the term *security* "to describe the combination of human and national security." "Defense and security are linked, but different, concepts. Defense primarily refers to states and alliances resisting physical attack by a third party. Defense is about the survival of the state and is not a discretionary activity. Security is a contested concept that can never be absolute. It is, therefore, to some extent, discretionary. It implies freedom from threats to core values both for individuals and groups. The decline in the incidence of inter-state war and the emergence of transnational threats, especially in the developed world, has resulted in greater political emphasis being placed on security rather than defense. Moreover, security has gradually evolved from the concepts of national and international security to the idea of human security" (UK MOD, January 2010, p. 76).

Levels

Security has many levels: a useful scale would run through the personal, local, provincial, national (sovereign government), trans-national (across sovereign states without involving sovereign governments), international (between sovereign governments), and supra-national (higher authority than sovereign governments).

Within the state: Britain recognizes national, regional, and local levels; the United States recognizes federal, state, city, and local levels of government; and Canada recognizes federal, provincial, and local government.

An academic analysis of crime used three levels (state, institution, and individual), although presumably we could add international crime (Kennedy & Van Brunschot, 2009, p. 8).

Increasingly, the authors recognize that the levels and domains are so interconnected or codependent that security managers need broad knowledge and awareness:

> Security is not the exclusive purview of state, or of institutional or individual actors, but rather depends on the intersection of these levels. These intersections are not necessarily hierarchical—individuals may undermine institutional security, just as institutions may undermine individual security. (Van Brunschot & Kennedy, 2008, p. 19)

Domains

Security crosses many domains. A student is most likely to study security in disciplines like criminology and policing (in courses or fields entitled *crime and justice*, *transnational crime*, *public safety*, and *public security*), health and medicine (*public health* and *health security*), economics, political economy, or development studies (*economic security*), political science and international studies (*national security*, *international security*, *peace and conflict*, *war studies*, and *peace studies*), and military or defense studies (*strategic studies*, *security studies*, *security management*, *defense management*, and *military science*). Some courses (*counter-terrorism* and *homeland security*) are so truly interdisciplinary that they could be taught in any of these disciplines.

Consequently, security is studied, at least implicitly, by a mix of disciplines, fields, and subfields, some of them ambiguous or contested. Many people fret about insecurity but have disciplinary biases or formative experiences that constrain their study of security, while security crosses the domains that academic disciplines and professional careers have tended to separate. Van Brunschott and Kennedy note this crossover of domains:

> Studying security is a multidisciplinary project. It is not possible to think about security without recognizing that boundaries between realms such as health, crime, and the environment, for example, are often blurred, both in theory and in practice. This means that we must draw on a number of different fields of study to make sense of how balancing risk leads to security (or insecurity). While the primary target of much of the work on security has been criminal justice agencies, particularly law enforcement, the issues raised in addressing hazards from health and natural disasters include public health officials, engineers, scientists, and others . . . Although we bring to the project our backgrounds in sociology and criminology, we maintain that security is a subject that has yet to be adequately covered by a specific discipline or in a satisfactory interdisciplinary fashion. Furthermore, concerns over security are never far from issues that pervade the public and private domains. While public health officials might concern themselves with flu epidemics and other transmissible diseases, for example, the goal of keeping populations healthy is ultimately a national and, increasingly, a global security issue for a vulnerable segment of the population, it also secures the public health system by alleviating it from having to deal with the expenditures incurred if such epidemics were to occur. (2008, pp. 17–18)

For most people, domains of concern include operational (Chapter 12), physical/site (Chapter 13), information, communications, and cyber (Chapter 14), transport (Chapter 15), and personal security (Chapter 16). The higher domains that concern everybody from the international to the personal level are national security, homeland security, international security, and human security, as described in the subsections below.

National Security

United States

The United States has institutionalized *national security* more than any other state, particularly in 1947 with the National Security Act, which established a National Security Council and National Security Adviser to the executive. For the DOD (2012b, p. 216), national security encompasses "both national defense and foreign relations of the United States" and is "provided by a military or defense advantage over any foreign nation or group of nations, a favorable foreign relations position, or a defense posture capable of successfully resisting hostile or destructive action from within or without, overt or covert."

Many internationalists and foreigners consider national security an inaccurate and possibly xenophobic concept, especially given increasingly international and transnational threats. In practice, most Americans use *national security* and international security interchangeably or to describe the same domains whenever politically convenient, while the newer term of *homeland security* has supplanted *national security*.

Canada

In 2003, the Canadian government established a Minister and a Department of Public Safety and Emergency Preparedness (Public Safety Canada). Public Safety Canada, as legislated in 2005, is not defined by national or homeland security, but is responsible for only domestic civilian authorities: the correctional service, parole board, firearms center, border services, the federal police, and the security intelligence service.

In April 2004, the Canadian government released its first National Security Policy (*Securing an Open Society*), which specified three core national security interests:

1. Protecting Canada and the safety and security of Canadians at home and abroad
2. Ensuring Canada is not a base for threats to our allies
3. Contributing to international security (Public Safety Canada, 2013).

The National Security Policy aimed at a more integrated security system and declared objectives in six key areas:

1. intelligence,
2. emergency planning and management,
3. public health emergencies,
4. transportation security,
5. border security, and
6. international security (Public Safety Canada, 2013).

The resulting institutional changes included the establishment of a National Security Advisory Council, an advisory Cross-Cultural Roundtable on Security, and an Integrated Threat Assessment Center.

In 2006, Public Safety Canada and the Department of National Defense (DND) created the Canadian Safety & Security Program "to strengthen Canada's ability to anticipate, prevent/mitigate, prepare for, respond to, and recover from natural disasters, serious accidents, crime and terrorism" (Public Safety Canada, 2013)—a scope more like American *homeland security*, although no department of Canada's government has any definition of homeland security.

The federal government still lacks a federal definition of either *security* or *national security*, although the Defense Terminology Standardization Board defines *national security* as "the condition achieved through the implementation of measures that ensure the defense and maintenance of the social, political and economic stability of a country" (Public Safety Canada, 2011, p. D.2). DND recognizes *national security* as counterterrorism, infrastructure security, cyber-security, and public safety and security generally—but not civilian border security (which falls under national *law enforcement*, for which the leading responsibility is Public Safety Canada) or military defense of Canada's borders or foreign interests. The *Policy on Government Security* (effective July 2009) defines the *national interest* as "the defense and maintenance of the social, political, and economic stability of Canada" (Public Safety Canada, 2011, p. D.2). Subsequently, Public Safety Canada has defined its mission "to ensure coordination across all federal departments and agencies responsible for national security and the safety of Canadians" (2013).

Britain

In 2008, the British government published its first *National Security Strategy*. In May 2010, a new political administration, on its first day, established a National Security Council (a committee to the Cabinet) and appointed a National Security Adviser. The Cabinet Office (2013) defines the National Security Council as "a coordinating body, chaired by the Prime Minister, to integrate the work of the foreign, defense, home, energy, and international development departments, and all other arms of government contributing to national security." Unfortunately, the Cabinet Office does not define national security. The UK MOD (2009, p. 6) defines national security as "the traditional understanding of security as encompassing 'the safety of a state or organization and its protection from both external and internal threats.'"

Homeland Security

United States

Justified mostly as a response to the international terrorist attacks of September 11, 2001 (9/11), on September 20, 2001, President George W. Bush announced that by Executive Order he would establish an Office of Homeland Security within the White House. The actual order (13228) was issued on October 8. The Office was established under the direction of Tom Ridge, formerly Governor of Pennsylvania, with few staff and no budget for distribution. The Homeland Security Act of November 25, 2002, established, effective January 2003, the Department of Homeland Security (DHS), which absorbed 22 prior agencies—the largest reorganization of U.S. government since the establishment of the Department of Defense in 1949.

In the first executive order, in many executive justifications, and in popular understanding, homeland security was equated with counter-terrorism, but counter-terrorism was always a minor part of departmentalized homeland security. Before 9/11, 46 federal agencies had some counter-terrorist responsibilities, according to the Congressional Research Service at the time (Perl, 2002, p. 9). The DHS absorbed few of them. Then, as now, U.S. counter-terrorism is conducted mostly by the intelligence agencies, the military services, the Federal Bureau of Investigation, and state and local law enforcement agencies, all of which lie outside of the DHS, although they coordinate. Most of the DHS' subordinate departments and activities manage border security, immigration, tariffs and customs, security within American waters, the security of infrastructure, natural risks, and emergencies in general.

The Executive Order of October 8, 2001, also created the Homeland Security Council (HSC) "to develop and coordinate the implementation of a comprehensive national strategy to secure the United States from terrorist threats or attacks" (Gaines & Kappeler, 2012).The HSC was almost the same as the

NSC, so the change attracted criticism. "The creation of the HSC essentially bifurcated the homeland security process: there were now two agencies reporting to the President that had policy authority over national security issues" (Gaines & Kappeler, 2012, p. 209). In May 2009, President Barack Obama merged the staff of the NSC and HSC, although their separate statutes remain.

On March 21, 2002, Bush signed an Executive Order (13260) that established the President's Homeland Security Advisory Council with a membership of no more than 21 people, selected from the private sector, academia, officials, and nongovernmental organizations. The Order also established four Senior Advisory Committees for Homeland Security: State and Local Officials; Academia and Policy Research; Private Sector; and Emergency Services, Law Enforcement, and Public Health and Hospitals.

Bush sought stronger executive powers, partly in the name of homeland security. On September 24, he announced the Uniting and Strengthening America by Providing Appropriate Tools Required to Intercept and Obstruct Terrorism Bill. This became the USA PATRIOT Act, which Congress approved with little deliberation (normally a bill of such length and consequence would be debated for years). The President signed it into law on October 26. The Act was long and conflated many issues but primarily increased the government's surveillance and investigative powers in order to "deter and punish terrorist acts in the United States and around the world" (Public Law 107–56, 2001).

On October 29, Bush issued the first Homeland Security Presidential Directive (HSPD). He would issue a total of 25 before leaving office in January 2009; during his two terms, he issued 66 National Security Presidential Directives, almost all of them after 9/11.

From 2001 to 2008, according to Google Ngram (http://books.google.com/ngrams), use of the term *homeland security* has risen from relative obscurity to surpass use of *national security*.

Canada

Public Safety Canada is formally defined by public safety and emergency preparedness (since 2003) and national security (since 2006) rather than homeland security, but its responsibilities include the national agencies for emergency management and border security, which in the United States fall under DHS. Public Safety Canada is responsible for criminal justice and intelligence, too, which in the United States fall outside of the DHS.

Britain

The British government has considered a department of homeland security but continues to departmentalize home, foreign, intelligence, and military policies separately. The Home Office is closest to a department of homeland security; it is officially described as "the lead government department for immigration and passports, drugs policy, counter-terrorism and policing" (Cabinet Office, 2013).

International Security

Most American political scientists acknowledge a field called *international relations*; some recognize a subfield called *international security*. The American Political Science Association recognizes *international security and arms control* as a "section." However, for ethical and practical reasons, the study of *international security* is not universally acknowledged. This is why Richard Betts advocated a subfield of international relations called *international politico-military* studies, which implies parity with other subfields such as *international political economy* (Betts, 1997). Some advocates of *international security* use it to encompass military, economic, social, and environmental hazards (Buzan, 1991).

In the 1980s and 1990s, increased recognition of globalization and transnationalism helped to drive attention toward international security, but use of the term *international security* has declined steadily since its peak in 1987, despite a small hump from 1999 to 2001, while use of *homeland security* has increased commensurately (http://books.google.com/ngrams).

Human Security

The United Nations and many governments and nongovernmental organizations recognize human security (freedom from fear or want). In 1994, the UN Development Program published its annual report (*Human Development*) with a reconceptualization of human security as freedom from fear or want across seven domains:

1. Economic security;
2. Food security;
3. Health security;
4. Environmental security;
5. Personal security;
6. Community security;
7. Political security (human rights).

In 2001, Japan initiated the international Commission on Human Security. In May 2003, it published *Human Security Now*, which asserted human freedoms from pervasive hazards such as pandemic diseases. In May 2004, the UN Office for the Coordination of Humanitarian Affairs (OCHA, 2003) created a Human Security Unit. It defines *human security* as "a concept concerned with the security of individuals and promoting the protection of individuals' physical safety, economic and social well-being, human dignity, and human rights and fundamental freedoms."

Human security grew as a valued concept particularly among those who work on international or global development and humanitarian affairs. It is now included in military doctrines for stabilization, counterinsurgency, and counterterrorism after excessive focus on homeland security and national security in the 2000s. For instance, in the context of counter-terrorism, human security has been defined as "freedom from fear or want for individuals or populations in terms of physical, economic, political, cultural and other aspects of security/absence of threat" (Beyer, 2008, p. 63).

Pedagogy Box 2.2 Human Security and British Military Stabilization Operations

"Security has traditionally been understood as National Security, concerning itself with territorial integrity and the protection of the institutions and interests of the state from both internal and external threats. However, increasingly, the understanding of security has been broadened to include the notion of Human Security, which emphasizes the protection of individuals who seek safety and security in their daily lives. Human security encompasses freedom from fear of persecution, intimidation, reprisals, terrorism and other forms of systematic violence as well as freedom from want of immediate basic needs such as food, water, sanitation, and shelter. Importantly, where the state lacks the ability to meet the human security needs of the population individuals tend to transfer loyalty to any group that promises safety and protection, including irregular actors. Of note:

- There are obvious overlaps between national and human security. For example, the presence and activities of violent groups both exacerbates the fragility of the state and undermines the safety and security of the people.
- A stable state must protect the most basic survival needs of both itself and its people. This includes the provision of human security for the population in addition to the control of territory, borders, key assets, and sources of revenue.
- A stable state exists within a regional context. As such it may import or export instability across its borders. Security issues that are outside of a host nation's direct influence will require regional political engagement." (UK MOD, 2009, p. 6)

Assessing Security

In assessing security, we could measure security as the inverse of the risks (Chapter 3), the hazards and threats (Chapter 4), or our exposure and vulnerability (Chapter 5). The choice between these options will depend on our available time and interest in a deeper assessment and the availability and our confidence in the data.

Subjectively, we could ask stakeholders how secure they feel or ask experts how secure something is. For instance, an important measure of the effectiveness of the criminal justice system is to ask the public how secure they feel. Ultimately, if the public does not feel more secure, the criminal justice authorities are failing, either to reduce crime or to persuade the public that security really has improved. Having said that, we must also realize some adjustments might need to be made for inaccurate cultural or social sensitivities (see Chapter 9), such as anti-police biases.

If the effectiveness of criminal justice were to be measured as simply the rate of crime, the authorities would be incentivized to report fewer crimes, or categorize crimes as less serious than they really were, whatever the real rate of crime. Moreover, crime rates can fall when the public adjusts to crime, such as by refusing to leave home, which would reduce public exposure to crime but would not be evidence for success in fighting crime.

Consequently, we should measure security by both crime rate and public perceptions of security and not assume that the crime rate is the superior measure just because events are more tangible than perceptions.

Capacity

This section defines capacity, explains the varying fungibility of different capacities, how capacity is traded with security, and how capacity (and thence security) tends to distribute inequitably.

Defining Capacity

Capacity is the potential to achieve something. Different capacities include the potentials to, for instance, acquire capabilities or deliver performance. When we identify capacity, we should define also what the capacity might be converted into, because capacities might be useful for one thing but not another. For instance, one organization's capacity for self-defense is different from another organization's capacity for investigation of crime.

Pedagogy Box 2.3 Definitions of Capacity

Unofficial

Capacity is "the ability or power to do something" (https://framenet.icsi.berkeley.edu). Incapacity is "the characteristics of a person or group and their situation that influence their capacity to anticipate, cope with, resist, and recover from the impact" (Wisner, Blaikie, Cannon, & Davis, 2004, pp. 11–13).

UN

Capacity is "a combination of all the strengths and resources available within a community, society, or organization that can be used to achieve agreed goals. Comment: Capacity may include infrastructure and physical means, institutions, societal coping abilities, as well as human knowledge, skills, and collective attributes such as social relationships, leadership, and management. Capacity also may be described as capability. Capacity assessment is a term for the process by which the capacity of a group is reviewed against desired goals, and the capacity gaps are identified for further action."

Coping capacity is "the ability of people, organizations, and systems, using available skills and resources, to face and manage adverse conditions, emergencies, or disasters" (UN Office of International Strategy for Disaster Reduction, 2009, pp. 2, 4).

Britain

"Capacity reflects the extent to which a country can absorb or manage a risk factor and take advantage of external stabilization." *Executive capacity* is "the ability of the state to deliver key functions," such as public health, education, and security (UK Strategy Unit, 2005, p. 38).

The Fungibility of Capacity

Since capacity is the potential for something, it must be converted into something else to be useful, but different forms of capacity are fungible into some things but not others. Financial capital is the most fungible form of capacity, since it can be spent on the defenses or actions that would control risks or counter threats. Within political units, economic capacity is the focus, because the economy can be a source of revenues and technologies and expertise that could be converted into other things. Declining, unstable, or inequitable economies suggest incapacity. For instance, in September 2012, the World Economic Forum surveyed more than 1,000 experts on global risks. Those experts ranked potential wealth gaps (severe income disparity) followed by unsustainable government debt (chronic fiscal imbalances) as the top two global risks, mostly because these risks suggest potential incapacity for controlling other risks, such as climate change (the third-ranked global risk) (World Economic Forum, 2013).

Some capacity remains somewhat fungible even after conversion into more specialized forms. For instance, military organizations are required for defense against major violent threats and are acquired with expensively trained personnel and specialized equipment but often are mobilized to rescue citizens from natural disasters, too.

By contrast, some capacities are so particular that they cannot be converted into much else. For instance, a state's built infrastructure, such as an airport, is expensive and practically not fungible. In an emergency, a road could be closed to road traffic and temporarily used to store assets or to accept aircraft, but is not convertible into a sea port or a power station, for instance. The underlying land can change use, but the infrastructure built on the land usually must be demolished before a change of use, and little material would be reusable.

Trading Capacity and Security

Increased capacity suggests the potential for increased security, but capacity and security are not the same: capacity needs to be converted or translated into security. Just being wealthy is not the same as being secure, although being wealthy suggests that we have the capacity to acquire defenses. Strategically, we would want to hold some capacity ready to convert it into controls on emerging risks; however, we would not want to hold all our capacity without converting some of it into controls because then we would not be controlling any risks. Thus, the achievement of security is an imperfect trade-off between capacity and security—between capacity reserved against emerging risks and capacity converted into controls on current risks.

Self-satisfaction about our capacity would be regrettable if we were to fail to convert that capacity into a required control on some intolerable risk, perhaps because we had failed to realize the risk or the control. For instance, before 9/11, the U.S. Government certainly failed to adequately control the increasing risks associated with religious terrorism, even though many persons (for instance: Hoffman, 2001), within and without the U.S. Government, had warned of increasing trends toward religiosity, lethal intent, capability, lethality, and anti-Americanism in terrorism. After 9/11, the U.S. Government converted colossal capacity into counter-terrorist, homeland security, defense, and military capabilities. Less capacity would have been required to control the risks when they were emerging than after they had emerged.

The Distribution of Capacity

In theory, incapacity suggests insecurity. In practice, small declines in capacity can lead to dramatic, nonlinear declines in security. In absolute terms, people without sufficient capacity do not have the potential to counter anything. Incapacity tends to correlate with exposure, vulnerability, and other concepts suggestive of insecurity, and these things to be highly interrelated. People who are poor or marginalized are more likely to be exposed to threats by living or working in dangerous areas, to lack defenses against threats, to lack the capacity to change their situation or recover from threats, and to lack official support. For instance, very poor people cannot afford to live except in infertile or highly hazardous areas, where they cannot build food reserves or protect themselves against natural disasters and such areas may be too remote from central official services to expect help.

Relative incapacity suggests a dramatic, nonlinear jump in the negative returns of an event. People with capacity can acquire the various controls that dramatically lower the risks, so when a negative event, such as an earthquake, occurs, negative returns are controlled to survivable levels. Conversely, people with incapacity cannot acquire any of those controls, so when the same event occurs for them, the negative returns are many times higher—they suffer a disaster or catastrophe.

Consequently, for some people, their exposure, vulnerability, and incapacity interact as very high risks of many types, while for others the risks are less numerous and lower in magnitude. Normally, risk does not distribute linearly across the population; instead, one large part of the population faces much greater risks than the other part (often a privileged minority) (Wisner, Blaikie, Cannon, & Davis, 2004, pp. 11–13).

Without outside help, the gap between those with capacity and those without tends to be stable or even grow, because negative risks most affect those without capacity and thereby reduce their capacity further. Consequently, many governments advocate interventions to improve the capacity of the deprived, particularly at the time of any intervention to recover from a negative event: "There is a strong relationship between long-term sustainable recovery and prevention and mitigation of future disasters. Recovery efforts should be conducted with a view towards disaster risk reduction" (Public Safety Canada, 2012, p. 78).

SUMMARY

This chapter has

- defined security,
- explored the analytical levels of security,
- reviewed the academic fields and functional domains of security, including national security, homeland security, international security, and human security,
- introduced the general principles of assessing security,
- defined capacity,
- explained how some types of capacity are more fungible,
- explained how capacity and security are traded off, and
- described how capacity distributes inequitably, usually for socio-political reasons.

QUESTIONS AND EXERCISES

1. What is the difference between security, safety, and defense?
2. Give examples of levels of security within a sovereign state.
3. Explain the difference between international security and national security.
4. How could a critic think of international security and national security as misleading?
5. What is the difference between national security and homeland security?
6. How have some governments departmentalized national security differently or similarly to how others have departmentalized homeland security?

7. Why is security interdisciplinary?
8. Why could the crime rate be a misleading measure of security?
9. What is the difference between security and capacity?
10. When would we not want to convert capacity into security?
11. Why would an authority be mistaken to assess its security by its capacity?
12. Why might one minority group within a state have much less capacity than another minority group?
13. Refer to how the domains of national security, homeland security, international security, and human security were described earlier in this chapter. In any of these domains, identify examples of capacity and defense.

Risk

This chapter defines risk, explains how usefully to describe a particular risk, explains how risks are categorized, introduces different statistical calculations of risk, and describes how to analyze and assess risks.

Defining a Risk

At most basic, risks are the potential returns from an event, where the returns are any changes, effects, consequences, and so on, of the event (see Chapter 7 for more on returns and events). As some potential event becomes more likely or the returns of that event become more consequential, the higher becomes the risk. Realizing risk as a resultant of these two vectors makes risk more challenging but also more useful than considering either alone.

Taken alone, either the likelihood or the return would be an unreliable indicator of the risk. For instance, in Table 3.1 the most likely scenario is the least risky (scenario 3); the scenario offering the highest return (scenario 1) is not the riskiest; the riskiest scenario (scenario 2) has neither the highest probability nor the highest return.

Risk is often conflated with other things, but is conceptually separate from the event, the threat that causes the event, and any other cause or source. Such conceptual distinctions help the analyst to clarify the risk, principally by tracing its sources through the process to potential returns. You could be certain about the threat or certain about what the returns would be if a threat were to cause a certain event but uncertain about the probability of the threat acting to cause that event. Similarly, I could be certain that a terrorist group means to harm my organization, but I would remain uncertain about the outcomes as long as I am uncertain about how the terrorist group would behave, how my defenders would behave, how effective the group's offensive capabilities would be, how effective my defensive capabilities are, and so on.

Another common semantic error is the use of the phrase "the risk of" to mean "the chance of" something. The *chance of something* amounts to a risk. To speak of *the risk of death* does not make much

Table 3.1 The Likelihood, Return, and Expected Return of Three Notional Scenarios

Scenario	Probability	Return	Expected return
1	10%	$1,500,000	$150,000
2	20%	$1,000,000	$200,000
3	70%	$1,000	$700

sense except as the *chance of death*. When we speak of the *risk* of something, literally we mean the potential returns associated with that thing. For instance, literally the risk of terrorism is the potential returns from terrorism, not the chance of any particular terrorist threat or event.

Pedagogy Box 3.1 Definitions of Risk

Unofficial

Risk is "a measurable uncertainty" (Knight, 1921, p. 26), "a measure of the probability and severity of adverse effects" (Lowrance, 1976), "the potential for unwanted or negative consequences of an event or activity" (Rowe, 1977), "a measurement of the chance of an outcome, the size of an outcome or a combination of both" (Ansell & Wharton, 1992, p. 4), "uncertainty and has an impact" (Carter, Hancock, Morin, & Robins, 1994, p. 16), "the product of the probability and utility of some future event" (Adams, 1995, p. 30), "a measure of the amount of uncertainty that exists" and relates "primarily to the extent of your ability to predict a particular outcome with certainty" (Heerkens, 2002, p. 142), "uncertain effect" (Chapman & Ward, 2003, p. 12), "a scenario followed by a policy proposal for how to prevent this scenario from becoming real" (Rasmussen 2006, p. 2), "an uncertain (generally adverse) consequence of an event or activity with respect to something that humans value" (IRGC, 2008, p. 4), or "the likelihood and potential impact of encountering a threat" (Humanitarian Practice Network, 2010, p. xviii).

Semantic analysis sometimes "frames" a concept as an actor, action, and object in some context. "The 'risk' frame crucially involves two notions—chance and harm" (Fillmore & Atkins, 1992, p. 80). Therefore, risk is "the possibility that something unpleasant will happen" or "a situation which puts a person in danger" (https://framenet.icsi.berkeley.edu).

United Nations

Risk is the "expected losses (of lives, persons injured, property damaged, and economic activity disrupted) due to a particular hazard for a given area and reference period. Based on mathematical calculations, risk is the product of hazard and vulnerability" (UN DHA, 1992). Risk is "the combination of the probability of an event and its negative consequences" (UN ISDR, 2009, p. 11).

Australia/New Zealand and International Organization for Standardization (ISO)

Up to 2009, the Australian/New Zealand standard had defined risk as "the chance of something happening that will have an impact on objectives." From 2009, it joined with the ISO to define risk as the "effect of uncertainty on objectives," which is "often expressed in terms of a combination of the consequences of an event (including changes in circumstances) and the associated likelihood of occurrence." "Organizations of any kind face internal and external factors and influences that make it uncertain whether, when[,] and the extent to which they will achieve or exceed their objectives. The effect this uncertainty has on the organization's objectives is 'risk'" (A/NZ, 2009, pp. iv, 1; ISO, 2009a, pp. 1–2).

Britain

Influenced by the Australian/New Zealand standards, the British Standards Institution (2000, p. 11) defined risk as a "chance of something happening that will have an impact upon objectives, measured in terms of likelihood and consequences." Nonetheless, the British government has no government wide definition. The National Audit Office (NAO) found that only 20% of departments (237 responded) of the British government reported a common definition within the department. The NAO defined risk as "something happening that may have an impact on the achievement of objectives as this is most likely to affect service delivery for citizens" (NAO, 2000, p. 1). The Treasury (2004, p. 49) defined risk as "uncertainty of outcome" and "combination of likelihood and impact." For the British Civil Contingencies Secretariat, risk is a "measure of the significance of a potential emergency in terms of its assessed likelihood and impact" (Cabinet Office, February 2013).

The Ministry Of Defense (2004, p. 3.4) has defined risk as "the chance of something going wrong or of the Department missing an opportunity to gain a benefit" (JSP525, May 2004: chapter 3, paragraph 4) and later (January 2010, p. 6) as "the consequences of the outcomes and how they could manifest themselves and affect defense business." "Military risk [is] the probability and implications of an event of potentially substantive positive or negative consequences taking place" (MOD, November 2009, p. 237).

Canada

Risk is "the combination of the likelihood and the consequences of a specified hazard being realized; refers to the vulnerability, proximity, exposure to hazards, which affects the likelihood of adverse impact" (Public Safety Canada, 2012, p. 81).

United States

Before the institutionalization of homeland security, the Federal Emergency Management Agency (FEMA) was the U.S. Government's effective authority on risk: "Risk means the potential losses associated with a hazard, defined in terms of expected probability and frequency, exposure, and consequences"

(Continued)

(Continued)

(FEMA, 1997, p. xxv). The Department of Homeland Security, which took charge of FEMA in January 2003, defines risk as "the potential for an unwanted outcome resulting from an incident, event, or occurrence, as determined by its likelihood and the associated consequence" (DHS, 2009, p. 111), although in the context of cyber risks a subordinate authority defined risk as "the combination of threat, vulnerability, and mission impact" (Cappelli, Moore, Trzeciak, & Shimeall, 2009, p. 32).

The Government Accountability Office (December 2005, p. 110) defines risk as "an event that has a potentially negative impact and the possibility that such an event will occur and adversely affect an entity's assets, activities, and operations."

The Department Of Defense (2010, p. 269) defines risk as the "probability and severity of loss linked to hazards."

Describing a Risk

A good description of risk helps analysis, recording, shared understanding, and communication. A good qualitative description of a particular risk should include the following:

- the temporal and geographical scope,
- the source of the potential event,
- the potential event,
- the probability of the potential event, and
- the potential event's returns.

This is a notional example of a good description: "Within the next year and the capital city, terrorists likely would attack a public building, causing damage whose costs of repair would range from $1 million to $2 million."

Pedagogy Box 3.2 Different Standards for How to Describe a Risk

The Australian/New Zealand and ISO standards (2009, p. 5) define a *risk description* as "a structured statement of risk containing the following elements: source, events, causes, and consequences." These standards prescribe *risk identification* as the second step in their 7-step process for managing risks. They define risk identification as a "process of finding, recognizing, and describing risks" including "risk sources, events, their causes, and their potential consequences" (see Chapter 8).

The Canadian Government generally follows ISO's guidance and does not define *risk description* but defines a *risk statement* as "a description of a risk, its likelihood, and its impact on any given environment" (Public Safety Canada, 2012, p. 85). Canadian federal guidance prescribes a description of the potential event, the natural environment, the meteorological conditions, and coincident vulnerability (Public Safety Canada and Defense Research & Development Canada, February 2013,

p. 16). The British Government's project risk management standard (PRINCE2®) prescribes a description of risk that includes cause, event, and effect (OGC, 2009).

The International Risk Governance Council (2008, p. 7) prescribes analysis of a risk by the following dimensions:

- degree of novelty (emerging, re-emerging, increasing importance, not yet managed);
- geographical scope;
- range of impacted domains;
- time horizon for analysis;
- time delay between risk and effects;
- hazard (ubiquitous, persistent, irreversible); and
- scientific or technological change (incremental, breakthrough).

A private British standard has prescribed the use of a table (see Table 3.2) in order to encourage a more "structured format" and fuller description of the risk, although readers might realize that this table looks more like a risk register or risk log (see Chapter 11) than a risk description.

Table 3.2 A *Structured Framework* for Describing Risk

1. Name of risk	[name]
2. Scope of risk	Qualitative description of the events, their size, type, number, and dependencies
3. Nature of risk	[category]
4. Stakeholders	Stakeholders and their expectations
5. Quantification of risk	Significance and probability
6. Risk tolerance/appetite	Objectives for control of the risk and performance
7. Risk treatment and control	Primary controls; confidence in existing controls; protocols for monitoring and review
8. Potential action for improvement	Recommendations to reduce risk
9. Strategy and policy developments	Identification of function responsible for developing strategy and policy

SOURCE: AIRMIC, ALARM, IRM, 2002, p. 6.

Categorizing Risks

Risks are routinely categorized by type. Categories help to communicate the scope of the risk, to assign the responsible authority to handle the risk, to understand the causes of the risk, and to suggest strategies for controlling the risk.

The subsections below describe categorizations as negative and positive risks, pure and speculative risks, standard and nonstandard risks, organizational categories, external levels, and higher functional categories.

Pedagogy Box 3.3 Prescriptions for Risk Categories

The Australian/New Zealand standard and ISO (2009a, p. 4) prescribe categorization of risks and list 6 categories (natural and competitive environmental; political; legal and regulatory; economic; socio-cultural; and technological). Similarly, the Canadian government prescribes a "risk taxonomy" — "a comprehensive and common set of risk categories that is used within an organization" (Public Safety Canada, 2012, p. 85). PRINCE2®, the official British project risk management standard, suggests categorizing risks at the end of "risk identification," before the "assessment," and offers 7 categories and 60 sub-categories. Another source on project management listed 10 categories and 64 sub-categories (Heerkens, 2002, p. 146). A typical government department or large commercial organization would identify even more subcategories. The World Economic Forum (in its latest annual report, "Global Risks 2013") identifies 50 global risks across 5 categories (economic, environmental, geopolitical, societal, and technological). By contrast, the International Risk Governance Council (2008, p. 6) recognizes just 4 categories of risk (natural, technological, economic, and environmental). Some project management authorities (such as the Association for Project Management) ignore risk categories entirely.

Negative and Positive Risks

The easiest but most neglected categorization of risk is to distinguish between negative risks (uncertain harm) and positive risks (uncertain benefit).

In general use, the noun *risk* is associated with harm, as in the phrase "a risk that this would happen" (Fillmore & Atkins, 1992, p. 81). The normative conception of risk as negative encourages actors to forget positive risks. Risk managers should remain aware of both positive and negative risks and not use confusing synonyms or conflated concepts to describe these categories. A disciplined analyst should look for potential allies and positive risks, so that, for instance, a government would not look on another country as a nest of negative risks alone and forget the chance of allies, trade, supplies, intelligence, and more. Although risk managers should always consider whether they have forgotten positive risks, in practice most risk managers are concerned with negative risks most of the time. Heerkens notes this below:

> With all due respect to the notion of capitalizing on opportunities, your time will probably be better spent focusing on trying to counteract threats. Experience tells us that you'll encounter many more factors that can make things bad for you than factors that can make things better. (Heerkens, 2002, p. 143)

Pedagogy Box 3.4 Official Conflation of Positive Risks

The reader might think that no responsible official could forget positive risks, but consider that the United Nations International Strategy on Disaster Reduction (2009, p. 11), the Humanitarian Practice Network (2010, p. 28), and the U.S. Government's highest civilian and military authorities on security and risk each define risk as negative (GAO, 2005, p. 110; DOD, December 2012, p. 267). In 2009, the ISO added "potential opportunities" after admitting that its previous guides had addressed only negative risks (p. vii). The word *opportunity* has been used by others to mean anything from positive hazard to positive risk, while the word *threat* has been used to mean everything from negative hazard to negative risk. For instance, the British Treasury and National Accounting Office (NAO, 2000, p. 1) have defined risk in a way that "includes risk as an opportunity as well as a threat" and the MOD (2010, p. 6) has defined "risk and benefit" together.

Pure and Speculative Risks

Another binary categorization of risk with implications for our analysis of the causes and strategies is to distinguish between pure (or absolute) and speculative risks. Pure risks are always negative (they offer no benefits) and often unavoidable, such as natural risks and terrorism. Speculative risks include both positive and negative risks and are voluntary or avoidable, such as financial investments. This distinction is useful strategically because the dominant responses to pure risks are to avoid them or to insure against them, while speculative risks should be either pursued if positive or avoided if negative. (Strategic responses are discussed more in Chapter 10.)

Standard and Nonstandard Risks

Standard risks are risks against which insurers offer insurance at standard rates, albeit sometimes parsed by consumers. Most standard risks derive from predictable causes, such as unhealthy behaviors, or frequent events, such as road traffic accidents, that give the insurer confidence in their assessments of the risks. Nonstandard risks tend to be risks with great uncertainty or great potential for negative returns, like those associated with war, terrorism, and natural catastrophes (although a few insurers specialize in these risks). To insure against a nonstandard risk, the consumer could negotiate a particular policy but might fail to find any insurer, in which case the consumer is left to retain or avoid the risk (see Chapter 10).

Organizational Categories

Organizations conventionally categorize risks by the organizational level that is subject to them or should be responsible for them. Although many different types of organizations can be identified, they generally recognize at least three levels, even though they use terms differently and sometimes incompatibly (see Table 3.3). Thus, all stakeholders should declare their understanding of categories, if not agree upon a common set.

We could differentiate risks within an organization by level (as in Table 3.3) or by the assets or systems affected by those risks. Table 3.4 shows how different authorities have categorized these risks; I have attempted to align similar categories.

Table 3.3 Organizational Levels, by Different Types of Organization

	Typical organization	British standard organization (BSI, 2000, p. 13)	British official or private organization (AIRMIC, ALARM, and IRM, 2002, p. 6)	British governmental organization (Cabinet Office, February 2013)	United States official organization	Military organization (for instance: MOD, 2009, August 2011, and November 2011)
Highest level	Corporate	Strategic/Top management	Strategic	Strategic or gold	Strategic	Strategic
Middle level	Division or Department	Middle management	Project/Tactical	Tactical or silver	Program	Operational
Lowest level	Group, Unit, or Team	Operational	Operational	Operational or bronze ("hands-on work")	Project or Operation	Tactical

Table 3.4 Areas of Risk Within the Organization, as Listed by Different Authorities, With Similar Areas Aligned

<table>
<tr><th>Waring and Glendon (1998, p. 7)</th><th>British Standards Institution (2000, p. 14)</th><th>Business Continuity Institute, National Counterterrorism Security Office, and London First (UK BCI 2003)</th><th>British Treasury (2004, p. 17)</th><th>Australian/New Zealand and ISO (2009a, p. 4)</th></tr>
<tr><td>-</td><td>-</td><td>-</td><td>-</td><td>Stakeholder relations</td></tr>
<tr><td>-</td><td>-</td><td>-</td><td>-</td><td>Structure</td></tr>
<tr><td>Objectives</td><td>-</td><td>-</td><td>Change (new policies, new projects, change programs, targets)</td><td>Policies, objectives, and strategies</td></tr>
<tr><td>Culture</td><td>-</td><td>-</td><td>-</td><td>Culture</td></tr>
<tr><td rowspan="3">Resources</td><td>People</td><td>Personnel</td><td rowspan="4">Operational (service or project delivery, capacity and capability, and risk management performance and capability)</td><td rowspan="3">Capabilities (resources and knowledge)</td></tr>
<tr><td>Finance</td><td>-</td></tr>
<tr><td>Infrastructure and physical plant</td><td>Physical assets</td></tr>
<tr><td>-</td><td>-</td><td>Systems</td><td>Information systems</td></tr>
</table>

Levels

Like security, risks can be categorized through a hierarchy of levels, say from the global level down to the personal (see Chapter 2).

Most organizations distinguish at least their internal risks from the external risks. The Australian/New Zealand and ISO standard prescribes, as the first step in managing risks, establishing both the organization's goals and other *internal* parameters and the parameters of the *external* environment. The external environment has at least 4 levels: international, national, regional, and local (ISO, 2009a, p. 4).

Higher Functional Types

Some authorities have offered basic universal categories that could be applied to anything, within or without the organization, up to the global level. Many authorities essentially agree on these categories, although the terms vary. Table 3.5 shows the different categories recommended by these different authorities, with similar categories aligned.

For instance, the International Risk Governance Council (2008, p. 6) recognizes 4 categories of risk (natural, technological, economic, and environmental). The World Economic Forum, in its latest annual report (Global Risks 2013), identifies 50 global risks across 5 categories: economic, environmental,

Table 3.5 Higher Categories of Risk, as Described or Prescribed by Different Authorities

Australian/ New Zealand and ISO, 1995–2009	Waring and Glendon (1998, p. 7)	UK Treasury (2004, p. 17)	UK MOD (January 2010, p. 6)	PRINCE2®, 1996–2009	World Economic Forum (2013)
Environmental	Climatic	Environmental	Resource and environment	Environmental	Environmental
Political	Political	Political	Geopolitical	Political	Geopolitical
Legal and regulatory	-	Legal and regulatory	-	Legal and regulatory	-
Socio-cultural	-	Socio-cultural	Social	-	Societal
Economic	Economic	Economic	Economic	Economic, financial, and market	Economic
-	-	-	-	Strategic and commercial	-
Internal	Organizational	Operational	-	Organizational, managerial, and human factors	-
Technological	Technological	Technological	Science and technology	Technical, operations, and infrastructure	Technological

geopolitical, societal, and technological. The Australian/New Zealand and ISO (2009a, p. 4) standard lists 6 categories (natural and competitive environmental, political, legal and regulatory, economic, sociocultural, and technological). PRINCE2® offers 7 categories and 60 subcategories. Another source on project management listed 10 categories and 64 subcategories (Heerkens, 2002, p. 146). A typical government department or large commercial organization would identify even more subcategories.

Simple Statistical Calculations and Parameters

This section describes the different ways to mathematically calculate risk, predictable return, expected return, Program Evaluation and Review Technique (PERT) expected return, range of contingencies, the range of returns, and risk efficiency.

Formulae for Risk

Risk, as defined here in its simplest qualitative form, is easy to formulate mathematically as the product (Risk) of probability (p) and the return (R), or: $Risk = p \times R$.

The formulations of risk can be made more complicated by adding exposure or vulnerability or even the hazard or threat. Different formulae produce risk by multiplying: frequency by vulnerability (BSI, 2000, pp. 20–21); threat by vulnerability (Humanitarian Practice Network, 2010, p. 28); hazard by vulnerability, in the context of natural risks (Wisner, Blaikie, Cannon, & Davis, 2004, pp. 49, 337); hazard, vulnerability, and incapacity, in the context of natural disasters (UN ISDR, 2009, p. 4; Public Safety Canada, 2012, p. 26); exposure, likelihood, and returns (Waring & Glendon, 1998, pp. 27–28); or vulnerability, threat, and returns, in the context of terrorism (Greenberg, Chalk, Willis, Khilko, & Ortiz, 2006).

Managers of natural risks, especially environmental risks and health risks, are more likely to use and prescribe formulae that multiply: hazard by vulnerability; hazard by exposure; hazard by vulnerability by exposure; or hazard by vulnerability by incapacity. Notional examples of appropriate or effective qualitative formulations of hazard and vulnerability (or exposure) are listed below:

- One person carrying a communicable pathogen coinciding with a person without immunity will lead to another infected person.
- The proportion of the population with communicable diseases multiplied by the number of uninfected but coincident and vulnerable persons gives a product indicating the number of newly infected persons (ignoring subsequent infections by newly infected persons).
- The number of people who are both exposed to a drought and lack reserves of food is the number of people who would starve without external aid.
- Coincidence between unprotected populations and armed invaders indicates the populations that will be harmed or displaced.
- The rate of crime in an area multiplied by the population in that area gives the number of people eligible for victims-of-crime counseling.
- If terrorists attack site *S* with an incendiary projectile and site *S* is both undefended against the projectile and flammable, then site *S* would be destroyed.

These formulae are justifiable anywhere where the event or returns are predictable given coincidence between a particular hazard and one or all of vulnerability, exposure, or incapacity. None of hazard, vulnerability, or incapacity necessarily includes probability, although uncertainty may be implicit in the assessment of a particular hazard or vulnerability (a higher rating of the hazard suggests more likely coincidence with the vulnerability; a higher rating of the vulnerability suggests a more likely failure of defenses).

Predictable Return or Event

In truth, given the formal logic in some of the formulae above that formally ignore probability, the product is a predictable return rather than an expected return (the commonest formulation of risk; see below).

In some formulae, the product is a predictable event, not a predictable return. For instance, Public Safety Canada (2012, p. 26) defines "a disaster" as a product of hazard, vulnerability, and incapacity. The disaster is a predictable event, given the presence of hazard, vulnerability, and incapacity.

Expected Return

Risk, in its simplest mathematical form, is the product of probability and return. If only one return were possible, this formula would be the same as the formula for the *expected return*. When we have many possible returns, the expected return is the sum of the products of each return and its associated probability. In statistical language, the expected return is a calculation of the relative balance of best and worst outcomes, weighted by their chances of occurring (or the weighted average most likely outcome). The mathematical formula is:

Figure 3.1 The Typical Formula for the Expected Return

$$ER = {}^{N}\Sigma_{i=1} (P_i \times R_i)$$

where:

ER = expected return

N = total number of outcomes

P_i = probability of individual outcome

R_i = return from individual outcome

For instance, if we estimate only two possible returns (either a gain of $20 million with a probability of 80% or a loss of $30 million with a probability of 20%) the expected return is 80% of $20 million less 20% of $30 million, or $16 million less $6 million, or $10 million.

Note that the expected return is not necessarily a possible return. In the case above, the expected return ($10 million) is not the same as either of the possible returns (+$20 million or –$30 million). The expected return is still useful, even when it is an impossible return, because it expresses as one number a weighted average of the possible returns. This bears remembering and communicating, because consumers could mistakenly assume that you are forecasting the expected returns as a possible return or even the predicted return.

The expected return does not tell us the range of returns. The expected return might be a very large positive value that we desire, but the range of returns might include very large potential negative returns. Imagine that we expect a higher profit from option *A* than option *B*, but the range of returns for option *A* extends to possible huge losses, while the range of returns for option *B* includes no losses. Risk averse audiences would prefer option *B*, but the audience would be ignorant of option *B*'s advantages if it received only the expected return. Hence, we should always report the expected return and the range of returns together.

Having said that, we need to understand that best or worst outcomes may be very unlikely, so the range of returns can be misleading too. Ideally, we should report the probabilities of the worst and best outcomes, so that the audience can appreciate whether the probabilities of the worst or best outcomes are really sufficient to worry about. We could even present as a graph the entire distribution of returns by their probabilities. Much of this ideal is captured by *risk efficiency*, as shown below.

Program Evaluation and Review Technique (PERT) Expected Return

If we identify many potential outcomes, then a calculation of the expected return might seem too burdensome, at least without a lot of data entry and a statistical software program. In that case, we could choose a similar but simpler calculation prescribed by the Program Evaluation and Review Technique (PERT), a project management technique originating from the US Navy. In this formula, we include only the worst, best, and most likely outcomes, and we weight the most likely outcome by a factor of 4.

The main problems with the PERT expected return are that the calculation excludes all possible returns except the worst, best, and best likely and the actual probabilities of each outcome.

The PERT formula may be preferable to the typical formula of expected return if consumers want to acknowledge or even overstate the most extreme possible outcomes.

Range of Contingencies

Many planners are interested in estimating the range of potential contingencies, where a contingency (also a scenario) is some potential event. Normally, planners are interested in describing each contingency with an actor, action, object, returns, space, and time. Such contingencies are not necessarily statistically described (they could be qualitatively described) but at least imply estimates of potential returns and can be used to calculate risk statistically.

Figure 3.2 PERT's Formula for the Expected Return

$$ER = (O + 4M + P) \div 6$$

where:

ER = expected return

O = the most optimistic return

M = the most likely return

P = the most pessimistic return

When lots of contingencies are possible, good advice, similar to PERT's advice, is to prepare to meet the likeliest contingencies and the worst contingencies (although judgments should be made about which of the negative contingencies has a high enough probability to be worth preparing for) and to shape the future toward the best contingency. Preparing in this way is often called contingency planning, scenario planning, or uncertainty sensitive strategic planning (Davis, 2003). However, judgments should be made about whether the worst and best contingencies are likely enough to be worth preparing for.

Range of Returns

The range of returns is the maximum and minimum returns (or the best and worst returns). Sometimes the difference between them is expressed, too, but the difference is not the same as the range. For instance, the range of returns from a project might be assessed from a profit of $2 million to a loss of $1 million—a difference of $3 million.

The range of returns is useful for decision makers who want to know the best and worst possible returns before they accept a risk and is useful for planners who must plan for the outcomes.

The difference (between the maximum and minimum or best and worst outcomes) is often used as an indicator of uncertainty, where a narrower difference is easier for planning. The difference is used as an indicator of exposure, too (in the financial sense, exposure to the range of returns). The statistical variance and standard deviation of all estimated returns could be used as additional indicators.

However, uncertainty is not measured directly by either the range of returns or the difference; also, the maximum and minimum returns may be very unlikely. Thus, the maximum and minimum returns should be reported together with the probabilities of each. You should also report the most likely return too. Indeed, PERT advocates reporting the most likely return as well as the worst (or most pessimistic) return and the best (or most optimistic) return.

Risk Efficiency

Some people have criticized the expected return for oversimplifying risk assessment and potentially misleading decision makers: "The common definition of risk as *probability multiplied by impact* precludes consideration of risk efficiency altogether, because it means risk and expected value are formally defined as equivalent" (Chapman & Ward, 2003). These critics prescribed measurement of the "adverse variability relative to expected outcomes, assessed for each performance attribute using comparative cumulative probability distributions when measurement is appropriate" (Chapman & Ward, 2003, p. 48).

This sounds like a complicated prescription, but the two criteria for risk efficiency are simple enough: the expected return should be preferable (either a smaller negative return or a larger positive return); and the range of returns should be narrower (sometimes we settle for a smaller maximum negative return or a larger minimum positive return).

By these criteria, an option would be considered preferable if its maximum negative return is lowest, the range of returns is narrowest, and the expected return is more positive. For instance, imagine that our first option offers a range of returns from a loss of $1 million to a gain of $1 million with an expected return of $0.5 million, while the second option offers a range of returns from a loss of $2 million to a gain of $20 million with an expected return of $0.25 million. The first option is more risk efficient, even though the second option offers a higher maximum positive return.

 Analyzing and Assessing Risks

The section discusses how you can analyze and assess risks. The subsections below discuss the importance of risk analysis and assessment, distinguish risk analysis from risk assessment, describe risk analysis, describe risk assessment, and introduce the different available external sources of risk assessments.

Importance

Risk analysis and assessment are important because if we identify the various things that contribute to the risks then we could control each of these things and raise our security. As one author has advised businesses in response to terrorism, "risk assessment and risk analysis are not optional luxuries" (Suder, 2004, p. 223). Another author has advised project managers to be intellectually aggressive toward the analysis of security and risk.

> In addition, be on the alert for new threats. Unfortunately, however, new threats will not necessarily be obvious. You should always be "looking for trouble." Be skeptical, aggressive, and relentless in your quest to uncover potential problems. As the saying goes, if you don't manage risk, it will manage you! (Heerkens, 2002, p. 151)

Placing Risk Analysis and Risk Assessment

Over the last fifteen years, increased awareness of risks and increased attention to security have discredited prior norms of analysis and assessment and suggested a requirement for more attentive risk analysis and assessment.

Given the increased salience of security and risk over the last two decades, we might expect rapid maturation of their analysis and assessment, but an academic investigation of different methods for assessing health, natural, and crime risks found that they "share some commonalities, but also have many differences" (Kennedy, Marteache, & Gaziarifoglu, 2011, p. 45). Authorities are either surprisingly vague about analysis and assessment, use the terms interchangeably, use terms that are clearly incompatible with the practices, or discourage formal methods of assessment in favor of more intuitive assessment (see Pedagogy boxes 3.5 and 3.6 below). For instance, NATO does not define them at all, the Humanitarian Practice Network (2010, p. xviii) defines risk assessment and risk analysis interchangeably, and the ISO uses *risk analysis* illiterately to mean risk assessment, while using *risk identification* to mean risk analysis.

To resolve this incompatibility, we need to go back to semantic analysis. Semantic analysts have identified a class of verbs that, when used in connection with risk, "represent the actor's cognitive awareness: know the risk, understand the risk, appreciate the risk, calculate the risks" (Fillmore & Atkins, 1992, p. 86). This description is a neat prescription for a process of analyzing and assessing risks, where knowing (identifying) and understanding the risks are parts of risk analysis, while appreciating and calculating the risks are parts of risk assessment:

1. Analyze the risks:
   a. Identify the risks.
   b. Understand the risks by relating them to their sources (see Chapter 4).

2. Assess the risks:
   a. Appreciate the associated likelihood and return of each risk.
   b. Calculate the relative scale, level, or rank of the risks.

This prescription is more literal and simpler than most other prescriptions (see below).

Risk Analysis

Risk analysis helps to identify and understand the risks ahead of risk assessment (appreciating and calculating the risk), which in turn is a practical step toward choosing which negative risks should be controlled and which positive risks should be pursued and how to communicate our risk management.

Analyzing the risk involves identifying the risk and disaggregating the risk from its source to its potential returns. (Diagrammatic help for analyzing risk is shown in Figure 4.3.) A proper analysis allows us to assess the likelihood of each part of the chain; if we had not assessed the risks, we could hardly imagine either controlling all the actual risks or efficiently choosing the most urgent risks to control. Poor analysis and assessment of risk leads to mismanagement of risks by, for instance, justifying the allocation of resources to controls on misidentified sources of risk or on minor risks. Better analysis of risk would not prevent political perversities, but would counter poor analysis. Consider current counter-terrorism strategy, which involves terminating the causes of terrorism. Tracing the causes means careful analysis of the risk through its precursors to its sources. If the analysis is poor, government would end up terminating something that is not actually a source or cause of terrorism.

Pedagogy Box 3.5 Other Definitions and Practices of Risk Analysis

Unfortunately, most authorities do not use the term *risk analysis* literally. Almost all refer to risk assessment but few refer to risk analysis; their references to risk analysis tend to mean risk assessment, while they use *risk identification* to mean literal risk analysis. In some standards, most importantly the Australian/New Zealand and ISO standard (2009, p. 6) and its many partial adherents (such as Public Safety Canada, 2012, and AIRMIC, ALARM, and IRM, 2002), *risk analysis* is an explicit step in the recommended process for managing risks. The Australian/New Zealand standard, the ISO, and the Canadian government each promise that risk analysis "provides the basis for risk evaluation and decisions about risk treatment." They define risk analysis as the "process to comprehend the nature of risk and to determine the level of risk," but this is risk assessment. Their *risk identification* ("the process of finding, recognizing, and recording risks") sounds more like *risk analysis*. The Canadian government refers to *hazard identification* as "identifying, characterizing, and validating hazards," which again sounds like analysis, and describes "identification" as one part of "assessment" (Public Safety Canada, 2012, p. 49). Some project managers refer to *risk identification* when they clearly mean *risk analysis*—they properly schedule it before *risk assessment*, but add *risk analysis* as a third step, ranking risks by our "concern" about them (Heerkens, 2002, p. 143).

Similarly, both the British Treasury and the Ministry of Defense have defined *risk analysis* as "the process by which risks are measured and prioritized," but this is another definition that sounds more like risk assessment. The British Civil Contingencies Secretariat ignores risk analysis and provides a more operational definition of assessment, where analysis is probably captured under "identifying" risks.

Risk Assessment

According to the semantic analysis above, all a risk assessment needs to do, after a risk analysis, is

a. Appreciate the associated likelihood and return of each risk

b. Calculate the relative scale, level, or rank of the risks

Risk assessment can be informal, subconscious, and routine. Some authors have pleaded for more insightful understanding rather than conventional wisdom or generalizable models. Molak writes, "The thought process that goes into evaluating a particular hazard is more important than the application of some sophisticated mathematical technique or formula, which often may be based on erroneous assumptions or models of the world" (1997, p. 8). According to Bracken, Bremmer, and Gordon, "Risk management is about insight, not numbers. It isn't the predictions that matter most but the understanding and discovery of the dynamics of the problems" (2008, p. 6).

Risk assessment is not just a formal step in a prescribed process but is something we do all the time. When you choose to walk across a street or enter a neighborhood, you have assessed the risks—however unconsciously or imperfectly. That process is often termed *dynamic risk assessment.* Although these skills include instinctive, automatic, and informal skills, they are subject to description and training.

Pedagogy Box 3.6 Other Definitions and Practices of Risk Assessment

United Nations

"Risk assessment is . . . a methodology to determine the nature and extent of risk by analyzing potential hazards and evaluating existing conditions of vulnerability that together could potentially harm exposed people, property, services, livelihoods, and the environment on which they depend" (UN ISDR, 2009, p. 11).

United States

"Risk assessment means a process or method for evaluating risk associated with a specific hazard and defined in terms of probability and frequency of occurrence, magnitude and severity, exposure, and consequences" (FEMA, 1997, p. xxv). For the GAO (2005, p. 110), risk assessment is "the process of qualitatively or quantitatively determining the probability of an adverse event and the severity of its impact on an asset. It is a function of threat, vulnerability, and consequences. A risk assessment may include scenarios in which two or more risks interact to create a greater or lesser impact. A risk assessment provides the basis for the rank ordering of risks and for establishing priorities for applying countermeasures." For DOD (2010, p. 269), risk assessment is "the identification and assessment of hazards."

Australian/New Zealand (2009) and ISO (2009a)

The Australian/New Zealand and ISO's definition of risk assessment ("the overall process of risk identification, risk analysis, and risk evaluation") is actually an operational definition of the process of assessing risks through three steps (which are also the second to fourth steps within a 7-step process of risk management: see Chapter 8):

1. Risk identification ("the process of finding, recognizing, and recording risks")
2. Risk analysis ("a process to comprehend the nature of a risk and to determine its level")
3. Risk evaluation ("the process of comparing the results of risk analysis with risk criteria to determine whether a risk and/international relations its magnitude is acceptable or tolerable")

Canadian

The Canadian government accepts the ISO's definition and process of risk management, but from October 2009 to October 2011 the Canadian government, with advice from the U.S., British, and Dutch governments, started the development of a federal method (All Hazards Risk Assessment process; AHRA), based on the first steps of the ISO process:

1. Setting the context: "a comprehensive understanding of the strategic and operating context of an organization," using its plans, environmental/situational assessments, and intelligence
   a. to "identify risk themes, defined as activities or phenomena of a particular interest to an institution"; and
   b. to produce "analysis" of future hazards and threats within the risk themes.
2. Risk identification: "the process of finding, recognizing, and recording risks," producing
   a. "a list of identified top priority threats and hazards (or risks)" by institution; and
   b. scenarios for each potential event.
3. Risk analysis: "to understand the nature and level of each risk in terms of its likelihood and impact."
4. Risk evaluation: "the process of comparing the results of risk analysis with risk criteria to determine whether a risk and/or its magnitude is/are acceptable or tolerable" (Public Safety Canada and Defence Research & Development Canada, February 2013).

(The published AHRA actually described the first 5 steps of the ISO's 7-step risk management process, but the fifth is the treatment or control of the risks and is clearly not part of risk assessment.)

British

The glossaries issued by the Treasury and MOD each defined risk assessment as "the overall process of risk analysis and risk evaluation," where *risk analysis* is "the process by which risks are measured

(Continued)

(Continued)

and prioritized" and risk evaluation is "the process used to determine risk management priorities by comparing the level of risk against predetermined standards, target risk levels[,] or other criteria." Each department subsequently developed *risk assessment* as, respectively, "the evaluation of risk with regard to the impact if the risk is realized and the likelihood of the risk being realized" (Treasury, 2004, p. 49) or the "overall process of identifying, analyzing[,] and evaluating risks to the organization. The assessment should also look at ways of reducing risks and their potential impacts" (MOD, November 2011).

The Civil Contingencies Secretariat defined risk assessment as "a structured and auditable process of identifying potentially significant events, assessing their likelihood and impacts, and then combining these to provide an overall assessment of risk, as a basis for further decisions and action" (Cabinet Office, February 2013).

Humanitarian Practice Network

Risk assessment (used interchangeably with risk analysis) is "an attempt to consider risk more systematically in terms of the threats in the environment, particular vulnerabilities and security measures to reduce the threat or reduce your vulnerability" (Humanitarian Practice Network, 2010, p. xviii).

IRGC

The International Risk Governance Council's *risk governance framework* refers to both "analysis" and "understanding" but does not specify these steps. Its separate process of managing risk starts with a step known as *risk preassessment*—"early warning and 'framing' the risk in order to provide a structured definition of the problem and how it may be handled. Pre-assessment clarifies the various perspectives on a risk, defines the issue to be looked at, and forms the baseline for how a risk is assessed and managed." The "main questions" that the assessor should ask are listed as follows:

- What are the risks and opportunities we are addressing?
- What are the various dimensions of the risk?
- How do we define the limits for our evaluations?
- Do we have indications that there is already a problem? Is there a need to act?
- Who are the stakeholders? How do their views affect the definition and framing of the problem?
- What are the established scientific/analytical tools and methods that can be used to assess the risks?
- What are the current legal/regulatory systems and how do they potentially affect the problem?
- What is the organizational capability of the relevant governments, international organizations, businesses and people involved? (IRGC, 2008, pp. 8–9)

The second step of the IRGC's 5-step process of managing risk is *risk appraisal*, which starts with "a scientific risk assessment—a conventional assessment of the risk's factual, physical, and measurable characteristics including the probability of it happening." The main questions that the assessor should ask are below:

- What are the potential damages or adverse effects?
- What is the probability of occurrence?
- How ubiquitous could the damage be? How persistent? Could it be reversed?
- How clearly can cause-effect relationships be established?
- What scientific, technical, and analytical approaches, knowledge, and expertise should be used to better assess these impacts?
- What are the primary and secondary benefits, opportunities, and potential adverse effects? (IRGC, 2008, p. 10)

Unofficial

Risk assessment is "the process of gauging the most likely outcome(s) of a set of events, situations[,] or options and the significant consequences of those outcomes" (Waring & Glendon, 1998, p. 21), "the combination of risk identification and risk quantification. The primary output of a risk assessment is a list of specific potential problems or threats" (Heerkens, 2002, p. 143), or "a consideration of the probabilities of particular outcomes, both positive and negative" (Kennedy & Van Brunschot, 2009, p. 4).

Crime Risk Assessment

Criminologists have prescribed the following questions for assessing risks:

- What type of threat or hazard are we facing?
- What types of data are needed?
- What are the sources of information available?
- What is the probability that the event would occur?
- How vulnerable are we?
- How exposed are we?
- How does information flow from the local to a higher level? (Kennedy, Marteache, & Gaziarifoglu, 2011, p. 34)

Dynamic Risk Assessment in Britain

In 1974, the British Parliament passed the Health and Safety at Work Act, which established the Health and Safety Commission (HSC) and the Health and Safety Executive (HSE) as responsible for the regulation of almost all the risks to health and safety arising from work. After a surge in deaths of firefighters in the late 1980s and early 1990s, the HSE served several improvement notices on the firefighting service, amounting to an order for better risk assessment. The Home Office (1997) recommended a

(Continued)

(Continued)

focus on the safety of personnel. The Fire Service Inspectorate (1998) agreed and ordered firefighters to perform a risk assessment before all deployments; the Inspectorate suggested that standard operating procedures could be developed for predictable scenarios—what became known as a "Dynamic Risk Assessment." The Civil Contingencies Secretariat defines "dynamic risk assessment" as a "continuing assessment appraisal, made during an incident or emergency, of the hazards involved in, and the impact of, the response" (Cabinet Office, February 2013).

Acknowledging the dynamic relationship between the emergency and firefighter, the Fire Service Inspectorate (1998) formalized a simple process:

1. Evaluate the situation, tasks, and persons at risk;
2. Select systems of work;
3. Assess the chosen system of work;
4. Assess whether the risks are proportional to the benefits:
   a. If yes, proceed with tasks.
   b. If no, evaluate additional control measures and return to step.

Some British police forces adopted the same model, particularly after the HSE prosecuted the Metropolitan Police for breaches of health and safety. However, increasingly police complained that Dynamic Risk Assessment was impractical, while some blamed health and safety rules for their reluctance to take risks in order to protect the public (such as when community police officers watched a civilian drown while they awaited rescue equipment). The HSE (2005) subsequently "recognized that the nature of policing necessitates police officers to respond to the demands of unpredictable and rapidly changing situations and reliance solely on systematic risk assessment and set procedures is unrealistic."

Sources of Risk Assessments

This section introduces the main available external sources of risk assessments: subject matter experts; structured judgments; and systematic forecasts.

Subject Matter Experts

External experts are useful for checking for external agreement with our internal analysis and assessment or for sourcing more expert assessments than we could source internally. Unfortunately, most risk assessments rely solely on surveys of other people, due to insufficient time, capacity, or (frankly) motivation for proper analysis and assessment, and the expertise of these respondents is often less than claimed.

The main problem with any survey is that objective experts are rarer than most people realize. Generally, procurers and surveyors report that they have surveyed *experts* or *subject-matter experts*, but do not measure or report expertise. For Public Safety Canada (2012, p. 90), which prescribes surveys of experts as complementary to objective evidence, a *subject-matter expert* is "a person who provides expertise in a specific scientific or technological area or on a particular aspect of a response."

Selection of experts involves choices: the more respondents, the more diversity of opinion, but adding more respondents also suggests wider recruiting of inferior experts. Our statistical confidence in the average response increases as we survey more people, although surveying more nonexperts or biased experts would not help.

Subject-matter expertise can suggest disengagement from wider knowledge. Probably everybody is subject to biases, and consumers prefer agreeable respondents. Even experts are subject to these biases, as well as political and commercial incentives.

For commercial, political, and personal reasons, many supposed experts are just the cheapest or most available or friendliest to the procurer. At the highest levels of government, often assessments of risks are made by informal discussions between decision makers and their closest friends and advisers, contrary to rigorous official assessments. Politicians often are uncomfortable accepting influence without political rewards or with methods that they do not understand. This dysfunction partly explains the George W. Bush administration's genuine confidence in its assessments in 2003 of the threats from the regime of Saddam Hussein and the opportunities from invading Iraq.

Political and commercial incentives help to explain the sustainment of poorly accredited academic experts or think tanks. In recent years, public confidence in experts of many types has been upset by shocks such as financial crises and terrorist attacks, suggesting we should lower our expectations or be more diligent in choosing our experts. For instance, in tests, most political experts performed little better than random when forecasting events five years into the future. Confident experts with deep, narrow knowledge ("hedgehogs" in Isaiah Berlin's typology of intellectuals) were less accurate than those with wide and flexible knowledge ("foxes"), although even foxes were not usefully accurate in forecasting events years into the future (Tetlock, 2006). Political scientists have a poor reputation for forecasting, perhaps because the phenomena are difficult to measure, they rely on small populations of data, they reach for invalid correlates, or they rely on unreliable judgments (unreliability may be inherent to political science if only because the subjects are politicized). Consequently, political scientists are highly polarized between different methods. While conscientious scientists attempt to integrate methods in order to maximize the best and minimize the worst, many political scientists form isolated niches (McNabb, 2010, pp. 15–28). Methods, data, and judgments are worst in the important fields of international security, war studies, and peace studies. Similarly, economists have received deserved criticism for their poor awareness of financial and economic instability in recent years.

All this illustrates the obvious principle that the risk assessor should be diligent when choosing experts. This is not to say that we should doubt all experts but that we should be more discriminating than is typical. We should carefully select the minority of all experts, even at the best institutions, who are objective, evidence-based, practical interdisciplinary thinkers.

Structured Judgments

We can structure the survey in more functional ways, as described in subsections below: Delphi survey; ordinal ranking; and plots of likelihood and returns.

Delphi Survey

The survey itself can be structured in more reliable ways. The least reliable surveys are informal discussions, particularly those between a small number of people under the leadership of one person, such as those commonly known as focus groups. Informal discussions tend to be misled by those most powerful in the perceptions of group members and by mutually reactionary, extreme positions.

Delphi surveys encourage respondents away from narrow subjectivity by asking them to reforecast a few times, each time after a revelation of the previous round's forecasts (traditionally only the median and interquartile range are revealed, thereby ignoring outliers). Interpersonal influences are eliminated by keeping each respondent anonymous to any other. This method helps respondents to consider wider empirical knowledge while discounting extreme judgments and to converge on a more realistic forecast. It has been criticized for being nontheoretical and tending toward an artificial consensus, so my own Delphi surveys have allowed respondents to submit a written justification with their forecasts that would be released to all respondents before the next forecast.

Ordinal Ranking

The respondent's task can be made easier by asking the respondent to rank the risk on an ordinal scale, rather than to assess the risk abstractly. The Canadian government refers to *risk prioritization* as "the ranking of risks in terms of their combined likelihood and impact estimates" (Public Safety Canada, 2012, p. 84). Essentially a risk ranking is a judgment of one risk's scale relative to another. Fewer ranks or levels (points on an ordinal scale) are easier for the respondent to understand and to design with mutually exclusive coding rules for each level. Three-point or 5-point scales are typical because they have clear middle, top, and bottom levels. More levels would give a false sense of increased granularity as the boundaries between levels become fuzzy.

Plotting Likelihood and Returns

A scheme for surveying more thoughtful assessments of risk would ask respondents to plot different types of risk in a single matrix by risk's two unambiguous multiples (likelihood and returns) (see Figure 3.3).

Indeed, the World Economic Forum (2013, p. 45) gives respondents a list of risks and asks them to rate both the likelihood and the impact (each on a 5-point scale). The World Economic Forum is able to calculate the risks for itself as a product of likelihood and impact. In its report, it presents the average responses for each risk's likelihood and impact on bar charts and as plots on a two-dimensional graph similar to that shown in Figure 3.3.

Naturally, given the opportunity, an even more accurate assessment would involve asking experts on the likelihoods (see Chapter 6) and other experts on the returns (see Chapter 7), from which we could calculate the risk.

Systematic Forecasts

In the 1990s, governments and supranational institutions and thence think tanks took more interest in producing their own forecasts of future trends and events. Initially, they consulted internal staff or external "futurists" and others whose opinions tended to be highly parochial. In search of more control, some have systematized forecasts that they might release publicly. These forecasts are based largely on expert judgments, but are distinguished by some attempt to combine theoretical or empirical review, however imperfectly.

Figure 3.3 A Risk Plot: Different Scenarios Plotted by Impact and Likelihood

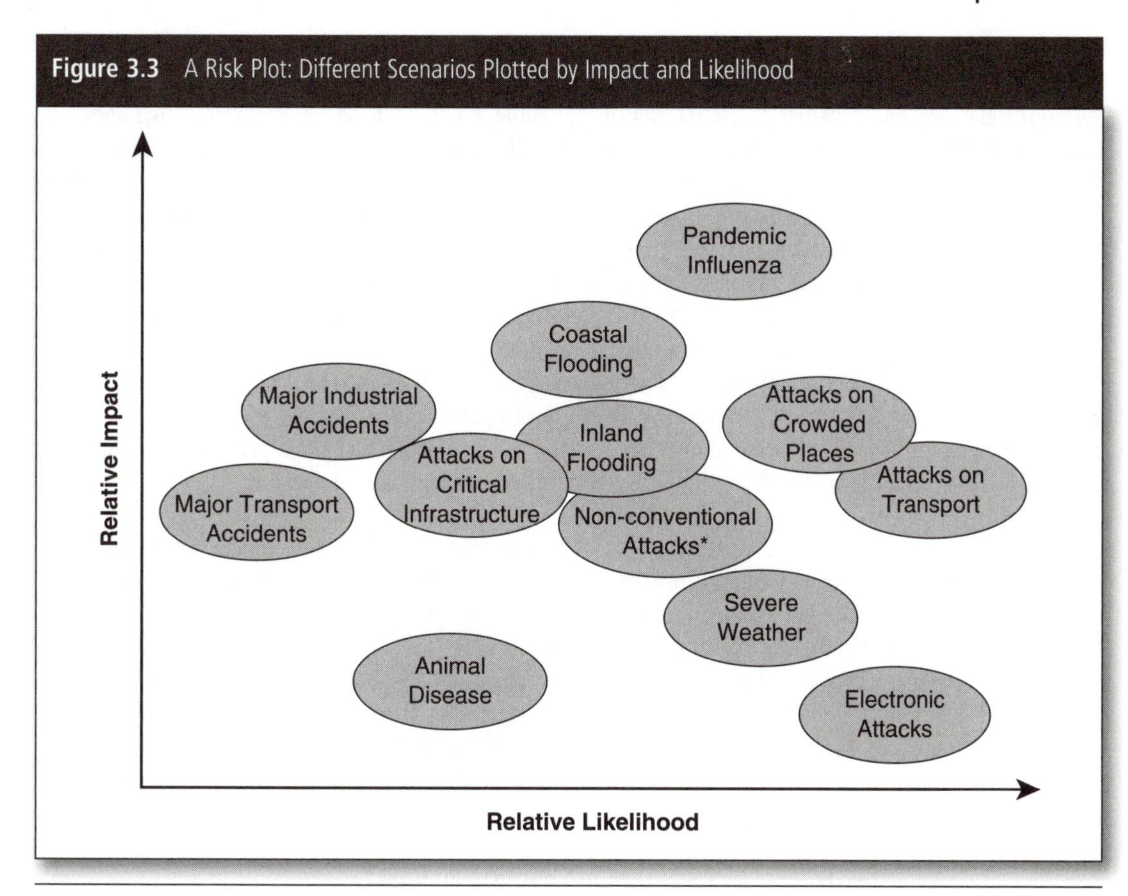

SOURCE: U.K. Cabinet Office, August 2008.

For instance, since 1997 the U.S. National Intelligence Council has published occasional reports (around every four years) on *global trends* with long horizons (inconsistent horizons of 13 to 18 years). In 1998, the British government's Strategic Defense Review recommended similar forecasts, so the Ministry of Defense established what is now the Development, Concepts and Doctrine Center, which since 2001 has published occasional reports on *global strategic trends* with a time horizon of 30 years (for the MOD, January 2010, p. 6, a trend is "a discernible pattern of change"). Annually since 2004, the British executive has produced a *National Risk Assessment* with a time horizon of five years—the published versions (since 2008) are known as "National Risk Registers of Civil Emergencies." In 2010, it produced a *National Security Risk Assessment* by asking experts to identify risks with time horizons of 5 and 20 years—this remains classified, but is summarized in the National Security Strategy (Cabinet Office, 2010, p. 29, 37; Cabinet Office, July 2013, pp. 2–4). Since 2011, the Canadian government has prescribed annual forecasts of "plausible" risks within the next five years, *short-term*, and 5 to 25 years in the future, *emerging* (Public Safety Canada and Defense Research and Development Canada, February 2013, p. 11). Since the start of 2006, the World Economic Forum has published annual forecasts of *global risks* (not just economic risks) with a horizon of 10 years.

Some think tanks are involved in official forecasts as contributors or respondents or produce independent forecasts with mostly one-year horizons. For instance, since 2008 the Strategic Foresight

Initiative at the Atlantic Council has been working with the U.S. National Intelligence Council on *global trends*. Since March 2009, around every two months, the Center for Preventive Action at the Council on Foreign Relations has organized discussions on plausible short- to medium-term contingencies that could seriously threaten U.S. interests; since December 2011, annually, it has published forecasts with a time horizon through the following calendar year. Toward the end of 2012, the Carnegie Endowment for International Peace published its estimates of the ten greatest international "challenges and opportunities for the [U.S.] President in 2013."

Official estimates are not necessarily useful outside of government: officials prefer longer term planning that is beyond the needs of most private actors; they also use intelligence that falls short of evidence; the typical published forecast is based on mostly informal discussions with experts. Some experts and forecasts refer to frequency or trend analysis or theory, but too many do not justify their judgments. Both the U.S. and British governments admit to consulting officials, journalists, academics, commentators, and business persons, but otherwise have not described their processes for selecting experts or surveying them. The Canadian government has been more transparent:

> Generally, the further into the future forecasts go, the more data deprived we are. To compensate for the lack of data, foresight practitioners and/or futurists resort to looking at trends, indicators etc. and use various techniques: Technology Mapping; Technology Road-Mapping; Expert Technical Panels, etc. These are alternate techniques that attempt to compensate for the uncertainty of the future and most often alternate futures will be explored. Federal risk experts can get emerging and future insights and trend indicators through community of practice networks such as the Policy Horizons Canada (http://www.horizons.gc.ca) environmental scanning practice group. (Public Safety Canada and Defense Research and Development Canada, February 2013, p. 11)

The World Economic Forum's survey is the most transparent: it asks respondents to assess, on a scale from 1 to 5, the likelihood of each of 50 possible events occurring within the next ten years. Additionally, it asked respondents to pick the most important risk (center of gravity) within each of the 5 categories of risk. It also asked respondents to link pairs of related risks (at least 3, no more than 10 such pairs). It used the results to identify the most important clusters of related risks, and then it explored these clusters through direct consultation with experts and focus groups.

SUMMARY

This chapter has:

- defined risk,
- explained how qualitatively to describe a risk more precisely and usefully,
- shown you different ways to categorize risks, including by
  - negative and positive risks,
  - pure and speculative risks,
  - standard and non-standard risks,

  - organizational categories,
  - levels, and
  - higher functional types,
- given you alternative ways to calculate risk and its parameters, including:
  - risk, by different combinations of probability, return, hazard, vulnerability, and exposure,
  - predictable return,
  - expected return,
  - PERT expected return,
  - range of contingencies,
  - range of returns, and
  - risk efficiency,
- shown how to analyze risks,
- shown how to assess risks, and
- introduced available external sources of risk assessments.

QUESTIONS AND EXERCISES

1. Identify what is good or bad in the different definitions of risk (collected earlier in this chapter).
2. Calculate the expected returns in each of the following scenarios:
   a. We forecast a 50% probability that we would inherit $1 million.
   b. The probability of a shuttle failure with the loss of all six passengers and crew is 1%.
   c. The probability of terrorist destruction of site *S* (value: $100 million) is 20%.
   d. If the project fails, we would lose our investment of $1 million. The probability of failure is 10%.
   e. One percent of our products will fail, causing harm to the user with a liability of $10,000 per failure. We have sold 100,000 products.
3. What are the expected returns and range of returns in each of the scenarios below?
   a. A military coalition has offered to arm an external group if the group would ally with the coalition. Survey respondents forecast a 60% probability that the group would stay loyal to the coalition. The group currently consists of 1,000 unarmed people.
   b. The coalition must choose between two alternative acquisitions: an off-road vehicle that could avoid all roads and therefore all insurgent attacks on road traffic, which account for 40% of coalition casualties; or an armored vehicle that would protect all occupants from all insurgent attacks. However, experts estimate a 20% probability that the insurgents would acquire a weapon to which the armored vehicle would be as vulnerable as would any other vehicle.
   c. The police claim that an investment of $1 million would double their crime prevention rate. Another authority claims that an investment of $1 million in improvements to electricity generation would enable street lights at night, which would triple crime prevention. Experts estimate the probability of success as 60% in the case of the police project, 50% in the case of the electricity project.

4. Consider your answers to question 3. In each scenario, how could you describe one option or alternative as risk efficient?
5. Describe the risks in the scenarios in questions 2 and 3.
6. Categorize the risks in the scenarios in questions 2 and 3.
7. What is the difference between the normal formula of expected return and the PERT expected return?
8. What are the advantages and disadvantages of asking experts to assess risk's level or rank?

Hazards, Threats, and Contributors

This chapter explains what is meant by the *sources* of risk, clarifies the differences between a source and its causes, defines hazards in general, and describes how threats differ from hazards. The following section describes how hazards are activated, controlled, and assessed. Sections then explain how to assess hazards and threats, the sources of positive risks (primarily *contributors*), and categorize hazards, threats, and contributors.

 The Sources and Causes of Risk

Sources

Hazards and threats are the sources of negative risk. As shown in sections below, the hazard and threat are different states of the same thing: The hazard is the source in a harmless state (such as a river remote to you), and the threat is the source in a harmful state (such as a flood that reaches you).

Poor analysis and loose language conflate hazard, threat, and risk, but they are separate concepts. The hazards and threats are sources of the risk in the sense that they are the actual actors or agents with the potential to harm, while the risk is the potential harm. For instance, the sources of the uncertain effects of political violence are the people who perpetrate such violence; the people (actors) cause the violence (event) that causes harm (returns). Neither the actors nor the event nor the returns are the same as the risk (the potential harm).

Sources are important to identify because many responses to risk instinctively seek to control the uncertainty or returns associated with the risk, in the process neglecting opportunities to terminate the sources. Even the simplest risks are usefully analyzed back to their sources and causes. For instance, a river, as a hazard, is one potential source of a flood; a flood is a threat to lives and property on the flood plain. The risks include potential drownings and potential property damage. If we want to terminate the source of the flood, we would need to prevent the river from ever flooding.

Pedagogy Box 4.1 Other Definitions of Sources

In the Australian/New Zealand and ISO standard (Australian and New Zealand Joint Technical Committee, 2009), a risk source is an "element which alone or in combination has the intrinsic potential to give rise to risk" (p. 6). The given example is a hazard. Some literature refers to risk sources as risk's "precursors" or risk's "objects" (Waring & Glendon, 1998, pp. 8–9).

Causes

A cause is the reason for some change. The words *source* and *cause* are often conflated, but they are separate concepts. The source of the risk is the hazard or threat: The cause of the threat is whatever activated the hazard into the threat. For instance, the river is a source for a flood. The threat (flood) is activated by unusual causes (such as unusual rainfall, high tides, saturated ground, poor drainage, a broken levee, etc.). The causes of the threat are separate to the normal sources of the river (such as rainfall, springs, tributaries, runoff) that do not normally cause a flood.

A good analyst pursues root causes. If we were to blame the flood on a broken levee, we should look for the causes of the broken levee (such as poor maintenance of the levee), which itself has causes (poor equipment, maintainers, leaders, or managers), and so forth until we reach the root causes.

Separation of the sources and causes is useful strategically because the causes could be terminated—often the most efficient way to terminate a risk. The advantages of such an analysis are obvious in the pursuit of health security, where the risks have multiple sources and causes.

> To prevent disease and injury, it is necessary to identify and deal with their causes—the health risks that underlie them. Each risk has its own causes too, and many have their roots in a complex chain of events over time, consisting of socioeconomic factors, environmental and community conditions, and individual behavior. The causal chain offers many entry points for intervention. (World Health Organization [WHO], 2009, p. 1)

An analysis of the causes and sources is usefully developed and communicated diagrammatically (see Figure 4.1).

In addition to simple causal chains, analysts could develop event trees (a diagram of events leading to other events), fault trees (a diagram of faults that caused other faults), or exposure trees (a diagram of causes and effects). For instance, Figure 4.2 shows a diagrammatic representation of an independent analysis of the root causes of crime in Haiti and the suggested solutions to those root causes.

Pedagogy Box 4.2 Synonyms of Risk Causes

The British Ministry of Defense (MOD) (2010a, p. 6) identifies risks by identifying their "driver" ("a factor that directly influences or causes change") and further differentiates a "ring road issue" ("a driver that is so pervasive in nature and influence that it will affect the life of everyone on the planet over the next 30 years").

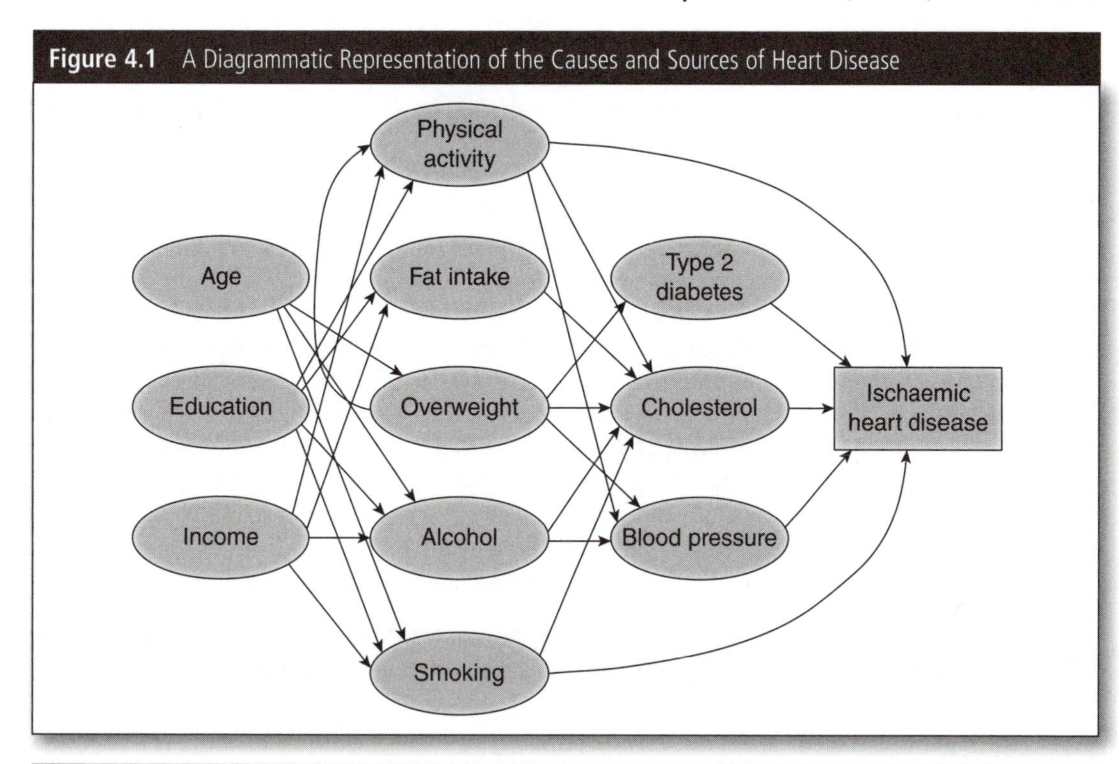

Figure 4.1 A Diagrammatic Representation of the Causes and Sources of Heart Disease

SOURCE: WHO, 2009, p. 2.

Figure 4.2 Analysis of the *Root Causes* of Crime in Haiti and the *Solutions* to Those Root Causes

Solutions	Root Causes		Proximate Causes		Problem
Transborder cooperation	***Weak border***	→	Transborder crime		
More female recruits	***Limited recruitment***	→	Weak police		
Graduate-level police academy	***Limited training***				
Vetted judiciary and new chambers	***Untried detainees***	→	Weak rule of law	→	Crime
Improved correctional facilities	***Prison breaks***				
Socio-economic improvement	***Social deprivation***	→	Social violence		

SOURCE: International Crisis Group, 2008.

Hazard

This section defines hazard, before following sections explain how hazards are activated into threats, how to control hazards, and how to assess hazards and threats.

Defining Hazard

A hazard is a potential, dormant, absent, or contained threat. Hazard and threat are different states of the same thing: The hazard is in a harmless state, the threat in a harmful state. The hazard would do no harm unless it were to change into a threat. For instance, a river is a hazard as long as it does not threaten us, but the river becomes a threat to us when it floods our property, we fall into it, or we drop property into it. As long as we or our property are not in the water, the river remains a hazard to us and not a threat. Hazards become threats when we are coincident with, enable, or activate the harmful state.

The hazard is the source of the event and of the associated risk, but it is not the same as an event or a risk. The risk is the potential returns if the hazard were to be activated as a threat. For instance, the risks associated with the flood include potential drownings, potential water damage, and potential waterborne diseases—these are all separate things to the threat (the flood).

A good analysis of the sources of a risk would be represented schematically as in Figure 4.3:

Figure 4.3 A Diagram Representing a Full Analysis of a Negative Risk From Source to Target

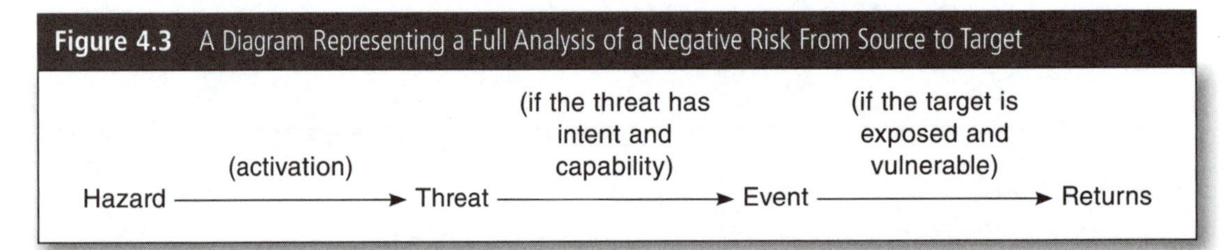

Pedagogy Box 4.3 Official Definitions of Hazard

UN

A hazard is "a threatening event, or the probability of occurrence of a potentially damaging phenomenon within a given time period and area." "Secondary hazards occur as a result of another hazard or disaster, i.e. fires or landslides following earthquakes, epidemics following famines, food shortages, following drought or floods" (United Nations Department of Humanitarian Affairs, 1992). A hazard is "a dangerous phenomenon, substance, human activity or condition that may cause loss of life, injury, or other health impacts, property damage, loss of livelihoods and services, social and economic disruption, or environmental damage" (United Nations Office for International Strategy for Disaster Reduction [UN ISDR], 2009, p. 7).

United States

The National Governors' Association, which helped to specify emergency management in the 1980s, defined a hazard as a "source of danger that may or may not lead to an emergency or disaster." The Federal Emergency Management Agency (FEMA) (1992) defined hazards as "an event or physical condition that have the potential to cause fatalities, injuries, property damage, infrastructure damage, agricultural loss, damage to the environment, interruption of business, or other types of harm or loss" (p. xxv). For the U.S. Department of Homeland Security (DHS) (2009), a hazard is a "natural or manmade source or cause of harm or difficulty" (p. 110). The U.S. Department of Defense (DOD) (2012b) defines a hazard as "a condition with the potential to cause injury, illness, or death of personnel, damage to or loss of equipment or property, or mission degradation" (p. 135). The Government Accountability Office (GAO) does not define hazard.

Australian/New Zealand and ISO

Australia/New Zealand and the ISO define a hazard as a "source of potential harm", where a hazard "can be a risk source"; they do not define threat (International Organization for Standardization, 2009a, p. 6).

British

The British Civil Contingencies Secretariat defines hazard as the "accidental or naturally occurring (i.e., non-malicious) event or situation with the potential to cause death or physical or psychological harm, damage or losses to property, and/or disruption to the environment and/or to economic, social and political structures" (U.K. Cabinet Office, 2013).

Initially, the MOD (2009a) defined hazard as "a source of potential harm, or a situation with a potential to cause loss, also an obstacle to the achievement of an objective." Later, the MOD (2011b) defined hazards as "accidental and non-malicious events, including naturally occurring events such as bad weather, flooding etc." (p. 14). The Treasury and National Audit Office (NAO) do not define hazard.

Canadian

A hazard is "a potentially damaging physical event, phenomenon, or human activity that may cause the loss of life or injury, property damage, social and economic disruption, or environmental degradation" (Public Safety Canada, 2012, p. 48).

Threat

This section defines threat and introduces ways to assess threats.

Defining Threat

A threat is an actor or agent in a harmful state. A threat is any actor or agent whose capacity to harm you is not currently avoided, contained, inactive, or deactivated.

Many risk managers and risk management standards effectively treat hazards and threats as the same or use the words *hazard* and *threat* interchangeably. Some analysts simply use one or the other word, whichever is favorite, whenever they identify a source of risk. Some of this favoritism is disciplinary: Natural risks tend to be traced to hazards but not threats, while human risks tend to be traced to threats but not hazards. Effectively, such analysis ignores the transition between hazard and threat. The hazard is a harmless state with potential to change into a threat; the threat is the same source, except in a harmful state. A threat could be changed into a hazard if it could be manipulated into a harmless state.

The routine conflation of hazard and threat is not satisfactory because it prevents our full differentiation of the harmless and harmful states and confuses our pursuit of the harmless state. Some authorities effectively admit as much by creating a third state in between. For instance, the Canadian government admits an *emerging threat*—"a credible hazard that has recently been identified as posing an imminent threat to the safety and security of a community or region" (Public Safety Canada, 2012, p. 35). Many commentators within the defense and security communities routinely describe "threats" as other countries or groups that are really hazards (because they have not made up their minds to harm or acquired sufficient capabilities to harm), so they use the term *imminent threat* or *clear and present danger* or even *enemy* to mean a literal threat. For instance, U.S. DOD (2012a, p. 47) refers to a *specific threat* as a "known or postulated aggressor activity focused on targeting a particular asset."

Uses and definitions of threat are even more problematic when they treat threats and negative risks as the same (see Pedagogy Box 4.4), just as some people treat opportunities and positive risks as the same.

Pedagogoy Box 4.4 Definitions of Threat

Unofficial

"Threats are the negative—or 'downside'—effects of risk. Threats are specific events that drive your project in the direction of outcomes viewed as unfavorable" (Heerkens, 2002, p. 143).

"A threat is a specific danger which can be precisely identified and measured on the basis of the capabilities an enemy has to realize a hostile intent" (Rasmussen, 2006, p. 1).

"Terrorist threats exist when a group or individual has both the capability and intent to attack a target" (Greenberg, Chalk, Willis, Khilko, & Ortiz, 2006, p. 143).

"We define threats, on the other hand, as warnings that something unpleasant such as danger or harm may occur... Hazards are associated with the present, possibly producing harm or danger right now. In contrast, threats signal or foreshadow future harm or danger, or the intention to cause harm or danger: harm has not yet been actualized and is merely a possibility" (Van Brunschot & Kennedy, 2008, p. 5). "[W]e identify the nature of the hazard under consideration and whether it constitutes a threat (suggesting impending or potential harm) or an actual danger today" (Kennedy & Van Brunschot, 2009, p. 8).

"A threat is anything that can cause harm or loss" (Humanitarian Practice Network, 2010, p. 28).

United States

The U.S. GAO (2005c) defines threat as "an indication of the likelihood that a specific type of attack will be initiated against a specific target or class of targets. It may include any indication, circumstance, or even with the potential to cause the loss of or damage to an asset. It can also be defined as an adversary's intention and capability to undertake actions that would be detrimental to a value asset... Threats may be present at the global, national, or local level" (p. 110).

The U.S. FEMA (2005) defines threat as "any indication, circumstance, or event with the potential to cause loss of, or damage to an asset. Within the military services, the intelligence community, and law enforcement, the term 'threat' is typically used to describe the design criteria for terrorism or manmade disasters" (pp. 1–2).

The U.S. Department of Homeland Security (DHS) (2009) defines threat as "a natural or man-made occurrence, individual, entity, or action that has or indicates the potential to harm life, information, operations, the environment, and/or property" (p. 111). The DHS assesses threat as the probability that a specific type of attack will be initiated against a particular target or class of target. The DHS estimates (categorically) the threat (mostly international terrorist threats) to urban areas; the results ultimately determine the relative threat by each state and urban area. To get there, it surveys senior intelligence experts on the intelligence in four categories (detainee interrogations; ongoing plot lines; credible open source information; and relevant investigations), then tasks its own analysts to judge the number of threat levels and the placement of target areas within one of these levels (U.S. GAO, 2008a, pp. 20–22).

The DOD Dictionary (2012b) does not define threat, but its definitions of threat assessment specify a threat as terrorist.

Researchers of nuclear and cyber security at Sandia National Laboratories define threat as a "person or organization that intends to cause harm" (Mateski et al., 2012, p. 7).

British

The British Standards Institution (BSI) (2000) defined threat as a "source or situation with potential to harm the organization's assets" (p. 11). Neither the British Treasury nor the NAO define threat. The Civil Contingencies Secretariat defined threat as "intent and capability to cause loss of life or create adverse consequences to human welfare (including property and the supply of essential services and commodities), the environment, or security" (U.K. Cabinet Office, 2013).

Initially, the U.K. MOD (2009a) defined threat as "the potential existence of a negative event of sufficient magnitude to imperil the achievement of one or more of the organization's objectives." The MOD added, truthfully but unfortunately, that threat is "often used in place of risk." Later, the MOD (2011a) defined threats as "deliberate and malicious acts, e.g. terrorist attacks" (p. 14).

Canadian

A threat is "the presence of a hazard and an exposure pathway" (Public Safety Canada, 2012, p. 94).

Activation of Hazards as Threats

Hazard and threat are different states of the same thing. Concepts that explain a hazard's transition to threat include activation, coincidence, enablement, and release from containment, as described in the subsections below.

Activity Related

Activation strictly means that some activity has changed the hazard into a threat. One useful analytical step is to list operational activities and to consider whether they could activate any of the available hazards (the resulting threats are best categorized as *activity related*). For instance, the foreign coalition in Afghanistan has activated hostility in conservative local groups by bringing education to girls. This was unavoidable given the coalition's objectives but still was subject to diplomacy and negotiation.

Coincident

Sometimes, it might be best to consider coincidence between target and hazard as sufficient for the hazard to become a threat, particularly for natural, inanimate, or passive hazards. For instance, any object on the ground could be considered a hazard that could trip us. The victim or target would activate the hazard by tripping over it; as long as the potential victim or target avoids the hazard, it remains a hazard. A hurricane remains a hazard until it veers toward our location.

Enabled

Sometimes activation is more akin to enablement. For instance, if an outside actor supplies a malicious but unarmed organization with arms, then that actor has enabled a threat.

Released

Sometimes a hazard only becomes a threat if its container were to be broken. For instance, if acid is contained in a sealed bottle, it is a hazard until we break the bottle. Similarly, if an imprisoned criminal is released or escapes and commits another crime, the criminal has transitioned from hazard to threat. A nation-state is sometimes described as contained when its neighbors are ready to stop its aggression.

Pedagogy Box 4.5 Remote Human Activations of Religious-Political Violence

Increasingly, security and risk managers must think more proactively and creatively about potential activations and their responses. For instance, Theo van Gogh was shot to death by a fellow Dutch citizen, who claimed vengeance for a short film (*Submission*) that criticized Islam's posture toward women. The actual threat was difficult to predict, given the millions of peaceful Dutch. The target too was uncertain: van Gogh had directed the film, but it had been written by a former Dutch legislator (Ayaan Hirsi Ali), and dozens of others were involved with production. The timing was unpredictable: The film was screened at different festivals in 2004; the Dutch public broadcaster showed the film on August 29; the threat acted on November 2. Only the targets were predictable and perhaps could have been protected with better security, yet individuals must trade security with freedom: van Gogh was killed while pedaling his bicycle on a public street in Amsterdam.

Similarly, in 2010, a pastor (Terry Jones) at a small church (Christian Dove World Outreach Center) in Gainesville, Florida, published a book titled *Islam Is of the Devil.* In July, he declared the ninth anniversary of the terrorist attacks of September 11, 2001, as "International Burn a Koran Day" and promised to burn copies of the Quran on that day. On September 9, he canceled his plan, under some official and clerical pressure, but on September 10, protests against his plan grew violent, particularly in Afghanistan and Pakistan, where clerics condemned the plan. On March 20, 2011, Jones "prosecuted" and burnt a Quran. On March 24, Afghan President Hamid Karzai condemned the act, but in the process publicized it. On April 1, protesters in Afghanistan killed at least 30 people, including seven employees of the United Nations Assistance Mission in Mazar-i-Sharif. On April 28, 2012, Jones and his followers burnt more Qurans, although this activation was controlled by more effective official condemnation and also relegated by other Muslim grievances. In fact, much political violence is activated only proximately by such remote events, obscuring longer-term and less tangible grievances. Terry Jones' actions were outside the control of the victims, but officials in the United States learnt better how to articulate their disapproval of his actions and tolerance of his right to free speech.

Some activations are within the control of the personnel that would be threatened. For instance, on February 22, 2012, U.S. military personnel incinerated a collection of documents removed from the library at Parwan Detention Facility in Afghanistan. After news leaked of some religious texts within the collection, 5 days of protests ended with at least 30 killed, including four U.S. soldiers. This particular activation must have seemed remote and unfair to the personnel who thought they were stopping prisoners from using the documents for illicit communications, but it was controllable. A later military investigation reported that Afghan soldiers had warned against the action and that the U.S. soldiers lacked cultural and religious awareness, since their cultural training amounted to a one-hour presentation on Islam (Source: Craig Whitlock, "US Troops Tried to Burn 500 Copies of Koran, Investigation Says," *Washington Post,* August 27, 2012).

 Controlling Hazards

Analysis in terms of hazard, activation, and threat helps to clarify how the hazard can be contained or avoided. A hazard is not forgettable—the hazard could become a threat, so the risk manager must often choose a strategy for keeping the source in its hazardous state. Hazards remain hazards to us so long as we avoid activating the hazard, avoid exposing ourselves to the hazard, control enablers, or contain the hazard.

Avoidance of Activation

The hazard can be controlled by simply not activating it, which is usually less burdensome than terminating the hazard. For instance, if an armed group has no intent to harm us, our interests, or our allies and if the situation would not change, then we would be silly to pick a fight with it. We may have other reasons to confront armed actors, but we would be wrong to describe a hazard as a threat in order to confront it, which illustrates the perversities of some claims during the 2000s to reduce terrorist *threats* at home by intervening in a foreign *hazard.*

Avoidance of Exposure

We can avoid hazards by simply avoiding coincidence. Imagine a malicious actor with the intent and capability to harm me (I am vulnerable) but located in some remote location from where it cannot threaten me (I am not exposed). The actor in that situation is a hazard but could become a threat by travelling to me; alternatively, I could coincide with it by travelling to meet it. For instance, criminals are hazards as long as we do not frequent the same area, but if we visit their active area, we would expose ourselves to criminal threats.

Controlling Enablers

Hazards sometimes are unable to harm us, but other actors could enable the hazard by providing new intents or capabilities. We would be able to prevent the threat by stopping the enablement. For instance, some states and international institutions seek to prevent proliferation of weapons, because those weapons could enable a malicious actor to threaten others.

Containment

Where we are uncertain of the hazards and threats, a simple starting step in identifying hazards and threats is to list the agents or actors in some situation and then ask whether their capacity to threaten is contained or not.

Hazards can be contained in physical ways. Familiar examples are acids or pathogens contained in some sealed container. Similarly, human actors can be described as contained if they are detained or deterred. Hazards can be contained in behavioral ways too. For instance, we could, in theory, comfortably work alongside an explosive device as long as we were confident that we would not activate its detonator. Containment can be extended with further precautions. For instance, an item that is suspected of being explosive could be fenced off or placed in a special container designed to withstand blast until the item could be dismantled.

Assessing Hazards and Threats

Hazard and threat assessments are widely required, but widely dissatisfying.

> Several advantages ensue from the ability to measure threats accurately and consistently. Good threat measurement, for example, can improve understanding and facilitate analysis. It can also reveal trends and anomalies, underscore the significance of specific vulnerability, and help associate threats with potential consequences. In short, good threat measurement supports good risk management. Unfortunately, the practice of defining and applying good threat metrics remains immature. (Mateski et al., 2012, p. 7)

Often a hazard or threat is assessed by its associated risk, which would be a conflation of concepts. For instance, the BSI (2000, p. 20) prescribed an assessment of a threat (it could be used as easily to assess hazards) on two dimensions: the consequences of any event caused by the threat and the frequency of events with that source. The product of these two dimensions is effectively the risk. The BSI considered higher products of these two dimensions as intolerable threats, but really, they are intolerable risks (see Table 4.1).

Hazard and threat assessments are typically dissatisfying also because they usually focus on either threat or hazard and neglect the other. Hazards rarely are assessed discreetly; threat assessments and

Table 4.1 An Unfortunate Assessment of *Threat* as Effectively Risk—A Product of Frequency and Consequence

	Infrequent	**Medium Frequency**	**Continuous**
Minor consequences	*Tolerable threat*	*Tolerable threat*	*Tolerable threat*
Medium consequences	*Tolerable threat*	*Medium threat*	*Medium threat*
Disastrous consequences	*Tolerable threat*	*Medium threat*	*Intolerable threat*

SOURCE: Based on U.K. British Standards Institution, 2000, p. 20.

risk assessments are more common but often lack realism without assessments of the hazards and of how easily the hazards could be activated as threats.

The subsections below discuss how hazards and threats can be identified, estimated on binary or continuous scales, and assessed by their likelihood of activation.

Pedagogy Box 4.6 Official Definitions of Hazard Assessments

The U.S. government has lots of human threat assessments and natural hazard assessments, but no definition of a generic hazard assessment. Similarly, Public Safety Canada (2012, pp. 49, 95) does not define hazard assessment but defines *hazard identification* ("the process of identifying, characterizing, and validating hazards") and *threat assessment* ("a process consisting of the identification, analysis, and evaluation of threats"). Even more narrowly, the British Civil Contingencies Secretariat defines a *hazard assessment* as "a component of the civil protection risk assessment process in which identified hazards are assessed for risk treatment" and defines hazard identification as "a component of the civil protection risk assessment process in which identified hazards are identified" (U.K. Cabinet Office, 2013).

Identifying Hazards and Threats

A necessary starting point is to identify the tangible actors or items that are in a hazardous state and to estimate their number. For instance, all roads are stages for traffic with which we could collide, so certainly other items of traffic are hazards. On the road surface itself will be other hazards, such as stones, with which we could collide, that could be tossed up by passing traffic into our path, or on which we could slip. The road surface might be disfigured by cracks or holes into which we could fall. Materials could fall onto the road from roadside hills. Precipitation could make the road slippery.

When lots of hazards are around, we can ease the identification burden by counting only those hazards of minimum scale or rank. For instance, per mile of road we could count the loose stones above a certain size or weight, count the number of holes above a certain width and depth, or the area of standing water of sufficient depth.

After an estimate of the hazards, we should estimate the entities that are already in a threatening state. Since a threat can be understood as an activated hazard, the analyst could search for threats by identifying hazards that have been activated (and the strategist should consider how to deactivate the threats).

Binary Versus Continuous Assessments

In practice, we often describe something as hazardous or not, or threatening or not, as if the states are binary (as if it either exists or not), but in theory, hazards and threats are on a continuous scale. Anything could be considered hazardous or threatening to some degree. We could trip over, collide with, or contract a disease from anything or anybody, but in practice, we usually ignore routine or minor hazards and would describe something as hazardous only if it were more hazardous than normal or it became a clear threat. For instance, we could take a road for granted, until the surface becomes pitted, loose, or wet, when we might describe the road as hazardous.

The road itself is inherently hazardous and each of these hazards makes the road more hazardous, so the road's hazardousness is on a continuous scale. However, in practice, we often forget about or ignore hazards until we realize that they have breached some threshold of acceptability, as if hazards lie on a binary categorical scale. Authorities and users could suddenly decide that the road is too hazardous to use if the holes, stones, or precipitation breach some threshold of scale.

This practical choice between a continuous and binary assessments of hazardousness is important to remember because it is a deliberate choice and a trade-off with consequences. Sometimes authorities include so many minor things as hazards or describe hazards in such detail that stakeholders cease to take the authorities seriously, while conversely sometimes they take major hazards for granted.

Assessing the Likelihood of Activation

The final part of a hazard assessment should focus on how easy the hazard would be to activate as a threat, leaving a later part of the assessment to focus on how threatening it would be if activated. Most threat assessments actually assess only the potential harm and rarely assess the actual potential for a threat to arise from a particular hazard.

Ease of activation could be measured as the inverse of the effectiveness of the controls on the hazard. For instance, a pathogen that is sealed inside a container, which is placed within a vault, within a locked building, within a guarded perimeter, becomes less likely to be activated as we put more containers around it. We could count the number of barriers to activation as an inverse measure of the ease of activation. A deeper analysis of hazardousness should identify the different processes by which the hazard could become a threat and should assess how easily each process could activate the threat.

A correspondingly deep assessment of the risks resulting from the source (the hazard) would include assessments of the probabilities of each stage in the journey from hazard through threat to risk (see Figure 4.3).

Sources of Positive Risks

Good analysis should identify not just negative hazards and threats but also the sources of positive risks—potential contributors that could be activated as some sort of positive partner, defender, or ally. The sections below define and analyze *opportunity*, *positive hazard*, *contributor*, *partner*, and *stakeholder*.

Opportunity

In general use, opportunity is defined as "a favorable juncture of circumstances" (Merriam-Webster's Dictionary), "a chance to do something or an occasion when it is easy for you to do something" (Longman), "a chance to do something, or a situation in which it is easy for you to do something" (Macmillan), "a time or set of circumstances that makes it possible to do something" (Oxford), or "an occasion or situation which makes it possible to do something that you want to do or have to do, or the possibility of doing something" (Cambridge). FrameNet defines opportunity as "a situation not completely under the agent's control and usually of a limited duration" that gives the agent "a choice of whether or not to participate in some desirable event."

In any general sense, an opportunity is a positive situation or good fortune (an antonym of *threatening situation*). Some risk analysts and managers use the word in this sense, such as where the International Organization for Standardization (2009a, p. vii) reminds us that "potential opportunities" should be considered and where many authorities suggest "take the opportunity" as a strategy.

However, some authorities define an opportunity as both a positive risk and the source (akin to a positive hazard) of a positive risk. Such authorities include managers of project and financial risks (Heerkens, 2002, p. 143; Hillson, 2003; O'Reilly, 1998) and the British government's Treasury, NAO, MOD, and project management standard (PRINCE2) (NAO, 2000, p. 1; U.K. MOD, 2011c, p. 7; U.K. Office of Government Commerce, 2009; U.K. Treasury, 2004). This is an unhelpful conflation, similar to the many uses of the word *threat* to mean both a negative hazard and a negative risk. Defining a positive risk as an opportunity is unnecessary because the term *positive risk* needs no synonym.

Positive Hazard

Hazard has no clear antonym, something like a sympathetic neutral, absent friend, well-wisher, hero, or angel. *Positive hazard* is the clearest antonym of negative hazard, just as we differentiate positive and negative risks. (*Opportunity* is sometimes used as the source of a positive risk, but we should not want to lose the unique meaning of opportunity as a favorable situation.)

Although hazard has an overwhelmingly negative connotation, the same source, depending on the situation, could become a threat or an ally, so analytically we would be justified to consider a hazard with both negative and positive potential. For instance, we might upset somebody enough that they want to harm us, or we could persuade them to help. Similarly, at the time of a foreign intervention, an armed militia might remain neutral (a hazardous condition) or side with local insurgents against the foreigners (a threatening condition), perhaps because the insurgents activate the hazard with bribes or because the foreigners activate the hazard by some negative interaction (as simple as accidental collateral harm to the militia). The neutral militia's potential as a contributor would be easy to forget. At the time of intervention, the foreigners could have engaged positively enough that the militia would have chosen to ally with the foreigners. The foreigners still should have rejected the offer if such an alliance were to offer intolerable negative risks, such as probable betrayal or defection after accepting arms, as sometimes occurred after foreign coalitions in Iraq and Afghanistan had allied with local militia.

Contributor

In my definition, a *contributor* is an actor or agent in a positive state—an antonym of threat. Other antonyms of threat include allies, defenders, guards, supporters, carers, helpers, donors, grantors, and aiders, but each has situational rather than generalizable meanings.

The only available official antonym of threat is *contributor*. The Canadian government refers to a contributor effectively as anything that contributes positively to the management of emergencies. It refers to contributors as "all levels of government, first receivers, healthcare and public health professionals, hospitals, coroners, the intelligence community, specialized resources, including scientific and urban search and rescue (USAR) resources, the military, law-enforcement agencies, non-government organizations, private sector contributors, and the academic community" (Public Safety Canada, 2012, p. 19).

Partner

The Canadian government differentiates a *contributor* from a *partner* ("an individual, group, or organization that might be affected by, or perceive itself to be affected by, an emergency") (Public Safety Canada, 2012, pp. 19, 71). The word *partner* is often used in the sense of ally, but in risk management, a partner could be sharing negative risks but not necessarily contributing positive risks, so the word *partner* does not mean the same as contributor.

Stakeholder

Practically every other actor is a hazard or an opportunity. This insight helps explain the common advice to consider *stakeholders* during practically any activity related to security or risk management. The British government has listed the following stakeholders in any business: own organization; donors and sponsors; suppliers and customers; design authorities; neighboring organizations; utility companies; insurers; emergency services; and local authorities (U.K. Business Continuity Institute, National Counterterrorism Security Office, & London First, 2003, p. 21).

A stakeholder such as a donor might seem like a certain contributor, but remember that an actor's state can change: A stakeholder could withdraw its support and declare neutrality (thereby becoming a hazard) or criticize the recipient's handling of its receipts (thereby becoming a threat).

Categorizing Hazards, Threats, and Contributors

Authorities tend to categorize risks, events, hazards, or threats in particular domains but have not agreed on the primary categories of hazards and threats, in part because of conceptual confusion between hazards and threats. I recommend four categories of hazards, threats, opportunities, and contributors, as described in the subsections below: natural, material, human/organizational, and human-caused or -made. With these categories, we can use Table 4.2 to code different actors or agents by their current relationship to us.

Table 4.2 A Table for Plotting Different Actors or Agents by Their Categorical Type and Their Current Relationship to Us, With Some *Notional Examples*

Type of Agent or Actor	Hazard	Opportunity	Threat	Contributor
Natural	*River*	*Water*	*Flood*	*Drinking water*
Material	*Cleaning fluid*	*Solar energy*	*Corrosive*	*Solar-generated electricity*
Human or organizational	*Infectious person*	*Neutral actor*	*Infection*	*Defender*
Human-caused or -made	*Landmine*	*Fuel*	*Improvised explosive device*	*Defensive weapon*

Pedagogy Box 4.7 Other Categories of Hazards and Threats

The International Risk Governance Council (IRGC) has suggested an unusually long list of "hazardous agents," but these are more illustrative than categorical (see Table 4.3).

Table 4.3 The International Risk Governance Council's List of Hazardous Agents

Category	Subcategories
Physical	*Ionizing radiation; nonionizing radiation; noise (industrial, leisure, etc.); kinetic energy (explosion, collapse, etc.); temperature (fire, overheating, overcooling)*
Chemical	*Toxic substances; genotoxic/carcinogenic substances; environmental pollutants; compound mixtures*
Biological	*Fungi and algae; bacteria; viruses; genetically modified organisms; other pathogens*
Natural forces	*Wind; earthquakes; volcanic activities; drought; flood; tsunami; wild fire; avalanche*
Socio-communicative	*Terrorism and sabotage; human violence (criminal acts); humiliation, mobbing, stigmatizing; experimentation with humans; mass hysteria; psychosomatic syndromes*
Complex combinations	*Food (chemical and biological); consumer products (chemical, physical, etc.); technologies (physical, chemical, etc.); large constructions, such as buildings, dams, highways, bridges; critical infrastructures (physical, economic, socio-organizational and -communicative)*

SOURCE: Renn, 2008, p. 7.

The Canadian government has defined two categories of hazard (technological and natural) and three categories of threat (accidentally human induced, intentionally human induced, natural) (Public Safety Canada, 2012, pp. 48, 94), but it also produced an incompatible "risk taxonomy" (see Table 4.4).

Table 4.4 The Canadian Government's "Taxonomy" of Threats and Hazards

Group	Category	Subcategories
Intentional	*Criminal*	*Terrorist; extremist; individual criminal; organized criminal; corporate or insider saboteur; corporate spy*
	Foreign state	*State-sponsored terrorist; spy; war belligerent*

(Continued)

(Continued)

Group	Category	Subcategories
Unintentional	*Social*	*Migration; social unrest and civil disobediences*
	Technical and accidental	*Spill; fire; explosion; structural collapse; system error yielding failure*
Health	*Pandemics and epidemics*	*Human health; animal health*
	Large-scale contamination	*Contaminant of drugs and health products; contaminant of food, water, or air; contaminant of the environment*
Emerging phenomena and technologies	-	*Biological science and technology; health sciences; (re)emerging health hazards; chemical components; emerging natural hazards; material science and engineering; information technologies*
Natural	*Meteorological*	*Hurricane; tornado or wind storm; hail, snow, or ice storm; flood or storm surge; avalanche; forest fire; drought; extreme temperatures*
	Geological	*Tsunami; earthquake; volcanic eruption; land or mud slide; land subsidence; glacier or iceberg effects; space weather*
	Ecological and global phenomena	*Infestations; effects of overexploitation; effects of excessive urbanization; global warming; extreme climate change conditions*

SOURCE: Public Safety Canada, 2013, p. 65.

The British Cabinet Office (2012b) has identified three categories of "emergency" events: natural, major accidental, and malicious.

Private analysts have suggested three categories of hazards (by which they meant also threats): terrorist, technological, and natural (Bullock, Haddow, & Coppola, 2013, p. 58).

We could use the World Economic Forum's five categories of risk (economic, environmental, geopolitical, societal, and technological) to categorize hazards and threats too.

Natural

A natural hazard is any natural phenomenon of potential harm. For instance, a flood is a natural hazard as long as it could harm us and has natural causes (such as rainfall). Note that a flood could have unnatural causes too, such as malicious sabotage of the levee. Some natural hazards can be activated by human behavior. For instance, some humans have turned harmless biological organisms into biological weapons; others have triggered earthquakes by aggressively fracturing the earth in pursuit of natural resources. These hazards are truly human-made but share other characteristics with natural hazards.

Natural sources of risk (such as a river) traditionally have been described as hazards and not threats, even when they are clearly causing harm and are properly categorized as threats (such as when a river is flooding a town), due to a linguistic bias toward natural hazards and human threats rather than natural threats and human hazards, but this is analytically misleading. Natural and human sources each can be hazards or threats.

Proper analysis should recognize natural threats whenever we coincide with a natural hazard in a harmful way. Clarification should emerge when we ask whether we are exposed and vulnerable (see Chapter 5) to the source: For instance, a person with a communicable disease (the hazard) would become a threat if we coincided with the person and we lacked immunity to the disease. Similarly, a drought would become a threat if we lacked reserves to cover the shortfall in the harvest (Wisner, Blaikie, Cannon, & Davis, 2004, pp. 49, 337).

One explanation for the favoritism toward the term *natural hazard* over *natural threat* is that natural agents have no human-like conscious intent. Like all hazards, natural hazards remain hazardous to us as long as we are not vulnerable and exposed, even though the same agents would be threats to anyone who is vulnerable and exposed. For instance, a flood or toxic contamination is a threat to anyone in the affected area, even while it remains a hazard to us until we travel into the affected area or it spreads into our area.

I suggest the following categories of natural sources:

- cosmic (for instance: solar storms; meteors),
- meteorological or weather and climatic (for instance: precipitation),
- tidal (high-tide floods),
- geomorphic (subsidence),
- seismic (earthquakes),
- volcanic (ejected lava or ash),
- incendiary (wildfires), and
- biological phenomena (diseases).

Note that some authorities refer to hydrological or hydrologic hazards as any water-related hazards, such as floods (Bullock, Haddow, & Coppola, 2013, pp. 58–59), which cross meteorological and tidal hazards and could be compounded by geological, seismic, volcanic, and incendiary hazards.

Pedagogy Box 4.8 Other Categories of Natural Hazards

The IRGC published a list of "natural forces" (wind, earthquakes, volcanic activities, drought, flood, tsunami, wild fire, avalanche), although it separated biological, chemical, and physical agents (such as radiation) that could be regarded as natural (see Table 4.3). The Canadian government defines a natural hazard as "a source of potential harm originating from a meteorological, environmental, geological, or biological event" and notes, as examples, "tornadoes, floods, glacial melt, extreme weather, forest and urban fires, earthquakes, insect infestations, and infectious diseases" (Public Safety Canada, 2012, p. 66). Like many insurers and reinsurers, Swiss Re Group defines natural catastrophes as "loss events triggered by natural forces."

Material

Material hazards (hazardous materials; HAZMATs) include entirely natural materials, such as fossil fuels, and human-made materials from natural sources, such as distilled fuels, that are somehow potentially harmful, such as by toxicity.

Inanimate material threats are easier than human or organized threats to measure objectively, in part because material threats do not have any conscious intent. For instance, biological and chemical threats (and hazards) are assessed often by their "toxicity" and measured by some quantity, perhaps as a concentration or rate in relation to some medium (such as milliliters of hazard per liter of water) or to the human body (such as grams of hazard per pound of body weight).

The activation of a threat from a hazardous material is usually human-caused (for instance, humans drill for oil and sometimes spill oil), so we should be careful to distinguish the human-caused threat (such as an oil spill) from the material hazard (the oil).

Some hazardous materials overlap human-made hazards (described later), such as explosive weapons (which are hazardous in themselves and contain hazardous materials).

Pedagogy Box 4.9 Official Definitions of Hazardous Materials

A *hazardous material* (HAZMAT) is "any substance, or mixture of substances, having properties capable of harming people, property, or the environment" (Public Safety Canada, 2012, p. 49). The U.S. DOD (2012b) does not define hazardous material but defines a *hazardous cargo* as a "cargo that includes not only large bulk-type categories such as explosives, pyrotechnics, petroleum, oils and lubricants, compressed gases, corrosives and batteries, but less quantity materials like super-tropical bleach (oxiderizer), pesticides, poisons, medicines, specialized medical chemicals and medical waste that can be loaded as cargo" (p. 127). Such materials are ubiquitous for commercial and household purposes, not just military purposes. The British Health and Safety Executive regulates the control of "substances hazardous to health," which are properly abbreviated to SHH but are often abbreviated to COSHH.

Human and Organizational

Human and organization actors are more analytically complicated than natural and material actors, so this section is longer. The subsections below define human and organizational actors and show how to assess human and organizational actors, introducing the new concepts of intent and capability.

Defining Human and Organizational Actors

Human hazards are human beings with the potential to threaten. Organizational hazards are organizations with the potential to threaten. Human and organizational hazards and threats are categorically different from human-caused or -made hazards and threats, which are described later.

These definitions should make clear that any human or organization is a hazard on some dimension, even if they were well meaning on most dimensions. For instance, someone who loves us could still accidentally trip us up or communicate a contagious disease. Human and organizational threats are best described by their intent and capabilities to harm, as described in the sections below.

Pedagogy Box 4.10 Official Definitions and Assessments of Human Hazards and Threats

The Canadian government has the most complicated analytical structure for human and organization actors. It separates

- generic threats (which include *intentional human-induced* threats);
- a *threat actor* or *malicious actor* ("an individual or group that attacks or threatens an asset, the government, or public safety and security");
- a *threat agent* ("an individual or group having the capability, intent, and/or motivation to pose a threat"); and
- *criminal activities* ("intentional human-caused actions or events, or omissions of duty, that constitute or may lead to a legal offense") (Public Safety Canada, 2012, pp. 20, 94).

The Canadian government lists six types of criminal threat:

- Terrorists
- Extremists
- Individual criminals
- Organized criminals
- Corporate insider saboteur
- Corporate spy

It separates foreign state threats from individual criminals, although some of the foreign state activities are criminal:

- State-sponsored terrorism
- Espionage
- War (Public Safety Canada, 2013, p. 65).

In another publication, the Canadian government has placed all malicious actors within a category termed ***intentional threats*** (Public Safety Canada, 2013, p. 65), which is differentiated from the effectively unintentional natural threats.

Similarly, the British government distinguishes natural and accidental events from "malicious attacks by both state and non-state actors, such as terrorists and organized criminals" (U.K. Cabinet Office, 2010, p. 25).

FEMA and other civil agencies of U.S. government recognize human-caused hazards, mainly in distinction from natural hazards, and mainly to mean terrorism (FEMA, 2005, pp. 1–2). In March 2009, a newly appointed U.S. Secretary of Homeland Security (Janet Napolitano) attempted to replace *terrorism* with *man-caused disasters*, although the attempt was ridiculed. Such a term is dissatisfying because it would conflate intentional and malicious threats with man-caused accidents.

(Continued)

(Continued)

In 2005, the U.S. GAO, after auditing threat assessment at the DHS, defined threat assessment as "the identification and evaluation of adverse events that can harm or damage an asset. A threat assessment includes the probability of an event and the extent of its lethality."

At that time, the DHS method of assessing threats to the homeland relied on official intelligence, mainly about actors who were plotting to harm the homeland. This intelligence was subcategorized in terms of the threat's intent, the threat's capabilities, the threat's "chatter" (as observed by U.S. intelligence) about its plots, and the "attractiveness" of the target area to the threat. Specific measures of the supply side included the total reports from the intelligence community that referred to the target area, the count of suspicious incidents, the count of investigations by the Federal Bureau of Investigation (FBI), the count of investigations by the Immigration & Customs Enforcement agency (ICE), and counts of the international visitors and vessels from "Special Interest Countries" (Masse, O'Neil, & Rollins, 2007; U.S. GAO, 2005b, 2008b).

In May 2008, the Diplomatic Security Service (established by the Department of State in 1985) created the Threat Investigations & Analysis Directorate, which consolidated the monitoring, analysis, and distribution of intelligence on terrorism directed against American citizens and diplomatic missions abroad and helps to determine for U.S. diplomatic missions the "threat ratings" that affect their security preparedness (U.S. GAO, 2009, p. 5). These threat ratings effectively use a 4-point scale to rate different types of threat (these types differentiate terrorists from other types of criminal) (see Table 4.5). Note that this method practically includes both hazards and threats.

Table 4.5 A Matrix for Representing the Threat Level by Level of "Impact on American Diplomats" and Different Categories of Threat

Level of Impact	Terrorism, International	Terrorism, Indigenous	Political Violence	Crime	Intelligence, Human	Intelligence, Technical
Critical (grave impact)						
High (serious impact)						
Medium (moderate impact)						
Low (minor impact)						

SOURCE: Based on U.S. GAO, 2009, pp. 7–8.

Assessing Human and Organization Actors

As the subsections below demonstrate, we could assess human and organization actors by identifying hazards and threats, and assessing intents and capabilities.

Identifying Human and Organizational Hazards

In the broadest sense, human hazards are easy to count as everyone in the same population, before we identify those that are known threats or contributors. Similarly, all organizations are hazards until we establish those that are threats or contributors. A proper analysis of the context should identify all the actors, code them as hazards, threats, or contributors, identify their relationships, and estimate their ease of activation or weakness of containment.

Pedagogy Box 4.11 Other Prescriptions for Identifying Human and Organizational Hazards

Many authorities, including the IRGC (2008, p. 20) and International Organization for Standardization (2009a), advocate attention to the "context," by which they mean analysis of the self and the surrounding actors. The IRGC usefully presents an image of an organization surrounded by

- the organization's own organizational capacity, which must contain hazardous employees and contractors;
- an "actor network" of politicians, regulators, commercial actors, news media, nongovernmental organizations, and general members of the public;
- a "political and regulatory culture" with "different regulatory styles; and
- a social climate.

Pedagogy Box 4.12 Estimating Criminal Threats

In order to estimate the number of criminal threats in a population or area, we could measure the supply side (in economic terms) by extrapolating from the known criminals in a past period, such as persons arrested, charged, convicted, or incarcerated. However, some of these types, such as arrested persons, would include false positives, and some types, such as currently incarcerated criminals, are in a hazardous state. Official crime rates underestimate the true rate of criminals in the general population. More crimes are reported than lead to convictions, and more crimes occur than are reported. Officials point out that popular fears cause people to think that fear-inspiring crimes are more frequent than they really are, but officials also have incentives to deflate crime, so the true rate of crime is difficult to induce. The U.S. Department of Justice's surveys suggest that people experience about twice as many crimes as arrests.

Certain crimes could be considered more serious and ranked accordingly relative to other crimes. If we could find no crimes of the particular type to measure, we could count all crimes as an indicator of criminal propensity in the area or population. Where criminal threats are estimated for a particular area, the estimate is sometimes known as *criminal terrain*.

Intent and Capability

Commentators tend to be too casual about declaring others as threats, so we should check for the two most conventional attributes of a threat: intent and capability. A proper threat analysis needs to assess the intent and capabilities of the threat, the different events that could be caused by the threat, the different returns by each event, and the target's exposure and vulnerability (the subjects of Chapter 5) to this particular threat. (This sort of analysis was shown in Figure 4.3.) Deeper analysis would allow us to separate hazards from threats by their differences in intent and capabilities. Scenario analysis would lead to forecasts of how a hazard or threat could switch to the other state given changes in intents or capabilities. Consider the simple, notional scenario below, which I will present as a series of logical steps in our analysis:

1. Terrorist group "T" currently has no intent or capability to harm our organization.
2. If terrorist group "T" were to discover our activity "A," then "T" would be aggrieved and thereby acquire the intent to harm our organization.
3. If terrorist group "T" were to discover method "M," then "T" would acquire the capability to defeat our defenses.

The following sections explain more about assessing intent and capability respectively.

Pedagogy Box 4.13 Official Assessments of Intent and Capability

The U.S. DHS (2010) notes that "[a]dversary intent is one of two elements, along with adversary capability, that is commonly considered when estimating the likelihood of terrorist attacks." Similarly, the Canadian government prescribes an assessment of the likelihood of a deliberate attack in terms of the actor's "intent" and the attack's "technical feasibility" (a combination of the actor's capability and the target's exposure and vulnerability) (Public Safety Canada, 2013, pp. 45–46).

The Humanitarian Practice Network (2010, p. 40) prescribes assessment of the threat's frequency, intent, and capability:

"When assessing a potential threat from a human source (adversary), determine whether they display the following three key characteristics:

- history—a past incidence or pattern of attacks on similar organizations.
- intent—specific threats, a demonstrated intention or mindset to attack.
- capability—the wherewithal to carry out an attack."

Intent

The subsections below respectively define intent and describe alternative ways to assess a threat's intent.

Defining Intent

Intent is a person's resolution or determination to do something. The intent to harm is fundamental to a deliberate threat. Indeed, FrameNet defines threat (noun) as something committed to harm and (verb) the expressed commitment to harm. Semantic analysts note that human actors are described with some goal when they cause harm or take risks. The actor's goal is expressed in four grammatical ways: intended gain, purpose ("what an actor intends to accomplish in performing the deed"), beneficiary ("the person for whose benefit something is done"), and motivation ("the psychological source of the actor's behavior") (Fillmore & Atkins, 1992, pp. 83–84).

A threat becomes more threatening as it becomes more intent on harming us. Human intent could be understood as deliberate (such as a malicious car driver) or accidental (a sleepy car driver). Natural and inanimate threats are best understood as having accidental or mechanistic intent, rather than deliberate intent: For instance, a landmine is designed to explode when something triggers the detonating mechanism, and a hurricane will follow a certain path. Neither has conscious intent, but each could coincide with a target in a predictably harmful way.

Assessing Intent

A good assessment of a human actor assesses the actor's current intent and the possibility of external or accidental activations of a threat from a hazard. For instance, most persons mean no harm to most other people most of the time, but they could be upset by some grievance or misled by some malicious entrepreneur, sufficient to become malicious toward us.

In practice, most assessments of intent are judgmental, but still we should prefer rigor and transparency over personal intuition or assumption, so we should consider and declare our coding rules. At simplest, we could judge whether the actor is sufficiently malicious, malignant, or misguided enough to harm us (the code would be binary: yes or no). This is a simple coding rule that could be declared to other stakeholders and be used to survey experts. We could collect finer codes by asking for a judgment on a 5-point scale—such as a whole number from 0 (no intent) to 4 (highest intent).

For instance, the U.S. Army provides a method for categorizing "enemies" on two dimensions: hostility and legal recognition as enemies (see Figure 4.4).

Figure 4.4 A Matrix for Analyzing Hazards and Threats by Their Hostility and Our Intent to Use Force (based on U.S. Army, 2008, Paragraph 1–43)

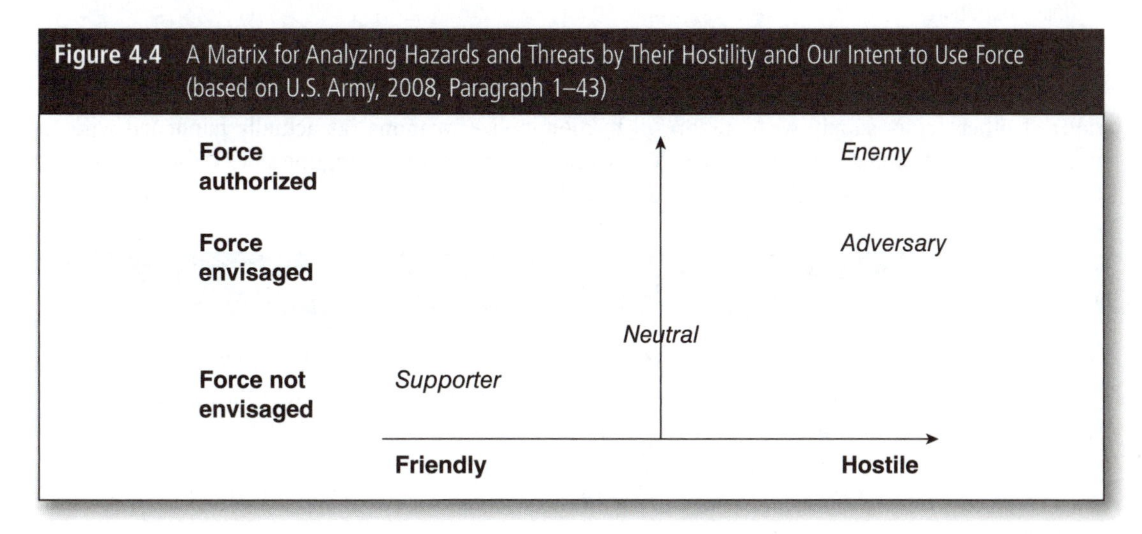

For analyzing stakeholders whose influence could affect resourcing, or any actors (like journalists) whose influence could affect at least our reputation, we could assess their intent along a dimension from support to opposition. We could add another dimension for influence, from fringe to mainstream (see Figure 4.5).

Figure 4.5 A Matrix for Analyzing Other *Actors* by Their Opposition/Support and Influence on Stakeholders

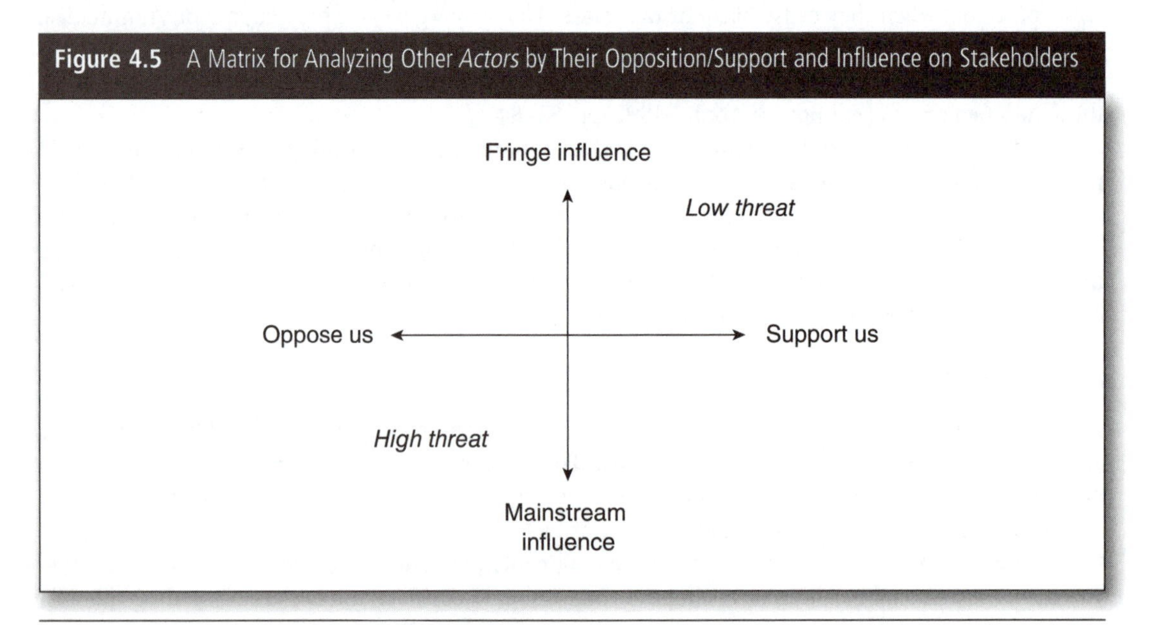

SOURCE: Based on U.K. Prime Minister's Strategy Unit, 2005, p. 29.

Capability

The subsections below respectively define a threat's capability and assess that capability.

Defining Capability

Intent to harm is necessary but not sufficient for a threat: The threat must have the capability to harm us. We could imagine another actor with malicious intent but no useful weapons (a hazardous condition). If other actors supply weapons or fail to monopolize weapons (as actually happened when a multinational coalition conquered Iraq in 2003 without securing former regime stocks) then the hazard could acquire capabilities sufficient to be considered a threat.

Pedagogy Box 4.14 Official Definitions of Capability

Many authorities define threat in terms of capability but fail to define capability, except as something that the target needs in respond to threats. Fortunately, the meaning of capability is consistent in those latter definitions: "a combination of resources" (Public Safety Canada, 2012) or "a demonstrable ability" (U.K. Cabinet Office, 2013) to do something.

Assessing Capability

The availability of weapons is a key indicator of human threat. Such availability is one enabler (alongside intent) of war and violent crime. Consequently, some indices of power, belligerence, or peacefulness include measures of the availability of weapons. An easy way to measure a threat's capabilities is to count their weapons or rank their weapons, from, for instance: no weapons, blunt objects, knives, hand guns, rifles, heavier weapons. Organizational capabilities can be measured objectively by counting threatening assets (such as weapons and personnel) or inputs (such as military spending).

Relative capabilities can be measured by comparing the other's capabilities against our capabilities (in the military, this process often is known as *net assessment*). We could also compare their offensive capabilities against our defensive capabilities. For instance, if the other is armed with only blunt instruments and we are armed with firearms or are protected behind materials proof against blunt instruments, then we should conclude that the other actor practically lacks capabilities to harm us and is therefore not a threat but a hazard (although we should remember that the hazard could become a threat by acquiring different weapons).

Human-Caused or -Made

Some hazards are best categorized as human-caused or -made, even if they contain or are derived from natural materials (for instance, biological weapons). Some of these hazards (such as landmines) are manufactured by humans deliberately, some are deliberately activated by humans (such as floods caused by terrorist sabotage), some are accidental (such as unintended pollution). Four clear categories (accidental, human activated, human manufactured, and technological) are described in the subsections below.

Pedagogy Box 4.15 Authoritative Concepts of Human-Caused or -Made Hazards and Threats

The United Nations International Strategy for Disaster Reduction (UN ISDR, 2009, p. 12) recognizes two types of human-caused or human-activated hazards: "technological hazard" and "socio-natural hazard." The U.S. FEMA (2005, pp. 1–2) recognized two types of human-caused hazard: "technological hazard"; and "terrorism." Similarly, the British Cabinet Office (2010, p. 25) distinguished "man-made accidents" from malicious actors (like terrorists).

The Canadian government clearly defines only technological hazard as an unnatural hazard but allows threats to include "intentional human-induced" and "accidental human-induced" threats (Public Safety Canada, 2012, p. 94). Its taxonomy separates intentional from unintentional threats and hazards, where the unintentional threats and hazards include a technical/accidental category separate from a social category.

Most insurers and reinsurers distinguish between *natural* and *man-made* catastrophes or disasters. For instance, Swiss Re Group defines man-made disasters as "loss events associated with human activities." United Nations agencies tend to refer to human catastrophes.

Accidental

Accidents are unintended events. Deliberate human-made hazards and accidents are usually conflated, but this is analytically imperfect because accidental and deliberate activities have very different legal and practical implications.

Pedagogy Box 4.16 Official Definitions of Accidental Hazards

The British Cabinet Office (2010, p. 25) distinguished "man-made accidents" from malicious actors (like terrorists). The Canadian government separates "intentional human-induced" from "accidental human-induced" threats (Public Safety Canada, 2012, pp. 94). Its taxonomy (Public Safety Canada, 2013, p. 65) lists technical and accidental events as

- spill,
- fire,
- explosion,
- structural collapse,
- system error yielding failure.

Human Activated

A human-activated threat has changed state from hazard to threat because of some human activity-note that this outcome could have been unintended (accidental). A human being could activate a threat by accidentally causing a grievance; another human being could engage in some activity (such as educating girls in a conservative part of Afghanistan) knowing that the activity could activate a grievance—in each case, the outcome is the same, but in one case, the outcome was accidental, while in the other, the outcome was an accepted risk. Similarly, one person could accidentally release a chemical threat from its container into a river, while another could knowingly change that same chemical into a chemical weapon. (*Man-caused* is a common adjective for hazards, but apart from being prejudicially gendered, it is often restricted to very contradictory behaviors, from terrorism to accidents. Man-caused literally includes both deliberate and accidental activities.)

Pedagogy Box 4.17 Unintentional Social Activation

The UN ISDR (2009) used the misleading term *socio-natural hazard* as "the phenomenon of increased occurrence of certain geophysical and hydrometereological hazard events, such as landslides, flooding, land subsidence, and drought, that arise from the interaction of natural hazards with overexploited or degraded land and environmental resources. This term is used for the circumstances where human activity is increasing the occurrence of certain hazards beyond their natural probabilities" (p. 12).

The Canadian government seemed to allow for human-activated human threats when it separated *social* unintentional threats and hazards from *accidental* threats and hazards (Public Safety Canada, 2013, p. 65).

Human Manufactured

Human-manufactured hazards and threats are material items that exist only because of a human constructive process. Human-manufactured hazards and threats include hazards and threats with no natural equivalents. By contrast, accidental and human-activated threats (such as a flood due to human error or sabotage) have natural relatives.

Almost any weapons are deliberately manufactured hazards. They are best categorized as hazards, since a typical weapon is harmless if left alone and only becomes a threat when activated by an actor (either accidentally discharged or used against a target by a human threat).

A landmine is an easy example. A landmine is some sort of explosive device activated when the target, usually a person or a vehicle, triggers the detonator. As long as the landmine remains undisturbed, it does no harm and remains a hazard. Helpful actors could contain the hazard by warning others of the hazard or controlling access to it. Malicious actors could seek to restore the hazard by removing it from its containment or could activate a greater threat by converting the landmine into an improvised explosive device (IED) that could be thrown at the target. The material hazardousness of a landmine can be measured by the weight or energy of the explosive filling, stealthiness (small size or weight and nonferrous materials imply stealthiness), and sensitivity of detonation mechanisms.

Technological

Technological risks are risks arising from technological failure, where the technology itself is the hazard (such as a part of an aircraft that falls on to a population below) or is the activator of a hazard (such as a drilling machine that activates an earthquake). In detail, a *technology risk* has been subcategorized as

1. *Technical risk*: "The set of technical problems associated with a new or emerging technology [such as] application of a new process, material, or subsystem before fully understanding the parameters that control, performance, cost, safe operating latitudes, or failure modes."

2. *Availability of competencies and complementary technologies required*: "Development of a new technology may require new technical skills, tools, and processes, or may require access to skills and tools already committed to other technology and product development efforts. Complementary technologies may be required to work in concert with the new technology, but may not be ready or implemented. In some cases, a critical resource is the technical know-how necessary to integrate the new technology into an existing system."

3. *Specification achievability*: "What we are referring to here is not the risk that the target specification has been properly selected based on the customer need and market requirements, but the risk that the technology performance is insufficient to meet the target specification. Examples include the possibility of shortfalls in parameters related to quality, speed, reliability, and cost." (Hartmann & Myers, 2001, pp. 37–38)

Unfortunately, human accidents often are categorized as "technological," which is misleading unless we mean that a technology has failed.

Pedagogy Box 4.18 Official Definitions of Technological Hazards

The UN ISDR (2009, p. 12) defines technological hazards as both accidental and deliberate ("originating from technological or industrial conditions, including accidents, dangerous procedures, infrastructure failures, or specific human activities"). Public Safety Canada (2012, p. 93) also defines technological hazard as both accidental and deliberate ("a source of potential harm originating from technology use, misuse, or failure"). (However, all its examples are accidental: "Examples of technological hazards include technical failures, mechanical failures, software failures, operator errors, process or procedure failures, structural failures, dependent critical infrastructure disruptions or failures.") By contrast, the U.S. FEMA (2005, pp. 1–2) defines technological hazards as unintended technical and material failures, such as leakage of a hazardous material.

SUMMARY

This chapter has

- explained the sources and causes of risk,
- defined hazard,
- defined threat,
- described how hazards can be activated as threats,
- explained how hazards can be controlled,
- described how to assess hazards and threats in general,
- defined and described the sources of positive risks, including opportunity, positive hazard, contributor, partner, and stakeholder,
- described natural sources,
- described material sources,
- described and assessed human and organizational sources, including by their intent and capabilities, and
- described human-caused and human-made sources, including accidental, human activated, human manufactured, and technological.

QUESTIONS AND EXERCISES

1. What is the difference between hazard and threat?
2. How could a hazard become a threat?
3. How could you prevent a hazard from becoming a threat?
4. How could the same thing be a hazard to us but a threat to others?
5. What would be different between a hazard assessment and a threat assessment?

6. Describe two ways in which you could practically assess hazards.
7. What mistakes should you expect in most uses of the term *threat*?
8. What is the difference between a negative hazard, positive hazard, threat, opportunity, and contributor?
9. Decide whether each of the following is best described as a negative hazard, positive hazard, threat, or contributor: neutral, enemy, ally, critic, attacker, supporter, acquaintance, skeptic, friendly neutral, opponent.
10. How could a journalist be a current hazard, threat, or contributor to your operational reputation?
11. What are the four main categories of hazards and threats?
12. Give an example of a threat that could be considered both natural and human-caused.

Target Vulnerability and Exposure

Having identified a hazard or threat (Chapter 4), we should identify the potential target and assess its vulnerability and exposure.

The main sections of this chapter describe what is meant by target, vulnerability, and exposure.

Target

This section defines target and introduces some simple ways to identify potential targets.

Defining Target

A target is the object of a risk or plan. The threat is the subject whose actions cause harm to the object. In the semantic frame *risk* two types of object are routine: a human victim ("the individual who stands to suffer if the harm occurs") or "a valued possession of the victim" (Fillmore & Atkins, 1992, p. 82).

Pedagogy Box 5.1 Official Definitions of Target

The North Atlantic Treaty Organization (NATO) (2008) defines a target as "the object of a particular action, for example a geographic area, a complex, an installation, a force, equipment, an individual, a group or a system, planned for captures, exploitation, neutralization, or destruction by military forces" (p. 2T2). The U.S. Department of Defense (DOD) (2012b) defines target as "an entity or object considered for possible engagement or other action" (p. 290). British and Canadian military authorities offer the NATO definition.

Identifying Targets

Identifying targets is a key step in assessing the risks associated with certain threats. Analytically, no threat should be identified except in relation to a particular target. (The proper analysis of all these concepts as they contribute to a risk is represented in Figure 4.3.) Targets can be identified by their attractiveness to threats and by their risk factors or indicators.

Targets as Attractive to Threats

In some way, targets are attractive to threats. We could assess the demand side by asking what sort of targets the threat demands. For instance, certain criminals target certain types of person—such as the more accessible, vulnerable, wealthy, different, or provocative types (from the threat's perspective). For rare threats like terrorists, we could review their rhetorical threats (as contained in the threat's speeches and policy statements). We could even measure the threat's focus on a particular target by measuring the proportion of this content that is focused on one target relative to other targets. This would be a more objective measure than simply asking people for their judgments of whether the group is a threat. An objective measure is useful because it might contradict or confirm our judgments.

Relating to the threat's demand for targets, we should measure the supply of such targets in an area of concern (sometimes called the *attractor terrain*). For instance, if we were concerned about potential targets for political terrorists, we could count the number of political representatives for the area or the value or size of official sites. If we were concerned about the potential targets for religious terrorists, we could count the number of religious sites in the area.

Authorities often seek to measure the scale or value of a socio-economy in an area as a measure of all targets, although such a measure would capture vulnerability, exposure, and capacity to respond to threat—not just attractor terrain. A separate suggestion for measuring the potential targets of terrorism is to measure population, socio-economic development (demographic characteristics, labor force demands, education, health services, production, and income), city development, and net trade (exports less imports) (Rusnak, Kennedy, Eldivan, & Caplan, 2012, p. 170). However, such measures capture vulnerability, exposure, and capacity to respond to threat—not just attractor terrain.

A useful categorical list of criteria by which a terrorist could select a target includes eight categories, remembered by the mnemonic "EVIL DONE":

1. Exposed
2. Vital
3. Iconic
4. Legitimate
5. Destructible
6. Occupied
7. Near
8. Easy (Clarke & Newman, 2006).

Given the resources, we should research the particular threat's intent and capability toward particular targets. Consider the simple, notional scenario below, which I will present as a series of logical steps in analysis:

1. Terrorist group "T" has the intent to harm our organization.
2. Terrorist group "T" is based near our organization's site "S." Thus, we should consider that site "S" is exposed to "T."
3. Terrorist group "T" currently does not have the capabilities to penetrate the defenses of site "S," so "S" is exposed, but the 100 employees within are not vulnerable.
4. If terrorists were to discover attack method "M," the defenses at site "S" would fail, and all 100 employees would be vulnerable.

Pedagogy Box 5.2 Crime Victimization

Unfortunately, victims of past crimes are more likely to suffer a future crime. British surveys in 1992 suggest that half of victims are repeat victims and that they suffer 81% of all reported crimes, of which 4% of victims experienced four or more crimes per year, or 44% of all crimes. Some people must have some collection of attributes (sometimes termed *risk heterogeneity*) that make them more vulnerable; perhaps an event (such as illness) makes the person more vulnerable (*event dependence*); perhaps a crime harms the person in such a way that makes him or her more vulnerable in the future; some people were always more susceptible to threats, a propensity that has been described as "increased vulnerability." For instance, past abuse acclimates the victim to abuse, while past success at abusing emboldens the abuser (Kennedy & Van Brunschot, 2009, pp. 65–67; Van Brunschot & Kennedy, 2008, p. 9). Training in crime prevention helped an experimental group of repeat victims to feel more informed about crime prevention, but unfortunately, it did not reduce their level of fear or the likelihood of victimization (Davis & Smith, 1994).

When looking for the specific attributes that make victimization more likely, we should be careful in our demographic assumptions. We could assume that the elderly and women are physically more vulnerable to crime, but while the elderly and women tend to report more fear of crime, young men suffer more crimes, partly because they attract competition from other young males, partly because young men are more socially active and thus more socially exposed (although women suffer more sexual crimes). Most crimes against young males are committed during the victim's social exposure, particularly where coincident with behaviors that liberate behavior, for instance, when out drinking alcohol at public bars. Most abuse of children, women, and the elderly occurs in the home, not in public settings. Despite the higher frequency of male targets, men report less fear (perhaps because they are socially or culturally conditioned to report less fear), while women normatively report more fear. Indeed, male victims of crime report less fear than female nonvictims report (Kennedy & Van Brunshot, 2009, pp. 32, 42–43).

Risk Factors, Indicators, Markers, and Correlates

Potential targets are often identified by situational or inherent factors that are usually termed *risk factors* (also *indicators*, *markers*, or *correlates*). Risk factors correlate with a particular risk but are not necessarily sources or causes. For instance, poverty is an indicator of a group's increased likelihood of suffering crime and disease, not because poverty causes criminals and pathogens, but because poverty is associated with the target's increased exposure and decreased capacity and with the threat's demand for targets. Similarly, poverty is an indicator of political instability, not because poverty causes governments to falter but because poverty correlates with high natural risks, private incapacity, and low government revenues.

Some potential targets are voluntarily vulnerable or exposed to the risk, for instance when somebody speculates on a business venture, and are described as "taking risks." Other potential targets are not necessarily voluntary, in which case they are described as "at risk," "in danger," or "running risks" (Fillmore & Atkins, 1992, p. 80). The adjective *risky* can be used to designate specific types of risk factor, such as "risky lifestyles" (Kennedy & Van Brunschot, 2009, p. 2).

 Vulnerability

This section defines vulnerability before introducing methods for assessing vulnerability.

Defining Vulnerability

Vulnerability essentially means that the target can be harmed by the threat. For instance, I would be vulnerable to a threat armed with a weapon that could harm me. The threat would cease if I were to acquire some armor that perfectly protects me from the weapon or some other means of perfectly countering the weapon.

Vulnerability is routinely conflated with exposure. In general use, vulnerability is "the state of being exposed to or likely to suffer harm" (FrameNet). The Humanitarian Practice Network (2010) defined vulnerabilities as "factors that increase an organization's exposure to threats, or make severe outcomes more likely" (p. 42). However, vulnerability and exposure are usefully differentiated (see the following section): essentially, vulnerability means that we are undefended against the threat, while exposure means we are subject to the threat.

Some definitions of vulnerability conflate risk. For instance David Alexander (2000, p. 13) defined vulnerability as the "potential for casualty, destruction, damage, disruption or other form of loss in a particular element," but this sounds the same as risk. Similarly, the Humanitarian Practice Network (2010, p. 28) defined vulnerability as "the likelihood or probability of being confronted with a threat, and the consequences or impact if and when that happens," but this also sounds the same as risk.

Pedagogy Box 5.3 Official Definitions of Vulnerability

UN

Vulnerability is the "degree of loss (from 0% to 100%) resulting from a potentially damaging phenomenon" (United Nations Department of Humanitarian Affairs [UN DHA], 1992) or "the characteristics and circumstances of a community, system, or asset that make it susceptible to the damaging effects of a hazard" (United Nations Office for International Strategy for Disaster Reduction [UN ISDR], 2009, p. 12).

United States

The U.S. Government Accountability Office (GAO) defines vulnerability as "the probability that a particular attempted attack will succeed against a particular target or class of targets" or (under *vulnerability assessment*) the "weaknesses in physical structures, personal protection systems, processes or other areas that may be exploited." The GAO used this definition in a dispute about assessments by the Department of Homeland Security (DHS) of the vulnerability of physical assets (see Pedagogy Box) (GAO, 2005c, p. 110; GAO, 2008a). The Department of Homeland Security (2009) defines vulnerability as "a physical feature or operational attribute that renders an entity open to exploitation or susceptible to a given hazard" (p. 112). In the context of cyber security, the GAO (2005b) defines vulnerability as "a flaw or weakness in hardware or software that can be exploited, resulting in a violation of an implicit or explicit security policy" (p. 10).

DOD (2012b, p. 329) defines vulnerability as "the susceptibility of a nation or military force to any action by any means through its war potential or combat effectiveness may be reduced or its will to fight diminished" or "the characteristics of a system that causes it to suffer a definite degradation (incapability to perform the designated mission) as a result of having been subjected to a certain level of effects in an unnatural (mad-made) hostile environment."

Australian/New Zealand and ISO

Vulnerability is the "intrinsic properties of something resulting in susceptibility to a risk source that can lead to an event with a consequence" (International Organization for Standardization, 2009a, p. 8).

British

The British Treasury and National Audit Office do not define vulnerability. The Civil Contingencies Secretariat defines vulnerability as "susceptibility of individuals or community, services, or infrastructure to damage or harm arising from an emergency or other incident" (U.K. Cabinet Office, 2013). In other documents, the government has used vulnerability as exposure.

"Britain today is both more secure and more vulnerable than in most of her long history. More secure, in the sense that we do not currently face, as we have so often in our past, a conventional threat of attack on our territory by a hostile power. But more vulnerable, because we are one of the most open societies, in a world that is more networked than ever before (U.K. Cabinet Office, 2010, p. 3)."

Canadian

The Canadian government defines vulnerability as "a condition or set of conditions determined by physical, social, economic, and environmental factors or processes that increases the susceptibility of a community to the impact of hazards" and notes that "vulnerability is a measure of how well-prepared and well-equipped a community is to minimize the impact of or cope with hazards" (Public Safety Canada, 2012, p. 97).

Assessing Vulnerability

This section introduces different schemes for assessing vulnerability by the target's defenses; the gap between the target's defenses and a particular threat; and the gap between the target's defenses and standard defenses.

Defenses

As a correlate of invulnerability, we could measure the target's defenses. For instance, the Humanitarian Practice Network (2010) prescribes measuring our "strengths" as "the flip-side of vulnerabilities" (p. 42).

We could measure our defensive inputs by scale or value. For instance, the defensive inputs at a site could be measured by spending on defenses, total concrete poured as fortifications, or total length of barriers at the site.

We should preferably measure the outputs—the actual defensive capabilities and performance, although this is usually more difficult than measuring inputs. The ideal measures of outputs are practical tests of defensive function. For instance, official authorities often send agents to attempt to pass mock weapons through baggage screening systems in airports as tests of airport security.

Pedagogy Box 5.4 Canadian Target Vulnerability Assessment

The Canadian government defines vulnerability assessment as "the process of identifying and evaluating vulnerabilities, describing all protective measures in place to reduce them[,] and estimating the likelihood of consequences" (Public Safety Canada, 2012, p. 97).

The "Target Capabilities List–Canada" is "a reference document that provides a generic model using common language and methodology to be used by Canadian response organizations and all levels of government to inventory the capabilities in place, analyze the gaps, and identify the tasks that must be completed to achieve preparedness goals." It "comprises 39 capabilities grouped according to 4 missions. They address 5 that are common to all capabilities, 8 pre-incident prevention and protection capabilities, 23 response capabilities, and 3 remediation and recovery capabilities" (Public Safety Canada, 2012, p. 92).

Target-Threat Gap Analysis

More particularly, we should identify a real threat (or imagine a real hazard as an activated threat) and compare our defensive capacity against the threat's offensive capacity. This sort of assessment is often termed a *gap analysis* since it looks for a gap between our defensive capacity and the threat's offensive capacity. For instance, we should be alarmed if we learn that a threat with a heavy caliber firearm has targeted a building that is not fortified against such a firearm.

Pedagogy Box 5.5 British Civil Contingencies Secretariat's Definition of "Capability Gap"

"The gap between the current ability to provide a response and the actual response assessed to be required for a given threat or hazard. Plans should be made to reduce or eliminate this gap, if the risk justifies it" (U.K. Cabinet Office, 2013).

Target-Standard Gap Analysis

In practice, we are often uncertain about any particular threat. Consequently, we usually measure our vulnerability to some standardized notional threats, such as chemical explosive weapons of a certain type or size.

Often vulnerability is judged subjectively, rather than measured objectively. Table 5.1 shows a 5-point coding scheme that produces one number between 1 and 5 as a rating of what level of capabilities the other would need in order to threaten the target. (Although this table was supposed to assess the threat level, it is a better measure of our vulnerability.)

The Canadian government has followed with a more complex scheme (see Table 5.2) for judgmentally coding the *technical feasibility* of an attack—this scheme actually measures both vulnerability and exposure.

Pedagogy Box 5.6 U.S. Diplomatic Vulnerability Assessments

The U.S. Department of State effectively measures the gap between the security standards and the actual security of overseas missions. The standards for overseas security are set by the Overseas Security Policy Board, chaired by the Assistant Secretary for Diplomatic Security, with representatives from U.S. government agencies that have a presence overseas. Each year, the Bureau of Diplomatic Security creates the Diplomatic Security Vulnerability List, which ranks sites according to their vulnerability. The Security Environment Threat ratings are determined by the Bureau of Diplomatic Security's Threat Investigations & Analysis Directorate (established May 2008) (GAO, 2009, pp. 5–7).

Table 5.1 A Scheme for Judgmental Coding of Vulnerability

Score	Determinants of Required Attack Capability Score
1 (high)	Highly specialized skills (requires highly specialized and rare skills such as operation of nuclear power plant, large-scale manufacturing, or precision or highly technical production operation in secret)
2	Specialty skills (such as hacking computers, piloting vehicles, or ability to plan and implement advanced coordinated operations)
3	Expert military skills (requires accurately positioned explosives, accurate firing, or using more sophisticated military weapons)
4	Basic military skills (including ability to handle personal weapons and carry out close quarter combat)
5 (low)	Volunteer or practical skills (can be carried out using only manual labor or school-educated personnel)

SOURCE: Greenberg, Chalk, Willis, Khilko, & Ortiz, 2006.

 Exposure

This section defines exposure and suggests ways to assess exposure.

Table 5.2 Canada's Official Coding Rules for the Technical Feasibility of an Attack

Technical Feasibility Score	Feasibility of Acquiring or Producing the Required Material Capabilities	Required Equipment	Access to the Target	Required Technical Expertise	Access to Critical Information
0.0	Almost impossible	Design must be customized, and/or manufacture requires state of the art capacity	Almost impossible	Controlled, advanced, and specialized	Almost impossible
0.5–1.0	Extremely difficult	Design must be customized, and/or manufacture is controlled	Extremely difficult	Advanced and specialized	Extremely difficult
1.5–2.0	Very difficult	Specialized	Very difficult	Advanced	Very difficult
2.5–3.0	Difficult	Some specialized components	Difficult	Partly advanced	Difficult
3.5–4.0	Easy	Manufacturing by standard equipment	Accessible	Minimal	Easily accessible
4.5–5.0	Ready	None	Very accessible	Low	Readily accessible

SOURCE: All Hazards Risk Assessment Methodology Guidelines 2012–2013, http://www.publicsafety.gc.ca/prg/em/emp/2013-ahra/index-eng.aspx, Public Safety Canada, 2013. Reproduced with the permission of Public Works and Government Services Canada, 2013.

Defining Exposure

Exposure often is treated as synonymous with vulnerability (and even risk), but exposure implies that we are subject to the threat, while vulnerability implies our lack of defenses against the threat. We are subject to the threat if we coincide with or are discovered by the threat in ways that allow the threat to target us.

FrameNet defines the verb *to expose* as to "reveal the true, objectionable nature of" something. In general use, *risk* is sometimes used as a verb to imply our voluntary exposure to some threat (as in: "I risked discovery by the enemy"). Risk is also used as a verb in front of some valued object representing what the actor has to lose (as in: "I risked my savings on that bet") (Fillmore & Atkins, 1992, pp. 97, 100–101). This use of the verb *risk* helps explain the dual meanings of exposure in the frame of risk: exposure to the threat and what we have to lose. In military contexts, exposure implies that we are under observation by a threat; but in financial contexts, exposure implies the things that could be lost. Thus, unfortunately, in security and risk analysis one word is used routinely with two different meanings, which I will term *threat exposure* (the more military context) and *loss exposure* (the more financial context).

Here I will focus on threat exposure (the target's revelation to the potential threat). If the hazard could not reach us or find us, we would not be exposed, whatever our vulnerability. This is a profound insight, because if we were confident that we are not exposed to a certain hazard, we would not need any defenses against that hazard (although we would need to be ready to acquire defenses if the hazard were about to discover or reach us). For instance, if we were confident that a communicable disease had been quarantined perfectly, we would not be justified in ordering mass immunization against that disease. We would not be exposed, so we would not need defenses.

Essentially any control of access is an attempt to control the potential target's exposure. Access controls include any attempt to manage the entry of actors or agents into some domain, for instance, by demanding identification of permitted persons before entry into a building or a password before access to some digital environment. As long as the access controls work perfectly, everything inside the perimeter remains not exposed to external threats, even though the perimeter would remain exposed. For instance, after 9/11, under new regulations, airline cockpit doors were supposed to be locked during flight, stopping the pilot's exposure to any threat in the passenger cabin during flight. The pilot remains vulnerable to the sorts of weapons (small knives, fists, and tear gas) used on 9/11, unless the pilot were equipped with a firearm, body armor, and a gas mask (some cockpit crew are certified to carry firearms), but the pilot is not exposed to any of these things as long as he or she remains on the other side of the door. Passengers in the passenger cabin would remain exposed to any threat in the passenger cabin, but their vulnerability would be reduced if joined by an armed Air Marshal prepared to defend them.

Pedagogy Box 5.7 Official Definitions of Exposure

The UN DHA (1992) does not define exposure but admits the *exposure time* of structures to earthquakes. The UN ISDR (2009, p. 6) defines "exposure" as the "people, property, systems, or other elements present in hazard zones that are thereby subject to potential losses" (p. 6).

NATO and U.S. government do not define exposure, but the NATO glossary (2008) and the DOD Dictionary (2012b) admit the concept by defining radiation *exposure dose*.

The International Organization for Standardization (2009a) standard defines exposure as the "extent to which an organization and/or stakeholder is subject to an event" (p. 7).

The British government, thanks to the Treasury being the lead department, treats exposure as would a financial manager: "the consequences, as a combination of impact and likelihood, which may be experienced by the organization if a specific risk is realized" (U.K. Treasury, 2004, p. 49) or "the range of outcomes arising from the combination of the impact of an event and the probability of the event actually occurring" (U.K. Ministry of Defense, 2009a).

The Canadian government does not define exposure but defines threat as "the presence of a hazard and an exposure pathway," and it noted that "exposure to hazards . . . affects" risk (Public Safety Canada, 2012, pp. 81, 94).

Assessing Exposure

For assessing exposure, we should measure exposure by area coincident with a particular hazard or threat, exposure by time, or some combination.

Exposure by Area

Someone's exposure to a threat could be defined by the space known to be coincident with that threat. For instance, crime tends to concentrate in certain areas (sometimes known as *hot spots*), perhaps because of local de-policing or a self-segregated community or some path-dependent accident of history. Someone's exposure to crime in that area increases as he or she spends more time travelling through, working in, or living in that same area. This repeat exposure helps to explain repeat victimization. Someone who becomes a victim of crime in a high-crime area and who does not move or change his or her behavior is just as likely to be a victim in the future (and past victimization may harm a person's capacity to avoid future crime). One study suggests that 10% of the crime map experiences 60% of crime, 10% of offenders are responsible for about 50% of offenses, and 10% of victims suffer about 40% of crimes (Kennedy & Van Brunschot, 2009, pp. 69–72).

We could measure the number or value of targets exposed. We could measure exposure spatially (such as the target area as a proportion of the total area or the target area's length of border or coastline as a proportion of total border or coastline) or in terms of flows (the number or scale of ports of entry, migrants, or trade). These sorts of measures could be combined mathematically in a single quotient (see Figure 5.1 for an example).

Pedagogy Box 5.8 Official Measures of Exposure

The UN ISDR (2009) noted that "[m]easures of exposure can include the number of people or types of assets in an area. These can be combined with the specific vulnerability of the exposed elements to any particular hazard to estimate the quantitative risks associated with that hazard in the area of interest" (p. 6). Similarly, the Humanitarian Practice Network (2010, p. 42) prescribed asking which persons travel through or work in the most exposed areas, which sites are most exposed to the threats, and which assets are most exposed to theft or damage.

Exposure by Time

We are exposed in time whenever the threat is coincident with us or knows where we are and can target us at that time. We could measure our exposure in time in either absolute terms (such as days exposed) or proportional terms (such as the fraction of the year). We could make the measure judgmental: For

Figure 5.1 A Formula for "Location Risk" (T_{iv}) Using Simple Measures of Exposure and Threat

$$T_{iv} = (T_i / T_v) / (({}^{N}\Sigma_{n=1} T_I)/({}^{N}\Sigma_{n=1} T_V))$$

n = individual target area

N = total area

T_v = value of target area

T_V = value of total area

T_i = crime incidents per target area

T_I = crime incidents across total area

SOURCE: Based on Rusnak, Kennedy, Eldivan, & Caplan, 2012, p. 169.

instance, one judgmental scheme assigns a value between 1 and 5 to correspond respectively with rare, quarterly, weekly, daily, or constant exposure (Waring & Glendon, 1998, pp. 27–28).

Natural threats are often cyclical or seasonal and predictable in duration, allowing us to calculate the proportion of time when we would be exposed if we were to reside in the area where a natural hazard occurred, such as a hurricane zone that experiences a hurricane season. If we knew that a threat was current, we could calculate the duration of our exposure if we were to travel through the area where the threat was active. Some of our behaviors allow us to calculate the duration of our exposure. For instance, we could calculate the time we spend travelling by automobile as a measure of our exposure to road traffic accidents. Similarly, we could calculate the time we spend travelling or residing in an area as a measure of our exposure to crime in that area.

SUMMARY

This chapter has

- defined target;
- introduced ways to identify targets, by their attractiveness to threats and their risk factors;
- defined vulnerability;
- described how to assess vulnerability, by our defenses, the gap between target defensive and threat offensive capabilities, and the gap between target defensive and standard offensive capabilities;
- defined exposure; and
- explained how to assess exposure by area and time.

QUESTIONS AND EXERCISES

1. Why could one thing be more likely than another to be a target of a threat?
2. Critique the unofficial and official definitions of vulnerability shown earlier in this chapter.
3. Practically, what could we measure in order to assess the vulnerability of a target?
4. Explain your favored choice of the official definitions of exposure shown earlier in this chapter.
5. Practically, what aspects of a potential target could we measure in order to assess exposure?

Probability and Uncertainty

The concepts of risk and hazard inherently include the concept of uncertainty: Risk is potential returns, and a hazard is a potential threat. This potential is a type of uncertainty. The sections of this chapter describe uncertainty and probability, including practical methods for identifying and assessing them.

Uncertainty

This section defines uncertainty, explains the difference between uncertainty and probability, explains the difference between uncertainty and risk, and introduces some practical ways to identify uncertainties.

Defining Uncertainty

Uncertainty is a lack of certainty, where certainty is "the personal quality of being completely sure" (FrameNet). Many other definitions would suggest that uncertainty, probability, and risk can be the same (see Pedagogy Box 6.1), but they are distinct, with important implications for how we assess and manage them.

Pedagogy Box 6.1 Definitions of Uncertainty

Unofficial

Uncertainty is "a lack of certainty, involving variability and ambiguity" (Chapman & Ward, 2002), "the absence of sufficient information to predict the outcome of a project" (Branscomb & Auerswald, 2001, p. 44), "an absence of information, knowledge, or understanding regarding the outcome of an action, decision, or event" (Heerkens, 2002, p. 142), or "the state of not being completely confident or sure" (FrameNet).

(Continued)

(Continued)

Australia/New Zealand

"Uncertainty is the state, even partial, of deficiency of information related to, understanding or knowledge of, an event, its consequence, or likelihood" (Australian and New Zealand Joint Technical Committee, 2009; International Organization for Standardization, 2009a, p. 2).

British

Uncertainty is "a condition where the outcome can only be estimated" (U.K. Ministry of Defense [MOD], 2009a).

Canada

Public Safety Canada (2012) does not define uncertainty but defines *uncertainty analysis* as "an analysis intended to identify key sources of uncertainties in the predictions of a model, assess the potential impacts of these uncertainties on the predictions, and assess the likelihood of these impacts" (p. 96).

The Difference Between Uncertainty and Probability

Uncertainty implies no assessed probability or likelihood, so an uncertain event implies a range of probabilities from 0% to 100%. *Certainty*, like *definitely*, implies a probability of 100%.

Pedagogy Box 6.2 Published Statements Comparing Uncertainty and Probability

"The practical difference between the two categories, risk and uncertainty, is that in the former, the distribution of the outcome in a group of instances is known (either through calculation a priori or from statistics of past experience), while in the case of uncertainty this is not true, the reason being in general that it is impossible to form a group of instances, because the situation dealt with is in a high degree unique. The best example of uncertainty is in connection with the exercise of judgment or the formation of those opinions as to the future course of events, in which opinions (and not scientific knowledge) actually guide most of our conduct" (Knight, 1921, Chapter 8, Paragraph 2).

"Properly speaking, the ability to describe the risk [chance] of failure inherent in a technical project implies some prior experience. It is not possible, for example, to talk meaningfully about a given project having a '10% probability of success' in the absence of some accumulated prior experience (such as a sample of similar projects of which 9 in 10 were failures). To the extent that a technical team is attempting to overcome a truly novel challenge, it may more properly be said to be facing uncertainty rather than risk. The distinction is more than academic. If the probabilities of failure can be reliably calculated, conditional on observable facts, risks can be easily managed" (Branscomb & Auerswald, 2001, p. 44).

The Difference Between Uncertainty and Risk

Since risks are potential returns, uncertainty is fundamental to our understanding of risk but is not the same thing. If something becomes certain (for instance: "we now know that she has died of malaria"), whatever prior risk had existed ("the chance of harm from contracting malaria") would cease to be a risk and we would be left with a certain event or outcome. If the event were impossible ("male mosquitoes cannot bite us") or would produce no returns ("that species of mosquito carries no pathogens"), then no risk would exist.

Identifying Uncertainties

As soon as we face any uncertainty (for example, "we don't know if that species can carry this pathogen"), we face a risk, so a good route to the identification of risk is to identify our uncertainties, even if we were so uncertain that we could not yet estimate the probability or returns.

We can look for uncertainties in areas known to be very uncertain. For instance, uncertainties concentrate in certain dimensions of any project (see Table 6.1).

International diplomatic, capacity-building, and stabilization missions are associated with particular uncertainties in similar dimensions (see Table 6.2).

The most extreme uncertainties are those that never occur to us. We could be undertaking routine activities oblivious to the risks. From one perspective, ignorance is bliss; from another perspective, ignorance is a failure of imagination or diligence.

Some uncertainties cannot be improved, or could not be improved without unreasonable burdens, so security and risk managers need to be comfortable with some level of uncertainty, without giving up their aggressive pursuit of certainty. A different skill is to persuade other stakeholders to accept the same comfort level as yours.

Table 6.1 Typical Aspects of Projects Where Uncertainty Is High

Dimension	Example Uncertainties
Scope	Extent of the work; ability to define work; design errors and omissions; customer-driven changes of scope
Time	Project duration; activity duration; time-to-market; launch date; timing of management reviews and approvals
Cost	Project costs; downstream manufacturing costs; inflations; currency exchange; budget
Resources	Quantity; quality; availability; skill match; ability to define roles and responsibilities
Technology	Customer expectations; probability of success; ability to scale-up; product manufacturability; design success
Organizational	Client's priorities and knowledge; coordination among departments
Market	User expectations; sales volume; pricing; market share; demographics; economy
Outside factors	Competitor actions; official regulations

SOURCE: Based on Heerkens, 2002, p. 145.

Table 6.2 Typical Causes of Uncertainty in International Missions

Dimension	Example Causes of Uncertainty
Actors	Numerous; poorly coordinated; incompatible expectations
Politics	Issue linkage; vested interests; grievances; distrust
Security	Restricted intelligence; opposition from uncommitted local and foreign actors
Time	Scheduling beyond the lifetime of political administrations
Resources	Shorter-term resourcing; underresourcing; interrupted resourcing; incompatible resources; unrequired resources; unmet requirements
Management	Turnover of managers; unprepared managers; insufficient managerial reach or authority
Activities	Change; reform
Environment	Natural hazards; poor infrastructure; poor public services; field operations

> However, despite your best efforts to identify and address threats, a large number of circumstances (think of them as slight threats) will remain that you won't be able to identify or have the resources to address. Further, too many things can happen that you simply cannot foresee or predict. That's why variability is inherent in projects.
>
> This inherent variability is impossible to manage away. Therefore, you must acknowledge it and accommodate it. Recognize, evaluate, estimate, and communicate its existence to your management and other stakeholders, as appropriate. (Heerkens, 2002, p. 152)

 Probability

This section defines probability, introduces methods for analyzing and assessing probability, and explains your different choices when sourcing data on probability.

Definitions

Probability, *likelihood*, and *chance* each mean the extent to which something could occur. Probability implies quantitative expressions (using numbers); likelihood and chance imply qualitative expressions (using words). Quantitatively, probability can be expressed as a number from 0 to 1 or a percentage from 0% to 100%.

The likelihoods run from no chance to certainty, but these words are routinely misunderstood and misused to mean narrower ranges. Likelihood is a potentially loaded word because it sounds similar to *likely*. (For instance, unfortunately, FrameNet defines likelihood as "the state or fact of being likely.") If you were to ask someone to estimate the likelihood of something, you might be leading them (however accidentally) to respond with an estimate of likely. Similarly, if we ask someone about the probability of something, they may infer that it is probable. If we asked someone to estimate the possibility, they might be led to think of something that is barely possible, not probable. The most loaded synonyms of chance are *risk* and *hazard*—words with overwhelmingly negative connotations. In general use, these words are used as verbs, as in *to risk* and *to hazard*, to mean taking the chance of harm to some valued object in pursuit of some goal (Fillmore & Atkins, 1992, pp. 87–88, 97). Unfortunately, no synonym or similar word is clear of potential bias, but chance seems to be least loaded and the word that surveyors should use when asking respondents for assessments.

Pedagogy Box 6.3 Other Definitions of Probability

Unofficial

Chance is "the uncertainty about the future" (Fillmore & Atkins, 1992, p. 81). Probability is "the extent to which something is probable"; likelihood is "the state or fact of being likely" (FrameNet). "Probability is the likelihood that the potential problem will occur" (Heerkens, 2002, p. 148).

Australian/New Zealand and ISO

Likelihood is "the chance of something happening" and "is used with the intent that it should have the same broad interpretation as the term 'probability' has in many languages other than English." Likelihood includes descriptions in "general terms or mathematically, such as a probability or a frequency over a given time period." "In English, 'probability' is often narrowly interpreted as a mathematical term" and defined as a "measure of the chance of occurrence expressed as a number between 0 and 1, where 0 is impossibility and 1 is absolute certainty" (International Organization for Standardization, 2009a, p. 7).

British

"The likelihood of a specific event or outcome occurring [,] measured as the ratio of specific events or outcomes to the total number of possible events or outcomes" (U.K. MOD, 2009a).

Canadian

Likelihood is "the chance of an event or incident happening, whether defined, measured, or determined objectively or subjectively." Probability is, "in statistics, a measure of the chance of an event or incident happening" (Public Safety Canada, 2012, pp. 60, 75).

United States

"Probability and frequency means a measure of how often an event is likely to occur. Frequency can be expressed as the average time between occurrences or exceedances (non-exceedances) of an event or the percent chance or probability of the event occurring or being exceeded (not exceeded) in a given year or longer time period" (U.S. FEMA, 1992, p. xxv). The Department of Defense (DOD) Dictionary (2012b) does not define probability, frequency, or uncertainty, but it lists an *uncertain environment* as an "operational environment in which host government forces, whether opposed to or receptive to operations that a unit intends to conduct, do not have totally effective control of the territory and population in the intended operational area" (p. 323).

Analyzing and Assessing Probability

The subsections below explain how to analyze probabilities, calculate probabilities mathematically, separate predictions from forecasts, separate the implausible from the plausible, and assess our confidence.

Using Analysis to Improve Assessment

An assessment of probability improves with assessments of probabilities within the analytical chain from source to risk. (A diagrammatic representation of this chain is shown in Figure 4.3.) Given good analysis of the risk from hazard to returns, the probability assessment is easier to handle. At the least, we should estimate the probability of the hazard being activated into a threat; the probability of the threat causing the event; and the probability of the event causing the returns.

Mathematically Calculating Probability

Given estimates of the probabilities of different events in a causal or analytical chain (sourcing estimates of probabilities is described in the higher section below), we can calculate their products or sums.

When we want to know the probability of both of two independent events occurring, we should multiply their probabilities. Events are independent if the occurrence of one event does not affect the probability of the other event. (Independent events are sometimes called consecutive events, given the misleading notion that they occur at different times.) If separate people tossed separate coins, or if you pulled a card from one deck of cards and pulled another card from a different deck of cards, the probabilities of these events are theoretically independent. If we toss a coin once, the theoretical probability of a head (the alternative is a tail) is 50%. If we toss two coins, the theoretical probability of getting two heads is 25% (50% multiplied by 50%). Similarly, if the probability of event type "A" is 10% and the probability of event type "B" is 50%, and both event types are independent of each other, then the probability of both "A" and "B" occurring is 50% of 10%, which equals 5%.

When we want the probability of either of two mutually exclusive events occurring, we should add the probabilities. Events are mutually exclusive if the occurrence of one precludes the occurrence of the other. For instance, when you toss a coin, the result can be either heads or tails, not both. If you pulled one card from a deck of cards, put the card aside, then pulled a second card, you could not pull the same card twice. Theoretically, the probability of tossing a coin and producing either a head or tail is 100% (50% plus 50%). If the probability of event type "A" is 10% and the probability of event type "B" is 50%, and either is possible but only one can occur, then the probability of either "A" or "B" occurring is 60% (10% plus 50%).

Predicting and Forecasting

Our assessment of probability is made easier if we separate the predictable from the forecastable. The concepts of forecasting and predicting are often treated as the same, but a prediction implies certainty (we would be *predicting* that an event *will* occur), while a forecast implies uncertainty (we would be *forecasting* that an event *could* occur). Given the ambiguity of these words, when using or consuming them, you should clarify their meaning.

Predictability is a useful concept because it can help you separate certainties from uncertainties in a scenario. Indeed, in any analysis or assessment, a useful attitude would be intellectually aggressive:

You should be tearing apart the scenario or situation looking for the events, actions, behaviors, or outcomes that are predictable in order to separate them from other things that are uncertain and require forecasting. Unfortunately, too many people throw up their hands at the first uncertainty and do not attempt to disaggregate the absolutely uncertain from the predictable and the forecastable.

Like a good description of risk, a good description of likelihood is more accurately expressed under specified conditions (such as "given saturated ground and an earthquake, then the probability of an earthslide is *z*"). Further specification of the sources, causes, and permissive conditions (under which an event would occur) would help us to increase the specificity of the scenario until the probability approaches certainty. For instance, if we proved certainty of a threat's capability and intent to harm a particular target and we proved certainty of the target's exposure and vulnerability to the threat, we should predict harm.

Consider the simple, notional scenario below, which I will present as a series of logical steps in our analysis and assessment of it:

1. If terrorists were to penetrate the defenses of site "S," all 100 employees would be exposed to the terrorists. (This is a conditional prediction of exposure.)
2. If terrorists were to attack with method "M," the defenses at site "S" would fail, and thus all 100 employees would be undefended (conditional prediction of vulnerability).
3. If terrorist group "T" were to discover our activity "A," then "T" would become aggrieved and acquire the intent to harm our employees (conditional prediction of intent).
4. The probability of terrorist group "T" discovering activity "A" is 50%. (This is a forecast of the probability of the intent being activated.)
5. The probability of terrorist group "T" discovering method "M" is 10% (a forecast of the probability of the capability being activated).
6. Thus, the probability of terrorist group "T" harming our employees at site "S" via method "M" is a product of the probabilities of "T" acquiring the intent (50%); "T" acquiring the capability (10%); our employees being vulnerable (100%); and our employees being exposed (100%). This product is 5%.
7. The expected return (see Chapter 3) at "S," given "T," "A," and "M," is harm to 5% of 100 employees, which equals five employees harmed.

The effective management of intelligence can lead to real predictions, while mismanagement of available intelligence is associated with blindness toward predictable events. For instance, on September 11, 2001 (9/11), when terrorists, sponsored by al-Qaida, flew hijacked airliners into the World Trade Center in New York and the Pentagon in Washington, DC, most observers were astounded at the terrorists' audacity: "In the aftermath of 9/11's devastation, it is easy to imagine that airplanes could again be used as weapons in future terrorist attacks, even though prior to this event we had not imagined such use" (Van Brunschott & Kennedy, 2008, p. 15).

In fact, 9/11 had close precedents. For instance, in December 1994, Algerian hijackers planned to detonate an Air France plane over the Eifel Tower in Paris (French police killed the hijackers while the plane was on the ground in Marseilles); and in 1995, al-Qaida planned to fly hijacked planes into the

Central Intelligence Agency headquarters. In time, we learnt also that some authorities had mishandled some of the intelligence on the plotters' preparations to hijack and to fly airliners. Most Americans had neglected the trends in religious terrorism and al-Qaida in particular before 9/11. Al-Qaida had demonstrated its increasing ambition and capacity through its preceding attacks, and itself was symptomatic of larger trends toward more ambitious terrorism. These trends led some commentators to recall such an event as "predictable" in the sense that some terrorists, somewhere, sometime, would attempt to fly planes into buildings. (They would not claim that 9/11 itself was predictable in time or space, just that attacks of the type were predictable somewhere, sometime.) Others effectively predicted the returns: "In terms of risk and disaster management, however, September 11 was a predictable if not predicted event: not so much in its organization but by globalization, and in its traumatic impact on mankind and international relations" (Suder, 2004, p. 2).

In recent years, we have heard some remarkable admissions of uncertainty by U.S. defense and security authorities. At the same time, we have heard some remarkable certainty from officials. For instance, on February 2, 2010, the U.S. Director of National Intelligence (Dennis C. Blair) told the Senate Intelligence Committee that a Jihadi attempt to attack within the United States was "certain" within the following 2 to 3 months.

Pedagogy Box 6.4 Official Definitions of Forecasting

The UN Department of Humanitarian Affairs (1992) defines a *forecast* as a "statement of statistical estimate of the occurrence of a future event" but admits that it "is used with different meanings in different disciplines, as well as 'prediction.'" The UN International Strategy for Disaster Reduction (2009) defines a "forecast" as a "definite statement or statistical estimate of the likely occurrence of a future event or conditions for a specific area" (p. 7).

Plausibility and Implausibility

Our assessment of probability is easier if we can ignore the implausible and assess the plausible. Uncertainty is so pervasive that it could be paralyzing. Indeed, risk or security managers often are criticized for finding risks everywhere and for imposing impractical advisories (such as bans on scissors that could cut or sports that could injure) to protect the public's health and safety.

This extremism is not helped by the popular cultural taste for fictional catastrophes and "black swans" (essentially: high impact, low probability events) (Taleb, 2007). If the advice is to be mindful of the possibility of events that rarely occur, the advice would be useful, but when the advice encourages planning for every imaginable event then the advice is impossibly burdensome. To pick a popular cultural example, many people have imagined an alien invasion of earth, but in the real world, no official authority has prepared for such an event because such preparations would be unjustifiably burdensome. We have no reason to assess the chance of aliens invading earth as possible, so we should prepare for other scenarios.

Despite a low probability, a high risk would still exist if the impact were very great, but if the impact is practically impossible, the risk is practically nonexistent. At the least, risk assessors need to remind themselves or their consumers that possible is not the same as probable. In most domains, plenty of higher probabilities can be assessed, so to assess every plausibility is not practical. At the same time, we should not dismiss some risks as practically impossible without admitting that they could change.

To be practical, when the number of potential events appear limitless, we should ignore any with a probability below some threshold. For instance, the British MOD's forecasts (2010a, p. 91) effectively ignore all potential events with a probability below 10% (since it defined possible with a probability above 10%) and forecasts only "credible strategic shocks" ("strategic shocks" are "high impact, low probability events").

Confidence

Given the choice, we should choose assessments or sources of assessments in which we have more confidence, perhaps because those assessments are produced from superior methods, superior sources, more genuine experts, or people who have been proven correct in the past. Sometimes authorities survey people on their confidence in forecasts.

The proper way to use ratings of confidence is to rely on the confident forecasts and ignore the unconfident forecasts (by whatever threshold you set between confidence and unconfidence). For instance, one group of experts might assess the probability of an event at 60%, another group at 50%. In order to choose between them, we could ask others to rate their level of confidence in each group; we could ask even the forecasters themselves to give their confidence in their own forecasts.

However, sometimes respondents or consumers confuse likelihood with confidence; for instance, sometimes consumers multiply the rating of confidence by the rating of likelihood to produce another rating of likelihood, but this is not theoretically justified or fair to the respondent. In order to discourage consumers from doing such a thing, intelligence analysts are advised to declare their confidence in their judgment and to follow their assessment of the probability "with the word 'because' and a response to complete the sentence that includes a list of key factors that support the judgment" (Pherson & Pherson, 2013, pp. 185, 188, 195).

Pedagogy Box 6.5 Official Canadian Method for Rating Confidence in Risk Assessments

Table 6.3 Canadian Official Confidence Levels

Confidence Level	Coding Rules
A	Very high confidence in the judgment based on a thorough knowledge of the issue, the very large quantity and quality of the relevant data, and totally consistent relevant assessments
B	High confidence in the judgment based on a very large body of knowledge on the issue, the large quantity and quality of the relevant data, and very consistent relevant assessments
C	Moderate confidence in the judgment based on a considerable body of knowledge on the issue, the considerable quantity and quality of relevant data, and consistent relevant assessments
D	Low confidence in the judgment based on a relatively small body of knowledge on the issue, the relatively small quantity and quality of relevant data, and somewhat consistent relevant assessments
E	Very low confidence in the judgment based on small to insignificant body of knowledge on the issue, quantity, and quality of relevant data and/or inconsistent relevant assessments

SOURCE: All Hazards Risk Assessment Methodology Guidelines, 2012–2013, p.25, Public Safety Canada and Defence Research and Development Canada, 2013. Reproduced with the permission of the Minster of Public Works and Government Services , 2013.

Sources of Data on Probability

This section explains different sources of data on probabilities: conversions of qualitative likelihoods, frequency data, judgments, and time horizons and periods.

Converting Qualitative and Quantitative Expressions

Studies show that most people do not interpret likelihoods or probabilities consistently or accurately. Some people are better at interpreting natural frequencies (such as "10 times out of 100") or bettor's odds ("10 to 1 odds on," which means "this event is ten times more likely to happen than not") than probabilities ("10%"). Most people fail to differentiate unfamiliar or extreme values: for instance, they are likely to fail to appreciate the full difference between 1 in 1,000 and 1 in 10,000. From good frequency data, we can calculate probability at such level of differentiation, but as numbers become smaller or larger, they become indistinguishably extreme to most people. Similarly, most people (other than mathematicians) do not accept a meaningful difference between 46% and 50%, although they would admit a profound difference between 100% and 0%. Consequently, judgments of the cardinal probability (for instance, 46%) of an event are unrealistically precise, so a more honest judgment is ordinal (say, 3 on a scale from 1 to 5).

Many respondents feel more comfortable assessing a probability in qualitative (textual) rather than quantitative terms. In theory, the literal meanings of different terms are easy to express quantitatively (as summarized in Table 6.4), but the general public's use and understanding of the terms are unreliable. For instance, people often use possible and probable interchangeably, but a possible event has a literal quantitative range from more than 0% (impossible) to less than 100% (certain), while a probable event lies between 50% and 100%.

In the public domain, at least, authors and respondents are incentivized toward less precise forecasts that are easier to deny or fit to events retrospectively. Even in confidential assessments, U.S. intelligence agents are advised to use the terms *may*, *could*, *might*, and *possibly* if they were not confident enough to use the more precise 7-point or 9-point scales of likelihood. When dealing with technically and politically complicated events (such as cyber attacks), the threats are rarely identified with certainty, so the investigator or intelligence agent is likely to use words like *possibly* in this context,

Table 6.4 Literal Qualitative and Quantitative Expressions of Probability

Qualitative Descriptor	Literal Quantitative Meaning (%)
Definite; certain; no doubt	*100*
Likely; probable	*More than 50*
Possible; could happen; plausible	*More than 0*
Even; as likely as not	*50*
Unlikely; improbable; doubtful	*Less than 50*
Impossible	*0*
Uncertain	*0–100*

although some advisers have reminded officials that such words "usually convey too little useful information to the reader" (Pherson & Pherson, 2013, p. 188). The typical published forecast is no more precise than a categorical judgment between unlikely or likely (in the American case) or unlikely, possible, likely, or certain (in the British case). This all leads to frustration for consumers who need forecasts of sufficient precision to be useful in risk calculations.

> For every prediction, there is a caveat. The reports lean heavily on words such as "could," "possibly," and "maybe." The lead-in to *Global Trends 2025* uses "could" nine times in two pages, and the report as a whole uses the word a whopping 220 times. The report also uses "maybe" 36 times. *Global Trends 2020* uses "could" 110 times. Add all of the caveats and conditionals, and a harsh critic might conclude that these reports are saying no more than that there is a possibility that something could happen at some point—and it might have a big effect . . . Exposing policymakers to "deep thoughts" about the future has value, but the failure to offer even broad ranges of probability estimates for outcomes is unfortunate. (Horowitz & Tetlock, 2012)

Pedagogy Box 6.6 Official Schemes for Converting Probabilities and Likelihoods

Different authorities use incompatible scales, qualitative terms, or quantitative interpretations of these terms. In Table 6.5, I have attempted to align some important standards, but they are inherently impossible to align perfectly, partly because their scales vary from 5 points to 10 points, partly because they use different terms, and partly because they use the same terms at incompatible points.

Table 6.5 Different Qualitative Scales for Likelihood or Probability

U.S. DOD	U.S. National Intelligence Council, 2002	U.S. Defense Intelligence Agency, 2010	Canadian Chief of Defence Intelligence	Australian/ New Zealand, 1995–2009, and ISO, 2009a	UK Cabinet Office, 2012a	United Nations, 2007
-	-	*Certain*	*Certain*	-	-	*Certain; imminent*
Frequent	*Almost certainly*	*Almost certainly; will*	*Almost certain; extremely likely*	*Almost certain*	*High*	
Probable	*Very likely*	*Very likely; very probable*	*Likely; probably*	*Likely*		*Very likely*
	Probably	*Probable; likely*	*Slightly greater than even*		*Medium high*	*Likely*

(Continued)

(Continued)

U.S. DOD	U.S. National Intelligence Council, 2002	U.S. Defense Intelligence Agency, 2010	Canadian Chief of Defence Intelligence	Australian/ New Zealand, 1995–2009, and ISO, 2009a	UK Cabinet Office, 2012a	United Nations, 2007
Occasional	*Even; likely*	*Even*	*Even*	*Possible*	*Medium*	*Moderately likely*
Remote	*Unlikely*	*Unlikely; improbable*	*Slightly less than even*	*Unlikely*	*Medium low*	*Unlikely*
Improbable	*Very unlikely*	*Very unlikely; very improbable*	*Unlikely; probably not*		*Low*	-
-	*Remote*	*Remote*	*Very unlikely*	*Rare*		-
-	-	*Impossible*	*No prospect*	-	-	-

SOURCES: Pherson & Pherson, 2013, pp. 188–190; U.S. Government Accountability Office, 1998, pp. 5–7.

Whatever qualitative terms are used, different users will interpret them differently. For instance, surveys of military officers and intelligence officials reveal that they interpret the word probably anywhere within a quantitative range from 25% to 90% (even though, literally, *probably* means greater than 50% to 100%). Worse, users interpret the word *probable* differently when the impacts are negative or positive—around 70% to 80% probability for positive impacts but around 40% to 50% for negative impacts.

The terms *unlikely*, *likely*, *most likely*, and *almost certainly* are normative in the intelligence community, but without standard quantitative interpretations. Some intelligence agencies have published tables of standard quantitative interpretations for each term, but still have not agreed a common standard, so these tables remain occasional guidance that officials often disregard (Pherson & Pherson, 2013, pp. 185–188, 191). A potential standard, created more than 50 years ago by an influential U.S. intelligence analyst, is shown in Table 6.6.

The British MOD has decided on similar schemes for intelligence (see Table 6.7) and global trends (see Table 6.8).

Interestingly, the British MOD allowed for quantitative separation between levels and an essentially illiterate scale for ease of differentiation between levels, while the Canadian Chief of Defence Intelligence has chosen a more literal and interval scale (see Table 6.9).

Unfortunately, many official authorities use more than one scheme, without clear justification. For instance, the British defense and security sector has used several different schemes for coding project risks, none with any declared mathematical or literal justification (see two examples in Table 6.10). The MOD eventually settled on a scheme for project risk management (see Table 6.11), but this remains incompatible with its schemes for intelligence or strategic trends (see Tables 6.7 and 6.8).

Table 6.6 A U.S. Intelligence Agent's Scheme for Converting Qualitative and Quantitative Expressions of Probability in Intelligence Analyses

Qualitative Descriptor	Quantitative Meaning (%)	
	Single Number	**Approximate Range**
Almost certainly; all but certain; highly likely; overwhelming odds	93	87–99
Probably; likely; we believe or estimate	75	63–87
Chances about even; we believe not or estimate not; we doubt	50	40–60
Probably not; Unlikely	30	20–40
Almost certainly not; almost impossible; highly unlikely; some slight chance	7	2–12
Impossible	0	0

SOURCE: Kent, 1963.

Table 6.7 A British Scheme for Converting Qualitative and Quantitative Expressions of Probability

Qualitative Descriptor	Quantitative Meaning (%)
Almost certain	More than 90
Highly probable or highly likely	75–85
Probable or likely	55–70
Realistic probability	25–50
Improbable or unlikely	15–20
Remote or highly unlikely	Less than 10

SOURCE: U.K. MOD, 2011b, p. 3.23.

Table 6.8 A British Scheme for Interpreting Qualitative and Quantitative Probabilities in the Context of Global Strategic Trends

Qualitative Probability	Quantitative Probability
Will [occur]	Greater than 90%
Likely, probably	60%–90%
May, possibly	10%–60%
Unlikely, improbable	Less than 10%

SOURCE: U.K. MOD, 2010a, p. 8.

(Continued)

(Continued)

Table 6.9 The Canadian Chief of Defense Intelligence's Scheme for Converting Qualitative and Quantitative Expressions of Probability

Qualitative Descriptor	Quantitative Meaning (Approximate %)
Certain; will [occur]; is [occurring]	100
Almost certain; extremely likely	90
Likely; probably	80
	70
Slightly greater than even chance	60
Even chance	50
Slightly less than even chance	40
Unlikely; probably not	30
	20
Very unlikely; little prospect	10
No prospect; will not [occur]	0

SOURCE: Based on Pherson & Pherson, 2013, pp. 188–190.

Table 6.10 British Examples of Incompatible Schemes for Interpreting the Quantitative Probabilities of Different Qualitative Levels

Probability Level in Qualitative Terms	U.K. Defense Procurement Agency	Carter, Hancock, Morin, and Robins (1996, p. 53)
Very high	>60%	-
High	40%–60%	30%–100%
Medium	20%–40%	10%–30%
Low	5%–20%	0%–10%
Very low	<5%	-

We could justify some fudging of the mathematics for practical reasons. For instance, proving certainty is often practically impossible, so for estimates of intelligence and forecasts of trends, the MOD allows a potential event to be coded as practically certain if the probability rises above 90%, or practically impossible if the probability falls below 10% (see Tables 6.7 and 6.8).

Table 6.11 One of the British MOD's Schemes for Categorizing Probabilities in the Context of Projects

Qualitative Level	Qualitative Interpretation	Quantitative Interpretation	Time Horizon
High	More likely than not	More than 60%	Within next year
Medium	As likely as not	30%–60%	Within 2–4 years
Low	Unlikely	Less than 30%	Within 4–10 years

SOURCE: Based on MOD, 2010b and 2011b.

Some schemes cannot be reconciled mathematically, even if we allow for practicalities. For instance, on a simple ordinal scale (low; medium; high) a British private standard chose an exponential distribution of probability (0%–2%; 2%–25%; 25%–100%) for negative outcomes but a normal distribution (0%–25%; 25%–75%; 75%–100%) for positive outcomes (Association of Insurance and Risk Managers, ALARM The National Forum for Risk Management in the Public Sector, & The Institute of Risk Management [AIRMIC, ALARM, & IRM], 2002, pp. 7–8). The British MOD has offered a different irregular distribution of probability on the same 3-point scale (see Table 6.11). The British executive has plotted the likelihood of terrorist and other malicious attacks within the next 5 years on a 5-point ordinal scale with apparent interval values (low; medium low; medium; medium high; high), but used a quantitative version with exponential values (0.005%–0.050%; 0.05%–0.50%; 0.5%–5.0%; 5%–50%; 50%–100%) in the context of natural and accidental risks (U.K. Cabinet Office, 2012a). Similarly, the Australian/New Zealand and ISO standard uses a 5-point ordinal scale (1, 2, 3, 4, 5) for coding likelihood, which is naturally interpreted as an interval scale, but the scale for coding probability has exponential values (0.001%–0.010%; 0.01%–0.10%; 0.1%–1.0%; 1%–10%; 10%–100%).

Frequency Data and Trend Analysis

The probability of future events often is inferred from past frequencies (see Table 9.2 for examples of real frequencies). A frequency is the number of events per defined unit of time, for example, "100,000 deaths to cancer per year." For the more frequent, well-observed, and unadaptive events, such as common diseases and accidents, statisticians can confidently assess future probabilities from past frequencies. For instance, if 1 million Americans die from a particular disease every year, we can confidently predict that 1 million Americans will die from that same disease next year. All other things equal (ignoring all other risk factors and assuming no changes), the probability of an average American dying from that disease next year is the number of forecasted deaths (1 million) divided by the total population (315 million), the product of which is 0.3%.

We can make our inferences more reliable by parsing the events by the conditions. For instance, road traffic accidents are very frequent, and the data are recorded in sufficient detail to produce thousands of events per year in areas as well-defined as cities, together with data on the types of vehicle, road, weather, season, and driver. Consequently, actuarial scientists can advise insurers with confidence about the probability of an accident within a certain period and area involving a driver of a certain age, gender, and occupation and with a certain vehicle. More complex statistical handling of frequency data is routine in most branches of insurance and financial risk management, which are associated with specialized disciplines or fields like actuarial science and stochastic modeling. These methods are too specialized for further description in this book, but any manipulation of frequency data, such as a calculation of a rate of deaths per population, would count as statistics.

Data become invalid if they do not accurately describe what they are supposed to describe. For instance, official crime rates run about half the rate of victimization rates (self-reported victims of crime in a survey population). The true crime rate is difficult to induce, because officials record fewer crimes than occur and are sometimes incentivized to deflate the rate, while victims both fail to report some of the crimes that they experienced and inflate crime in general, but the true crime rate is closer to the victimization rate than the official crime rate (Kennedy & Van Brunschot, 2009, pp. 63–65).

Some data are invalid due to poor choices about correlates. For instance, data on interpersonal violence within a state have been used as an indicator of the state's propensity to violence, but this correlate illustrates something called the *ecological fallacy*—an inference about behavior at a higher level from aggregate data on units at a lower level.

Consumers may not be motivated, allowed, qualified, or resourced to investigate the accuracy of the data. The dilemma for the conscientious consumer of statistics is that longer-term historical data are suggestive of more confidence if we assume unchanging phenomena, but less confidence if we suspect fundamental change in the real world. Statistical methods have suffered crises of confidence after the Latin American debt crisis in the 1980s, the Asian economic crisis in the late 1990s, the surge in terrorism on and after September 11, 2001, and the global economic and fiscal crisis from 2008 (Suder, 2004, p. 178).

Statistically, fewer data implies less confidence. We can be confident in frequency data where events are numerous, accurately observed, and their causes do not change. Car drivers can mature in their compliance with regulations, but otherwise, driver types are not remarkably adaptive (short of a shock, like a road traffic accident), in part because driving and accidents are regular enough that the risks are treated as familiar. However, historical data would be misleading if we were to expect the causes of the phenomenon to change somehow. For instance, criminal behavior would seem stable until some innovation that rapidly spreads through the criminal population.

Data on highly dynamic or adaptive behaviors are least reliable. Data on terrorism are particularly problematic because terrorism is actually infrequent compared to most other crimes. Additionally, the data are corrupted by poor reporting of most terrorist events, official secrecy, and politicization. Finally, terrorism is an adaptive behavior. Consequently, relying on data from a previous decade to forecast terrorist behavior in the next decade is foolish. Many analysts prefer subjective judgments, based on more qualitative data, rather than rely on statistical modeling (Greenberg, Chalk, Willis, Khilko, & Ortiz, 2006).

When dealing with dynamic or adaptive behaviors, our forecast would need to be theoretical as well as empirical. In any domain, due diligence includes checking the validity of our data or of our sources. Sometimes, the highest authorities fail us. For instance, in April 2004, the U.S. State Department released its latest annual *Patterns of Global Terrorism*, which claimed that the frequency of terrorism had declined in 2003. The George W. Bush administration claimed that the data were proof of its counter-terrorism policy and of reduced risks from terrorism. However, two independent academics showed that the numbers literally did not add up and that in fact terrorism had increased. After they published their findings in a newspaper and a journal, the State Department terminated the publication (Krueger & Laitin, 2004).

Surveying Judgments

Ideally, we would become sufficiently expert in the theories in order to estimate the likelihood of future behaviors, but we could forego our own review of the theories in favor of a survey of other experts. We could ask respondents to assess the probability of an event occurring within some period of time, to forecast when an event would occur, or if they would agree with a prediction of an event within a period of time.

Freely available survey results, such as those reported by journalists, are materially attractive even though the respondents are unlikely to be experts. Such surveys often ask how the respondent will behave (such as vote) and rarely ask the likelihood of something happening, but they may ask whether the respondent thinks that something will occur or change. For instance, survey items often ask whether the respondent believes that crime will increase in a certain area. The proportion of respondents who agree could be used as a probability; although this method has little theoretical justification, it may be the best we could do with limited time or resources.

Any consumer faces some basic statistical choices (for instance, we should select the median rather than mean response because medians are less sensitive to outlier responses) and some methodological choices (for instance, a "Delphi Survey" would ask the respondents to reforecast more than once in reaction to the most recent responses, anonymously revealed—this helps respondents to converge around the most realistic responses: see Chapter 3).

Time Horizons and Periods

Frequency data over long periods of past time can be used confidently to calculate probabilities over short periods of future time. For instance, if we were confident in data suggesting that an area suffered 1,000 murders each decade and we predicted no change in the rate, then we could confidently forecast 100 murders next year.

For less frequent events, we might forecast the period within which the next event would occur. Extending a longer period as the scope for an event increases the certainty of the event. Usefully, we could choose a time period within which we think an event is certain (has a probability of 100%) and make inferences about lower probabilities earlier in the period. Imagine that the data shows that a crime of a particular type occurred just once in the last decade in our area; we could infer a 10% chance of such a crime occurring within the next year in our area. Trend analysis captures change by, for instance, finding that a certain crime rate has doubled every decade and forecasting that the crime rate will double again over the next decade (assuming all other things equal).

Always try to talk about time in defined units (days, weeks, months, years, decades, centuries). Too often, commentators talk about short-, medium-, and long-term risks, without any standard interpretation of these terms. At the least, time should be periodized in relation to a known unit or a start or end point. For instance, the British government's project management standard (PRINCE2) assesses a risk's "proximity" in terms of project time: imminent, within stage, within project, beyond project (U.K. Office of Government Commerce, 2009).

SUMMARY

This chapter has

- defined uncertainty,
- explained the difference between uncertainty and risk,
- explained how to find and identify uncertainties,
- defined probability and likelihood,
- explained how to analyze probability,
- explained how to mathematically calculate probability,
- explained how to separate predictable and forecastable things,
- explained how to separate plausible and implausible things,
- noted the motivation for a separate assessment of confidence,
- explained how to convert qualitative and quantitative expressions of probability,
- explained how to use frequency data to infer probabilities,
- referred to expert judgments on probabilities, and
- explained how to use time to infer probabilities.

QUESTIONS AND EXERCISES

1. What is the difference between uncertainty and probability?
2. What is the difference between uncertainty and risk?
3. Where in a project would you expect to identify more uncertainty?
4. In what areas of an overseas mission is uncertainty most inherent?
5. What is the difference between probability and likelihood?
6. What misunderstandings should you worry about when surveying people about their estimates of likelihood or probability?
7. How does good analysis of a risk back to its source help an assessment of probability?
8. Why should we attempt to separate the predictable from the forecastable?
9. How could we avoid assessing an infinite number of plausible scenarios?
10. How should you use and not use a reported confidence in a probability assessment?
11. Give the literal meanings of the following words as a quantitative probability or probability range:
    a. certain
    b. uncertain
    c. possible
    d. probable

e. likely
f. definite
g. might happen
h. will happen
i. could happen
j. more likely than not to happen
k. improbable
l. impossible
m. unlikely

12. What is the difference between a frequency and a probability?
13. What sorts of behaviors can be forecasted accurately with past frequencies?
14. Assume that events of a certain type occur at a linear frequency of 120 events per year:
    a. How many events can we predict next month?
    b. What is the probability of just 60 events next year?
    c. What is the probability of an event tomorrow?
    d. What is the probability of one event occurring tomorrow and another the day after?
    e. What is the probability of a single event either occurring or not occurring tomorrow?

Events and Returns

This chapter defines returns (one of the two main concepts that make up a risk), events, issues, and incidents, explains how events are assessed, shows how returns are categorized, and gives practical advice on how to assess returns.

Defining Returns

The returns of an event are the changes experienced by an affected entity. The returns are experienced by or affect the holders of the risk or those exposed to the risk, such as investors or victims.

The term *returns*, as used in this book, includes many other concepts, such as effects, outputs, outcomes, costs, losses, profits, gains, benefits, consequences (the U.S. government's favorite), or impacts (the British government's favorite). These other terms are inconsistently used and defined. For instance, the Canadian government refers to both consequences and impacts to mean slightly different things.

Pedagogy Box 7.1 Official Types of Returns

Outcome

Outcomes are "a description of salient features of the future strategic context, with an associated level of confidence" (U.K. Ministry of Defense [MOD], 2010a, pp. 5–6).

Effect

"An effect is a deviation from the expected—positive and/or negative" (Australian and New Zealand Joint Technical Committee, 2009, p. 1).

(Continued)

(Continued)

Impact

The *impact* is "the amount of loss or damage that can be expected from a successful attack on an asset. Loss may be monetary, but may include loss of lives and destruction of a symbolic structure" (U.S. Government Accountability Office [GAO], 2005b, p. 110). The U.S. Department of Defense (DOD) Dictionary does not define this term.

Impact is the "scale of the consequences of a hazard, threat or emergency expressed in terms of a reduction in human welfare, damage to the environment and loss of security" (U.K. Cabinet Office, 2013). Impact is the "consequence of a particular outcome (may or may not be expressed purely in financial terms)" (U.K. MOD, 2011c, p. Glossary 2).

"The term impact is used to estimate the extent of harm within each of the impact categories [people; economy; environment; territorial security; Canada's reputation and influence; society and psycho-social]. When describing a composite measure of impacts (considering more than one impact category), the term consequence is applied" (Public Safety Canada, 2013, p. 22).

"Impact is the seriousness or severity of the potential problem in terms of the effect on your project" (Heerkens, 2002, p. 148).

Consequence

For U.S. Department of Homeland Security (DHS) (2009), the *consequence* is "the effect of an event, incident, or occurrence" (p. 109). "Consequences mean the dangers (full or partial), injuries, and losses of life, property, environment, and business that can be quantified by some unit of measure, often in economic or financial terms" (U.S. Federal Emergency Management Agency [FEMA], 1992, p. xxv). The consequence is "the expected worse case or reasonable worse case impact of a successful attack. The consequence to a particular can be evaluated when threat and vulnerability are considered together. This loss or damage may be long- or short-term in nature" (U.S. GAO, 2005b, p. 110). The U.S. DOD Dictionary does not define this term.

The consequence is "the outcome of an event affecting objectives." It "can be certain or uncertain and can have positive or negative effects on objectives" (International Organization for Standardization, 2009a, p. 8). The "consequences of an event" include "changes in circumstances" (Australian and New Zealand Joint Technical Committee, 2009, p. 1).

For Canadian government, a consequence is "a composite measure of impacts (considering more than one impact category)" (Public Safety Canada, 2013, p. 22).

For the British Civil Contingencies Secretariat, consequences (plural) are the "impact resulting from the occurrence of a particular hazard or threat, measured in terms of the numbers of lives lost, people injured, the scale of damage to property and the disruption to essential services and commodities" (U.K. Cabinet Office, 2013).

Cost and Benefit

In U.S. government, *costs* are "inputs, both direct and indirect," while a *benefit* is the "net outcome, usually translated into monetary term; a benefit may include both direct and indirect effects" (U.S. GAO, 2005b, p. 110). The U.S. DOD Dictionary does not define any of these terms.

Harm

Harm is "a potential unwelcome development" (Fillmore & Atkins, 1992, p. 82). The British Civil Contingencies Secretariat defines harm as the "nature and extent of physical injury (including loss of life) or psychological or economic damage to an individual, community, or organization" (U.K. Cabinet Office, 2013).

Defining Event

An event is an occurrence in time or "a thing that happens or takes place" (FrameNet). Events, as occurrences, include accidents, wars, attacks, structural failures, etc. The returns of the event are separate things, such as death or injury.

The event is useful to identify because we could calculate the risk more accurately after assessing the likelihood of the event occurring and the returns from such an event. Analytically, we should imagine how an actor could cause an event and imagine the returns.

Returns and events are routinely conflated, sometimes for justifiable convenience when the returns are unknown. For instance, people often talk about a potential accident as a risk, where the real risk is the potential harm from the accident (Fillmore & Atkins, 1992, p. 87). Similarly, the British Civil Contingencies Secretariat defines a *contingency* as a "possible future emergency or risk" (U.K. Cabinet Office, 2013), but the potential emergency (event) cannot be the same as the potential returns (risk).

Conflation of events and returns is colloquially justifiable, but not analytically justifiable. Strictly speaking, we would be wrong to talk of a potential accident or potential war or potential building collapse as a risk (each is a potential event, but not a potential return); we should be self-disciplined enough to talk of a potential event with which we should associate potential returns (risks), while keeping the event and the returns separate.

Pedagogy Box 7.2 Official Definitions of Event

In the Australian/New Zealand and ISO (International Organization for Standardization, 2009a, p. 6) standard, an event is "an occurrence or change of a particular set of circumstances," where an "event can be one or more occurrences and can have several causes" and "can consist of something not happening."

For U.S. DHS (2009) an *occurrence* is "caused by either human action or natural phenomena that may cause harm and may require action. Incidents can include major disasters, emergencies, terrorist attacks, terrorist threats, wild and urban fires, floods, hazardous materials spills, nuclear accidents, aircraft accidents, earthquakes, hurricanes, tornadoes, tropical storms, war-related disasters, public health and medical emergencies, and other occurrences requiring an emergency response" (p. 110).

In Canadian government, an *event* is "a significant occurrence that may or may not be planned and may impact the safety and security of Canadians" (Public Safety Canada, 2012, p. 37).

The British government does not offer a standard definition of event, but the Civil Contingencies Act of 2004 refers to an "event or situation" that causes significant harm as an emergency (U.K. Cabinet Office, 2013).

Defining Issue and Incident

An issue or an incident is an event that requires a response. In general use, an *issue* is "an important topic for debate or resolution", while an *incident* is either "an occurrence" or "a disruptive, usually dangerous or unfortunate event" (FrameNet). Issues are useful to separate from other events, because issues require further action, while other events can be ignored.

Pedagogy Box 7.3 Official Definitions of Incident and Issue

The British Civil Contingencies Act of 2004, and thence the Cabinet Office, does not define event but identify *incident* ("an event or situation that requires a response from the emergency services or other responders") and regularly use the phrase *event and situation* in definitions of various emergencies (U.K. Cabinet Office, 2013). The British government has been keen to conceptualize issue, particularly in the context of defense acquisition projects. For the U.K. MOD (unpublished), an *issue* is "a significant certain occurrence differentiated from a risk by virtue of its certainty of occurrence and by the fact that it should be accounted for in Planning and Scheduling activities and not Risk Management."

The Canadian government does not define issue but defines *incident* in a similar way, as "an event caused by either human action or a natural phenomenon that requires a response to prevent or minimize loss of life or damage to property or the environment and reduce economic and social losses." The government goes further to describe *incident management* as "the coordination of an organization's activities aimed at preventing, mitigating against, preparing for, responding to, and recovering from an incident" (Public Safety Canada, 2012, p. 52). For the Humanitarian Practice Network (2010, p. xvi) a *critical incident* is "a security incident that significantly disrupts an organization's capacity to operate; typically life is lost or threatened, or the incident involves mortal danger."

Assessing Events and Issues

When we declare an event as an issue or incident, already we have assessed it as more important than events that are not issues or incidents. The importance of events can be ranked on an ordinal scale. The Australian/New Zealand standard (Australian and New Zealand Joint Technical Committee, 2009) uses a 5-point ordinal scale (from 1 to 5; or from *insignificant*, *minor*, *moderate*, *major*, to *catastrophic* respectively). The British government effectively adopted the same scale (although *major* became *significant*) (U.K. Cabinet Office, 2012a).

Events are often ranked by certain words, such as *disruption*, *crisis*, *emergency*, *disaster* and *catastrophe*, and *shock*, as explained in the subsections below.

Disruption

A disruption is "a disturbance that compromises the availability, delivery, and/or integrity of services of an organization" (Public Safety Canada, 2012, p. 28).

Crisis

The British Standards Institute defines a crisis as "an inherently abnormal, unstable and complex situation that represents a threat to the strategic objectives, reputation or existence of an organization," but the Civil Contingencies Secretariat essentially defines it as an emergency (U.K. Cabinet Office, 2013).

For Canadian government, a crisis is "a situation that threatens public safety and security, the public's sense of tradition and values, or the integrity of the government. The terms 'crisis' and 'emergency' are not interchangeable. However, a crisis may become an emergency. For example, civil unrest over an unpopular government policy may spark widespread riots" (Public Safety Canada, 2012, p. 20).

Emergency

The UN (UN Department of Humanitarian Affairs [DHA], 1992) defines an emergency as "a sudden and usually unforeseen event that calls for immediate measures to minimize its adverse consequences."

Britain

In Britain, the Civil Contingencies Act (2004) (U.K. Cabinet Office, 2013) defines an emergency as "an event or situation which threatens serious damage to human welfare [or] to the environment of a place in the United Kingdom, or war, or terrorism that threatens serious damage to the security of the United Kingdom." The Civil Contingencies Secretariat went on to define an emergency as "an event or situation which threatens serious damage to human welfare in a place in the UK, the environment of a place in the UK, or the security of the UK or of a place in the UK." The British MOD (2011c) defines an emergency as "an event or situation which threatens serious damage to the human welfare, security or environment of the UK" (p. Glossary-2).

The British Cabinet Office categorizes three types of events that could count as emergencies:

1. Natural events
2. Major accidents
3. Malicious attacks

The British Civil Contingencies Secretariat defines a *major accident* as an emergency and defines an *accident* as an "unplanned, unexpected, unintended and undesirable happening which results in or has the potential for injury, harm, ill-health or damage" (U.K. Cabinet Office, 2013).

Since 2010, the British Cabinet Office has separated local emergency from national emergency and defined three levels of national emergency:

1. Level 1: Significant emergency—central government nominates a lead government department to support other stakeholders.
2. Level 2: Serious emergency—central government directs the emergency management.
3. Level 3: Catastrophic emergency—central government directs the emergency management.

Canada

Public Safety Canada (2012, pp. 29, 65) defines an emergency as "a present or imminent event that requires prompt coordination of actions concerning persons or property to protect the health, safety, or welfare of people, or to limit damage to property or the environment."

In Canada, the Emergencies Act of 1988 envisioned mostly regional emergencies but defines a *national emergency* as "an urgent and critical situation of a temporary nature that

a. seriously endangers the lives, health, or safety of Canadians and is of such proportions or nature as to exceed the capacity or authority of a province to deal with it, or

b. seriously threatens the ability of the Government of Canada to preserve the sovereignty, security, and territorial integrity of Canada,

and that cannot be effectively dealt with under any other law of Canada."

The Emergencies Act recognized four types of events as emergencies:

1. *Public welfare emergency*: "Results or may result in a danger to life or property, social disruption or a breakdown in the flow of essential goods, services or resources, so serious as to be a national emergency," and is "caused by a real or imminent
   a. fire, flood, drought, storm, earthquake or other natural phenomenon,
   b. disease in human beings, animals or plants, or
   c. accident or pollution."
2. *Public order emergency*: "Arises from threats to the security of Canada and that is so serious as to be a national emergency."
3. *International emergency*: "An emergency involving Canada and one or more other countries that arises from acts of intimidation or coercion or the real or imminent use of serious force or violence and that is so serious as to be a national emergency."
4. *War emergency*: "War or other armed conflict, real or imminent, involving Canada or any of its allies that is so serious as to be a national emergency."

In "the context of continuity of constitutional government," the Canadian government differentiates events on a 3-point scale of their returns:

1. "Level 1 event: an event that disrupts work to a limited extent within a primary location but does not require the relocation of an entire organization or institution."
2. "Level 2 event: an event that compromises an entire building in such a way that an organization or institution cannot perform its functions and that a partial or total relocation to a nearby secondary location becomes necessary."
3. "Level 3 event: an event that requires that an entire organization or institution be relocated to an alternate site outside of the national Capital Region" (Public Safety Canada, 2012, pp. 58–59).

Disaster and Catastrophe

Anyone who routinely talks about some events as disasters or catastrophes effectively uses a two-level scale (disaster or catastrophe; other events). Insurers, at least, use these terms to describe events with negative returns above well-defined thresholds. Catastrophe and disaster are often used interchangeably, but many insurers and reinsurers differentiate *natural catastrophes* from *man-made disasters*. By contrast, United Nations agencies tend to refer to natural disasters and human catastrophes. Yet the UN Office for International Strategy for Disaster Reduction (ISDR) (2009) defines disaster without any reference to either human or natural sources, as "a serious disruption of a community or a society involving widespread human, material, economic, or environmental losses and impacts, which exceeds the ability of the affected community or society to cope using its own resources" (p. 4).

The British Civil Contingencies Secretariat defines *catastrophic emergency* as "an emergency which has an exceptionally high and potentially widespread impact and requires immediate central government direction and support"; it defines disaster as an "emergency (usually but not exclusively of natural causes) causing, or threatening to cause, widespread and serious disruption to community life through death, injury, and/or damage to property and/or the environment" (U.K. Cabinet Office, 2013).

Public Safety Canada (2012, p. 26) defines disasters as both natural and human-caused. It does not define a catastrophe, but uses the French word *catastrophe* in translation of the English word disaster. A disaster is "an event that results when a hazard impacts a vulnerable community in a way that exceeds or overwhelms the community's ability to cope and may cause serious harm to the safety, health, or welfare of people, or damage to property or the environment" (Public Safety Canada, 2012, p. 26).

Strategic Shocks

The MOD adds *strategic shocks*, which are "high impact events that have the potential to rapidly alter the strategic context" or result "in a discontinuity or an abrupt alteration in the strategic context" or "dislocates the strategic context from the trends that have preceded it." Past examples include the public breach of the wall dividing Berlin in 1989, the terrorist attacks of September 11, 2001, and the global financial crisis of 2007–2008 (U.K. MOD, 2010a, pp. 5–6, 91).

 Categorizing Returns

The returns of major risks have multiple dimensions. The most typical categorization is between material and human returns. For instance, the consequences of terrorism have been coded from 1 to 5 on two dimensions: humans killed or injured and economic costs (Greenberg, Chalk, Willis, Khilko, & Ortiz, 2006). Swiss Re Group, like most insurers and reinsurers, measures *losses* in terms of total economic losses; insured property claims; and human casualties.

Unfortunately, official authorities prescribe some diverse terms of and categories of returns. Table 7.1 shows my attempt to align their categories.

 Assessing Returns

Returns can be assessed judgmentally on ordinal scales or measured in economic, organizational, operational, human, environmental, or territorial/geopolitical terms, as explained in sequential subsections below.

Judgmentally Estimating Returns

Returns can be judged or communicated on ordinal scales. A scale may be as simple as *low*, *medium*, and *high* and has the advantage of easy interpretation as interval steps.

Table 7.1 Official Prescribed Categories of Returns, Aligned

U.S. DHS (2009, p. 109)		United Nations Development Program (1994)		U.K. Cabinet Office (2012a, pp. 3, 29, 37)		British Civil Contingencies Secretariat (U.K. Cabinet Office, 2013)		Public Safety Canada (2013, p. 23)	
Consequences	Strategic mission or governance	Consequences	Physical damage	Harm	National security	Impact	Loss of security	Impact	Territorial security
			Emergency operations						Canada's reputation and influence
	-		Environmental impact		Natural environment		Damage to environment		Environment
	Human health and safety		-		Human welfare		Reduction in human welfare		People
			Deaths	Impact	Fatalities				
			Injuries		Illness or injury				
	Psychological effects		-		Psychological impact				Society and psycho-social
	-		Social disruption		Social disruption				
	Economics		Disruption to economy		Economic harm				Economy

Pedagogy Box 7.4 Official Methods for Rating Returns

The British MOD judges impacts on three levels and three dimensions. Each harm or impact is ranked on a scale from 0 to 5 (see Table 7.2).

Table 7.2 British MOD's (2010b and 2011a) Standard Scale of Impacts

Impact Level	Impact on Achievement of Strategic Aim	Impact on Performance	Management Action Required if the Risk [Event] Occurred
High	Major impact	Important reduction	Major
Medium	Significant impact	Moderate reduction	Significant
Low	Minor	Some effect	Moderate

The U.S. DOD standard, which has been used in civilian government and the commercial sector too, uses a 4-point scale of negative consequences by three different dimensions (see Table 7.3).

Table 7.3 The U.S. DOD's Standard Scale of Impacts

Catastrophic	Death	System loss	Severe environmental damage
Critical	Severe injury or occupation illness	Major system damage	Major environmental damage
Marginal	Minor injury or occupational illness	Minor system damage	Minor environmental damage
Negligible	Less than minor injury or occupational illness	Less than minor system damage	Less than minor environmental damage

SOURCE: U.S. GAO, 1998, p. 7.

The UN's Threat and Risk Unit standardized a 5-point scale of impacts by three dimensions (see Table 7.4).

Table 7.4 The UN's Standard Scale of Impacts

Critical	Death or severe injury	Total loss of assets	Loss of programs and projects
Severe	Serious injury	Major destruction of assets	Severe disruption to programs
Moderate	Nonlife threatening injury and high stress	Loss or damage to assets	Some program delays and disruptions
Minor	Minor injuries	Some loss or damage to assets	Minimal delays to programs
Negligible	No injuries	Minimal loss or damage to assets	No delays to programs

SOURCE: UN Department of Peacekeeping Operations, 2008.

The World Economic Forum (2013, p. 45) asks respondents to estimate the impact of a possible event on a purely numerical 5-point scale (1–5).

Objectively Measuring Returns

Returns can be estimated in terms of many objective measures, such as event frequency (accidents or news media mentions), value of losses, inputs (budget, time, or personnel allocated), or product performance (specifications satisfied, capability delivered, customer satisfaction, reliability, usage).

The subsections below collect typical measures of material, economic, organizational, operational, human, environmental, and territorial returns.

Economic Returns

Economic returns include:

- financial gains and losses,
- direst economic gains and losses, such as reduced trade,
- indirect economic gains and losses, such as increased transaction costs due to damaged communications, and
- flow changes, such as the flows of goods and services that will not be produced or delivered due to damages to material things such as productive assets and infrastructure.

Material damages can be measured by the financial costs of damages, losses, or replacements. For instance, Public Safety Canada (2013, p. 28) prescribed measures of direct economic loss (such as the value of lost stores or equipment, the repair costs, and the replacement costs), but it separated material losses from the economic value of environmental and human losses.

Material returns can be measured by the scale of the items, area, or population affected. For instance, over 2 days in 1871, a great fire in the city of Chicago burnt more than 2,000 acres of urban land, destroyed 28 miles of road, 120 miles of sidewalk, 2,000 lampposts, and 18,000 buildings, and cost more than $200 million in property damage.

Monetary measures of returns are the most fungible. For financial officers and accountants, returns are typically measured as profit or loss.

Insurers and reinsurers tend to measure the financial cost of insured claims and to regard the sum of insured and uninsured losses as the *total economic losses*. For instance, in 2012, Swiss Re Group counted certain events as natural catastrophes or man-made disasters if their total losses breached $90.9 million or their associated insured property claims reached at least $45.8 million (or $18.3 million for shipping claims or $36.6 million for aviation claims).

Pedagogy Box 7.5 Canadian Schemes for Assessing Economic Losses

The Canadian government has published a useful scheme for judgmentally assessing direct economic losses by

- buildings,
- infrastructure,
- machinery and equipment,
- residential housing and contents, and
- raw materials.

It prescribes a judgmental assessment of the indirect economic losses by

- production or service provision losses due to the paralysis of productive activities;
- higher operational costs due to destruction of physical infrastructure and inventories or losses to production and income;
- lost production due to linkage effects, such as when suppliers cannot find alternative markets to their lost markets;
- additional costs incurred due to the need to use alternative means of production or provision of essential services; and
- costs of required government responses to the emergency.

These indirect economic losses can be mitigated by indirect benefits, primarily

- shift in consumer demand or spending on alternative products or services;
- change in the productivity of assets, such as when a flood waters and nourishes productive land;
- labor reallocation, such as when workers are more productive to compensate for lost productive capacity; and
- reconstruction activity, such as the products and services required during repair and reconstruction.

The Canadian government prescribed an ordinal scale to rank total economic impacts by total estimated economic losses (see Table 7.5).

Table 7.5 The Canadian Government's Rating of the Impact on the Economy

Impact Rating	Economic Loss (Canadian Dollars)
None	None
0.0	$10 million
0.5	$30 million
1.0	$100 million
1.5	$300 million
2.0	$1 billion
2.5	$3 billion
3.0	$10 billion
3.5	$30 billion
4.0	$100 billion
4.5	$300 billion
5.0	$1,000 billion

SOURCE: All Hazards Risk Assessment Methodology Guidelines, 2012–2013, p.30, Public Safety Canada and Defence Research and Development Canada, 2013. Reproduced with the permission of the Minster of Public Works and Government Services, 2013.

Organizational Returns

Organizational returns are often neglected in favor of more material measures, but serious organizational returns include corporate reputation, scale and direction of new media coverage, management effort, personnel turnover, and strategic impact. Some ways could be found to measure these returns in fungible financial terms, but usually the returns are intangible enough to discourage measuring them at all.

Pedagogy Box 7.6 Canadian Assessments of Organizational Returns

Public Safety Canada recommends at least rating the extent to which hierarchical levels or jurisdictions are affected or required in response (see Table 7.6).

This rating would be modified by the period of response:

Table 7.6 The Canadian Government's Rating of the Magnitude of Response to an Emergency

Rating	Response Magnitude
None	None
0	Some local general response, but no specialized response
1	Some local specialized response, and surveillance and monitoring from federal authorities
2	Multiregional general response, and notification from federal authorities
3	Multifunctional, multiregional specialized response, and notification from federal authorities
4	Multifunctional, multijurisdictional, specialized response, and mobilization from federal authorities
5	Multifunctional, national and international, specialized response, and rapid mobilization from federal authorities

SOURCE: All Hazards Risk Assessment Methodology Guidelines, 2012–2013, p.32, Public Safety Canada and Defence Research and Development Canada, 2013. Reproduced with the permission of the Minster of Public Works and Government Services, 2013.

- 1 week (add 0.5)
- 1–3 weeks (add 1.0)
- 3–10 weeks (add 1.5)
- 2–8 months (add 2.0)
- 8–24 months (add 2.5)
- 2–6 years (add 3.0)
- 6–20 years (add 3.5)

Canada also ranks the impact on Canada's reputation, a method that could be adapted for any organization:

1. Insignificant damage to Canada's reputation and influence–Minor, short-term, and localized reaction that is limited to small groups of individuals and has no repercussions for Canada or Canadians.
2. Minor damage to Canada's reputation and influence–Minor, medium- to long-term, international reaction by groups of individuals that has a minor effect on Canada or Canadians.
3. Significant damage to Canada's reputation and influence–Significant, short- to medium-term, international reaction by groups of individuals, foreign governments, and/or organizations that has a medium term effect on Canada and Canadians.
4. Major damage to Canada's reputation and influence–Major, short- to medium-term, widespread reaction by large groups, foreign governments and/or organizations that has a long lasting effect on Canada and Canadians.
5. Severe damage to Canada's reputation and influence–Major, long-term, widespread reaction by large groups, foreign governments and/or organizations that has a lasting effect on Canada and Canadians. (Public Safety Canada, 2013, p. 42)

Operational Returns

The outputs, performance, or effectiveness of projects, programs, activities, strategies, campaigns, missions, and operations are routinely assessed, usually in terms of operational effectiveness, which is another form of return.

Pedagogy Box 7.7 British Military Assessments of Operational Returns

British military operational "assessment is the evaluation of progress, based on levels of subjective and objective measurement in order to inform decision-making."

"There are three broad categories of assessment that should produce the answers to the following three questions, first, did we do, properly, the things that we set out to do; second, was what we set out to do, the right thing; and finally, is the combination of things that we are doing getting us to where we want to be?

Answers to the first are provided by Measurement of Activity (MOA). MOA is defined as: assessment of task performance and achievement of its associated purpose. It is an evaluation of what actions have been completed rather than simply what has been undertaken . . .

(Continued)

(Continued)

Answers to the second are provided by Measurement of Effect (MOE). MOE is the assessment of the realisation of specified effects. It is concerned with effects, both intended and unintended. Drawing on various measurements and perspectives, it assists progress measurement, highlights setbacks and supports planning... Finally, answers to the third are provided by Campaign Effectiveness Assessment (CEA). CEA is evaluation of campaign progress based on levels of subjective and objective measurement in order to inform decision-making." (U.K. MOD, 2009b, p. 210)

British military intelligence authorities measure the extent to which desired "effects" have been achieved, "tasks" have been performed, "activities" have worked as intended, and "targets" have been damaged (U.K. MOD, 2011b, pp. 4.9–4.10).

Human Returns

Human returns are the changes experienced by human beings. Typically, human returns are measured as deaths, injuries, disability-adjusted life years, economic cost, and changes of situation, as described in subsections below.

Pedagogy Box 7.8 Official Definitions of Human Returns

Many authorities do not define human returns beyond illustrative examples. For instance, in Britain, the Civil Contingencies Act (2004) defines an emergency in part by "serious damage to human welfare," which includes "loss of human life, human illness or injury, homelessness, damage to property, disruption of a supply of money, food, water, energy, or fuel, disruption of a system of communication, disruption of facilities for transport, or disruption of services related to health." The Civil Contingencies Secretariat is vaguer about a *mass casualty incident*, as "causing casualties on a scale that is beyond the normal resources of the emergency services."

The Canadian government allows for "impacts on people" to include deaths, injuries (including psychological), and displacements or deprivations of basic necessities of life (Public Safety Canada, 2013, p. 23).

Deaths

Deaths are normally measured as fatalities due to an event, mortality rate (deaths per unit population), and frequencies (deaths per unit time).

In the context of terrorism, *mass casualty* tends to mean at least 5 dead and *high casualty* tends to mean at least 15 dead.

Death is one of the severest human returns, but a focus on deaths can underestimate other returns, such as injuries, disabilities, loss of life expectancy, psychological stress, health costs, and injustices.

Injuries

An injury is any damage to the body. (*Wound* implies a puncture wound or an injury due to violence.) An injury could cause death, but normally we measure deaths and survivable injuries separately.

Injuries can be measured as a rate, as a frequency, by number on the body, and on a scale (normally described by *severity*). For instance, the Canadian government recognizes a high degree of injury as "severe harm that affects the public or compromises the effective functioning of government following a disruption in the delivery of a critical service" (Public Safety Canada, 2012, p. 51).

Injuries can be categorized by location on or in the body, medical cause (for instance, toxic, traumatic), or event (for instance, road traffic accident, sports).

Injuries, like deaths, have economic value in the tort system and health system (see below).

DALYs

Disability-adjusted life years (DALYs) are the years of healthy life lost across a population due to premature mortality or disability caused by some event or threat. The DALY is a useful measure because it places two separate measures (deaths; injuries) on the same measure, helping to equate the returns. For instance, one source might affect few people but kill most of them, while another source severely disables everyone it affects but kills few of them directly.

Pedagogy Box 7.9 Official Definitions and Measures of DALYs

The World Health Organization (WHO) calculates the DALYs for a disease or injury as the sum of

- the years-of-life-lost due to premature mortality in the population (YLLs; calculated from the number of deaths at each age multiplied by a standard life expectancy of the age at which death occurs) and
- the years-lost-due-to-disability (YLDs; the product of the frequency of incident cases in that period, the average duration of the disease, and the severity of the disability on a scale from 0—the code for perfectly healthy—to 1—the code for death; years lost in young or old age are discounted nonuniformly by around 3%) (WHO, 2009, p. 5).

This method remained unchanged from 1990 until the Global Burden of Disease Study (2012) adapted the method:

- The YLLs and YLDs are summed, as before;
- the YLLs are calculated similarly, except they are calculated from age-sex-country-time-specific estimates of mortality by cause, multiplied by the standard life expectancy at each age;
- the YLDs are calculated as prevalence of disabling conditions by age, sex, and cause, weighted by new disability weights for each health state, without any discount or weighting by age.

The Canadian government prescribes the consolidation of the impacts on people in terms of DALYs and prescribes conversion of estimated DALYs into an *impact rating* from 0 to 5 (see Table 7.7).

(Continued)

(Continued)

Table 7.7 The Canadian Government's Rating of the Impact on People by DALYs

Impact Rating	Total DALYs (Injuries and Fatalities)	Equivalent Adult Fatalities
None	0	0
0.0	40	1
0.5	120	3
1.0	400	10
1.5	1,200	30
2.0	4,000	100
2.5	12,000	300
3.0	40,000	1,000
3.5	120,000	3,000
4.0	400,000	10,000
4.5	1,200,000	30,000
5.0	4,000,000	100,000

SOURCE: All Hazards Risk Assessment Methodology Guidelines, 2012–2013, p.27, Public Safety Canada and Defence Research and Development Canada, 2013. Reproduced with the permission of the Minster of Public Works and Government Services, 2013.

Economic Value

Since outcomes can be measured by imperfectly competitive dimensions, assessors naturally search for a fungible measure, which tends to be financial, but this can seem too insensitive or calculated, especially when fatalities are measured economically. The economic value of a particular fatality can be calculated from past inputs, such as the sunk cost of education, and lost future outputs, such as lost earnings.

A life lost or injured has financial value in insurance and the tort system (although insurance or legal liability would not be engaged in every case).

Many medical authorities (such as the American Medical Association) and government authorities issue standard "schedules" for assessing the economic worth of injuries, for use by adjusters in insurance claims, employers in compensation of injured employees, and judges in tort cases. The first calculation normally expresses the impairment locally on the body, specific to the part of the body (down to the finger or toe or organ), the scale of the impairment, and the type of injury. Multiple impairments are then combined and expressed as the resulting impairment to the whole body. This overall impairment is combined with the occupation of the victim and the age of the victim according to prescribed codes and formulae. The final product of all this is normally a "rating" of the victim's "final permanent disability rating" or "physical impairment for employment," on a scale from 0% (no reduction of earning potential) through progressively more severe partial disability to 100% (permanent total disability).

Pedagogy Box 7.10 Official Compensation for Terrorism

Since 1984, the U.S. government has offered financial compensation (in the form of money or tax relief) for deaths and injuries suffered by resident victims of crime, usually to the value of a few tens of thousands of dollars. In 1996 (following mass casualty terrorism at a bombed federal office in Oklahoma City in 1995), this offer was extended to resident victims of terrorism, even if abroad at the time. Victims of terrorism on September 11, 2001, were compensated under an additional federal scheme, whose payouts far exceeded payouts by charities or insurers. From all sources, the seriously injured and the dependents of each killed victim received $3.1 million per victim on average, except emergency responders, who received $4.2 million on average. Payouts varied with projected lifetime earnings (Dixon & Kaganoff Stern, 2004).

Since the 1960s, the British government has offered to victims of violent crime compensation by type of injury, with a current range from £1,000 to £500,000 (effective November 2012). In January 2012, the British government decided to include (effective April 2013) British victims of terrorism abroad since 2002.

Pedagogy Box 7.11 Official Compensation in Afghanistan

The International Security Assistance Force (ISAF) (since December 2001) in Afghanistan has compensated Afghanis for deaths or injuries or damage to livelihoods that are collateral to its military operations but have political and military implications. In recent years, ISAF has valued an Afghani life at $2,500 (the payment is not necessarily made in U.S. dollars); typically, an injury is compensated with some local commodity, such as a goat. However, after U.S. Army Staff Sergeant Robert Bales was accused of killing 16 unarmed Afghanis, within the same month ISAF compensated $50,000 for each of these lost lives and $11,000 for each injured survivor.

Changes of Situation

Changes of situation include forced migration or displacement from normal place of residence, homelessness, loss of work, separation from family, loss of rights, and injustice.

Pedagogy Box 7.12 Mass Evacuation

The British Civil Contingencies Secretariat defines a *mass evacuation* as a movement of at least 100,000 people from danger to safety, a medium-scale as 1,000 to 25,000 people, and a small-scale as up to 1,000 people (U.K. Cabinet Office, 2013).

Environmental Returns

Natural environmental damage can be assessed in economic terms when agriculture or some other economically productive use of the area is affected. Otherwise, an environmental regulator or assessor refers to statutory scales of value or legal precedents before seeking to impose a fine on or compensation from the perpetrator. Biologists and geographers may assess environmental damage in lots of nonfungible direct ways, such as animals killed, species affected, and the area of land or water affected. The land area is the most fungible of these measures.

Pedagogy Box 7.13 Canadian Assessment of Natural Environmental Harm

After a natural disaster, the Canadian government uses the area affected to modify the ranking of the magnitude of official response (see Table 7.6), where a damaged area of 400 square kilometers would raise the ranking of official response by 1.0 (see Table 7.8).

Table 7.8 The Canadian Government's Modification of Consequences Magnitude (Table 7.6) by Geographical Area Affected

Extent Rating	Area Damaged (up to, square kilometers)
0.0	50
+0.5	150
+1.0	500
+1.5	1,500
+2.0	5,000
+2.5	15,000

SOURCE: All Hazards Risk Assessment Methodology Guidelines, 2012–2013, p.33, Public Safety Canada and Defence Research and Development Canada, 2013. Reproduced with the permission of the Minster of Public Works and Government Services, 2013.

The Canadian government would add another 0.5 to the magnitude if the sum value of the natural environmental damage was 9 after summing as many of the following criteria that might apply:

- Loss of rare or endangered species (value: 2)
- Reductions in species diversity (value: 1)
- Loss of critical/productive habitat (value: 2)
- Transformation of natural landscapes (value: 0.5)
- Loss of current use of land resources (value: 1)
- Loss of current use of water resources (value: 2)
- Environmental losses from air pollution (value: 0.5)
- Duration of environmental disruption
  - 3–10 weeks (value: 0.5)
  - 2–8 months (value: 1)
  - 8–24 months (value: 1.5)
  - 2–6 years (value: 2)
  - 6–20 years (value: 2.5)

Territorial/Geopolitical Insecurity

Separate to an assessment of harm to a natural environment, we may need to assess declining security of a geopolitical unit, such as sovereign territory, a city, or province. This would be a routine measure in unstable countries or countries with porous or contested borders, such as Pakistan, Afghanistan, Columbia, the Philippines, and Somalia, where central government is not in control of all of its territory most of the time.

Pedagogy Box 7.14 Canadian Assessment of Territorial Insecurity

In the context of a loss of territorial control or security, Public Safety Canada (2013, pp. 39–41) assesses the area affected (see Table 7.9), the duration, and the population density affected.

Table 7.9 The Canadian Government's Ranking of Territorial Loss or Insecurity

Extent Rating	Area Damaged (up to, square kilometers)
0.0	50
+0.5	150
+1.0	500
+1.5	1,500
+2.0	5,000
+2.5	15,000

SOURCE: All Hazards Risk Assessment Methodology Guidelines, 2012–2013, p.40, Public Safety Canada and Defence Research and Development Canada, 2013. Reproduced with the permission of the Minster of Public Works and Government Services, 2013.

This magnitude score would be modified by duration:

- 1 hour (subtract 2)
- 1–3 hours (subtract 1.5)
- 3–10 hours (subtract 1)
- 0.5–1 day (subtract 0.5)
- 3–10 days (add 0.5)
- 20 days to 1 month (add 1)
- 1–3 months (add 1.5)
- 3–12 months (add 2)
- 1–3 years (add 2.5)
- 3–10 years (add 3)
- More than 10 years but not permanent (add 3)
- Permanent (add 3.5)

It would also be modified by population density:

- 0.1 persons per kilometer (subtract 1)
- 0.3 persons per kilometer (subtract 0.5)

(Continued)

(Continued)

- 3 persons per kilometer (add 0.5)
- 10 persons per kilometer (add 1)
- 30 persons per kilometer (add 1.5)
- 100 persons per kilometer (add 2)

SUMMARY

This chapter has

- defined returns,
- defined events,
- defined issues and incidents,
- showed how to assess events,
- explained how to categorize returns, and
- explained how to assess returns—judgmentally on an ordinal scale and objectively by their economic, organizational, human, environmental, and territorial/geopolitical returns.

QUESTIONS AND EXERCISES

1. What is the difference between returns and events?
2. What is the difference between issues and other events?
3. Why are issues usefully separated from other events?
4. Why are DALYs useful?
5. How could deaths be a misleading measure of human returns?
6. Why might stakeholders resist your economic valuation of human returns?
7. Search for a real event that someone else has described as a "disaster" or "catastrophe." Look at the official categories of events and decide which categories apply to the event.
8. Choose two real disasters or catastrophes and compare their "impact" using the official methods shown early in this chapter.
9. Choose a real disaster or catastrophe and use the Canadian method for assessing its economic returns.
10. Choose a real example of organizational failure or crisis, such as an organization caught breaking the law or delivering poor service or products. Use the Canadian method for assessing the organizational returns.
11. Choose a real official operation, such as an official attempt to provide some new service, acquire something, or counter some threat. Use the British military method for assessing operational returns.
12. Identify an environmental disaster. Use the Canadian method to assess the environmental returns.
13. Identify a state that has experienced changes in its territorial or geopolitical control. Use the Canadian method to assess these changes.

PART II

Managing Security and Risk

This (second) part of the book builds on good analyses and assessments of security and risks by explaining how to manage security and risks. Chapter 8 will help the reader to design and to develop an organization's cultures, structures, and processes to more functionally manage security and risk. Chapter 9 explains why different people have different sensitivities to different risks, that is, why different people tend to be oversensitive to certain types of risks while tolerating others. Chapter 10 explains how to choose controls and strategies in response to risks. Chapter 11 shows how we should record risks, communicate to stakeholders about our understanding and management of security and risks, monitor and review our current management, and audit how others manage security and risk.

Definitions of Risk Management

Unofficial

Some authors distinguish *strategic risk management*, which "addresses interactions between pure and speculative risks," such as when investors defer their investments in an area because of the area's natural risks or when resources for security are cut in response to increased financial uncertainty (Waring & Glendon, 1998, p. 14).

Others distinguish *uncertainty management* as "managing perceived threats and opportunities and their risk implications but also managing the various sources of uncertainty which give rise to and shape risk, threat[,] and opportunity" (Chapman & Ward, 2002, p. 10) or "the process of integrating risk management and value management approaches" (Smith, 2003, p. 2).

Risk governance is "the identification, assessment, management and communication of risks in a broad context. It includes the totality of actors, rules, conventions, processes and mechanisms and is concerned with how relevant risk information is collected, analysed and communicated, and how management decisions are taken. It applies the principles of good governance that include transparency, effectiveness and efficiency, accountability, strategic focus, sustainability, equity and fairness, respect for the rule of law and the need for the chosen solution to be politically and legally feasible as well as ethically and publicly acceptable" (International Risk Governance Council, 2008, p. 4).

UN

Risk management is "the systematic approach and practice of managing uncertainty to minimize potential harm and loss" (United Nations Office for International Strategy for Disaster Reduction, 2009, p. 11).

United States

Risk management is "a continuous process of managing—through a series of mitigating actions that permeate an entity's activities—the likelihood of an adverse event and its negative impact. Risk management addresses risk before mitigating action, as well as the risk that remains after countermeasures have been taken" (U.S. Government Accountability Office, 2005b, p. 110) or "the process of identifying, assessing, and controlling risks arising from operational factors and making decisions that balance risk cost with mission benefits" (U.S. Department of Defense, 2012b, p. 267).

Australian/New Zealand and ISO

Risk management is the "coordinated activities to direct and control an organization with regard to risk" (International Organization for Standardization, 2009a, p. 2). "In this standard, the expressions 'risk management' and 'managing risks' are both used. In general terms, 'risk management' refers to the architecture (principles, framework[,] and process) for managing risks effectively, and 'managing risk' refers to applying that architecture to particular risks" (Australian and New Zealand Joint Technical Committee, 2009, p. v).

Canadian

"Risk management is the use of policies, practices, and resources to analyze, assess, and control risks to health, safety, the environment, and the economy" (Public Safety Canada, 2012, p. 83).

British

"Risk management means having in place a corporate and systematic process for evaluating and addressing the impact of risks in a cost effective way and having staff with the appropriate skills to identify and assess the potential for risks to arise" (U.K. National Audit Office, 2000, p. 2). It encompasses "all the processes involved in identifying, assessing and judging risks, assigning ownership, taking actions to mitigate or anticipate them, and monitoring and reviewing progress," which "includes identifying and assessing risks (the inherent risks) and then responding to them" (U.K. Treasury, 2004, p. 49). The Civil Contingencies Secretariat defines risk management as "all activities and structures directed towards the effective assessment and management of risks and their potential adverse impacts" (U.K. Cabinet Office, 2013).

Risk management is the "development and application of management culture, policy, procedures and practices to the tasks of identifying, analyzing, evaluating and controlling the response to risk" (U.K. Ministry of Defense, 2011c).

Cultures, Structures, and Processes

This chapter explains how to design and develop an organization so that it more functionally manages security and risk. Organizational design conventionally recognizes three main dimensions of an organization, and this chapter's sections study each of these in turn: culture, structure, and process.

Cultures

A culture is a collection of the dominant norms, values, and beliefs in a group or organization. This section explains why security and risk managers should pay attention to culture, how they can assess a culture, and how they can develop a culture to be more functional.

Why Develop Culture?

Of the three main dimensions of an organization (culture, structure, process), culture is probably the easiest to neglect and most difficult to observe and change. Some standards of risk management now prescribe explicit attention to an organizational culture and urge development of a culture that is supportive of risk management and is congruent with the structure and process of risk management. The culture needs to support the structures and processes of risk management; an organization is less likely to manage risks well if its members normatively think of risk management as too burdensome, silly, pointless, or alien. For instance, developing the perfect process for how personnel are supposed to keep the office secure would be pointless if our personnel normatively ignore the process or encourage colleagues to ignore the process. Cultures are also important factors in how different risks are tolerated or rejected (see Chapter 9).

Some failures to manage security or risk correctly could be due to poor or incomplete training, but too often leaders would blame personnel competences and neglect to consider whether the culture needs attention. The personnel could be perfectly trained in the processes and perfectly aware of the authorities and responsibilities, but nonetheless not value or normatively comply with the processes or structures.

Pedagogy Box 8.1 Official Prescriptions for a Risk Management Culture

The British Standards Institution (2000) noted that the "role of culture in the strategic management of organizations is important because: the prevailing culture is a major influence on current strategies and future chances; and any decisions to make major strategic chances may require a change in the culture." It identified failures of risk management "due, at least in part, to a poor culture within the organization" despite the organization's proper attention to the process (p. 21).

Similarly, the International Risk Governance Council (2008, pp. 6, 20) noted that organizations and societies have different "risk cultures" that must be managed as part of risk management.

The Australian/New Zealand and ISO standard (International Organization for Standardization, 2009b) stresses in one of its 11 "principles for risk management" that risk management should take account of "human and cultural factors" and that the "framework" should be tailored to and integrated into the organization.

Assessing Culture

Culture is difficult to observe because it is less tangible than structure and process, but a researcher could directly observe organizational personnel in case they betray normative noncompliance with, negative valuations of, or incorrect beliefs about security and risk management.

The researcher could survey personnel with classic questions such as "Do you believe risk management is important?" or "Do you follow prescribed processes when nobody else is watching?"

Sometimes, a bad culture is betrayed by repeated failures to implement processes, to exercise authority, or to take responsibility for risk management. Ideally, such repeated failures should be observed currently by regular monitoring and reviewing and should prompt an audit that would diagnose the root causes (as discussed in Chapter 11).

Developing a Culture

Changing a culture is difficult, but obvious solutions include exemplary leadership, more awareness of the desired culture, more rewards for compliance with the desired culture, more punishments for noncompliance, and more enforcement of compliance.

Of course, we should also consider whether the negative culture is a reaction to something dysfunctional in the structure or process. For instance, perhaps employees are copying noncompliant leaders; perhaps employees have good reason to dislike some of the prescribed processes, such as processes that are too burdensome or that incorrectly assess certain risks. If the structure or process is at fault, the structure or process needs to change positively at the same time as we try to change the culture positively.

Ultimately, culture is changed and maintained only by congruence with structure and process, training of and communication to personnel of the desired culture, and cultural congruence across all departments and levels from managers downwards.

Pedagogy Box 8.2 Developing a "Security Culture"

"Much of the focus in security management tends to be on specific operational needs, such as security policies and plans, but there is also a need to take a step back and look at how to develop a culture of security within the organization, including developing capacity. One of the most important priorities is to make sure that all staff know the organization and its mission in any given context. It is not uncommon for many staff, including national staff, not to know much about the agency that they represent. Staff need to be told what the organization is about . . . In addition, treat security as a staff-wide priority, not a sensitive management issue to be discussed only by a few staff members behind closed doors. Specifically:

- Make sure that all staff are familiar with the context, the risks and the commitments of the organization in terms of risk reduction and security management.
- Make sure that all staff are clear about their individual responsibilities with regard to security, teamwork and discipline.
- Advise and assist staff to address their medical, financial and personal insurance matters prior to deployment in a high-risk environment.
- Be clear about the expectations of managers and management styles under normal and high-stress circumstances.
- Make security a standing item (preferably the first item) on the agenda of every management and regular staff meeting.
- Stipulate reviews and if needed updates of basic safety and security advice, as well as country-wide and area-specific security plans, as described above.
- Invest in competency development. It is not uncommon for aid agencies to scramble to do security training when a situation deteriorates. Investment should be made in staff development, including security mitigation competences, in periods of calm and stability.
- Ensure that security is a key consideration in all program planning.
- Perform periodic inspections of equipment by a qualified individual, including radios, first aid kits, smoke alarms, fire extinguishers, intruder alarms and body armor.
- Carry out after-action reviews (AARs). The focus is on assessing what happened and how the team acted in a given situation, not on individual responsibilities. It is a collective learning exercise." (Humanitarian Practice Network, 2010, pp. 13–14)

Structures

Structures are patterns of authorities and responsibilities. The authorities are those departments or persons assigned to determine how security and risk should be managed. The responsible parties are supposed to manage security and risk as determined by the authorities. The three subsections below respectively explain why the development of structure is important, give advice on developing the internal structure of an organization, and give advice on developing functional relations between organizations.

Why Develop Structure?

Structure is important because security and risk receive improper attention when the responsibilities or authorities are unclear or dysfunctional. The risk manager's role in advocating risk management is indicated by parts of the Australian and British governments that formally refer to lower risk managers as "risk champions."

Structure is important also to outsiders who want to know with whom to communicate. Imagine a stakeholder who wants to contribute to your security but cannot find the best authority within the organization (or cannot find an interested authority)—the wasted time, effort, and frustrations count as unnecessary transaction costs, could damage your reputation, and reduce the chances of future opportunities.

Structure is important to the efficiency of an organization, since clearer authorities and responsibilities reduce the transactions costs and redundant activities associated with confused or redundant authorities.

Developing Internal Structure

Understandably, most actors are private about their security and risk management structures, but we know that the structures of organizations are pulled in many directions by resource constraints, bureaucratic interests, political issue-linkage, and simple path-dependency, so organizational structure is commonly suboptimal, particularly in very small or poor organizations and in very large organizations (which have more resources but are subject to more vectors).

Two main trade-offs are within the control of the organizational designer: the trade-off between managerial control and burden and the trade-off between domain and cross-domain expertise.

Trading Managerial Control With Burden

Organizational designers need to be careful that they do not vacillate between:

- lots of well-specified authorities that are overwhelmed by responsibilities and inefficiently dispute each other, and
- poorly specified authorities that are unaccountable or unsure.

They should be careful too not to vacillate between:

- highly centralized management, which should be materially efficient but is remote from lower managers and possibly unaware of managerial practices at lower levels, and
- decentralized management, which could be more efficient for the system as a whole, if lower managers are self-motivated and skilled, but also hide dysfunctional practices from higher managers (Newsome, 2007, pp. 18–22).

Trading Domain and Cross-Domain Expertise

Traditionally, within government and large commercial organizations, the official centers of excellence or influence have been the departments of finance, defense, intelligence, internal or homeland security, and information management. Each of these departments offers some generalizable skills in risk or security management, but none can offer expertise across all departments and domains.

A small organization or operation is likely to be specialized in a certain domain. For instance, a financial services provider is specialized in financial risks. In large organizations, with cross-domain functions, domain specializations are required within departments, but are problematic across departments. In recent decades, this tension between intra- and inter-domain expertise has been seen in the success with which official and private organizations have successfully raised awareness of risk and security management and their structures and processes, while failing to manage all risks equally.

Some organizations have appointed directors of risk management or of security with cross-domain responsibilities: many of the persons are accountants, information technology experts, or former military or law enforcement personnel. Their professional pedigree should inspire some confidence, but each domain is particular and cannot offer experience or expertise across all domains. Cross-domain security and risk management needs cross-domain experience and expertise. This sounds rational, but naturally some people are more open to wider knowledge and skills than others ("foxes" are preferred over "hedgehogs"—to recall Isaiah Berlin's typology).

Security and risk managers from different domains can be stereotyped (although stereotypes allow for many exceptions). For instance, stereotypical financial officers are good at assessing the stark financial risks of projects (such as potential lost investment) but are less qualified to assess the technical risks (such as potential technological failures) that would compound the financial risks (such as the extra costs of urgently procuring an off-the-shelf replacement for the intended product of a failed project).

Stereotypical security and defense professionals are good at estimating the capabilities that they would want to use, but they are less qualified to assess technically the products that potential suppliers would offer them in order to deliver those capabilities. Good examples can be found in British government procurement of defense equipment (see Pedagogy Box 8.3); most democratic governments have experienced similar problems. Consequently, private advocates of technology risk management urge project managers to hold regular reviews of the technology risks with "technology champions and a peer group of subject-matter experts."

> As technologies move from the research bench to product development, there is an inherent tension between the technology champions and the product chief engineer. The technologist creates new concepts, new surprises, and new risks. He or she is optimistic, is successful if his or her ideas are adopted, and may overstate the merits. The chief engineer, on the other hand, tries to solve problems, avoid surprises, and minimize risk; he or she is successful if the product meets the specification on schedule, irrespective of the technology used. (Hartmann & Myers, 2001, pp. 37–38)

Similarly, stereotypical information managers and information security managers are experts in information technologies, but they have proven less competent at managing the risks of procurement. Most infamously, in 2002, the British National Health Service launched a National Programme for Information Technology with a budget of £6.2 billion, but after costing more than twice as much, most of its projects were canceled in 2011 by a different political administration, on the recommendation of a new Major Projects Authority.

Stereotypical intelligence or internal security professionals have proved themselves better at identifying threats than at procuring solutions. For instance, the U.S. Department of Homeland Security has been caught out procuring unproven technologies, such as systems ("puffers") designed to test the human body for the scent of explosives. From 2004 to 2006, the Transportation Security Administration acquired 116 systems at 37 airports, despite poor detection and availability rates during tests. All were deleted at a procurement cost of at least $30 million.

Pedagogy Box 8.3 The Structure of British Defense Procurements, 2000–2013

For decades the British Ministry of Defense (MOD) has struggled to procure equipment on time, within budget, and with the capabilities specified. In the 2000s, after many procedural changes, the main structural change was the merger of the Defence Procurement Agency and the Defence Logistics Organisation to form Defence Equipment and Support (DE&S). Savings were expected from consolidation of redundant assets and colocation of most staff at a site near Bristol. At the time of the merger in April 2007, the two parent organizations employed 27,500 people. In fiscal year 2009, DE&S received a budget of £13 billion and employed 25,000 people. However, the costs of improving staff skills absorbed most of the potential savings accrued from shedding staff, while the disruption retarded the new agency's performance, although urgent operational requirements (UORs) also contributed.

One preexisting managerial dysfunction was not changed: Almost annually, the House of Commons Committee of Public Accounts complained that program managers rotated in on short tenures of 2–3 years without accountability for the performance of programs that typically ended after their tenure:

> There is poor accountability for long-term equipment projects, such that no-one has had to answer for this prolonged failure of management. Senior Responsible Owners do not remain in post long enough to ensure continuity on large scale programs, making it difficult to hold anyone responsible for whether they succeed or fail. (U.K. MOD, 2011c, pp. 6, 8)

In early 2009, the MOD commissioned a report (known as the Gray Report, after Bernard Gray, the lead author), which found that the MOD's equipment acquisitions had arrived on average 5 years late and collectively cost £35 billion more than planned. Gray reported that the MOD was unfocused, "with too many types of equipment being ordered for too large a range of tasks at too high a specification." Gray reported that the acquisitions system had retarded military operations.

The programs with the worst time and budget overruns and rates of postponement or failure related to armored and fighting vehicles. In May 2011, the National Audit Office (NAO) reported that the MOD had initiated 8 armored vehicle projects since May 1992 at a sunk cost of £1,125 million.

- Three projects (Tactical Reconnaissance Armoured Combat Equipment Requirement; Multi-Role Armoured Vehicle; Future Rapid Effect System Utility Vehicle) had been canceled or suspended without delivering any vehicles and at a total cost of £321 million.
- Three projects (Future Rapid Effect System Specialist Vehicle; Warrior Capability Sustainment; Terrier Armoured Engineering Vehicle) remained delayed without delivering any vehicles at a total sunk cost of £397 million and total forecasted costs of £9,105 million.
- Only two projects (Viking All-Terrain Vehicle [Protected]; Titan and Trojan Engineering Vehicles) had delivered the required vehicles, but the numbers were comparatively trivial (total 166 vehicles required at a sunk cost of £407 million).

The report concluded that "given the expenditure of over £1.1 billion since 1998 without the delivery of its principal armoured vehicles–the Department's standard acquisition process for armoured vehicles has not been working."

Meanwhile, new vehicles or upgrades for legacy vehicles were required urgently for operations in Afghanistan (from 2001) and Iraq (from 2003). The British Army had sent some tracked fighting vehicles to Iraq and Afghanistan that were difficult to sustain and employ. British ground forces required more survivable versions of its wheeled logistical, liaison, patrol, and "force protection" vehicles. At first, the British upgraded legacy vehicles, which would be easier to sustain and to adapt after operations in Iraq and Afghanistan, but during 2007, the government authorized more substantial new models and upgrades to existing models. In 2007, about 40 UORs related to five types of armoured vehicle:

- two American-produced base models for Heavy Protected Patrol Vehicles (same as the American class known as Mine-Resistant Ambush Protected Vehicles); and
- three upgraded legacy vehicles–a better protected, armed, and automotively improved version (the Bulldog) of the FV432 (tracked) armoured personnel carrier, an armored and armed version of the BvS 10 (Viking) light articulated tracked all-terrain vehicle (previously procured for amphibious and arctic operations), and a ruggedized, partially armoured, and armed version (WMIK) of the most numerous four-wheeled vehicle (Land Rover).

Most logistical ("B") vehicles also required a protection kit. Many more types of new models of vehicle would be procured–mostly "off-the-shelf"–in following years, few of which would be required beyond current operations. Most of these vehicles arrived on operations during the period of net withdrawal rather than net reinforcement. Some never fulfilled the UORs that had been used to justify them.

The NAO blamed the Ministry (including implicitly the ministers) for poor planning and biases toward naval and aerial platforms.

> [T]he cycle of unrealistic planning followed by cost overruns has led to a need to regularly find additional short-term savings. Areas of the Defence budget where there have been lower levels of long-term contractual commitment, such as armoured vehicles, have borne the consequences of decisions to fund large scale and long-term projects in other sectors.

The NAO blamed the MOD also for specifying high capability goals, then failing to compromise given the technology available.

> Complex requirements have been set which rely on technological advances to achieve a qualitative advantage over the most demanding potential adversaries. However, for vehicles procured using the standard acquisition process there has not been an effective means to assess the costs, risks and amount of equipment needed to meet these requirements in the early

(Continued)

(Continued)

> stages. These demanding requirements often reduce the scope to maximize competition which in turn can lead to cost increases, delays to the introduction of equipment into service and reductions to the numbers of vehicles bought to stay within budgets. (U.K. NAO, 2011, p. 6)

The NAO suggested that the MOD could improve its standard acquisitions process by learning from UORs, which identify incremental requirements and technological opportunities beyond current acquisitions but warned that the MOD would need to combine planning for full sustainment and value for money beyond current operations. The NAO recommended that the MOD should improve its technological awareness and pursue evolutionary development within realistic technological opportunities.

> Firm delivery deadlines and budgets could further ensure realism in setting requirements. This could be achieved by engaging more closely with industry to assess vehicle requirements, based on mature technology, that are initially sufficient–and better than vehicles already in service–but having the potential for future development. The Department should consider buying vehicles in batches, with each subsequent batch offering improved capabilities within a lower initial budget approval, but based on a common vehicle design to minimize any differences in logistic support and training requirements. (U.K. NAO, 2011, p. 11)

The NAO had not fully investigated the structure, process, or culture of acquisitions, and some anonymous officials complained that the NAO was better at identifying past failings than solutions and better at blaming the MOD than the political decisions with which the MOD must comply. The political administration (Labour Party, 1997–2010) was not prepared to cut any procurement program during its many wars but instead incrementally trimmed the funding or projects from practically all programs, many of which consequently could not achieve their specified capabilities.

The budgeting system also created structural problems. As in the United States, national government in Britain is paid for from annual authorizations, within which the MOD matches money to programs, with little spare capacity at the time, so when one program overran its budget or suffered a cut in budget, money was robbed from other programs or the program's activities or objectives were cut. The Committee of Public Accounts found that from 2006 to 2011 the MOD had removed £47.4 billion from its equipment budget through 2020–2021, of which 23% (£10.8 billion) covered armored vehicle projects. The Committee recommended that the MOD "should ensure that future procurement decisions are based on a clear analysis of its operational priorities, and must challenge proposals vigorously to ensure they are both realistic and affordable. Once budgets have been set, they must be adhered to. The Department's inability to deliver its armoured vehicles programme has been exacerbated by over-specifying vehicle requirements and using complex procurement methods" (U.K. MOD, 2011c, p. 5).

The Treasury was most influential over UORs, since it capped the budget for all UORs and often meddled with individual UORs, with the result that MOD departments fought mostly internally over the few UORs that could be approved–those approved tended to be the cheaper UORs. Since the users of the products of these UORs often were multiple or inconsistent, the user was weakly represented in these decisions. Special Forces were the most consistent and politically supported users, so tended to enjoy the best success rate, but often with undesirable outcomes for other users. For instance, the MOD acquired a new light machine gun for the whole army—it had satisfied the requirement from the special forces for an ambush weapon but was practically useless in most of the long-range defensive engagements in Afghanistan. Similarly, the MOD acquired lots of small fast unarmoured vehicles that were useful for special operations but soon deleted from the fleet. Some of the vehicles that were acquired via UORs met justifiable UORs (the more survivable vehicles were most required), but they were usually acquired without training vehicles, so users often first encountered new types of vehicles only after deploying.

The Labour government had promised to publish Gray's report in July 2009 but reneged until October, then deferred most consideration until the next Strategic Defence Review. A national election (May 6, 2010) delayed that review.

On February 22, 2011, 9 months after taking office as Defence Secretary Liam Fox announced his first reforms of the MOD's procurement process, which he condemned as "fantasy defence procurement" and a "conspiracy of optimism." He promised that procurement projects would not proceed without a clear budgetary line for development, procurement, and deployment. He announced a Major Projects Review Board (under his own chairmanship) to receive quarterly updates on the MOD's major programs—first the 20 most valuable projects, followed by the rest of the 50 most valuable projects. The Board met for the first time on June 13, 2011. Following the meeting, the MOD asserted that

> Any project that the Board decided was failing would be publicly "named and shamed." This could include a project that is running over budget or behind expected timelines. This will allow the public and the market to judge how well the MOD and industry are doing in supporting the Armed Forces and offering taxpayers value for money.

The Defence Reform Unit's report was published on June 27, 2011. The Report made 53 wide-ranging recommendations, the most important of which was for a smaller Defence Board, still chaired by the Defence Secretary, but without any military members except the Chief of Defence Staff. The three Service Chiefs were supposed to gain greater freedom to run their own services. The services would coordinate primarily through a four-star Joint Forces Command. The MOD would form separate Defence Infrastructure and Defence Business Services organizations. Another recommendation was to manage and use senior military and civilian personnel more effectively, transparently, and jointly, with people staying in post for longer, and more transparent and joint career management. An implementation plan was expected in September 2011, for overall implementation by April 2015. The process of acquisition was not expected to change, although the structure would. The Select Committee on Defence (U.K. House of Commons, 2011b, Paragraph 207) recommended that the MOD should appoint "suitably experienced independent members" to the Board.

On September 12, 2011 (speaking to the Defence & Security Equipment International show in London), the Defence Secretary claimed that Britain's "forces in Afghanistan have never been so

(Continued)

(Continued)

well-equipped." In Afghanistan at that time, British forces employed about 10,000 military personnel and 22 different models of armored vehicle at a cost in 2011 of £4 billion (from contingency reserve, above the core defense budget of £33.8 billion in fiscal year 2011–2012). The U.K. MOD was in the middle of a 3-month study into the Army's future vehicle fleet—clearly most of the armoured or fighting vehicles returning from Afghanistan (by the end of 2014) would not be required for the core fleet; some could fill core requirements but the cost of repatriating, reconfiguring, and sustaining even these vehicles would be prohibitive in an era of austerity.

On May 14, 2012, Defence Secretary (since October 2011) Philip Hammond announced to the House of Commons his latest reforms.

> Under the previous Government, the equipment plan became meaningless because projects were committed to it without the funding to pay for them, creating a fantasy program. Systematic over-programming was compounded by a "conspiracy of optimism", with officials, the armed forces, and suppliers consistently planning on a best-case scenario, in the full knowledge that once a project had been committed to, they could revise up costs with little consequence. It was an overheated equipment plan, managed on a hand-to-mouth basis and driven by short-term cash, rather than long-term value. There were constant postponements and renegotiations, driving costs into projects in a self-reinforcing spiral of busted budgets and torn-up timetables. Rigid contracting meant that there was no flexibility to respond to changed threat priorities or to alternative technologies becoming available. It is our armed forces and the defense of our country that have ultimately paid the price for that mismanagement. The culture and the practice have to change.
>
> We will move forward with a new financial discipline in the equipment plan. There will be under-programming rather than over-programming, so that we can focus on value rather than on cash management. That will give our armed forces confidence that once a project is in the program, it is real, funded, and will be delivered, so that they can plan with certainty.

Hammond announced that further reductions in British commitments to the most expensive programs (aircraft and aircraft carriers), on top of reductions since 2010 in military and civilian personnel, bases, and other assets and equipments, finally had eliminated the gap, worth £38 billion (then worth US$61 billion), between commitments and budgets out to 2020. (Over the next 10 years, the MOD planned to spend nearly £160 billion on the acquisition of equipment and data systems, including, for the first time, a "contingency reserve" fund worth £4 billion. Only £4.5 billion of that spending was allocated to new or upgraded armored vehicles. The annual budget was worth £34.4 billion in the fiscal year in which he made his announcement. For the year beginning April 2013, the annual budget would be £34.1 billion.)

On January 31, 2013, after the Treasury had cut future funding, the MOD announced the first fully funded defense equipment procurement plan to be reviewed by the NAO, worth £60 billion over 10 years (although this is also the period that some economists forecasted for continuing public austerity).

Developing Interorganizational Coordination

Coordination between organizations implies benefits such as mutually improved security and reduced collective costs. The Humanitarian Practice Network (2010, pp. 17–18) promised the following benefits:

- A better alert system: Agencies receive a fuller picture of actual or possible security threats or alerts in their environment, which increases the chances of avoiding an incident. This can be supported by a "communications tree" using mobile phones, e-mail, and radio. It can also be supported by a common emergency radio channel.
- Better risk assessment: A central record of all incidents and near misses in a given operating environment is a better basis for a risk assessment than a partial or incomplete record.
- Strategic and tactical monitoring and analysis of the operating environment and its security implications: Every agency has to do this and will normally contact others informally to obtain information. Where there is trust and confidentiality is respected, it is possible to collaborate in a more structured way.
- Cost-effective extra capacity or services: Rather than each agency individually carrying the costs of bringing in or hiring additional skills, specialists can be brought in on a collective basis. The costs for a training event on security can also be shared.
- Liaison and engagement with the authorities: Rather than negotiating individually, agencies can potentially make a stronger and more consistent case together.
- Advocacy with donors: If the security situation deteriorates and several agencies conclude that they need extra financial resources for additional mitigating measures, they may be able to make a more effective case with donors collectively.

Security coordination implies deliberate cooperation, more than commercial relationships, political alliances, or rhetorical friendships. For instance, after 9/11, the United States signed many bilateral agreements with other governments in which both governments stated their shared commitment to fighting terrorism; sometimes the United States promised money to help the other government develop its counter-terrorist capacity; however, few of these early agreements specified how the two governments were supposed to coordinate their counter-terrorist activities, to measure their coordination, or to hold each other accountable for their coordination. Meanwhile, other governments, with whom the United States had made no new agreements, coordinated better (Newsome, 2006).

No international standard for interorganizational coordination has been agreed, but the Humanitarian Practice Network (2010) noted the following common practices:

- Informal networking, for example, periodic meetings or an informal network of security focal points.
- Interagency security measures, such as a shared residential guard network, sharing of field-level security focal points, or security training.
- Introducing security as a theme in existing interagency working groups.
- Interagency security and safety offices, which can be independently resourced and led, or hosted by nongovernmental organizations.

An interagency security mechanism may have several functions, including

- Convening security meetings
- Providing security alerts, cross-checking unconfirmed information, and facilitating information dissemination
- Carrying out risk assessments and pattern and trend analysis and communicating the results in threat reports
- Providing introductory security briefings, as well as technical assistance and advice to individual agencies, and training
- Crisis management: Providing support with contingency planning and facilitating in-extremis support; for example, if an agency suffers a critical incident such as a kidnapping, the platform might be able to provide additional analysis and support through local networks.
- Liaison with governmental authorities, international and national military forces, including UN peacekeeping forces, and private security companies (p. 19).

Coordinating security between organizations is not easy, even when objectively each organization has a self-interest in coordination. Commercial competition inhibits coordination, although security against third-party threats does not need to affect commercial competitiveness. Many private actors assume that official authorities will protect them, but officials cannot be expected to follow every private actor or activity, particularly in remote locations. Some private actors inflate their self-reliance, without realizing the benefits of coordination or the interdependency of risks. Table 8.1 summarizes the possible impediments and approaches to coordination.

As an example from Table 8.1, consider structural or geographical separation as a barrier to coordination between organizations. A commonly understood solution is to exchange "liaison officers." For instance, the British national government sends Government Liaison Officers to local Emergency Control Centers, the Ministry of Defense appoints Joint Regional Liaison Officers to each of the Emergency Control Centers, and local governments appoint a "Host Organization Lead Officer" to manage mutual aid. Organizations are supposed to appoint (news) Media Liaison Officers too.

 Processes

A process is a series of actions or activities toward some end. The subsections below explain why the development of a prescribed process of security and risk management is important and gives examples of standard processes to choose from.

Why Develop Process?

Each of us has a process for managing the risks of everyday life, but not all processes can be perfect, and we should not allow every possible process. With useful experience or guidance, we could develop a process that reminds us to perform actions or activities that are necessary to proper security and risk management. As an organization, we should standardize that process to help managers perform closer to the ideal. A standard process also helps interoperability and communications between personnel and organizations. Most authorities or standards today prescribe or suggest a process by which risk or security is supposed to be managed (see Table 8.2).

Table 8.1 Impediments and Approaches to Security Coordination

Impediments		
Category	**Examples**	**Approaches**
Material	*Resource constraints*	*Resource pooling, risk sharing, shared controls, review risk assessments, and efficiency of controls*
	Physical separation	*Liaison officers and communications*
Cultural and social	*Linguistic or cultural differences*	*Multicultural employees or experts*
	Self-reliance culture	*Set coordination as a corporate objective*
	Internally oriented culture	*Develop external orientations*
	Pursuit of relative gains	*Reward absolute gains*
Structural and strategic	*Competing objectives*	*Cooperative objectives*
	"Buck-passing" (passing one's own responsibilities to another)	*Accountability to a third party*
	Redundant authorities	*Consolidate authorities*
	Ambiguous responsibilities	*Define responsibilities*
Procedural and Personnel	*Ill-defined or incompatible processes*	*Standardize a process*
	Lack of expertise	*Train or employ experts*
Political	*Political issue linkage*	*Prohibit changes outside of major policy changes*
	Politicization	*Nonpartisanship*
	Political sensitivities	*Compartmentalized information assurance*

SOURCES: Based on Newsome, 2006; Newsome & Floros, 2008; Newsome & Floros, 2009.

Choosing Between Processes

Standard processes are usually communicated visually as a list, series, or cycle of steps. As far as I know, all standard processes have at least three steps. For instance, British government has defined risk management with three steps (identifying, assessing, and responding to risks), although it has prescribed processes with four to six higher steps and much explanatory text on the lower steps and activities (U.K. Treasury, 2004, pp. 9, 13). The U.S. government has no standard but the GAO's five-step process (see Table 8.2) is probably the most authoritative and specified within U.S. government, so for these reasons, at least, it deserves fuller description here (although I do not consider it ideal).

Table 8.2 The U.S. GAO's Process for Managing Risk in More Detail

Higher Step	Summary of Activities	Example Activities	Example Outcomes
Establish our strategic goals, objectives, and constraints	Gather information on our ends and means	Discovery of what the strategic goals are attempting to achieve and of the steps needed to attain the goals	Information on our desired end states; our strategic goals and subordinate objectives; the activities required to reach objectives; our priorities, milestones, and outcome-related performance measures; and the limitations or constraints that would affect outcomes
Assess risks	Identify key elements of potential risks	Analyze threats; estimate vulnerability of assets; identify consequences of threats to assets	Information on threats, vulnerabilities, and potential outcomes
Evaluate alternative responses	Evaluate alternative controls on the risks	Consult outside experts on the controls; cost-benefit analysis of controls	Information on the effectiveness and costs of alternative controls; specifications for the controls
Select responses	Consider and choose between alternatives, given information from previous step and other managerial information, such as funding	Establish organization's risk tolerance; establish managerial valuation of controls and assets	Information on managerial choices between controls and allocation of resources
Implement and monitor the responses	Implement controls and a system for updating our security	Implement the controls according to the strategy; test the controls periodically; relate to peer and to higher risk management	System for monitoring effectiveness of risk management; system for developing risk management in response to new assessments or lessons learned

SOURCE: Based on U.S. GAO, 2005c.

Illustrating the inconsistencies within U.S. government, the DHS (2009, p. 111) recognizes a *risk management framework* as a "planning methodology that outlines the process" in six effective steps (see Table 8.3).

The most internationally influential process since 1995 is the Australian/New Zealand standard (also the ISO process since 2009), with seven well-established higher steps. It defines the "risk management process" as the "systematic application of management policies, procedures, and practices to the activities of communicating, consulting, establishing the context, and identifying analyzing, evaluating, treating, monitoring, and reviewing risk." It distinguishes the process from the "framework" (the "set of components that provide the foundations and organizational arrangements for designing, implementing, monitoring, reviewing, and continually improving risk management throughout the organization") (ISO, 2009a, pp. 2–3). Other authorities refer to processes, "frameworks," and "models" interchangeably (Australian and New Zealand Joint Technical Committee, 2009, pp. 13–21).

The steps of these processes largely align (see Table 8.3), although some processes are missing important steps. For instance, much theoretical work would support establishment of our internal objectives and the external context at the start of the process and prescribes communication with stakeholders throughout the process, but these steps are explicit in few of the processes in Table 8.3. The British Treasury's guidance, the Australian/New Zealand/ISO standard (2009), and the International Risk Governance Council (2008, p. 7) each treat *communication* as a continuous activity throughout the process. The Australian/New Zealand/ISO standard treats *monitoring and reviewing* too as a continuous activity, but the British Treasury does not specify these activities. The Australian/New Zealand/ISO standard refers to good communications, monitors, and reviews leading to "mature" or "enhanced" risk management that shows continual improvement, full accountability for risks, application of risk management to all decision making, continual communications about risk, and full integration of risk management into organizational structure.

Pedagogy Box 8.4 The ACTION Process for Managing Criminal Risks

1. **A**ssessing risk (mostly by identifying criminal threats and hazards and their potential victims)
2. Making **C**onnections (largely between criminals and between criminals and targets)
3. Setting **T**asks to control the risks (mostly preventing crime and preparing to respond to crime)
4. Collecting **I**nformation about the effectiveness of the controls
5. Refining the **O**rganization (properly structuring authorities, responsibilities, monitoring, training, and decision making)
6 **N**otifying others (mostly communicating about the risks and controls to stakeholders) (Kennedy & Van Brunschot, 2009, p. 125)

SUMMARY

This chapter has

- defined culture,
- explained why we should care to develop the culture of security and risk management,
- advised on how to assess a culture,
- advised on how to develop a culture,
- defined structure,
- explained why the design and development of organizational structures is important,
- given advice on developing the internal structure of an organization,
- shown how to develop relations between organizations,
- defined process, and
- compared different standard processes.

Table 8.3 Different Processes for Managing Risks, With Their Equivalent Steps Aligned

Australian/ New Zealand (1995) and ISO (2009)	Carter (1994, pp. 71–73)	Waring and Glendon (1998, pp. 8–9, 25)	Turnbull and Internal Control Working Party (1999)	U.K. NAO (2000, pp. 42–44)	U.K. Prime Minister's Strategy Unit (2002); U.K. Treasury (2004)	U.S. GAO (2005c)	U.S. FEMA (2005)	U.S. DHS (2009, p. 110)	Public Safety Canada (2011a, p. 14); also follows ISO (2009)	International Risk Governance Council (2008)
Establish the context	-	*Set policy*	*Set objectives*	*Clarify objectives*	*Understand context*	*Set strategy*	-	*Set goals and objectives*	-	*Preassessment*
Identify risks	*Identify risks*	*Identify hazards*	*Identify and evaluate risks*	*Identify risks*	*Identify risks*	*Assess risks*	*Identify threats*	-	*Ongoing hazard analysis*	
Analyze risks	*Evaluate risks*	*Assess hazards and consequences*		*Assess risks*	*Assess risks*		*Assess values of assets*	*Identify assets*	*Analyze impact on critical infrastructure*	*Appraisal*
		-					*Assess vulnerabilities*	-	*Determine aggravating or mitigating factors*	
Evaluate risks		*Estimate risks*					*Assess risks*	*Assess risks*	*Risk analysis*	*Characterization and evaluation*
Treat risks	*Control risks*	*Evaluate controls*	*Treat risks*	*Respond to risks*	*Respond to risks*	*Evaluate alternative responses*	*Consider mitigation options*	*Prioritize and implement protection programs and resiliency strategies*	*Recommendations to decision makers*	*Management*
		Select control				*Select response*				
	Mitigate	*Implement*				*Implement and monitor*				
Monitor and review	*Improve*	*Monitor*	*Review*	*Monitor and review*	*Review*			*Measure performance*	-	
		Audit								
		Review						*Take corrective action*		
Communicate and consult		-	*Communicate*	-	*Communicate and learn*	-	-	-	-	*Communication*

QUESTIONS AND EXERCISES

1. Why does culture matter?
2. Give some symptoms of a dysfunctional culture.
3. Why might personnel fail to follow a process, despite extensive training in the process?
4. How could you assess a culture?
5. Describe the conventional ways to develop a culture.
6. When might we assess a culture as dysfunctional but change the structure or process?
7. What is the difference between authority and responsibility?
8. Why would your internal organizational structure matter to security managers or risk managers outside of your organization?
9. What are the two main trade-offs that an organizational designer faces when structuring risk management within an organization?
10. What is good or bad about security and risk management authorities that are
    a. highly centralized,
    b. highly decentralized,
    c. highly specified, or
    d. unspecified?
11. Of what should you be wary, when promoting a security and risk manager from one domain within the organization to responsibilities in another domain or across domains?
12. What are the five main categorical impediments to interorganizational coordination?
13. How could we mitigate problems associated with geographical separation of two cooperating organizations?
14. How could we develop the cultures of two organizations that are supposed to be cooperating but tend to self-reliance?
15. How could we change a tendency for one organization to pass its responsibilities to another organization?
16. What should we do in response to complaints from two organizations that they manage risks differently?
17. What could we agree with another organization if both organizations are worried about political linkage of our shared management of security or risk with irrelevant issues?
18. Why should managers not be allowed to choose their own process for managing security or risk?
19. Reconsider the U.S. and Australian/New Zealand processes.

   a. What is different and the same between them?
   b. Develop a process that combines the best of both.

20. Reread Pedagogy Box 8.3 above about the structure of British defense acquisitions.
   a. Identify examples of imperfect authorities.
   b. Identify examples of imperfect responsibilities.
   c. Identify examples of procedural failures.
   d. What sort of organizational culture would you expect as a result of or in support of the identified structural and procedural failings?
   e. What were the structural reforms introduced in 2011?
   f. What were the procedural reforms introduced in 2011?
   g. What further structural or procedural reforms would you recommend?

Tolerability and Sensitivity

This chapter reviews human sensitivity to and toleration of different risks. Awareness of risk tolerance is useful strategically because the strategist normally would seek to control intolerable risks but not control tolerable risks. To control all risks would be more burdensome and unnecessary, although more sensitive stakeholders may force us to do so. Sometimes the security and risk manager's job includes managing the sensitivities of different stakeholders in order to mitigate the dysfunctions associated with distorted sensitivities.

The sections below define sensitivity and tolerability, describe the cultural and social drivers of sensitivity, describe the psychological and situational drivers of sensitivity, and compare some real risks and sensitivities.

Defining Tolerability and Sensitivity

Risk tolerance implies that we are prepared to live with the risk without further action. *Risk sensitivity* or *risk averseness* implies that we are less tolerant than others of risks in general or of a particular risk. Clearly, the opposite of risk sensitivity is *risk insensitivity* but is normally termed *risk tolerance* or *risk seeking* (although risk tolerance implies passive acceptance, while risk seeking implies active pursuit). Risk insensitivity at higher authorities has been conceptualized as risk permissiveness or lack of regulation (Jablonowski, 2009, Chapter 6). These terms have many synonyms: See Pedagogy Box 9.1 below.

These terms imply conscious awareness of risks and of our response to risks, but people are often unaware of risks yet effectively tolerate them. Rationally, we would expect people to accept positive risks and avoid negative risks in general, but people sometimes lack sufficient awareness or time or sense to behave rationally. When we talk about some people being more tolerant of risk, we should not imply that those people have no sensitivity to risk, just that relative to other people they are less sensitive to risks in general or perhaps a particular risk. Risk sensitivity can change, so a person who has seemed relatively risk seeking to date may seem risk sensitive in old age. (Situational, psychological, social, and cultural drivers of risk sensitivity are discussed in the other sections, below.)

Pedagogy Box 9.1 Definitions of Sensitivity, Tolerability, and Synonyms

UN

Acceptable risk is "the degree of human and material loss that is perceived by the community or relevant authorities as tolerable in actions to minimize disaster risk" (UN Department of Humanitarian Affairs [DHA], 1992, p. 16) or "the level of loss a society or community considers acceptable given existing social, economic, political, cultural, and technical conditions" (UN Office for International Strategy for Disaster Reduction [ISDR], 2009, p. 1).

International Risk Governance Council (IRGC)

A risk is "'acceptable' (risk reduction is considered unnecessary), 'tolerable' (to be pursued because of its benefits and if subject to appropriate risk reduction measures), or, in extreme cases, 'intolerable' and, if so, to be avoided" (IRGC, 2008, p. 13). "The term 'tolerable' refers to an activity that is seen as worth pursuing (for the benefit it carries) yet it requires additional efforts for risk reduction within reasonable limits. The term 'acceptable' refers to an activity where the remaining risks are so low that additional efforts for risk reduction are not seen as necessary" (Renn, 2008, p. 28).

International Organization for Standardization

Risk attitude is the "organization's approach to assess and eventually pursue, retain, take, or turn away from risk." *Risk appetite* is the "amount and type of risk that an organization is willing to pursue or retain." *Risk tolerance* is the "organization's or stakeholder's readiness to bear the risk after risk treatment in order to achieve its objectives." *Risk aversion* is the "attitude to turn away from risk." The ISO, followed by the Canadian government, also refers to *risk perception*—"a stakeholder's view on a risk," a perception that "reflects the stakeholder's needs, issues, knowledge, beliefs, and values" (International Organization for Standardization, 2009a, pp. 8–9).

Canada

Risk tolerance is "the willingness of an organization to accept or reject a given level of residual risk" (Public Safety Canada, 2012, p. 86).

Britain

PRINCE2 defines risk tolerance as "the threshold levels of risk exposure, which, when exceeded, require the risk to be escalated to the next level of management" (U.K. Office of Government Commerce, 2009, p. 260).

The British Standards Institute (BSI) defines risk tolerance as "risk reduced to a level that can be tolerated by the organization" (BSI, 2000, p. 11).

Risk appetite is the "amount of risk which is judged to be tolerable and justifiable" (U.K. Treasury, 2004, p. 9), the "total amount of risk that an organisation is prepared to accept, tolerate or be exposed to at any point in time" (U.K. Ministry of Defense, 2011c), or the "willingness of an organization to accept a defined level of risk" (U.K. Cabinet Office, 2013).

Cultural and Societal Drivers of Sensitivity

Risk sensitivity varies between individuals, groups, departments, societies, and countries in ways that can be described as cultural. This section focuses on varying organizational and societal sensitivities.

Organizational Sensitivity

Different organizations have different sensitivities due to internal decisions, strategies, and cultures. The Australian/New Zealand and ISO standard (International Organization for Standardization, 2009b) admits that "human and cultural factors" can change an organization's sensitivity. The BSI (2000, p. 21) noted that "the prevailing culture is a major influence on current strategies and future chances." At that time, the British government found that 42% of British government departments (n = 237) regarded themselves as more risk averse than risk taking, although 82% supported innovation to achieve their objectives (U.K. National Audit Office, 2000, p. 5).

> Civil service culture—that is the values, ethos, ethics and training underpinning departments' management approaches—has traditionally been risk averse. This is partly because departments have tended to associate risk taking with increasing the possibility of something going wrong, of project failure or financial loss which could lead to Parliamentary and public censure. Conversely, in successful private sector companies well managed risk taking is considered to be important because companies have an incentive to improve service delivery to customers which is key to them maintaining and extending their competitive advantage. (U.K. National Audit Office, 2000, p. 2)

Societal Sensitivity

Societies, from the smallest community to transnational religions, tend to different cultures and thus tend to different attitudes toward risk (although globalization is a driver toward commonality). The IRGC (2008, pp. 6, 20) noted that organizations must recognize the surrounding "political cultures" and "risk culture, which impacts on the level for risk tolerance (or risk aversion), and the degree of trust in the institutions responsible for risk governance." If they act internationally, they must "accept and account for the variety of risk cultures around the world, as these will require different methods of, particularly, management and communication."

All cultures are peculiar to their societies, but different societies can be linked by common cultures or similar cultures that can be described. For instance, Protestant societies celebrated steady hard work as the path to wealth and tended to frown on risk-taking behaviors in general, including gambling (a speculative risk), although they seem to have been friendliest to capitalist speculation (certainly, Protestantism and capitalism are correlated historically).

By contrast, more fatalistic cultures and societies (perhaps because of strong beliefs in divine will) tend to be less sensitive to pure risks, although high religiosity is associated with taboos on gambling.

Traditional societies tend to encourage recklessness as proof of the individual's credibility to provide for or defend their prospective partners or followers. These cultures are seen in traditional warrior societies and criminal gangs and also in insecure societies where people are expected to take risks in order to survive.

In many societies, risks are high by foreign standards but are regarded locally as routine or unavoidable for practical as well as cultural reasons. For instance, more than 90% of road traffic deaths occur in low- and middle-income countries, where simple controls are not required or enforced, such as seat belts (which reduce the chance of death in a crash by 61%), collision-triggered air bags, energy absorbing structures, and speed restrictions (World Health Organization, 2009, p. 26). Locals may be cognizant of their higher risks but nevertheless cannot do much about them; foreign tourists effectively accept the same risks when they use local transport.

As societies develop, they accrue more material affluence and security and forms of credibility that discourage recklessness. They may develop a "postmodern" "risk society" that is hypersensitive to social risks, such as potential crime, and to economic risks, such as potential interruptions in the supply of manufactured goods, but hyposensitive to other risks, such as potential environmental damage from increased industrial manufacture (Beck, 1992, 1995).

Some authors have extended the idea of a risk society to a society that is hypersensitive to political violence and is easily manipulated by its government.

> The underlying logic of this response—in which demands for security are established on the basis of the manipulative creation of insecurity—leads to a high anti-democratic political environment . . . Underlying the vulnerability of a population to manipulation in a politics of security—at the hands of the security industry and its political masters—is a pervasive psychological vulnerability . . . The politics of security relies on an extreme sensitivity to threats of violence: sensitivity out of all proportion to actual levels of risk. (Cox, Levine, & Newman, 2009, p. x)

Personal Drivers of Sensitivity and Insensitivity

In practice, risk sensitivity is highly variable across persons and groups and is dynamic within the lifecycle of these actors as they react to risks, interact with each other, and mature. Some of the variance and dynamism is objective (for instance, a person who is exposed to a risk should be more sensitive to it than a person who is not exposed), but most people are subjective, so their sensitivities are likely to be inflated or deflated for parochial or even irrational reasons. Some authors like to describe risk as an unavoidably "mental construct" and remind us that any risk assessment must reflect inherently psychological "risk perceptions" (Renn, 2008, p. 21).

The more detailed situational, psychological, and social drivers of sensitivity are summarized in Table 9.1 and described in the subsections below: loss averseness, a focus on returns instead of likelihood, inflation of negative pure risks, proximity, anchoring, cognitive availability, unrepresentativeness, base-rate neglect, maturation, misinformation, real situations, lack of personal control, distrust, and group psychology.

Loss Averseness

In general, people are loss averse, meaning that they are disproportionately sensitive to losses than gains. For instance, imagine a choice between an investment from which you could earn a sizeable profit but also face a 25% probability of losing all of your investment and another investment with the same chance of winning the same profit but a 84% chance of losing just 30% of your investment. The expected returns are practically the same in both cases, but most people would be repulsed by the option in which they could lose everything. (This response would be justified by analysis of the range

Table 9.1 Drivers of Risk Sensitivity and Insensitivity

Drivers of Risk Insensitivity	Drivers of Risk Sensitivity
Remoteness to the risk	*Proximity to the risk*
Deteriorating memory of the risk	*Anchoring in the experience of the risk*
Youth, irresponsibility, and testosterone	*Maturity, responsibilities*
Traditional cultures	*Socio-economically developed societies*
Informed awareness of the risk	*Misinformation about the risk*
Trusted regulation and authorities	*Rule breaking*
Objective expertise about the risk	*Subjective biases against the risk*
Group support	*Personal exposure*
Hypothetical situations	*Real situations*
Voluntary thrills	*Involuntary violence and medical risks*
Speculative risks	*Pure risks*

of returns: In one case the range runs from total loss to profit; in the other the range runs from a loss of 30% of total investment to profit. The latter is less uncertain and has a smaller worst-possible return.)

In economic language, people tend to have a nonlinear loss function: They become loss averse at a quicker rate than the losses become more likely. If a person were speculating just once on a potential high loss, the loss averseness could be described as rational (better not to bet at all rather than accept the chance of losing everything). If the person were able to bet many times and the odds of gains were favorable each round, even if a high loss were possible in any round, the person could rationally justify placing the bet many times, expecting a net gain over the long run. Professional gamblers think rationally in terms of net gains over the long run, but most people are nonlinearly loss averse.

Returns Focused

In general, people tend to focus on the potential returns more than the probability of those returns. In fact, most people are so bad at understanding the difference between probabilities that they often ignore probabilities altogether. In effect, their risk calculation overstates the returns and understates the likelihood, with the result that they obsess about potential highly negative events just because they would be highly negative, while neglecting much more likely but less negative events. This helps explain the popular cultural attention to low likelihood, high impact negative events ("shocks" or "black swans") and inflated popular fears about the most harmful and spectacular but least likely crimes, such as mass murder.

> Equally, if crime is judged to have severe consequences, and the outcome is vivid and affect-laden, then that individual is likely to be insensitive to probability variations. That individual is unlikely to feel better if he or she is told that the chances of victimization are rather slight. (Jackson, 2006, p. 258)

In fact, people inflate the likelihood of both negative and positive things, so they tend to be both over-confident about winning a bet and over-expectant of crime and other bad things.

When asked to assess a risk, typically, people will not consciously think in terms of likelihood or returns but will assess some feeling about the risk, even if it is subconsciously biased by their particular bias toward the likelihood or returns. Consequently, surveyors should ask respondents to assess the likelihood or returns separately. Nevertheless, most people probably assess the likelihood and returns of any particular event the same, based on their one feeling about the risk. For instance, the World Economic Forum (2013, p. 45) has found that respondents rated the likelihood and impact of each given risk similarly; a strict statistical interpretation of the results would suggest that highly likely events tend to be highly impactful and that unlikely events tend to be inconsequential, but the real world shows otherwise: More likely events (such as normal precipitation) tend be less consequential than less likely events (such as hurricanes).

Inflation of Negative Pure Risks

People are generally loss averse and speculative risk seeking, so they tend to overestimate negative pure risks (that they cannot control) and positive speculative risks (that they can voluntarily take), while ignoring many risks in between. For instance, most people tend to be underconfident about avoiding a natural disaster but overconfident when they gamble. Most people tend to overestimate all sorts of pure risks, like violent crime, while underestimating more speculative negative risks, such as driving a car fast on a public road. Pure risks make the spectator feel like a powerless victim of fate. Speculative risks are voluntary and thus give the speculator a sense of control.

Proximity

People will feel more sensitive to a risk that is more proximate in time or space (say, when they are travelling through a stormy area) than when they are remote to the risk (say, when the last storm recedes into the past). This proximity is correlated with anchoring, as explained below.

Psychological Anchoring

When people experience an event, they tend to be psychologically "anchored" in the experience and more sensitive to the associated risks. For instance, persons who experience a road traffic accident today likely would be more sensitive to the risks associated with road traffic accidents tomorrow than they were yesterday. Over time, or with therapy or distractions or maturation, memory tends to deteriorate or become less salient, and the sensitivity declines, but a particularly formative or shocking experience may anchor the person's sensitivity forever, even manifesting as a medical condition, such as post-traumatic stress disorder.

Cognitive Availability

People do not need to experience the event directly to become anchored in it, as long as the experience is available to them in some captivating way, such as visual images of the events or personally related, emotionally delivered verbal accounts by those who experienced it. More immersive or experiential media, such as movies and video games, increase the effect. The *cognitive availability* of the event produces effects similar to direct experience of the event. For instance, most people in the world were very remote to 9/11 in geographical terms but were shocked by the images and accounts and felt more sensitive toward terrorism risk. Normal human reactions to 9/11 were understandable and rational, since audiences were learning about a real event with implications for risks everywhere.

Cognitive availability can mislead the audience. People are more likely to recall risks associated with striking images or experiences than risks that are less cognitively available (even if they are objectively higher). The great interest that popular culture takes in fictional violent crime and that journalists take in real violent crimes contributes to a general perception that violent crimes are more frequent than they really are. Survey respondents often report high levels of fear but are imprecise about the threats, although they blame crime in general, the surrounding area in general, or certain demographics, and they refer to a recent crime as evidence of increasing frequency. This high but abstract fear has been termed *free-floating fear*. Such fear is very frustrating for police and public safety professionals when they succeed in lowering crime without lowering the public's fears of crime (although sometimes such professionals are less willing to admit that minor crimes and social disorder often increase even while the rates of serious crime or overall crime decrease).

Consequently, people can feel more sensitive to remote risks just because they become more aware of them, not because the risks are becoming more proximate. For instance, elderly people were found to be more fearful when they had frequent visitors; these frequent visitors tended to remind the elderly about all the things to worry about, whereas people with less visitors received fewer reminders and developed less fear. Similarly, the self-reported fears of violent crime among residents of Winnipeg, Manitoba, surged after they received broadcasts from a television station in Detroit, Michigan, 1,000 miles away, where the news reports were dominated by crime. Winnipeg's crime rate had not changed (Kennedy & Van Brunschot, 2009, pp. 31–32).

The availability bias is easy to manipulate by officials, journalists and their editors, and entertainers—anybody with capacity to release striking images or conceptualizations to a mass audience (remember the earlier description of "risk society").

Unrepresentativeness

People also take cognitive shortcuts through their memory to cases that seem "representative" of a new case, even when the cases are not provably representative at all. For instance, one person could blame a surge in youth crime on bad parenting because of a memory of bad parents whose child turned to crime, while another person could blame the same surge on poverty because of a memory of a deprived child who stole food.

Base-Rate Neglect

Worse, most people are naturally underempirical: They react to the most available and proximate events rather than check the longer-term rate or trend. This dysfunction is called also *base-rate neglect*.

Perversely, people tend to tolerate frequent negative events, like road traffic events, even though they would not accept similar losses of life concentrated in shorter periods of time. Some risks are tolerated because they are familiar, routine, and distributed regularly over time. (Road traffic is justified also for rational reasons, such as social, economic, and personal gains.) Road traffic killed one American every 16 minutes in 2010 (see Table 9.2): This frequency perversely suggests routine risk; moreover, driving is voluntary. This helps explain why people are much more sensitive to infrequent small losses of life to terrorism than to frequent losses of life to road traffic (Renn, 2008, p. 23).

Maturation

Maturation suggests less base-rate neglect (and less anchoring and unrepresentative cases), although unfortunately most people do not mature significantly in this respect once they reach adulthood.

Young children tend to be insecure and inexperienced with risks, but as they enter adolescence, they tend to act more recklessly, particularly toward thrill-seeking speculative risks; youth and masculinity is associated with testosterone, a natural hormone that has been shown (in females too) to peak at the same time as reckless behavior. As people age or mature, testosterone production tends to fall naturally and they tend to gather experiences of risks and responsibilities (such as dependent families) that encourage them to be more sensitive.

Yet older people, like very young children, naturally tend to focus on very short-term concerns and can even behave more recklessly (for instance, rates of sexually transmitted disease increase after retirement, after a trough in middle age). Thus, over a typical lifetime, risk sensitivity would fall lowest in adolescence and early adult years, peak in middle age, and decline in old age (except to short-term risks).

The role of age and gender is noticed even among experts. For instance, the World Economic Forum (2013, p. 50) found that its younger respondents (40 years old or younger) and female respondents were more pessimistic about both the likelihood and impact of negative risks in general (on average, women rated the likelihood as 0.11 higher and the impact as 0.21 higher on a 5-point scale) and economic risks in particular. Older respondents (officials and politicians tended to be found in this group) were more pessimistic about particular risks (prolonged infrastructure neglect; failure of climate change adaptation; rising greenhouse gas emissions; diffusion of weapons of mass destructions), but presumably for professional reasons, rather than any age-related sensitivity. (The World Economic Forum surveyed more than 1,000 experts, mostly from business, academia, nongovernmental organizations, and government.)

Misinformation

When people feel uninformed about a risk, they tend to overestimate low risks, while underestimating high risks (*assessment bias*). In fact, people can be more comfortable with certainty about a high risk than uncertainty about the level of risk, in part because uncertainty drives them to fear the worst. Informed awareness of the risk helps to lower sensitivity, even when the risk turns out to be worse than feared! For instance, a person living for years with undiagnosed symptoms probably wonders whether the underlying condition is harmless or deadly (a wide range of returns). That person might be relieved to receive a firm medical diagnosis, even if the prognosis does not include recovery, just because the diagnosis relieves some of the uncertainty. In some sense, the uncertainty was a negative event in itself, since it was worrying and stressful.

Objective expertise usually leads to informed awareness. Inexpert familiarity with negative risks tends to cause inflation of those risks. For instance, almost everyone has heard of cancer, but few people objectively understand the chances by different sources or causes—consequently, they react viscerally to anything that they believe could be carcinogenic. Conversely, as long as their exposure is voluntary, people will expose themselves to things such as sunlight, tanning machines, nicotine, alcohol, or sexually transmitted pathogens that are much more carcinogenic than practically harmless but externally controlled agents like fluorinated water.

Experts should be able to identify a risk that outsiders either inflate (because they fear it) or deflate (because they do not understand why they should fear it). However, disciplinary biases could drive experts within a particular domain to misestimate, leaving us with a dilemma about whether to believe the in-domain or out-domain experts. For instance, the World Economic Forum (2013, p. 51) found that economists assessed economic risks, and technology experts assessed nanotechnology risks, as lower than external experts assessed these same risks, while environmental experts assessed environmental risks higher than others assessed them.

Real Situations

In hypothetical situations, people tend to claim more recklessness or bravery than they would exhibit in real situations. For instance, if asked how they would behave if they saw a stranger being robbed, most people would claim to defend the victim, but in practice, most people would not. This is an issue for risk managers who might use data gathered from respondents on their risk averseness in hypothetical or future scenarios—most respondents claim less sensitivity than they would show in the real world, and their responses could be manipulated easily by the framing of the question.

Lack of Control

People are more sensitive to risks that they feel that they cannot control or are under the control of remote persons or groups, such as official regulators. Resentment is more likely if the controllers are seen to be incompetent or separate, such as by ethnicity or religion or class. Perversely, people can be insensitive to voluntary risks if they think they can control them even if they cannot. For instance, alcoholics and tobacco smokers tend to underestimate the addictiveness of alcohol or nicotine and tend to underestimate the health risks (Renn, 2008, p. 22).

People tend to accept surprisingly high risks so long as they are voluntary and thrilling or promise intrinsic or social rewards despite the negative risks, such as driving cars fast or playing contact sports. In a sense, these are speculative risks. Indeed, people effectively tolerate probable net losses when they bet against a competent oddsmaker, but complain about unlikely and smaller losses over which they have less control, such as being short changed. Most people are more sensitive to pure risks, like terrorism, than objectively higher risks, like driving a car (hundreds of times more lives are lost in car accidents than to terrorism), in part because driving is a speculative risk (at least in the sense that it is voluntary) (see Table 9.2).

Distrust

Most people are keen on controls on negative risks so long as the controls do not impact their lives, but they are distrustful of controls that affect them. In fact, people are happy to complain about all sorts of pure risks and how poorly they are controlled by higher authorities, but also complain when controls are imposed without consultation, affect personal freedoms, or use up resources that could be used elsewhere. Surveys can produce contradictory responses, such as majority agreement that a risk is too high and needs to be controlled, but majority disagreement with any significant practical controls that might be proposed.

Risk sensitivity decreases when the speculative behavior is institutionalized within trust settings or regimes that the speculator perceives as fair and universal. When rule breaking is exposed, risk sensitivity increases (as well as altruistic punishment) (Van Brunschot & Kennedy, 2008, p. 10). For instance, decades ago most people had confidence in the banking system, but since financial crises and scandals in 2008 they became more sensitive to financial risks and more distrustful of the financial system.

People can be keen on punishing rule breakers even if the punishment of a few is bad for themselves; their motivation makes evolutionary and rational sense if such punishment improves future compliance with rules—this motivation is known as *altruistic punishment*.

Sometimes this blame is justified, particularly when a minority of people break the rules and expose the rest of us to increased risks. For instance, we should feel aggrieved if a colleague allowed a friend to bypass the controls on access to a supposedly secure area and that friend stole our property or attacked us. Similarly, many people blamed a handful of financial speculators for the financial crisis in 2008 and proposed punitive measures such as stopping their employment, stopping their income bonuses or salary rises, or taxing their high earnings before the crisis (a tax known by some advocates as a "Robin Hood" or "windfall" tax). A contradiction arises when a risk grows uncontrolled and perhaps manifests as a shocking event while most people had not supported controlling the risk, but most people still would seek to blame others.

Group Psychology

Individuals tend to be vulnerable to social contagion or peer pressure. Groups tend to encourage members toward reckless behavior as long as the majority is unaffected ("peer pressure"). Groups naturally provide members with the sense of shared risks, collective protection, and cohesion. Groups can exploit any of these effects by actively encouraging recklessness in return for membership or credibility within the group. On the other hand, where the group is risk sensitive but a new member is risk insensitive, the group would encourage the member to conform to the group.

 Real Risks and Sensitivity

Partly because of the subjective biases and drivers described above, most people are oversensitive to some very unlikely events, like shark attacks or winning the lottery, and undersensitive to much likelier events, like road traffic accidents or gambling losses. In many domains, people simply ignore risk or the easy management of risk, such as when they are impulsive or passionate. The subsections below compare some important real risks with typical sensitivities to those risks: pair bonding, procreation, war initiation, avoidable diseases, space travel, air travel, road travel, violence, terrorism, and sharks.

Pair Bonding

Most of us will ignore or accept very high risks as long as they are socially, emotionally, or sexually attractive, familiar, or normative. Pursuit of such risks could be described as rational so long as we expect rewards such as belonging or happiness, but most people are unrealistic about the positive risks, blind to the negative risks, and neglectful of easy controls on the negative risks.

For instance, most people will marry or seek a lifelong romantic relationship and claim that they are doing so for love rather than material gain. In many ways, the trajectory is admirable and exhilarating—why interrupt something so natural and emotional with caution and negotiation? Yet a lifelong commitment faces much uncertainty because of the long term of the commitment and the comparative immaturity of the parties. Part of the impulsiveness is biochemical and has been compared to intoxication or addiction. The elevation of the biochemicals (such as serotonin) typically subsides within 18 to 36 months of "falling in love," although the longer-term parts of love could persist. Love seems to be some combination, varying by individual experience, of friendship or companionship, attachment or commitment, and sexual lust or attraction.

In effect, most people celebrate their romantic and emotional impulses, bet on lifelong love, and even eschew easy controls on the risks that would make lifelong love easier to achieve. Popular culture is full of celebratory stories about people who impulsively make commitments despite little experience with their partners, opposition from close family or friends, official barriers, or poverty.

Unfortunately, few people achieve lifelong love and the costs of a failed partnership are great. Even though most people expect "'til death do us part" and forego a prenuptial agreement when they marry, most first marriages end in divorce (see Table 9.2). A typical wedding cost $27,000 per average American couple in 2011 (according to TheKnot.com). A divorce could cost a few thousand dollars, if both parties would not contest the divorce, but a typical divorce is more expensive (about $40,000 for the average couple in direct legal costs alone) and is associated with other negative returns, such as opportunity costs (which could add up to hundreds of thousands of dollars), changes of financial arrangements, residency, and employment, stress, and loss of custody of property and children.

If humans were rational in their pairing and procreating, they would rarely need help or fail, but historically all societies have developed norms, cultures, and institutions intended to direct human behaviors toward lifelong pairing and procreation and toward gender roles and codependency. The ideals of love, lifelong pairing, and marriage have natural origins and rewards, but each is partly socially constructed. Some of these structures are to the benefit of couples or society as a whole, but some are counter-productive. For instance, many people feel trapped in marriages by fears of the inequities of divorce. In traditional societies, men have most of the rights and benefits, while women have few alternatives to marriage and even can be forced to marry. In return, men are expected to provide for their wives and children; their failure to provide is often the sole allowable grounds for a female-initiated divorce. Societies that are legally gender-equal or -neutral still culturally and effectively treat provision as a masculine role. Many public authorities still promise greater alimony payments and widowed pensions to women than men on the obsolete grounds that women are helpless without men. Family legal systems in developed societies tend to favor women during disputes over child custody and separation of assets (even though in traditional societies they tend to favor men). These norms, cultures, and institutions effectively change the risks by gender, but couples and parents, when starting out, are largely oblivious to these structures.

Some couples choose not to separate but are not happy together. Naturally, a dissatisfactory pairwise commitment could be rational, given the material efficiencies of living together, the redundancy in the pair when one is incapacitated, and the costs of separation. Some people make perfectly rational calculations that a relationship is a hedge against future incapacity; some people simply expect to gain from a more affluent partner or from an employer or government that has promised benefits to partners; some people stay unhappily together for the sake of their marriage vows, their children, or religious and other socially constructed reasons. Some economists would argue that all humans are making rational, self-interested calculations all the time, but most people, at least consciously, report that their romantic pairings are emotional, not rational (Bar-Or, 2012).

Procreating

Most adults will have children during their lifetime, even though child rearing is very expensive and offers few material efficiencies (unlike a childless adult pairing). For many parents, the emotional rewards of parenting are incalculable and outweigh all material costs, but parents also tend to underestimate the material costs. The U.S. Department of Agriculture estimates the direct expense of rearing an American child from birth in 2011 through age 17 at around $235,000 for a middle-income family, excluding higher education expenses around $30,000 to $120,000. The average cost of tuition and fees for the 2011/12 school year as $8,244 for a public college and $28,500 for a private one. The indirect costs and opportunity costs for the parents are likely to add up to a sum at least double the direct costs (Lino, 2012).

In addition to the financial risks are the potential psychological and emotional returns: Parents, like romantic partners, must face many disappointments in the choices made by their dependents; tragically, a child could reject his or her parents, fall ill, or die; if the parents separate, likely one parent would be left with little custody. Yet most people, when they choose to have children, do not care to predict the negative risks realistically, or they choose to accept whatever comes. The emotional rewards of rearing children may be described as rational, although this would be conflating too much of the rational with the emotional. Some may have rational reasons to procreate, such as future reliance on children for support during the parental generation's retirement, although many parents would object ethically to such reasons. Of course, for many people procreation is an accident of recreation: They never meant to have children at that time or with that person, but sexual rewards are difficult to ignore. Sexual impulsiveness helps to explain the high rate of sexual acts without protections against either pregnancy or sexually transmitted diseases.

War Initiation

For sovereign states, a clearly high risk is potential defeat in war. Most states are at peace most of the time, but when they enter wars, they tend to be overoptimistic or simply feel that they have no choice (perhaps because the alternative is capitulation without fighting). Less than 60% of belligerents will win their wars (as defined in the Correlates of War dataset for the last 200 years or so), and this proportion is inflated by states that bandwagon belatedly with the winning side. More than one-third of war initiators (such as a state that attacks another state without provocation) will lose, despite their implicit confidence in victory at the time they initiated. This overconfidence can be explained partly by the political and social pressures for governments to throw their weight around or to comply with belligerent stakeholders or to divert stakeholders from other issues. Official overconfidence must be explained partly by poor official risk assessments too.

Avoidable Disease

People naturally accept some risks that are seen as unavoidable or routine, such as the lifetime chance of cancer (about 40%) or heart disease (about 25%). Less rational is voluntary engagement in activities—primarily smoking, alcohol abuse, unhealthy eating, and sedentary lifestyles—that dramatically increase the risks: Some activities easily double the chances. In fact, most prevalent cancers and heart diseases are entirely "avoidable" (see Table 9.2).

Table 9.2 Actual Risks and Sensitivity to Risks

Outcome or Return	Frequency or Probability	Example Reasons for		Data Sources
		Sensitivity	Insensitivity	
Divorce	About 50% per marriage; Annual divorce rate is equivalent to 0.36% of population (2010)	Proximate experience; maturation	Social norms; emotional and sexual drivers; inexperience	U.S. National Center for Health Statistics, Centers for Disease Control and Prevention
Defeat in major international wars (each more than 1,000 combat deaths, all belligerents)	41% of all belligerents, 35% of initiators, 1814–1994	Experience of defeat; pacific stakeholders	Experience of victory; belligerent stakeholders; poor risk assessment	Correlates of War dataset
Posttraumatic stress disorder	About 30% of U.S. soldiers who served in Iraq, 2003–2008	Information	Social norms	U.S. Department of Defense (DOD)
Cancer	42% per lifetime; 64% of those with cancer will die of cancer	Proximate experience	Familiarity; regular frequency	Macmillan Cancer Research
Fatal heart disease	About 25% per lifetime, 50% per smoker or obese person	Symptoms or prognosis	Volunteerism; sense of control	U.S. National Center for Health Statistics
Space shuttles destroyed on missions	1.0% projected, 1.5% actual (1981–2011)	Failed mission	Successful mission	U.S. National Aeronautics and Space Administration (NASA)
Military casualties	2% wounded, 0.25% killed of all U.S. military personnel deployed to Afghanistan or Iraq, 2001–2011	Expectation or experience of deployment	Social and political norms and rewards; acceptance of objectives; speculative thrills	U.S. DOD
Road traffic fatalities	0.020% of low- and 0.022% of middle-income country residents per year (2004); 0.016% of Americans per year (2010); 0.006% of Britons per year (2010)	Proximate experience; more exposed or vulnerable vehicle	Regular frequency; voluntary participation in driving	World Health Organization; U.S. National Highway Traffic Safety Administration; U.K. Office of National Statistics

(Continued)

Table 9.2 (Continued)

Outcome or Return	Frequency or Probability	Example Reasons for Sensitivity	Example Reasons for Insensitivity	Data Sources
All violent crimes	0.4% of Americans per year (2010)	Violence; sense of lack of control	Confidence in law enforcement	U.S. Federal Bureau of Investigations
Murders	0.005% of Americans per year (2010)			
Fatalities by guns	0.01% of Americans per year (0.003% of Americans due to firearm crimes alone) (2010)			U.S. Centers for Disease Control and Prevention
Fatalities due to terrorism, 2000–2006	0.0002% of Americans per year; 0.00002% of Britons per year; 0.007% of Iraqis per year; 0.0001% of global residents per year	Irregular frequency; recency of events; violence	Revelations of greater risks; familiarity	Global Terrorism Database at the National Consortium for the Study of Terrorism and Responses to Terrorism (START)
Fatalities while aboard commercial airlines	0.00001 per flight	Recent aircraft accident	Confidence in regulation	U.S. Centers for Disease Control and Prevention
Fatalities due to shark attacks	<0.0000003% of Americans per year	Sensationalism; misinformation	Understanding of shark behavior	U.S. Centers for Disease Control and Prevention

Space Travel

The National Aeronautics and Space Administration (NASA) effectively accepted that 1% of space shuttle missions would end in failure with the almost certain loss of everyone aboard, a high risk, but one justified by the great scientific, economic, political, and military benefits. The actual rate would be 1.5% of missions. A fatality per flight is 150,000 times less frequent on an airliner than a space shuttle (see Table 9.2).

Air Travel

Air travel is often described as the safest mechanical way to travel, but this statement illustrates a difficulty with frequency data: Frequencies often do not fairly compare dissimilar events. Air safety is rigorously regulated and inspected, whereas individual car owners and drivers effectively regulate their own safety, outside of infrequent and comparatively superficial independent inspections. Consequently, an average aircraft flight is much less likely to cause fatality than an average car journey. Yet the fatalities of air travel seem large because a catastrophic failure in an aircraft tends to kill more people per failure. Consequently, an air accident is much less frequent but more newsworthy than a typical road accident.

Moreover, an air passenger can feel lacking in control of the risks, whereas a car driver can feel in control (a situation that tends to decrease sensitivity to risk). For all these reasons, people tend to be more sensitive to the risks of air travel than car travel. Yet road travel kills more than 600 times more Americans than air travel kills. Even though people take more road journeys than air journeys, road traffic is more deadly than air travel, both absolutely and as a rate per miles travelled (see Table 9.2).

Road Travel

In 2010 (the safest year on American roads in recorded history), road traffic killed nearly 32,885 Americans (16.3 per 100,000 inhabitants), an average of 90 persons per day, and injured 2,239,000 Americans (724 per 100,000 inhabitants), an average of 6,134 persons per day.

Americans take many more journeys by car than by aircraft, so the higher number of Americans killed on the roads is partly a function of increased exposure to road traffic. Car travel seems less risky when the measures capture exposure: in 2010, the National Highway Traffic Safety Administration observed 0.0011 fatalities per 100,000 miles travelled, 12.64 fatalities per 100,000 registered motor vehicles, and 15.65 fatalities per 100,000 licensed drivers.

The risks increase with voluntary behaviors, such as reckless driving, telephone use, or intoxication. About 30% of Americans will be involved in an alcohol-related car accident at least once during their lifetime (see Table 9.2).

Violence

People are sensitive to violence of all kinds because the perpetrator's intent seems outside of the victim's control (although sometimes intent is activated by the target), and violence suggests severe effects on the unprotected human body. Potential harm from violence is certainly a pure risk, whereas driving and firearm ownership are voluntary and might be experienced as thrilling. Most types of violent crimes, including homicides, have declined in America since the 1980s. Violent crimes are a minority of all crimes, but in 2010 Americans suffered more than 1.2 million murders, rapes and sexual assaults, robberies, and aggravated and simple assaults (408 per 100,000 inhabitants). Tragically, some victims experienced more than one of these crimes. More than 2.2 times as many Americans die in road traffic accidents than are murdered (14,748, or 4.8 per 100,000 inhabitants, in 2010, another declining year for murders).

Private firearm ownership also has declined (from a high of 54% of households in 1994 to lows of 40%, according to Gallup's surveys); nevertheless, firearm crimes have not declined as a proportion (around 80%) of crime. Most deaths by firearms are suicidal, but suicides do not trouble most other people; instead, people worry more about external uses of firearms against them. Firearm crime started to rise after a trough in 2000 (road traffic fatalities have continued to decline since then). In 2010, in America 11,078 homicides were committed with firearms (3.6 per 100,000 residents); the deaths and injuries attributable to firearms cost America $68 billion in medical costs and lost work (data source: Centers for Disease Control).

Most Americans are genuinely scared of firearm crime. Indeed, these fears drive much of the defensive demand for guns. Nevertheless, sensitivity to firearm crime is countered by the freedoms to own and bear arms. Some cities and states legislated against firearm ownership or carriage, but national political interest in firearm control did not change significantly until after a series of mass murders with firearms occurred in 2012. At the end of 2012, the political administration pushed for more restrictive federal legislation. This event illustrates the potential for "shocks" (unusual events) to change popular or political sensitivity.

Terrorism

Many more Americans are murdered for nonpolitical reasons that are murdered by terrorism, but terrorism attracts more sensitivity. Everybody should feel more sensitive to political violence after shocking events like the terrorist attacks in the north-eastern United States of September 11, 2001. (Use of the term *terrorism risk* rose about 30 times from 2000 to 2005, according to Google Ngram.) Rationally, high lethality (nearly 3,000) on one day (9/11) demonstrates the capacity of terrorism to kill more people at once, but nonterrorist Americans and road traffic accidents each killed many more times more Americans even in 2001, and 2001 was an extreme outlier for terrorist-caused deaths. Road traffic and nonterrorist Americans are consistently more deadly and costly every year.

From 9/11 through 2012, nonterrorist Americans murdered more than 600 times more Americans (180,000) within the United States than terrorists murdered (less than 300 U.S. citizens, excluding U.S. military combatants) both in the United States and abroad. Fewer Americans were killed by terrorism in that period than were crushed to death by furniture.

In the most lethal year (2001) for Americans due to terrorism, road traffic killed more than 10 times more Americans than terrorism killed. During the seven calendar years (2000–2006) around 9/11 and the U.S. "war on terror," terrorism killed about 80 times fewer Americans than road traffic accidents killed. During that same period, road traffic killed 300 times more Britons than terrorism killed. Even in Iraq, during the peak in the insurgency and counter-insurgency there, terrorism killed about the same proportion of the Iraqi population as the proportion of the British population that was killed by road traffic. The rate of road traffic deaths in low- to middle-income countries ran 200 to 220 times greater than the rate of terrorism deaths globally.

Terrorism does threaten political, social, and economic functionality in ways that typical road traffic accidents and ordinary murders cannot, but terrorism is not as costly in direct economic costs. For 2000, the U.S. National Highway Traffic Safety Administration estimated $230.6 billion in total costs for reported and unreported road traffic accidents, excluding the other costs of traffic, such as environmental and health costs due to emissions from automobile engines. The terrorist attacks of September 11, 2001, (the costliest ever) cost around $40 billion in insured losses.

Terrorism, like any crime, is a pure risk for the victim; its violence and seeming irrationality prompts visceral sensitivity. Moreover, terrorism is infrequent and concentrated in time. Some authors have pointed out that governments have rational, self-important, and manipulative reasons (such as desires to avoid scrutiny, link other issues, or sell otherwise unpopular policies) for inflating terrorism and other violent threats to fundamental national security ("the politics of fear"; "the politics of security") (Cox, Levine, & Newman, 2009; Friedman, 2010; Mueller, 2005, 2006).

Political and popular obsessions with terrorism declined in the late 2000s, when economic and natural catastrophes clearly emerged as more urgent. In Britain, the Independent Reviewer of Terrorism Legislation admitted that the most threatening forms of terrorism deserve special attention but pointed out that objectively terrorism risks had declined and were overstated. "Whatever its cause, the reduction of risk in relation to al-Qaida terrorism in the United Kingdom is real and has been sustained for several years now. Ministers remain risk averse—understandably so in view of the continued potential for mass casualties to be caused by suicide attacks, launched without warning and with the express purpose of killing civilians." He took the opportunity to describe terrorism, in the long-run, as "an insignificant cause of mortality" (5 deaths per year, 2000–2010) compared with total accidental deaths (17,201 in 2010 alone), of which 123 cyclists were killed by road traffic, 102 military personnel were killed in Afghanistan, 29 Britons drowned in bathtubs, and 5 Britons were killed by stings from hornets, wasps, or bees (Anderson, 2012, pp. 21–22, 27).

Terrorism is still risky, but the main lesson in all this is that terrorism tends to be inflated at the expense of other risks.

Sharks

Many people have phobias of harmless insects, birds, and even ephemeral things (such as clouds). Some of these phobias are difficult to describe rationally but are more likely where the source is considered strange, unpredictable, or indistinguishable from harmful versions or relatives. Hazards with the potential for great, random, unconscious, or irrational violence tend to occupy inordinate attention. These hazards include terrorists and other premeditated violent criminals (who are much less frequent than nonviolent criminals) and animals such as sharks.

Most species of sharks do not have the physical capacity to harm humans and are wary of humans (humans kill millions of wild sharks per year). Almost all attacks by sharks on humans are by a few unusually large species, almost always by juveniles developing in shallow waters who mistake humans for typical prey; in most attacks, the shark makes a single strike, does not consume anything, and does not return for more. Having said that, a single strike could be fatal if, say, it severs an artery or causes the victim to breathe in water. In some cases sharks have attacked humans who seem unusually vulnerable or numerous, such as after shipwrecks.

Shark attacks are extremely rare, but popular culture devotes considerable attention to shark lethality. Sharks kill 0.92 Americans per year, while trampolines kill 1.10 Americans per year, rollercoasters 1.15, free-standing kitchen-ranges 1.31, vending machines 2.06, riding lawnmowers 5.22, fireworks 6.60, dogs 16.00, sky diving 21.20, furniture 26.64 by crushing, and road traffic 33,000 (Zenko, 2012). Of course, we should remind ourselves that frequencies can be misleading because they tend to ignore dissimilar parameters such as exposure. One explanation for the low number of people actually killed by sharks is the low exposure of people to sharks: very few people swim with sharks. Nevertheless, sharks are much less dangerous to humans than most humans believe.

SUMMARY

This chapter has

- defined risk sensitivity and tolerability,
- explained different organizational cultural sensitivities,
- reviewed different societal sensitivities,
- described the many personal psychological, social, and situational drivers of sensitivity, including:
    - loss averseness,
    - a focus on returns over likelihood,
    - inflation of negative risks,
    - proximity,
    - psychological anchoring,

  - o cognitive availability,
  - o unrepresentativeness,
  - o base-rate neglect,
  - o maturation,
  - o misinformation,
  - o real situations over hypotheticals,
  - o lack of personal control,
  - o distrust, and
  - o group psychology,
- and compared real risks to popular sensitivities, including:
  - o pair bonding,
  - o procreating,
  - o war initiation,
  - o avoidable disease,
  - o space travel,
  - o air travel,
  - o road travel,
  - o violence,
  - o terrorism, and
  - o sharks.

QUESTIONS AND EXERCISES

1. What is the difference between risk sensitivity and risk tolerance?
2. What descriptive inaccuracies are suggested when describing someone as risk sensitive or risk insensitive?
3. Why might a particular society be more sensitive to
   a. speculative risks,
   b. pure risks,
   c. reckless, demonstrative behavior,
   d. poorly regulated road traffic,
   e. socio-economic risks, or
   f. political violence?
4. What is meant by *nonlinear loss averseness*?
5. When people consider a risk, do they tend to focus on the likelihood or the returns?
6. If we were to survey people on their assessments of both the likelihood and returns at the same time, how might the results be corrupted?
7. Which of the following would people typically most overestimate or underestimate:
   a. positive speculative risks,

b. negative speculative risks, or
c. pure risks?

8. How do rules affect risk sensitivity?
9. What sorts of controls is somebody likely to oppose even if he or she agrees that the risk needs to be controlled?
10. What is altruistic punishment, and how can it be justified?
11. What is the difference between proximity, anchoring, and availability as drivers of risk sensitivity?
12. Why might a group become more sensitive to a risk despite becoming more remote to it?
13. Explain why somebody might be less sensitive in the short term to events of one type than events of another type despite both types of events occurring at the same frequency over the long term.
14. Explain why a person's risk sensitivity typically changes over a lifetime.
15. Explain why different types of information about a risk could either lower or raise sensitivity to the risk.
16. Why might an individual's risk sensitivity be different when alone or with a group?
17. Why might one person be more sensitive to risks under certain regulators than others?
18. Why might somebody's real sensitivity to risk vary from their expectations?
19. Give some examples of how societies and cultures discourage sensitivity to romantic pair bonds and procreation.
20. Why are people generally more sensitive to the risks of air travel than road travel?
21. Why do people tend to overestimate violent crimes?
22. Why is popular culture more interested in shark attacks than dog attacks?
23. Humans are more often the victims of dog attacks than shark attacks, but why might the actual risks of shark attacks be greater?

Controls and Strategies

This chapter explains controls and strategies—the actual things under our control that affect our risks. The two main sections of this chapter define control and explain when and why controls are applied to risks and define strategy and explain when and why to choose between available strategies in response to risk.

Control

This section defines control, explains how to separate tolerable from intolerable risks that you should control, explains the trade-off between intolerability and practicality, explains why sometimes even tolerable risks are controlled, and explains why different stakeholders can have different levels of toleration and control at the same time.

Defining Control

A control is anything that was intended to or effectively does reduce a risk (see Table 10.1 for official definitions). If a control reduces a risk, the precontrol state of the risk is usually known as the *inherent risk*, while the postcontrol state is usually known as the *residual risk*.

The control is not necessarily an absolute solution to the risk. It may reduce a risk to a still intolerable level or to an only temporarily tolerable level. Consequently, good risk management processes prescribe monitoring the risk, even after control.

Establishing Tolerable Risks

Most authorities and standards prescribe the establishment of a risk tolerability threshold, below which a negative risk is tolerable and above which it should be controlled.

Since stakeholders, managers, and risks are diverse, authorities and standards normally leave users to find their own tolerability threshold and do not prescribe where the threshold should fall, although project managers have been advised to tolerate risks that score less than 30–40 on a 100-point scale (Heerkens, 2002, p. 148). In international security, some writers imply that strategists should not tolerate

Table 10.1 Official Definitions Relating to Risk Controls and Strategies

	Australian and New Zealand Joint Technical Committee (2009); International Organization for Standardization (2009a)	**U.K. Treasury (2004)**	**U.K. MOD**	**U.K. Civil Contingencies Secretariat (U.K. Cabinet Office, 2013)**	**Public Safety Canada (2012)**
Control	"a measure that is modifying risk," including a "process, policy, device, practice, or other actions which modify risk."	"any action . . . taken to manage risk"; an internal control is "any action, originating within the organization, taken to manage risk" (p. 50).	"any action taken by management to enhance the likelihood that established objectives and goals will be achieved" (2009a); "The coordination of activity, through processes and structures that enable a commander to manage risk and deliver intent" (2009b, p. 234).	A risk control is "measures to reduce the likelihood of an emergency occurring from a given risk, and/or implement measures to mitigate the impacts of that emergency should arise." A control is "the application of authority, combined with the capability to manage resources, in order to achieve defined objectives."	-
Treatment	"a process to modify risk"	-	-	"process of determining those risks that should be controlled (by reducing their likelihood and/or putting impact mitigation measures in place) and those that will be tolerated at their currently assessed level" (countermeasures are "precautionary actions to protect the public")	"the process of developing, selecting, and implementing risk control measures"

	Australian and New Zealand Joint Technical Committee (2009); International Organization for Standardization (2009a)	**U.K. Treasury (2004)**	**U.K. MOD**	**U.K. Civil Contingencies Secretariat (U.K. Cabinet Office, 2013)**	**Public Safety Canada (2012)**
Capability	-	-	-	"a demonstrable ability to respond to and recover from a particular threat or hazard"	"a combination of resources that provides the means to prevent, protect against, respond to, and recover from emergencies, disasters, and other types of incidents. In capability-based planning, a capability includes the following elements: planning, organization, equipment and systems, training, and exercises, evaluations, and corrective actions"
Strategy	effectively the same as risk treatment	"the overall organizational approach to risk management as defined by the Accounting Officer and/or Board" (p. 50)	Risk mitigation is "reduction of the exposure to, probability of, or loss from risk" (2011c).	"the level (above tactical level and operational level) at which policy, strategy and the overall response framework are established and managed"	("strategic emergency management plan") "an overarching plan that establishes a federal government institution's objectives, approach, and structure for protecting Canadians and Canada from threats and hazards in their areas of responsibility and sets out how the institution will assist with coordinated emergency management" (p. 90)

(Continued)

Table 10.1 (Continued)

	Australian and New Zealand Joint Technical Committee (2009); International Organization for Standardization (2009a)	U.K. Treasury (2004)	U.K. MOD	U.K. Civil Contingencies Secretariat (U.K. Cabinet Office, 2013)	Public Safety Canada (2012)
Inherent risk	-	"the exposure arising from a specific risk before any action has been taken to manage it" (p. 49)	"the risk found in the environment and in human activities that is part of existence" (2009a) (note: this conflates pure risks or natural risks)	-	-
Residual risk	"the risk remaining after risk treatment"	"the level of risk remaining after internal control has been exercised [and] the exposure in respect of that risk" (p. 9); "the exposure arising from a specific risk after action has been taken to manage it and making the assumption that the action is effective" (p. 49).	"the remaining level of risk after risk control measures have been implemented" (2009)	-	"risk that remains after implementing risk mitigation measures" (p. 80)

negative risks until their probabilities approach zero, given the high negative returns of strategic failure in international war:

> [A]ny strategic argument which seeks to direct and inform practice needs to satisfy certain conditions so that the desired end is, in fact, achieved by the means recommended and employed. The rationality of such arguments does not depend upon making out a plausible or acceptable case for the recommended action, but in showing that the result is either highly probable or certain. (Reynolds, 1989, p. 29)

Visually, identifying tolerable risks involves assessing the risks, assessing our tolerability level or threshold, and plotting the risks on a linear scale, where risks higher or lower than the threshold would be intolerable (see Figure 10.1).

However, individually tolerable risks could interact or vector together as a single *compound risk* that is intolerable. For instance, we could choose to assess criminals individually and find their associated risks tolerable, but if those criminals were to cooperate or to be analyzed as a homogenous group, then the risks associated with the group might become intolerable.

Pedagogy Box 10.1 Prescriptions for Establishing Tolerability

The Australian/New Zealand and ISO standards (International Organization for Standardization, 2009a, p. 8) prescribe in their risk management process a step termed *risk evaluation*—meaning "the process of comparing the result of risk analysis with risk criteria to determine whether the risk and/or its magnitude is acceptable or tolerable." (The Canadian government too follows the definition and the process.)

The International Risk Governance Council (IRGC) (2008, p. 6) prescribed a step called *characterization and evaluation* (separating tolerable from intolerable risks).

The Humanitarian Practice Network (2010) describes the "threshold of acceptable risk" as "the point beyond which the risk is considered too high to continue operating; [it is] influenced by the probability that an incident will occur, and the seriousness of the impact if it occurs" (p. xix).

Figure 10.1 Conceptualizing Inherent and Residual Risks

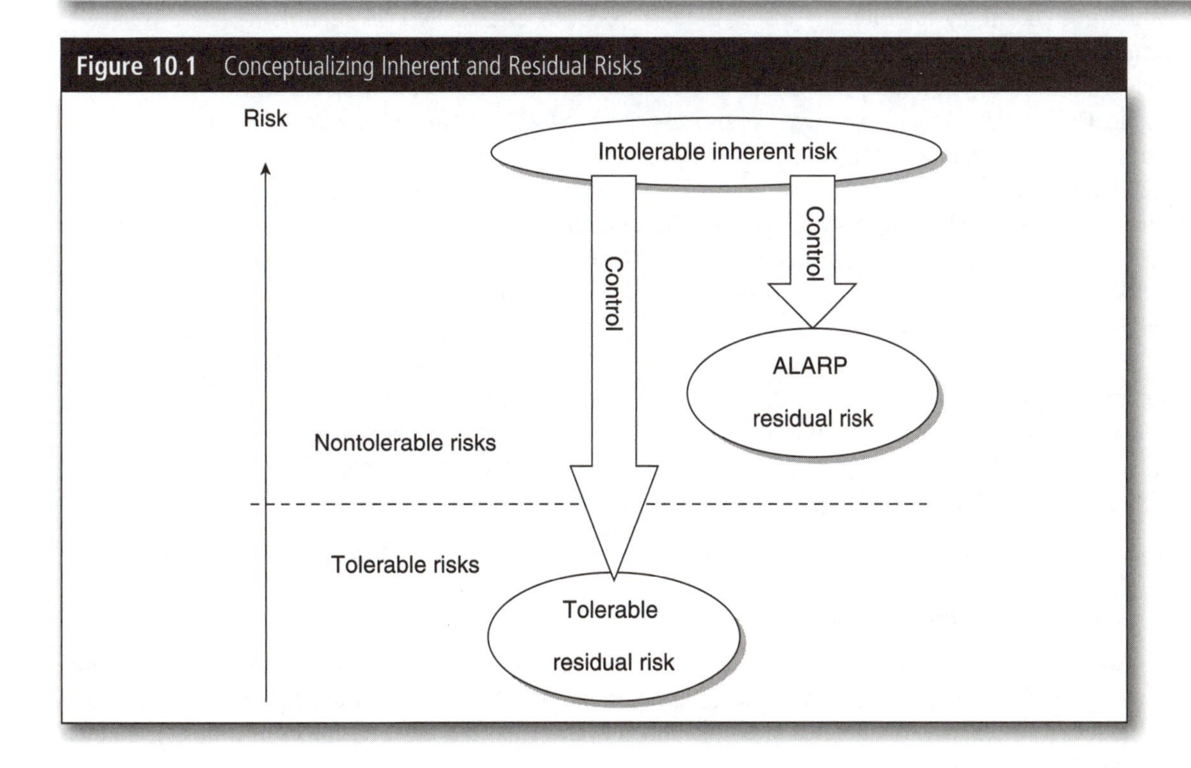

Intolerability Versus Practicality

Ideally, we would seek to control intolerable risks until the residual risk is tolerable. However, sometimes the controls would be impractical or unjustifiably burdensome, in which case risk managers might accept a residual risk level that is higher than the tolerability level. If so, on practical grounds, they would effectively tolerate a level of risk that they would not tolerate otherwise. This level is described sometimes as the ALARP (as low as reasonably practical) level. Some authors talk of a constant "risk balance" or "security dynamic"—a balance between our tolerance of the risks, our resources available to control the risks, and our values (Van Brunschot & Kennedy, 2008, pp. 12–13).

Naturally, the ALARP level could be used unscrupulously to justify a multitude of sins, such as laziness or meanness, but ALARP levels are everywhere, even though most are unadmitted. For instance, law enforcement authorities ideally would like to eliminate crime, but they would need to track every activity of every person, which would be impractical, unethical, and stressful. In effect, some level of crime becomes "acceptable" (Kennedy & Van Brunschot, 2009, p. 4). Similarly, regulation of transport systems seeks to promote but not to guarantee safety; otherwise the transport systems would grind to a halt under the burden of inspections and reports.

Pedagogy Box 10.2 ALARP Food Risks

Since 1995, the Food and Drug Administration (FDA), which oversees the safety of most foods, medical devices, and medical drugs in the United States, has published a tolerability level for insect parts in food, even though surveys of food consumers show that most consumers, rhetorically at least, would not knowingly tolerate any insect parts in food. In effect, the FDA regards its "food defect action levels" (such as more than 75 insect parts per 50 grams of flour or more than 60 insect parts per 100 grams of chocolate) as ALARP levels: "The FDA set these action levels because it is economically impractical to grow, harvest, or process raw products that are totally free of non-hazardous, naturally-occurring, unavoidable defects" (U.S. FDA, 2005).

Tolerance of an ALARP level could introduce new risks, such as potential collapse of public confidence in the authority that tolerated the ALARP level before some associated public shock revealed such tolerance to the public. For instance, from 2004 to 2007, U.S. consumers were shocked by a series of revelations of meat from diseased livestock in the human food chain. Effectively, authorities had knowingly tolerated diseased meat in the food chain, while most consumers had been unaware. In 2009, new U.S. federal laws took effect that outlawed diseased meat from being passed for human consumption. In 2012, British consumers were shocked by revelations that meats routinely sold in supermarkets, fast food outlets, and restaurants as beef had been identified genetically as horse meat, mostly from continental European sources, causing a collapse in confidence in European-wide regulation of food labelling.

Controlled Tolerable Risks

Sometimes, scrupulous authorities assess a risk as tolerable but are forced to control it anyway by outside stakeholders, sometimes for unnecessary reasons. For instance, a natural risk manager might have assessed the chance of a hurricane as tolerably low and allocated most resources to control the much higher chance of drought, but the public in an unaffected region could become alarmed by a hurricane in a neighboring region and demand observable defenses against hurricanes, even if neighboring risks were unrelated.

Pedagogy Box 10.3 Controlled Tolerable Food Risks

Consumers of food tend to be alarmed by harmless and even nutritious "defects" (such as insect parts) that they could see in their food, more than by harmful and nonnutritious defects (such as artificial pesticides and hormones and natural diseases) that they cannot see. Consequently, consumers demand food that has fewer observable defects than the FDA specifies, but this encourages food suppliers to use more pesticides in order to reduce insects—thereby increasing the risks associated with pesticides. This is a trend that the FDA discourages: "It is FDA's position that pesticides are not the alternative to preventing food defects. The use of chemical substances to control insects, rodents, and other natural contaminants has little, if any, impact on natural and unavoidable defects in foods" (U.S. FDA, 2005).

Incompatible Tolerability

Sometimes different stakeholders effectively work alongside each other with different tolerability levels. For instance, during recent multinational coalition operations in Afghanistan (since 2001), Iraq (since 2003), and other countries, soldiers from developed countries have been instructed not to travel without armed or armored protection, while indigenous personnel were issued inferior levels of protection, and some "third-party" nationals in the employ of civilian contractors were expected to work without any protection at all.

These incompatible tolerability levels reflect the different risk sensitivities within each national culture and organizational culture, and the different practical constraints on each actor's controls.

In some cases, incompatible sensitivities or controls may not matter to cooperative operations, but they could interfere with interoperability. For instance, in Afghanistan and Iraq, foreign personnel often were forbidden from entering high-risk areas that local personnel had been ordered to enter, while local personnel often demanded equipment of the same survivability as used by foreign troops. Similarly, local personnel often accused foreign personnel of deferring too readily to remote strike weapons, such as air-to-ground missiles launched from aircraft, that sometimes cause collateral civilian casualties, while foreign personnel often accuse local personnel of lacking care in the use of their portable firearms against civilians misidentified as enemies.

Strategies

This section defines risk management strategies, describes existing prescribed strategies, describes the 6 "T" strategies, and combined or balanced strategies.

Defining Strategy

A *risk management strategy* is any purposeful response to insecurity or risk; the strategy might be emergent or subconscious, but must aim to affect security or risk. The strategy is usefully distinguished from the controls—the particular actions used to change a particular risk, such as a guard acquired as part of a protective strategy. (Many authorities on risk management have offered a set of recommended responses to risk or approaches to security that they usually term *treatments*, *approaches*, *responses*, or *strategies*. Unfortunately, many authorities use these terms interchangeably for strategy or control.)

Pedagogy Box 10.4 Other Definitions of Risk Management Strategies

Some risk management standards refer to *approaches* toward security or managed risks. Some private commentators use both terms (*strategy* and *approach*) (Van Brunschot & Kennedy, 2008, pp. 165–166). The Humanitarian Practice Network is unusual for talking about both *risk management strategies* and *security strategies*. It defines (2010) a *security strategy* as "the overarching philosophy, application of approaches, and use of resources that frame organization security management" (p. xviii). Business managers, grounded in marketing strategies and corporate strategies, are comfortable referring to any purposeful response as a risk management strategy (Branscomb & Auerswald, 2001, Chapter 4).

The ISO prescribes seven strategies but does not define strategy, although it seems to regard "risk treatment" ("a process to modify risk") as inclusive of strategy. The Canadian government follows ISO, with some reservations.

The British Standards Institution has largely followed the ISO, but the British government has not ordered departments to follow any common standard. The British Treasury (2004) defines a risk management strategy as "the overall organizational approach to risk management as defined by the Accounting Officer and/or Board" (p. 50). The British Ministry of Defense (2011c) has definitions of military strategy but none of risk management strategy, although it defines "risk mitigation" as "reduction of the exposure to, probability of, or loss from risk" (pp. 6–7).

Strategy is well defined in military contexts. For instance, the United States Department of Defense (DOD) dictionary (2012b) defines it as "a prudent idea or set of ideas for employing the instruments of national power in a synchronized and integrated fashion to achieve theater, national, and/or multinational objective." Nevertheless, military strategists traditionally have not mentioned risk directly, although they routinely refer to security. In the last two decades, many governments have introduced risk management as a supplement or alternative to traditional security and defense strategies. For instance, in 2001, the DOD published a Quadrennial Defense Review with a declaration that "managing risks is a central element of the defense strategy" (p. 57). Some academics have encouraged or noticed the shift: "Strategy is no longer a question of defeating concrete threats in order to achieve perfect security; it has instead become a way of managing risks" (Rasmussen, 2006, p. 11). Nevertheless, the DOD has no definition of risk management strategy or security strategy, although the U.S. Defense Acquisition University prescribes strategies for managing acquisition projects and other departments routinely list strategies for managing security in certain domains, such as counter-terrorism.

Existing Strategies

The Australian/New Zealand standard (since 1995) and ISO (International Organization for Standardization, 2009a, pp. 9–10) offer a set of seven strategies that has proved most appealing, but not perfect, partly because some of the seven strategies overlap (see Table 10.2). For instance, *retaining* the risk is written to include both negative and positive risks, which overlaps with *pursuing* a positive risk. Similarly, *changing the consequences* involves mostly controlling the consequences of a potential event, but, as written, includes also the retention of financial reserves, which would not directly control the consequences at all and is better placed as a substrategy of *retaining* the risk. The ISO standard is followed by the Canadian government, among others, but the Canadian government is dissatisfied with the ISO strategies and recently (2013) published a cursory development, which remains ongoing.

Trade associations tend to follow the ISO, otherwise prescriptions tend to be contradictory. For instance, the Humanitarian Practice Network (2010, pp. 28, 50, 55) identified three risk management strategies, three overlapping security strategies, and two variations of the risk management strategies, for eight overlapping approaches that actually shake out as substrategies to three of the seven strategies offered by the ISO (see Table 10.2).

Similarly, two criminologists have categorized just three strategies/approaches (*prepare and make ready*, *respond*, *recover and prevent*), within which they conflated many competing optional approaches. For instance, within "*preparedness and readiness*" they effectively conflated transferring risks, avoiding risks, defending against threats, and preventing negative events—each of which is different to preparing or making ready for an event. The only natural separation between "*preparing*" and "*responding*" is chronological (you should prepare to respond to an attack in case it happens; it if happens you should respond). Finally, "*recover and prevent*" included an optional approach ("*prevent*") that naturally belonged in the first stage but was mentioned in all three stages. Fairly, they admitted "some degree of slippage with respect to the notions of preparedness and prevention" (Van Brunschot & Kennedy, 2008, p. 184).

Official authorities have tended to focus their risk management strategies on project risks, such as the U.S. Defense Acquisition University's four uncontentious strategies (*avoid*; *control*; *accept*; *transfer*). Other official authorities are focused on security strategies such as *preparedness*, *resilience*, *continuity*, and any other of a total of nine synonyms that largely mean *controlling the negative consequences* (see below) of a potential event—which is only one of the seven strategies offered by the ISO.

The Institute of Chartered Accountants of England and Wales (Turnbull, 1999) suggested four effective strategies (see Table 10.2), which were most influential on British government. Subsequently, the Treasury prescribed (and most other departments adopted) five risk management strategies known as the "five Ts" (U.K. Ministry of Defense [MOD], 2011c, pp. 6–7). The British government's project management standard (PRINCE2) follows similar strategies but knows them by other words. These five Ts also contain impractical overlaps and separations. For instance, *treating* and *terminating* risks involve essentially the same activities—terminating the risk would be the ultimate effect of perfectly treating the risk.

The Six "T" Strategies

Clearly, the current offerings are dissatisfactory. The authoritative prescriptions do not agree on even the number of strategies. Some of their strategies align neatly, but some contain substrategies that are placed under different strategies by different authorities. Some strategies are separated but are really

Table 10.2 Different Prescriptions and Definitions of Risk Management Strategies

Turnbull (1999)	Australian/ New Zealand and International Organization for Standardization (2009a, pp. 10–11)	Public Safety Canada (2013, p. 56)	International Risk Governance Council (2008, pp. 12–13)	PRINCE2 (U.K. Office of Government Commerce, 2009)	U.K. Treasury and MOD (2011c, pp. 6–7)	Newsome (2014)
Accept (negative risks and perhaps positive risks)	Retain the risk (negative or positive risks): "acceptance of the potential benefit of gain, burden of loss, from a particular risk."	"Retaining the risk by choice"	Accept ("risk reduction is unnecessary")	Accept (negative risks)	Tolerate (negative risks): "A risk may be acceptable without requiring any specific action to be taken. Even if not acceptable, the organisation may not have the ability to manage the risk, or the cost of doing so might be disproportionate to the potential benefit gained. In these cases, senior management may decide that the level of risk is tolerable and within the organisation's risk appetite."	Tolerate (negative risks), including watch and retain.
Terminate or avoid (negative risks)	Avoid (negative risks): "decision not to be involved in, or to withdraw from, an activity in order not to be exposed to a particular risk"; Remove the risk source.	"Avoiding the risk by deciding not to continue with the activity that gives rise to the risk" "Removing the source of the risk"	Avoid "intolerable risks"	Avoid or fallback (negative risks) or reject (positive risks)	Terminate (negative risks): "The option to change, suspend or terminate an activity, process or service, should only be considered when there is no conflict with the organisation's objectives and stakeholder expectation."	Terminate (negative risks), including: defer; withdraw; prevent the source or cause; prevent negative returns.
-	-	-	-	-	Possibly: "take the opportunity."	Turn negative into positive.
Possibly: "accept" positive risks.	Take (negative risks) or increase (positive risks).	-	Pursue "benefits"; Retain.	Enhance or exploit (positive risks).	Take the opportunity (positive risks): "In mitigating a threat (e.g. transfer or treat), it may be possible to gain	Take the chance of positive returns.

Turnbull (1999)	Australian/ New Zealand and International Organization for Standardization (2009a, pp. 10–11)	Public Safety Canada (2013, p. 56)	International Risk Governance Council (2008, pp. 12–13)	PRINCE2 (U.K. Office of Government Commerce, 2009)	U.K. Treasury and MOD (2011c, pp. 6–7)	Newsome (2013)
					additional benefit, i.e. identifying [a] resource that can be used elsewhere to benefit the organization."	
Transfer (negative risks), including by insurance or out sourcing.	Share: "form of risk treatment involving the agreed distribution of risk with other parties."	"Sharing the risk with another party"	Transfer	Transfer (negative risks) or share (negative and positive risks).	Transfer (negative risks): "It may, in certain circumstances, be appropriate to transfer risks. Risks may be transferred in order to reduce the risk exposure to the organisation, or because another organisation is more capable of managing the risk."	Transfer (negative and positive risks), including by insurance; tort; charity; guarantor; partner; or contractor.
Treat (negative risks)	Change the likelihood (both negative and positive risks). Change the consequences, (including: finance the risk: "contingent arrangements for the provision of funds to meet or modify the financial consequences should they occur.")	"Changing the likelihood" "Changing the consequences" "Reducing exposures or vulnerabilities"	Reduce (negative risks)	Reduce (negative risks)	Treat (negative risks): "This is the most likely initial response to risks, and involves taking controlling action—preventative, corrective, directive or detective. There may still be some residual risk after control action has been taken, which may require further use of Treat or Tolerate strategies."	Treat (negative risks), including controlling the returns (by preparedness, mitigation, resilience, continuity, or recovery); controlling the likelihood.
-	-	-		-	-	Thin (negative risks), by diversifying the risks or distributing the exposure.

variations of each other. Some offerings are very narrow. Most surprising, no authority admits *diversification*, a routine strategy in many domains, especially finance. Similarly, no authority explicitly admits the possibility of *turning* a risk from negative to positive.

Semantic analysts have identified in general use a class of verbs (such as *avoid, reduce, minimize,* and *eliminate*) representing human attempts to change risk. They identified another class of verbs (such as *incur, entail, offer,* and *involve*) representing the object's situational or voluntary relationship with the risk. A final class of verbs (such as *assume, face, shoulder,* and *bear*) represents a victim's relationship with the risk (Fillmore & Atkins, 1992, pp. 86–87). These words suggest a minimum of three strategies: treat—which sometimes extends to terminate, take, and tolerate.

Combining these observations, I offer six "Ts" (tolerate, treat—which sometimes extends to terminate, turn, take, transfer, and thin the risk), rationalizing the competing prescriptions, with a more practical taxonomy and due emphasis on strategies that are usually conflated or forgotten. The sections below explain these six strategies.

Tolerate

The strategy of toleration might be known elsewhere as one of *assumption* or *acceptance*, but these terms are often confused with *taking* the risk, which implies pursuit of a positive risk (see below).

Tolerating the risk would eschew any control on the risk (although this should not imply forgetting about the risk). We could choose to tolerate the risk, even if it were higher than our threshold for intolerability, if we were to decide that the benefit of controlling the risk would not be justified by the cost of controlling the risk.

Tolerating the risk means eschewing any additional control but is not the same as eschewing any management of the risk. Tolerating the risk should imply either watching or retaining the risk, either of which might be treated elsewhere as a separate strategy but is properly treated as an option within the strategy of tolerating the risk, as described in subsections below.

Watch

While we tolerate a risk, we should watch the risk in case the risk changes. Such a watch implies, in practice, periodic reassessment of the risk level. If the risk were to fall, we would feel more justified in tolerating the risk. If the risk were to rise, we should consider a new strategy (probably *treat* the risk).

Retain

A strategy of "retaining the risk" implies that the owner of the risk is holding or building reserves against the potential negative returns. For instance, if we feared a poor harvest and could not find or afford an insurer or donor who would promise to supply any shortfall in our supply of food, we should build reserves of food. Similarly, if we invest in a new commercial venture but decide that insurance against financial failure would be too costly, we should hold or build financial reserves that could pay for the costs of failure. Retaining the risk is the main alternative to *transferring* the risk to some outside actor (such as an insurer or partner).

Treat (and Sometimes Terminate)

If we were to decide that we could not tolerate a risk, we should treat the risk. Treating the risk means the application of some control to a risk in order to reduce the risk, ideally to a tolerable level, possibly until we terminate the risk. A strategy of termination includes *prevention* of things like the threat's intent or capabilities or our exposure to threats (see below). Prevention might be defined elsewhere as treating the risk (see, for instance, Heerkens, 2002, p. 150), but prevention implies termination of the risk.

Opportunities to terminate the risk are often forgotten in the haste to prevent the risk growing. Termination is attractive because we could eliminate the risk entirely. This outcome would comply with the adage "prevention is better than cure" and with the commercial manager's desire for the most efficient strategy, but not if the burden of treatment becomes prohibitive. The burden may persuade us to accept a technically intolerable residual risk, but one as low as reasonably practical (ALARP).

As described in the four subsections below, treating or terminating the risk can be achieved in four main ways: reducing our exposure to the source; reducing the source's threatening intent; reducing the source's threatening capabilities; or reducing the potential negative effects of an event. For instance, we could park our car outside of the area where car thieves operate (reducing exposure), equip the car with an alarm that discourages attempts to break into the car (controlling the threat's intent), acquire windows that resist break-ins (controlling the threat's capabilities), or use our least valuable car (controlling the negative effects).

Pedagogy Box 10.5 Official Definitions of Prevention

The UN Office for International Strategy for Disaster Reduction (ISDR) (2009) defined *prevention* in only this sense (as "the outright avoidance of adverse impacts of hazards and related disasters") (p. 9). Similarly, the UN Department of Humanitarian Affairs (DHA) (1992) defined prevention as "encompassing activities designed to provide permanent protection from disasters. It includes engineering and other physical protective measures, and also legislative measures controlling land use and urban planning."

U.S. Department of Homeland Security (DHS) (2009) defines prevention as "actions taken and measures put in place for the continual assessment and readiness of necessary actions to reduce the risk of threats and vulnerabilities, to intervene and stop an occurrence, or to mitigate effects" (p. 110).

The Canadian government defines prevention as "actions taken to eliminate the impact of disasters in order to protect lives, property, and the environment, and to avoid economic disruption." A *preventive control* is "a plan or process that enabled an organization to avert the occurrence or mitigate the impact of a disruption, crisis, or emergency" (Public Safety Canada, 2012, p. 73).

Reduce Exposure

Reducing our exposure to the sources of risk would reduce their opportunities to harm us. Reducing exposure involves any of four sub-strategies: deferring our exposure to the sources; avoiding exposure; withdrawing from exposure; or containing the hazard.

Defer

We could choose to defer our acceptance of the risk. The word *defer* implies that we are not currently exposed to the risk but that we reserve the option to undertake the risk at a later point. For instance, we could decide that an investment is too negatively risky this year, so we could defer a review of the decision to next year in case the risk might have changed to a state that is worth pursuing.

Avoid

The word *avoid* implies that we want to do something without exposing ourselves to a negative risk. For instance, we could decide that we should intervene in a lawless area in order to terminate the threats at their geographical source—this is a strategy of termination. An alternative strategy is to intervene in the area whenever the threats are not present, perhaps in order to build local capacity or provide humanitarian aid—this strategy is one of avoidance.

Pedagogy Box 10.6 Canadian Definition of Risk Avoidance

The Canadian government defines *risk avoidance* as "an informed decision to avert or to withdraw from an activity in order not to be exposed to a particular risk" (Public Safety Canada, 2012, p. 82).

Withdraw

A strategy of withdrawing from the risk implies that we are currently exposed to the risk, but we choose to stop our exposure to the risk. For instance, we could be operating in some city where the chance of political violence rises to an intolerable level, at which point one of our choices is to move somewhere else.

Contain

Containing the hazard could be achieved by preventing the hazard from reaching us, or preventing ourselves from coinciding with the hazard. For instance, if a flood were to reach us it would be a threat, but if we could construct some diversion or barrier the flood would not reach us. Similarly, a river that routinely floods a narrow valley could be dammed. Similarly, a criminal could be detained.

Sometimes, containment temporarily contains a hazard until it returns to its threatening state. Worse, containment could strengthen the hazard. For instance, detention of criminals is criticized for bringing criminals together where they can further radicalize and prepare each other for further crime, without providing opportunities for renunciation of crime or the take up of lawful employment. Indeed, more criminals return to crime after detention (this return is known as *recidivism*) than return to lawfulness.

Sometimes, an attempt to contain a hazard might reduce the frequency of minor events but not all events. For instance, a dam would terminate minor floods, but if flood waters could overflow the dam then we would have less frequent but more catastrophic floods.

Some strategies of containment have costs that are underassessed by the author of the strategy: often the domain, such as flood prevention, in which the risk manager is working, is imperfectly competitive with the domain, such as natural biodiversity, that suffers the costs of the measures. For instance, from the environmentalist's perspective, damming a valley is likely to damage its natural environment in ways that are not justified by the decreased chance of flooding in the town.

Reduce Intent

Since a threat necessarily must have intent and capability to harm us, we could keep a hazard in its hazardous state or return a threat to it hazardous state by terminating the source's threatening intent.

The three main substrategies are reduce the causes of the activation of such intent; deter intent; and reform intent.

Reduce the Causes of Activation

The causes of the threat include the activation of the hazard into a threat. Prevention of the causes would prevent the threat from arising from the hazard.

Prevention is particularly appropriate in domains such as preventable diseases: helping people to give up behaviors such as smoking is far cheaper than treating smokers for lung cancer; vaccinating against a pathogen is ultimately cheaper than treating the diseases caused by the pathogen. Similarly, prevention of climate change would be more effective and efficient (1% to 2% of global GDP until 2050) than treating the effects (5% to 10% of global GDP until 2050) (Swiss Re, 2013, p. 13). Similarly, preventing human hazards from acquiring the intent or capabilities to behave as terrorists is more efficient than defending every potential target from every potential threat.

Prevention is attractive in international relations, too, where the negative returns can be enormous. For instance, the British government has long advocated for more international cooperation in the assessment and control of potential conflicts.

> More effective international responses to reduce risks of instability—and thereby prevent crises—are possible. Prevention is much more humane and far less costly than crisis response . . . The underlying causes of conflict need to be tackled . . . In many cases, the suppression of violent crises has not addressed the dynamics of tension or political conflict, and thus has not reduced the risks of future armed conflict. (U.K. Prime Minister's Strategy Unit, 2005, pp. 4, 22)

However, proactive control of some causes of activation may activate other threats. The British government's high-minded advocacy in 2005 for more international cooperation in the assessment and control of international risks looked hypocritical after the largely bilateral U.S.-British invasion of Iraq in 2003, which stimulated an insurgency there and vengeful terrorism at home, such as when four British Muslims killed themselves and 52 others in suicide bombings on public transport in London, July 7, 2005, having recorded messages that blamed British foreign policy.

Pedagogy Box 10.7 Reducing the Causes and Sources of Disease

"Most scientific and health resources go toward treatment. However, understanding the risks to health is key to preventing disease and injuries. A particular disease or injury is often caused by more than one risk factor, which means that multiple interventions are available to target each of these risks. For example, the infectious agent Mycobacterium tuberculosis is the direct cause of tuberculosis; however, crowded housing and poor nutrition also increase the risk, which presents multiple paths for preventing the disease. In turn, most risk factors are associated with more than one disease, and targeting those factors can reduce multiple causes of disease. For example, reducing smoking will result in fewer deaths and less disease from lung cancer, heart disease, stroke, chronic respiratory disease, and other conditions. By quantifying the impact of risk factors on diseases, evidence-based choices can be made about the most effective interventions to improve global health" (World Health Organization, 2009, p. 1).

Deter

Deterring the threat means dissuading the hazard from becoming a threat. For instance, most national efforts to build military capacity are explicitly or effectively justified as deterrent of potential aggressors. So long as potential aggressors are deterred, they remain in a hazardous state and do not reach a threatening state.

Deterring the threats would reduce the frequency of negative events. For instance, at physical sites, security managers often seek to draw attention to their alarms, cameras, and guards in order to increase the chances that the potential threat would observe these measures and be deterred. However, encouraging observation of our defensive measures could help the potential threat to discover vulnerabilities, such as fake alarms, misdirected cameras, and inattentive guards. For the purpose of deterrence, ideally, defensive vigilance and preparedness should be observable without being counter-able.

We could seek to detain or kill or otherwise punish people for having the intent to harm. This action may reduce the threat's capabilities directly and deter others from becoming similar threats, although sometimes punishment (particularly in counter-terrorism) becomes vengeful rather than purposefully deterrent.

Pedagogy Box 10.8 Another Definition of Deterrence

The Humanitarian Practice Network (2010, pp. xvi, 55) recognizes a "deterrence approach" as a "security strategy" or "an approach to security that attempts to deter a threat by posing a counter-threat, in its most extreme form through the use of armed protection."

Reform

We could also seek to reform or turn around someone's harmful intent. Postdetention programs, such as supervision by parole officers and suspended sentences, seek to reduce recidivism mainly by containment and deterrence, but some programs include mandatory participation in seminars and suchlike that aim to reform the former prisoner's intent. Much counter-terrorism since the 2000s is focused on persuading people that terrorism is morally wrong, to renounce terrorism, and to speak out against terrorism.

Reduce Capabilities

Reducing threatening capability involves controlling the hazard's acquisition of capability or reducing the threat's acquired capabilities.

Counter the Acquisition of Capabilities

Preventing the potential aggressor from acquiring the capabilities to threaten us is the objective behind the many strategies called "counter-proliferation," which aim to reduce the supply of arms to hazardous actors (such as unfriendly states, insurgents, and terrorists). Countering acquisition is easy to confuse with containing the hazard but is not the same strategy. For instance, while seeking confirmation as U.S. Secretary of State, Senator John Kerry told the Senate's Foreign Relations Committee (January 24, 2013) about current U.S. strategy toward Iranian nuclear weaponization: "We will do what we must do to prevent Iran from obtaining a nuclear weapon, and I repeat here today, our policy is not containment [of a threat]. It is prevention [of acquisition], and the clock is ticking on our efforts to secure responsible compliance."

Given that a group's capabilities include personnel, this strategy could focus on countering the group's recruitment.

Reduce Acquired Capabilities

Once the threat has acquired threatening capabilities, we could aim to reduce those capabilities by removing, damaging, or destroying them. For instance, law enforcement involves confiscating weapons, war involves attacks on enemy arms and the supply chain, and health care includes destruction of pathogens, toxins, and other sources of health risks.

Sometimes personnel are targeted in order to reduce threatening capabilities. Counter-terrorism sometimes includes campaigns to persuade people to separate from terrorist groups. An alternative is to kill them. A terrorist who has already attacked and is not dissuadable or detainable is more justifiably killed. However, prevention of terrorism has too often involved extra-judicial killing of terrorist hazards, rather than containing, deterring, or reforming the sources, and has often generated new grievances. In fact, terrorist groups, particularly religious terrorist groups, are more cohesive and motivated after lethal attacks on them, even if their capabilities are degraded (Post, 1987). If we were to fail to kill the leader of a group that is still in a hazardous state (it had not chosen to threaten us), we would provide the leader with justifiable intent to retaliate against us. Even if the leader had chosen to be a threat already, killing the target erodes the rule of law and encourages similar actions against our own leaders.

Controlling Negative Effects

We could control or reduce the negative effects that would arise from a potential event. Termination of the risk would be achieved if we went so far as to prevent any negative effects from the threat's capabilities. For instance, imagine that a criminal leader has chosen to threaten us and orders the criminal gang to take up small arms against us. If we were to acquire for all our assets a material armor that is perfectly proof against small arms (and we were to ban all unarmored activities), our operations would become invulnerable to small arms. As long as the criminal gang does not acquire weapons that threaten our armor, and the armor works perfectly, we would have prevented all risks associated with that gang. In theory, the gang could innovate a threat to our defenses, a reminder that we should watch risks for change.

Controlling the negative effects is a strategy that could be known by many other words that are more precise, such as *defense, deterrence, protection*, and *preparedness*. Defense, as the capacity to defeat the attack, is focused on reducing the likelihood of a successful attack, as is deterrence. Some defensive measures, like most forms of preparedness, are focused on reducing the negative returns of an attack. For instance, guards could be employed to prevent human threats from attacking more vulnerable or valuable things, such as interior personnel and assets, and to deter any attacks in the first place—in either case, their effect is to reduce the likelihood of a successful attack. Other acquisitions, such as the armor worn on the bodies of the guards, are acquired more to reduce the negative effects of any attack than to reduce the likelihood of an attack.

The strategy of controlling the negative effects is known by (unfortunately) nine other terms that are highly synonymous but rarely admit their common objective or the existence of other synonyms, and are often poorly defined: protecting the targets, preparing to defend or protect against the threat, planning for contingencies, mitigating the negative returns, managing consequences, building resilience against disruption, responding to the event, continuing operations despite the event, or recovering from the event.

Protection

For the U.S. DHS (2009), *protection* is the "actions or measures taken to cover or shield from exposure, injury, or destruction. In the context of the NIPP [National Infrastructure Protection Plan], protection includes actions to deter the threat, mitigate the vulnerabilities, or minimize the consequences associated with a terrorist attack or other incident" (p. 110).

For the British Civil Contingencies Secretariat, *civil protection* is "organization and measures, under governmental or other authority, aimed at preventing, abating or otherwise countering the effects of emergencies for the protection of the civilian population and property" (U.K. Cabinet Office, 2013).

For the Humanitarian Practice Network (2010, pp. xviii, 55, 71) the *protection approach* is "a security strategy" or "approach to security" that "emphasizes the use of protective devices and procedures to reduce vulnerability to existing threats, but does not affect the level of threat." It later added that reducing vulnerability under this approach can be done "in two ways, either by hardening the target or by increasing or reducing its visibility," but the latter reduces the likelihood not the returns.

Preparedness

For the UN, *preparedness* is the "activities designed to minimize loss of life and damage, to organize the temporary removal of people and property from a threatened location and facilitate timely and effective rescue, relief and rehabilitation" (UN DHA, 1992) or "the knowledge and capacities developed by governments, professional response and recovery organizations, communities, and individuals to effectively anticipate, respond to, and recover from, the impacts of likely, imminent, or current hazard events or conditions" (UN ISDR, 2009, p. 9).

For U.S. Federal Emergency Management Agency (FEMA) (1992) preparedness is "those activities, programs, and systems that exist prior to an emergency that are used to support and enhance response to an emergency or disaster." For U.S. DHS (2009), preparedness is the

> activities necessary to build, sustain, and improve readiness capabilities to prevent, protect against, respond to, and recover from natural or manmade incidents. Preparedness is a continuous process involving efforts at all levels of government and between government and the private sector and nongovernmental organizations to identify threats, determine vulnerabilities, and identify required resources to prevent, respond to, and recover from major incidents. (p. 110)

For the British Civil Contingencies Secretariat, preparedness is the "process of preparing to deal with known risks and unforeseen events or situations that have the potential to result in an emergency" (U.K. Cabinet Office, 2013).

Contingency and Scenario Planning

The term *contingency planning* literally means planning to meet different contingencies (future issues), although it is sometimes used to mean preparedness (for instance, Heerkens, 2002, p. 150).

For the UN, contingency planning is "a management tool used to ensure that adequate arrangements are made in anticipation of a crisis" (UN Office for the Coordination of Humanitarian Affairs [OCHA], 2003) or "a management process that analyses specific potential events or emerging situations that might threaten society or the environment and establishes arrangements in advance to enable timely, effective, and appropriate responses to such events and situations" (UN ISDR, 2009, p. 3). For the Humanitarian Practice Network (2010, p. xv) contingency planning is "a management tool used to ensure adequate preparation for a variety of potential emergency situations," while *scenario planning* is "forward planning about how a situation may evolve in the future, and how threats might develop [and] reviewing the assumptions in plans and thinking about what to do if they do not hold."

For Public Safety Canada (2012) a *contingency plan* is "a plan developed for a specific event or incident" (p. 17).

For the British Civil Contingencies Secretariat, a contingency is the "possible future emergency or risk that must be prepared for," a contingency plan is a "plan prepared by a particular authority specifying the response to a potential incident within its area of jurisdiction," and a civil contingency planning is "civil protection provisions made for the preparation and planning of a response to and recovery from emergencies" (U.K. Cabinet Office, 2013). For the MOD (2009b) a contingency plan is "a plan which is developed for possible operations where the planning factors have identified or can be assumed. This plan is produced in as much detail as possible, including the resources needed and deployment options, as a basis for subsequent planning" (p. 234).

Mitigation

For the UN, *mitigation* is the "measures taken in advance of a disaster aimed at decreasing or eliminating its impact on society and environment" (UN DHA, 1992) or "the lessening or limitation of the adverse impacts of hazards and related disasters" (UN ISDR, 2009, p. 8).

For the U.S. government, mitigation is "any action taken to eliminate or reduce the long-term risk to human life and property from hazards" (U.S. FEMA, 1999), "ongoing and sustained action to reduce the probability of or lessen the impact of an adverse incident" (U.S. DHS, 2009, p. 110), or "the capabilities necessary to reduce loss of life and property by lessening the impact of disasters" (U.S. DHS, 2011).

For Public Safety Canada (2012), it is the "actions taken to reduce the impact of disasters in order to protect lives, property, and the environment, and to reduce economic disruption" (p. 63).

"Mitigation . . . aims at reducing the negative effects of a problem" (Heerkens, 2002, p. 150).

Consequence Management

Consequence management sounds much like mitigation. The Canadian government defines *consequence management* as "the coordination and implementation of measures and activities undertaken to alleviate the damage, loss, hardship, and suffering caused by an emergency. Note [that] consequence management also includes measures to restore essential government services, protect public health, and provide emergency relief to affected governments, businesses, and populations" (Public Safety Canada, 2012, p. 17). The British Civil Contingencies Secretariat defines consequence management as the "measures taken to protect public health and safety, restore essential services, and provide emergency relief to governments, businesses, and individuals affected by the impacts of an emergency" (U.K. Cabinet Office, 2013).

Resilience

Resilience is "the ability of a system, community, or society exposed to hazards to resist, absorb, accommodate to and recover from the effects of a hazard in a timely and efficient manner, including through the preservation and restoration of its essential basic structures and functions. Comment: Resilience means the ability to 'resile from' or 'spring back from' a shock" (UN ISDR, 2009, p. 10).

Resilience is the "adaptive capacity of an organization in a complex and changing environment" (International Organization for Standardization, 2009a, p. 11).

The U.S. DHS (2009) defined resilience as "the ability to resist, absorb, recover from, or successfully adapt to adversity or a change in conditions" (p. 111).

In Britain, "resilience reflects how flexibly this capacity can be deployed in response to new or increased risks or opportunities" (U.K. Prime Minister's Strategy Unit, 2005, p. 38), the "ability of the community, services, area, or infrastructure to detect, prevent, and, if necessary, to withstand, handled and recover from disruptive challenges" (U.K. Cabinet Office, 2013), or is the "ability of an organization to resist being affected by an incident" (U.K. MOD, 2011c, p. Glossary-3). *Community resilience* is "communities and individuals harnessing local resources and expertise to help themselves in an emergency, in a way that complements the response of the emergency services" (U.K. Cabinet Office, 2013).

In Canada, resilience is "the capacity of a system, community, or society to adapt to disruptions resulting from hazards by persevering, recuperating, or changing to reach and maintain an acceptable level of functioning" (Public Safety Canada, 2012, p. 80).

Recently, the World Economic Forum asserted the greater importance of "national resilience" to "global risks."

> In the wake of unprecedented disasters in recent years, "resilience" has become a popular buzzword across a wide range of disciplines, with each discipline attributing its own working definition to the term. A definition that has long been used in engineering is that resilience is the capacity for "bouncing back faster after stress, enduring greater stresses, and being disturbed less by a given amount of stress". This definition is commonly applied to objects, such as bridges or skyscrapers. However, most global risks are systemic in nature, and a system—unlike an object—may show resilience not by returning exactly to its previous state, but instead by finding different ways to carry out essential functions; that is, by adapting. For a system, an additional definition of resilience is "maintaining system function in the event of disturbance". The working definition of a resilient country for this report is, therefore, one that has the capability to 1) adapt to changing contexts, 2) withstand sudden shocks and 3) recover to a desired equilibrium, either the previous one or a new one, while preserving the continuity of its operations. The three elements in this definition encompass both recoverability (the capacity for speedy recovery after a crisis) and adaptability (timely adaptation in response to a changing environment). (World Economic Forum, 2013, p. 37)

The World Economic Forum chose to break down resilience into three characteristics (robustness, redundancy, resourcefulness) and two measures of performance (response, recovery).

a. "Robustness incorporates the concept of reliability and refers to the ability to absorb and withstand disturbances and crises. The assumptions underlying this component of resilience are that: 1) if fail-safes and firewalls are designed into a nation's critical networks, and 2) if that nation's decision-making chains of command become more modular in response to changing circumstances, then potential damage to one part of a country is less likely to spread far and wide."

b. "Redundancy involves having excess capacity and back-up systems, which enable the maintenance of core functionality in the event of disturbances. This component assumes that a country will be less likely to experience a collapse in the wake of stresses or failures of some of its infrastructure, if the design of that country's critical infrastructure and institutions incorporates a diversity of overlapping methods, policies, strategies or services to accomplish objects and fulfill purposes."

c. "Resourcefulness means the ability to adapt to crises, respond flexibly and—when possible—transform a negative impact into a positive. For a system to be adaptive means that it has inherent flexibility, which is crucial to enabling the ability to influence of resilience. The assumption underlying this component of resilience is that if industries and communities can build trust within their networks and are able to self-organize, then they are more likely to spontaneously react and discover solutions to resolve unanticipated challenges when larger country-level institutions and governance systems are challenged or fail."

d. "Response means the ability to mobilize quickly in the face of crises. This component of resilience assesses whether a nation has good methods for gathering relevant information from all parts of society and communicating the relevant data and information to others, as well as the ability for decision-makers to recognize emerging issues quickly."

e. "Recovery means the ability to regain a degree of normality after a crisis or event, including the ability of a system to be flexible and adaptable and to evolve to deal with the new or changed circumstances after the manifestation of a risk. This component of resilience assesses the nation's capacities and strategies for feeding information into public policies and business strategies, and the ability for decision-makers to take action to adapt to changing circumstances." (pp. 38–39)

The World Economic Forum chose to assess national resilience to global risks as a system of five "core subsystems" (economic, environmental, governance, infrastructure, and social) and thus advocated assessing the resilience of each of the five subsystems by each of the five components of resilience.

Separately, survey respondents suggested that national resilience has seven characteristics or attributes: politicians' ability to govern; healthy business-government relations; efficient implementation of reforms; public trust of politicians; low wastefulness of government spending; measures to control corruption; and government services for improved business performance.

Response

The World Economic Forum places recovery as a part of resilience, but U.S. emergency management always has separated response as a "phase" of emergency management before recovery.

> [Response is the] activities that address the short-term, direct effects of an incident, including immediate actions to save lives, protect property, and meet basic human needs. Response also includes the execution of emergency operations plans and incident mitigation activities

> designed to limit the loss of life, personal injury, property damage, and other unfavorable outcomes. As indicated by the situation, response activities include applying intelligence and other information to lessen the effects or consequences of an incident; increasing security operations; continuing investigations into the nature and source of the threat; ongoing surveillance and testing processes; immunizations, isolation, or quarantine; and specific law enforcement operations aimed at preempting, interdicting, or disrupting illegal activity, and apprehending actual perpetrators and bringing them to justice. (U.S. DHS, 2009, p. 111)

Continuity

The management of emergency, consequence, or continuity essentially means the same thing as resilience.

The British Civil Contingencies Secretariat defines *continuity* as "the grounding of emergency response and recovery in the existing functions of organisations and familiar ways of working" and defines "business continuity management" as "a management process that helps manage risks to the smooth running of an organization or delivery of a service, ensuring that it can operate to the extent required in the event of a disruption" (U.K. Cabinet Office, 2013). Public Safety Canada (2012) defines *business continuity management* as "an integrated management process involving the development and implementation of activities that provides for the continuity and/or recovery of critical service delivery and business operations in the event of a disruption" (pp. 7–8).

Recovery

Continuity might overlap *recovery*—although recovery might imply outside aid, such as by the UN, which would mean that the risk had been transferred. The UNHCR defined recovery as a focus on how best to restore the capacity of the government and communities to rebuild and recover from crisis and to prevent relapses into conflict. "The UN ISDR (2009) defined recovery as "the restoration, and improvement where appropriate, of facilities, livelihoods and living conditions of disaster-affected communities, including efforts to reduce disaster risk factors" (p. 9).

The U.S. DHS (2009) defined recovery as

> the development, coordination, and execution of service- and site-restoration plans for affected communities and the reconstitution of government operations and services through individual, private sector, nongovernmental, and public assistance programs that identify needs and define resources; provide housing and promote restoration; address long-term care and treatment of affected persons; implement additional measures for community restoration; incorporate mitigation measures and techniques, as feasible; evaluate the incident to identify lessons learned; and develop initiatives to mitigate the effects of future incidents. (p. 111)

The Canadian government defined recovery as "actions taken to repair or restore conditions to an acceptable level after a disaster" and noted that recovery includes "the return of evacuees, trauma counseling, reconstruction, economic impact studies, and financial assistance." It also referred to response —"actions taken during or immediately after a disaster to manage its consequences and minimize suffering and loss" —noted examples— "emergency public communication, search and rescue, emergency medical assistance, evacuation, etc." (Public Safety Canada, 2012, pp. 78, 81).

For the British Civil Contingencies Secretariat, recovery is the "process of rebuilding, restoring, and rehabilitating the community following an emergency." Linked to recovery, is *remediation*: "restoration of a built or natural environment that has been destroyed, damaged, or rendered hazardous as the result of an emergency or disasters" (U.K. Cabinet Office, 2013).

Turn

We could effectively terminate the risk by turning the source or cause in our favor. For instance, rather than kill the leader of the criminal gang, we could ally with it against another threat or offer a cooperative return to lawful activities.

The strategy of turning the risk offers more than either terminating or taking the opportunity because it turns a negative into a positive risk.

We would never want to turn a positive risk into a negative risk, but we could do so unintentionally, for instance, by upsetting an ally until the ally turns against us. Moreover, a strategy of turning a negative into a positive risk could fail and could introduce new risks from the same source. At worst, an alliance could expose us to a temporary ally that ends up a threat. For instance, from 2007, the U.S.-led coalition in Iraq chose to pay rents and to arm various militia or insurgent groups in return for their commitment to stop attacks on coalition targets; some of these groups helped to combat others who remained outside of the coalition, but some eventually turned their new arms on the coalition. The continuing lawlessness and multiple duplicities in Iraq were permissive of such chaos. At worst, an alliance could expose us to a threat that is only pretending to be an ally.

A strategy of turning threats into allies can be tricky too because of reactions from third parties. For instance, many victims of the criminals would feel justifiably aggrieved if you offered cooperation with the criminals without justice for the victims. Some other criminals could feel that their further crimes would be rewarded by cooperation or feel aggrieved that you chose not to cooperate with them.

Take

Taking a risk is a deliberate choice to pursue a positive risk, even if negative risks are taken too. The strategy of taking risk is known elsewhere as a strategy of pursuing, enhancing, or exploiting positive risks. (The British Treasury, and thence most of British government, has called the strategy "taking the opportunity," but I have found that users conflate its intended meaning with any strategic response to risk, as in "taking the opportunity" to do anything but nothing.)

Taking risk could include accepting some potential negative returns, so long as we are simultaneously pursuing positive risk. For instance, any speculative risk includes the chance of gaining less than we expected or even a loss. Taking a risk does not need to mean avoidance of potentially negative returns, just to mean pursuit of potential positive returns.

Taking the risk would seem obvious if we estimate a large chance of positive outcomes and no chance of negative outcomes. Nevertheless, many people take speculative risks despite a much higher chance of loss than of gains. In fact, against a competent bookmaker, most bets have negative expected returns, but plenty of people make such bets in pursuit of an unlikely big win.

Even if the chance of positive outcomes is higher than of negative outcomes, we should still not take the risk if the cost of taking the risk outweighs the potential positive returns or at least the expected return (see Chapter 3). Taking the risk may necessitate investments or expenditures of resources. For instance, many business ventures involve hefty investment in the hope of future profits or returns on investment. Sometimes investors must take highly subjective decisions about whether the potential positive returns outweigh the potential loss of the exposed investment.

Finally, taking the risk may involve unobserved risks. For instance, we could agree to make a hefty investment after having estimated that positive returns are highly likely, yet that investment might leave us without reserves against unrelated negative risks, such as potential collapse in our health or income while awaiting the returns on our investment.

Transfer

Transferring the risk means that we transfer some of the risk to another actor. We could pay an insurer for a commitment to cover any negative returns, hope to sue the liable party through the tort system, rely on charity to cover our losses, rely on some guarantor to compensate us, share the risk with business partners, or share risks with contractors.

The most likely alternative to transferring the risk is to retain the risk—relying on our internal resources to cover negative returns. Retaining the risk is a form of tolerating the risk, whereas transferring the risk implies that we cannot tolerate the risk. Retaining the risk makes better sense if we were to believe that the other actor could not or would not cover our negative returns.

The sub-sections below discuss the six main vectors for transferred risk: insurers; tort systems; charities; guarantors; partners; and contractors.

Pedagogy Box 10.9 UN Definition of Risk Transfer

The UN ISDR (2009) defines *risk transfer* as "the process of formally or informally shifting the financial consequences of particular risks from one party to another whereby a household, community, enterprise, or state authority will obtain resources from the other party after a disaster occurs, in exchange for ongoing or compensatory social or financial benefits provided to that other party" (p. 11).

Insurers

Insurers accept a premium (usually a financial price per period of coverage) in return for accepting some responsibility for a risk (usually a promise to pay monies toward the financial costs that you would suffer due to agreed events).

Insurers cover some risks at standard rates—these standard risks are easier for the insurer to assess, such as potential harm from road traffic accidents, home fires, and work-related injuries. Traditionally, most potential insurees were forced to retain risks associated with war, terrorism, natural disasters, and other risks that insurers liked to write up as "acts of god," either because insurers refused to insure against such risks, given their greater uncertainty, or because few consumers could afford the premiums (or because consumers were less trusting of the insurer who would insure against such risks). In recent decades, particularly since the terrorist attacks of 9/11 (September 11, 2001), governments have guaranteed insurers against higher losses associated with these risks, promised to cover the losses directly, or legislatively forced insurers not to exclude such risks. These official actions have encouraged insurers and insurees and discouraged retention of risk. Consequently, take-up of political risk and terrorism insurance has jumped 25%–50% since 9/11.

However, at the same time, legal disputes between insurer and insuree over huge losses have discouraged potential insurees in certain domains. Insurers sometimes disagree with the insured party about whether the insured is covered against a certain negative return. For instance, the insurers of the twin towers in Manhattan that collapsed on September 11, 2001, tried to claim that the source was domestic terrorism (because the terrorists, although foreign by citizenship and sponsorship, were passengers and hijackers of planes that had taken off from American airports), which was not covered, rather than international terrorism, which was covered.

Sometimes insurers find that incoming claims run ahead of their reserves or their reinsurers' reserves, so in theory the insuree could be left retaining all the risk even after paying for insurance, although governments can choose to guarantee insurers.

Tort System

The tort system is the legal system that allows parties to bring claims of wrongdoing, harm, or injustice against another party.

The tort system is an uncertain instrument and a negative risk given that a court could disagree with the claimant's case against a liable party, leaving the claimant with legal costs or an order to pay the other party's legal costs. The tort system is useless to us if the court is biased against us, the liable party has insufficient reserves or assets to cover our losses, or the liable party is able to evade a court's judgment.

The effectiveness of the tort system varies by time and space. For instance, the United States has a strong tort system and highly accountable public services, where service providers and suppliers complain that their liabilities make business difficult, whereas Britain has a weak tort system and poorly accountable public services, where consumers complain that service providers and suppliers are too willing to make promises for which they are practically not liable (except in terms of lost customers).

Charities

Charities accept risks that otherwise would not be covered by those exposed, perhaps because they are too poor in material terms or too poorly represented. Charities often appear in response to crisis. For instance, some persons chose to manage donations of money in response to Storm Sandy in the northeastern United States in October 2012, and others chose to volunteer their labor. Most international aid is essentially charitable, although some quid pro quo, such as preferential trade, might be implied.

Charities are the least certain of the actors to which we could transfer our risks, since they themselves usually rely on voluntary donations and their reserves tend to be unpredictable and particular in form. Unlike insurers with whom we contract, charities are under no obligations, so they can choose not to cover our losses.

Guarantors

Guarantors promise to cover our negative returns. Guarantors could be as simple as a relative who promises to help out if our business fails or as authoritative as a government that promises to pay "benefits"/"entitlements" if we lose our jobs or become too ill to work. Some guarantors effectively preempt the tort system by promising to pay us compensation if some representative causes us injury or injustice. For instance, in order to encourage business, many governments guarantee residents against losses due to riots, terrorism, or other organized violence.

However, guarantors sometimes choose not to honor their commitments. Ultimately few governments are beholden to any independent judicial enforcement of their promises, so any official guarantee is effectively a political risk. For instance, governments often guarantee to compensate businesses against mass lawlessness or political violence in order to encourage business within their jurisdiction, but after widespread riots in Britain in August 2011, the British government was criticized for its incremental interpretation of who was eligible for compensation and how quickly their businesses should be restored, leading eventually to official clarification of its future interpretation.

Partners

We could persuade another party to coinvest or codeploy—effectively sharing the chance of lost investment or mission failure. However, a coinvestor could sue us for false promises or incompetence or some other reason to blame us disproportionately for the losses—effectively using the tort system to transfer the risk back to us. Similarly, political partners can blame each other for shared failures.

Contractors

Contractors who agree to provide us with some service or product effectively share the risk of their nonperformance, such as a failure to deliver a service on time or as specified. Contractual obligations may mean nothing in the event of nonperformance if the contractor does not accept those obligations, refuses to compensate us for nonperformance, is not found liable by the tort system, or does not have the reserves to cover our losses.

Thin the Risk

Thinning the risk is a strategy known usually as diversification. It is a unique strategy that does not terminate, turn, take, transfer, or treat any particular risk but nevertheless reduces our total risk by spreading or thinning our loss exposure across more diverse types of risks, sites, partners, providers, etc. You could take on more types of risk while reducing your total negative risk, although at the same time you may reduce your potential positive returns.

Readers may be most familiar with diversification in financial risk management. The simplest example of nondiversification is a situation where one investor has speculated all his or her resources on one venture. Whatever the likelihood of failure, the investor has exposed all his or her resources to a failure in that venture. Alternatively, the investor could invest all the same resources in two ventures. Even if the likelihood of failure is the same for both ventures, the total risk has fallen, without reducing either the likelihood of an individual failure or total exposure. This is mathematically true because total loss is possible only if both ventures fail rather than one venture fails. If the likelihood of failure is 50%, the likelihood of total loss from investing in one venture is 50%, but the likelihood of total loss from investing in two ventures is 25% (50% multiplied by 50%; the two events are independent or consecutive, so their probabilities are multiplied when we want to know the probability of both events occurring). Our total risk has thinned because our exposure to any one negative event has thinned, not because the likelihood of any event or our total exposure has changed.

Although diversification is applied routinely to financial risks, it can be applied to any risk. For instance, imagine that we are operating in an area where terrorists are plotting to destroy our operations. Instead of operating in a single city with a 20% chance of total loss (\$$x$), we could spread our operations equally over two cities (\$$0.5x$ per city), each with an independent (consecutive) 20% chance of loss within that city. The probability of total loss (\$$x$) would shift from 20% to 4% (20% multiplied by 20%).

However, thinning or diversifying the risks could involve new costs. For instance, operating in two cities might be more expensive than operating in one city (if only because we have foregone the efficiencies of scale or centralization).

Moreover, thinning or diversifying the risks often reduces the chance of the best outcome at the same time as it reduces the chance of the worst outcome. For instance, if we operate in one city, as specified above, the chance of not losing any of $x is 80%, but across two cities, the chance is 64% (80% multiplied by 80%). The way to justify reductions in the likelihoods of both the best and worst outcomes is to realize that the range of returns has narrowed (thus, we face narrower uncertainty over the range of possible outcomes) and the chance of the worst outcome has fallen (this combination of effects fulfills *risk efficiency*—see Chapter 3).

Combining and Balancing Strategies

Ideally, we want the single most efficient strategy. For instance, we would not want to purchase very expensive controls on the negative returns of a potential event if we could freely persuade a hazardous actor not to cause the event.

In practice, we often combine strategies in response to a collection of risks, even in response to one risk, in order to combine the best of different strategies. For instance, we might seek both to terminate a risk while we seek to control its potential negative returns in case termination does not work. The Humanitarian Practice Network (2010) notes that "[i]n practice, a good security strategy needs a flexible combination of approaches" (p. 56).

We should combine strategies that hedge against one another failing. We should also combine strategies when risks lie on four polarized dimensions, as described in the subsections below: negative versus positive risks; pure versus speculative risks; unknown versus known causes and sources; and uncontrollable and controllable causes and sources.

Negative and Positive Risks

The most basic strategic response to risk is to maximize positive risks and minimize negative risks. For this reason, PRINCE2 starts its strategic recommendations with a question about whether the risks are positive or negative (although the authority misleadingly uses the terms *threat* and *opportunity*). British Prime Minister Tony Blair once advocated to government a similar strategy, where risk management is "getting the right balance between innovation and change on the one hand and avoidance of shocks and crises on the other" (Strategy Unit, November 2002, foreword). The IRGC (2008, p. 4) agrees that the "challenge of better risk governance" is "to enable societies to benefit from change while minimizing the negative consequences of the associated risks."

Pure and Speculative Risks

Relatedly, we should minimize pure risks and speculate in the most positive risks. Indeed, some authors have defined risk management as an "activity seeking to eliminate, reduce and generally control pure risks . . . and to enhance the benefits and avoid detriment from speculative risks" (Waring & Glendon, 1998, p. 3).

These strategic approaches to pure and speculative risks can be known by specific terms, such as the following:

- *Strategic risk management*, which "addresses interactions between pure and speculative risks" (Waring & Glendon 1998, p. 14). For instance, your exposure to natural disaster (natural risk) could deter investors (financial risk), or a potential financial crisis (financial risk) suggests potential collapse in outside resourcing of your security.

- *Enterprise risk management*, which "addresses interactions between pure and speculative risks" (Waring & Glendon 1998, p. 14) or is "making use of methods and processes to capitalize on opportunities or avoid hazards to meet institutional goals" (Kennedy & Van Brunschot, 2009, p. 28).
- *Integrated risk management* is "a continuous, proactive and systematic process to understand, manage and communicate risk from an organization-wide perspective and to support strategic decision making that contributes to the achievement of an organization's overall objectives" (Public Safety Canada, 2012, p. 56), or a "multi-agency approach to emergency management entailing six key activities—anticipation, assessment, prevention, preparation, response, and recovery" (U.K. Cabinet Office, 2013).
- *Uncertainty management*: "[M]anaging perceived threats and opportunities and their risk implications but also managing the various sources of uncertainty which give rise to and shape risk, threat and opportunity" (Chapman & Ward, 2002, p. 54), or "the process of integrating risk management and value management approaches" (Smith, 2003, p. 2).
- *Risk efficiency*: "Successful risk management is not just about reducing threats to project performance. A key motive is the identification of opportunities to change base plans and develop contingency plans in the context of a search for risk efficiency, taking an aggressive approach to the level of risk that is appropriate, with a view to long-term corporate performance maximization" (Chapman & Ward, 2002, p. 54).

Unknown and Known Causes and Sources

The IRGC (2008, p. 6, 16–17) recommends categorization of risks by our "knowledge about the cause-effect relationships" (our "knowledge challenge"), where each category would suggest a different response. The IRGC recommends placing a risk in one of four categories: simple, complex, uncertain, or ambiguous.

1. *Simple risks*, such as home fires, where the causes are obvious, "can be managed using a 'routine-based' strategy, such as introducing a law or regulation."
2. *Complex risks* arise from "difficulties in identifying and quantifying causal links between a multitude of potential causal agents and specific observed effects. Examples of highly complex risks include the risks of failures of large interconnected infrastructures and the risks of critical loads to sensitive ecosystems." They "can be addressed on the basis of accessing and acting on the best available scientific expertise, aiming for a 'risk-informed' and 'robustness-focused' strategy. Robustness refers to the degree of reliability of the risk reduction measures to withstand threatening events or processes that have not been fully understood or anticipated."
3. *Uncertain risks* arise from "a lack of clarity or quality of the scientific or technical data. Highly uncertain risks include many natural disasters, acts of terrorism and sabotage, and the long-term effects of introducing genetically-modified species into the natural environment." They "are better managed using 'precaution-based' and 'resilience-focused' strategies, with the intention being to apply a precautionary approach to ensure the reversibility of critical decisions and to increase a systems' coping capacity to the point where it can withstand surprises."

4. *Ambiguous risks* result "from divergent or contested perspectives on the justification, severity, or wider meanings associated with a given threat. Risks subject to high levels of ambiguity include food supplements, hormone treatment of cattle, passive smoking, some aspects of nanotechnology, and synthetic genomics." The "appropriate approach comprises a 'discourse-based' strategy which seeks to create tolerance and mutual understanding of conflicting views and values with a view to eventually reconciling them."

Uncontrollable and Controllable Causes and Sources

Similarly, in search of categories of risk that would be easier to act upon, Robert Kaplan and Anette Mikes (2012) suggested, and the World Economic Forum endorsed (2013, p. 36), the management of risks by the extent to which their sources and causes were controllable. They effectively combined judgments of positive versus negative, pure versus speculative, and internal versus external risks to suggest three categories:

1. *Preventable risks*: "These are internal risks, arising from within the organization, that are controllable and ought to be eliminated or avoided. Examples are the risks from employees' and managers' unauthorized, illegal, unethical, incorrect, or inappropriate actions and the risks from breakdowns in routine operational processes." The correct response is to set rules demanding behaviors that prevent these risks.
2. *Strategy risks*: "Strategy risks are quite different from preventable risks because they are not inherently undesirable. A strategy with high expected returns generally requires the company to take on significant risks, and managing those risks is a key driver in capturing the potential gains." To me, strategy risks sound like speculative risks, so the correct response is to treat the risks in order to minimize the negative and maximize the positive. (Kaplan and Mikes advise us "to reduce the probability that the assumed risks actually materialize and to improve the company's ability to manage or contain the risk events should they occur." Their general point was that rules-based prevention would be too exclusive for strategy risks.)
3. *External risks*: "Some risks arise from events outside the company and are beyond its influence or control. Sources of these risks include natural and political disasters and major macroeconomic shifts." The World Economic Forum (2013, pp. 9, 36) endorsed external risks as "global risks" and characterized "most" of the global risks in its reports as "difficult to predict" with "little knowledge on how to handle such risks." To me, external risks sound like pure risks, to which the correct responses are avoidance or insurance (or some other form of transference). Kaplan and Mikes advise us to "focus on identification (they tend to be obvious in hindsight) and mitigation of their impact." The World Economic Forum advises us to focus on resilience.

SUMMARY

This chapter has

- defined control,
- given advice on establishing tolerable risks,

- explained the trade-off between intolerance and practicality,
- explained why sometimes tolerable risks are controlled,
- explained why some stakeholders could be working together with incompatible levels of toleration and controls,
- defined strategy,
- reviewed and aligned existing prescriptions for strategies,
- explained the six rationalized "T" strategies:
    - tolerate, which includes
        - watching and
        - retaining
    - treat and terminate, which includes
        - reducing exposure, by any of
            - deferring,
            - avoiding,
            - withdrawing, or
            - containing,
        - reducing threatening intent, by any of
            - reducing the causes of activation,
            - deterring threats, or
            - reforming threats,
        - reducing threatening capabilities, by any of
            - countering the acquisition of capabilities or
            - reducing acquired capabilities,
        - controlling the negative effects of any threatening event, which includes many official synonyms, including
            - protection,
            - preparedness,
            - contingency planning,
            - mitigation,
            - consequence management,
            - resilience,
            - response,
            - continuity, and
            - recovery,
    - turn,
    - take,
    - transfer, to any of
        - insurers,
        - the tort system,
        - charities,
        - guarantors,

        - partners, or
        - contractors, and
    - thin (diversify).
- explained how to balance and combine strategies in response to
    - negative and positive risks,
    - pure and speculative risks,
    - unknown and known sources and causes, and
    - uncontrollable and controllable sources and causes.

QUESTIONS AND EXERCISES

1. What is the difference between a control and a strategy in response to risk?
2. What do we call risks before and after controls have been applied to them?
3. What is a compound risk?
4. How could we justify tolerating a risk that has been assessed as intolerable?
5. If someone tells us that they cannot control an intolerable risk, what unjustifiable reasons should we worry about them not admitting?
6. Why might a tolerable risk be controlled?
7. Why might different contributors to an activity work alongside each other with different controls on the same risk?
8. Forecast an operational problem when contributors work alongside each other with different controls on the same risk.
9. Which of the six "T" strategies is illustrated by each of the following examples:
    a. staying out of an insecure area,
    b. exiting a risky area,
    c. offering amnesty to a human threat,
    d. offering an alliance with a human threat,
    e. investing in a new business,
    f. investing in access controls at a port,
    g. agreeing to join a new business venture,
    h. building reserves against potential losses,
    i. planning for emergencies,
    j. moving operations to a country that guarantees compensation if I were to suffer losses to political violence,
    k. accommodating a threat's political grievances against me,
    l. moving operations to a city where I could easier sue the local police if I were to suffer losses to political violence,

m. moving my shipping to a country with a larger charity supporting victims of shipping disasters,
n. moving my shipping to a country that provides publicly financed screening of all shipping containers for threats before they are loaded on my ships,
o. moving my shipping to a country that prevents insurers from excluding terrorism,
p. moving my operations to a country that promises never to tax my earnings,
q. persuading an opposition group to join an alliance,
r. assassinating an opposition group's leader,
s. moving operations to a safer city,
t. splitting my operations between two sites of effectively the same profile,
u. persuading a group that its hostile intent toward me is mistaken.

10. What is the correct strategic response to a tolerable risk?
11. What sorts of sources of a risk are more justifiable terminated?
12. What sorts of objections should we expect when turning a risk?
13. How could we unintentionally turn a positive risk into a negative risk?
14. What sorts of expected returns and range of returns would justify taking a risk?
15. Why might you reasonably disallow taking a risk even if it offers a positive range of returns?
16. What are the six vectors for transferring or sharing risks?
17. With what sorts of actor should we not transfer or share risks, even if they were willing to do so?
18. Name as many as possible of the nine synonyms for strategies or activities that seek to control potential negative returns.
19. How does thinning (diversifying) our risks reduce our total risk without reducing any particular risk?
20. What are the typical disadvantages of thinning the risks?

Recording, Communicating, Assuring, and Auditing

This chapter explains how to record the risks that you have assessed and how you have managed them, how to communicate information on security and risk, how to monitor and review how your stakeholders are managing their security and risk, and how to audit how other others manage their security and risk.

 Recording Risk

This section describes why recording information about risks and risk management is important and often required by higher authorities and how practically you should record such information.

Requirement

A good process for managing risk should include the deliberate maintenance of some record (also known as a *register* or *log*) of your assessments of the risks and how you are managing the risks. Such a record is useful for institutional memory, transparency, accountability, assurance and compliance, and communication.

Pedagogy Box 11.1 Other Requirements for Risk Records

Since 1995, the Australian/New Zealand and ISO (International Organization for Standardization, 2009a, p. 12) standard has prescribed a "risk register."

(Continued)

(Continued)

Following the ISO standard, the Canadian government expects each federal and regional authority principally involved in emergency management to maintain a risk register (Public Safety Canada, 2012, p. 85). In 2011, the Canadian federal government finished a standard risk assessment methodology that specified annual assessments from the departments, which Public Safety Canada would compile as a single risk register (Public Safety Canada, 2013, p. 59).

The British government participated in the development of a standard for managing projects (PRINCE2) that advises users to maintain a *log* of project risks. In 1996, the government released PRINCE2 for general use. The British Ministry of Defense (MOD) subsequently prescribed a *register* of project risks.

In 2004, the British Parliament passed legislation (Civil Contingencies Act) that designated primary authorities during an emergency and ordered them to maintain assessments of risks related to emergencies. National government maintains a National Risk Assessment (the publicly available version is the National Risk Register). In addition, the Cabinet Office Briefing Rooms, where the political executive convenes emergency meetings, includes a Central Situation Cell, which collates information as the Common Recognized Information Picture–a "single, authoritative strategic overview of an emergency or crisis that is developed according to a standard template and is intended for briefing and decision-support purposes" (U.K. Cabinet Office, 2013).

Practical Records

In practice, the record is usually a table or spreadsheet of information related to risk. Today, such information is easily maintained in digital software. Word processing software would be adequate; users generally use simple spreadsheet software; more dedicated risk and security managers might acquire a specialized risk management software; some software is configured for specialized domains, such as financial risks and maritime risks.

The task is relatively simple technically, but can be burdensome, and many standards differ on what information should be recorded. Consequently, many responsible parties fail to complete the task perfectly.

The standards in the public domain differ but generally agree with my basic specifications below:

- Each identified risk should be recorded on a separate register or log or sheet, starting with a unique code for identification and filing.
- The information should include any dates when the risk was identified, the register was opened, the register was modified, and the risk should be reviewed.
- The author of the information as well as the responsible parties ("owners") and those affected ("holders") should be recorded.
- The risk should be described, categorized, and assessed.
- The controls, strategies, and other activities involved in managing the risk should be recorded.

Pedagogy Box 11.2 Other Risk Register Descriptions

Specifications of the register/log can be vague, such as a "record of information about identified risks" (International Organization for Standardization, 2009a, p. 12). The Canadian government has more usefully defined a risk register as "a list of identified risks and related information used to facilitate the monitoring and management of risks." It observed that "the risk register is generally in the form of a table, spreadsheet, or database and may contain the following information: statement or description of the risk, source of the risk, areas of impact, cause of the risk, status of action of sector network, existing controls, risk assessment information, and any other relevant information" (Public Safety Canada, 2012, p. 85).

Private authorities on project risk management have advocated a tabulated description of each risk that could be used as a risk register (see Table 3.2). PRINCE2 prescribed a simple list of information on each risk (see Table 11.1).

Table 11.1 The PRINCE2 Risk Log

Risk identifier [unique code]:
Author:
Date registered:
Description:
Risk category:
Impact:
Probability:
Expected return:
Proximity [in time]:
Response [strategy]:
Countermeasures [controls]:
Owner [of this risk]:
Actionee [implementer of response]:
Date of last update:
Current status [active or closed]:

SOURCE: U.K. Office of Government Commerce, 2009, p. 260.

Communicating Risk

Risk records can be used to communicate the risks to other stakeholders, but they tend to be restricted to the few stakeholders who need or can be trusted with all the information. Consequently, few owners have released complete records publicly, except as required by legislation or regulation. The subsections below describe the requirement for communicating risk and the alternative ways in which you could visually communicate risks.

Requirement

Communication of risk assessments and information about your management of the risks is useful for external confidence and transparency and is a necessary vehicle in compliance with external reviews, monitors, and audits.

Pedagogy Box 11.3 External Requirements for Communicating Risks

Of the standard processes of risk management identified earlier in this book (see Table 8.3) only the Australian/New Zealand and ISO standard, the International Risk Governance Council (IRGC), and two departments of British government specified the communication of risks. The Canadian government generally follows the ISO and defines *risk communication* as "the imparting, receiving, and/or exchanging of clear, credible, and timely information about the existence, nature, form, likelihood, severity, acceptability, treatment, or other aspects of risk to improve decision-making in risk management" (Public Safety Canada, 2012, p. 83).

The Australian/New Zealand and ISO (International Organization for Standardization, 2009a) standards stressed that communication was less a separate step in a sequential process than a continual activity. The IRGC (2008) stated the same:

> Communication is of the utmost importance. It enables stakeholders and civil society to understand the risk itself. It also allows them to recognize their role in the risk governance process and, through being deliberately two-way, gives them a voice in it. Once the risk management decision is made, communication should explain the rationale for the decision and allow people to make informed choices about the risk and its management, including their own responsibilities. Effective communication is the key to creating trust in risk management. (p. 15)

Similarly, the Humanitarian Practice Network (2010, p. 14) prescribed continual communication of security plans:

- A plan is a piece of paper. Paper does not reduce any risks. Plans need to be shared, explained, and implemented.
- A good plan today may no longer be appropriate 6 months from now. If the situation evolves, review the analysis and plans.

- People not familiar with security plans and procedures cannot adhere to them. All staff and visitors need to be briefed as soon as they arrive and after any important changes are made.
- Good implementation depends on competencies. The best possible plan falls apart without the knowledge and skills to implement it. Some aspects of security management require specialized knowledge or skills.
- Effective security management depends to a degree on practice. Practicing—through simulations and training—is vital.

Pedagogy Box 11.4 British Official Communications of Risks

The British Civil Contingencies Act (2004) obliged the principal emergency responders to "arrange for the publication of all or part assessments made and plans maintained . . . so far as is necessary or desirable for the purpose of:

1. preventing the emergency,
2. reducing, controlling or mitigating the effects of an emergency, or
3. enabling other action to be taken in connection with an emergency."

Subsequent guidance defined a Community Risk Register as first "a register communicating the assessment of risks within a Local Resilience Area which is developed and published as a basis for informing local communities and directing civil protection workstreams," later "an assessment of the risks within a local resilience area agreed by the Local Resilience Forum as a basis for supporting the preparation of emergency plans." An *emergency plan* is a "a document or collection of documents that sets out the overall framework for the initiation, management, co-ordination and control of personnel and assets to reduce, control or mitigate the effects of an emergency" (U.K. Cabinet Office, 2013).

Guidance obliged local authorities to communicate information that would improve public *risk awareness* but forbade them from releasing sensitive information, such as would be useful to threats. As soon as an event is certain, public authorities are supposed to "warn and inform" the public and to advise on how to respond (U.K. Cabinet Office, 2012c, Chapter 7).

Confidentially, the British government maintains a National Risk Assessment. The simplified, publicly available version is the National Risk Register. In August 2008, the British executive released its National Risk Register for the first time, but only as a simplified plot of 12 national risks, with some description of the risks and their relative scale, but no practical descriptions of how these risks had been assessed or managed. It has released updates in 2010 and 2012. The National Steering Committee on Warning and Informing the Public was created in 1997 as a quasi-independent organization to provide advice and guidance to emergency managers in national and regional governments.

(Continued)

(Continued)

In emergencies, the Central Situation Cell of the Cabinet Office communicates the Common Recognized Information Picture to emergency responders and holds a Common Operating Picture (a "single display of information collected from and shared by more than one agency or organisation that contributes to a common understanding of a situation and its associated hazards and risks along with the position of resources and other overlays of information that support individual and collective decision making") (U.K. Cabinet Office, 2013). *Strategic communication* (essentially the message that the government wants to release) is coordinated through cross-departmental Information Strategy Groups. Each group produces a National Information Strategy. During domestic emergencies, normally the group would be chaired by someone from the Home Office; during international diplomatic and military operations, an official from the Foreign & Commonwealth Office (FCO) would chair.

Alternative Ways to Communicate Risks

The subsections below discuss some visual ways to communicate risk assessments: risk scales or ladders, risk matrices, heat maps, risk radars, and risk maps.

Risk Scales or Ladders

The simplest way to communicate a risk is to tell consumers whether a risk exists or not. This implies an effective scale, with only two possible values (risk or no risk). Owners often release the risk in this form casually or informally, such as a statement containing a description of some risk.

More formally, owners communicate risk via explicit *scales* (sometimes called *ladders*) with 3 points or 5 points. Military and diplomatic sites traditionally have advertised 3-point *threat levels* at different physical sites, but they essentially mean risk levels.

However, even 5-point scales have been criticized for communicating too little information to be useful. At the same time, they have been criticized for suggesting more certainty or precision than was justified.

Pedagogy Box 11.5 U.S. Homeland Security Communications

The Homeland Security Advisory System or *homeland threat level* was first released by the newly established U.S. Office of Homeland Security in late 2002. This scale included the levels *severe*, *high*, *elevated*, *guarded*, and *low*, which were colored red, orange, yellow, blue, and green, respectively. The George W. Bush administration changed the level 17 times from 2002 through 2006, but never below elevated, prompting complaints that the administration was holding the level artificially high for political reasons and causing subordinate authorities to control risks inefficiently. The first Homeland Security Secretary (Tom Ridge) later recalled that the administration had pressured him to raise the level before the national election in 2004 (Ridge & Bloom, 2009). Meanwhile, state and local authorities complained that the level was not specific enough. At first, these authorities ordered increased security whenever the level rose, but without more information they could not know where to reallocate resources. (In March 2003, the U.S. Conference of Mayors estimated that cities alone were spending $70 million every week on additional homeland security measures due to heightened levels.) They demanded more intelligence so that they could control the specific risk by, for instance, ordering an increased police presence around the railway system if the intelligence suggested an increased threat to trains. In practise, intelligence was preferable to any abstract threat level. Most consumers were issued only the homeland threat level; since this changed between one of the three highest levels for poorly justified reasons, consumers became neglectful.

For this and other reasons, in 2009, a bipartisan panel recommended reducing the number of levels from five to three, but the scale was not replaced until April 2011, when DHS implemented the National Terrorism Advisory System (NTAS), which occasionally and temporarily issues a statement specifying an elevated terrorist threat or an imminent terrorist threat, each with a specified date of expiration. The default option is no statement of threat. Effectively, the NTAS is a 3-point scale but is never communicated on any scale. Instead, each statement is issued as a single-page document describing the threat.

Pedagogy Box 11.6 British Terrorism Risk Communication

Since August 2006, the British government has published its assessment of Britain's terrorism threat level on a 5-point scale (low–an attack is unlikely; moderate–an attack is possible but not likely; substantial–an attack is a strong possibility; severe–an attack is highly likely; critical–an attack is expected imminently). The threat level remained at the fourth level except for a jump to the highest (fifth) level during short periods during August 2006 and June–July 2007. This practical constancy was not useful to public consumers; the British government issued no guidance on public responses by threat level. In September 2010, threat levels were separated for "Northern Ireland-related terrorism" and "international terrorism," since then the international terrorist threat level has dropped as low as the middle (third) level, and the Northern Ireland-related terrorist threat level has dropped as low as Level 2.

Risk Matrices

Risk matrices are the most recognizable ways to communicate risk, thanks to their simplicity and frequent use, although matrices typically oversimplify the records on which they are based and often use misleading scales or risk levels.

Conventional risk matrices are formed by two dimensions representing returns and likelihood respectively. A fair and transparent matrix should have symmetrical scales on each dimension and should admit that the risk in each cell is a product of these dimensions. This mathematical consistency produces risk levels each with a definite order and clean boundaries. For instance, Table 11.2 shows a simple risk matrix with symmetrical 3-point scales on each dimension and with risks calculated as products of the scales.

Table 11.2 A Simple Risk Matrix With Symmetrical Scales and Mathematically Correct Products

High likelihood (3)	*Medium risk (3)*	*Medium-high risk (6)*	*High-high risk (9)*
Medium likelihood (2)	*Low-medium risk (2)*	*Medium risk (4)*	*Medium-high risk (6)*
Low likelihood (1)	*Low risk (1)*	*Low-medium risk (2)*	*Medium risk (3)*
	Low impact (1)	***Medium impact (2)***	**High impact (3)**

The Australian/New Zealand and ISO standards (Australian and New Zealand Joint Technical Committee, 2009) introduced a risk matrix with symmetrical 5-point dimensions (each scale is numbered 1–5, although the qualitative explanations are poorly differentiated) and four risk levels that are consistent with the risk scores produced from the dimensions. Subsequently, the UN's Threat and Risk Unit chose a risk matrix with symmetrical 5-point dimensions and six risk levels (see Table 11.3).

Unfortunately, many risk matrices assign risk levels that are not mathematically justified and are misleading. For instance, Table 11.4 shows a risk matrix used by a commercial company for its risk assessments; the matrix and its legend show four discrete qualitative risk levels but do not show that these levels are mathematically irregular and overlapping: acceptable risks (1–3); risks subject to review (2–5); undesirable risks (6–9); and unacceptable risks (10–20). These risk levels effectively overstate the impact and understate the likelihood; some risks were placed in a higher level when the impact is high and the likelihood is low than when the likelihood is high and the impact is low. This may have been deliberate, such as to acknowledge the layperson's overvaluation of high impact over high likelihood events of the same risk level, but the reasons should be explained.

Communicators who want risks to be interpreted consistently should use risk ladders or matrices that are symmetrical and assign risk levels that are congruent with the mathematics. Consumers should check for these things or ask the communicator to explain the divergence.

Table 11.3 The UN's Standard Risk Matrix

Critical impact (5)	*Low (5)*	*Medium (10)*	*High (15)*	*Critical (20)*	*Critical (25)*
Severe impact (4)	*Low (4)*	*Medium (8)*	*High (12)*	*High (16)*	*Critical (20)*
Moderate impact (3)	*Negligible (3)*	*Low (6)*	*Medium (9)*	*High (12)*	*High (15)*
Minor impact (2)	*Negligible (2)*	*Low (4)*	*Low (6)*	*Medium (8)*	*Medium (10)*
Negligible impact (1)	*No determinable risk (1)*	*Negligible (2)*	*Negligible (3)*	*Low (4)*	*Low (5)*
	Unlikely (1)	**Moderately likely (2)**	**Likely (3)**	**Very likely (4)**	**Certain or imminent (5)**

SOURCE: UN Department of Peacekeeping Operations, 2008.

Table 11.4 A Risk Matrix With Asymmetrical Dimensions and Risk Levels

Catastrophic impact (4)	*Risk subject to review (4)*	*Undesirable risk (8)*	*Unacceptable risk (12)*	*Unacceptable risk (16)*	*Unacceptable risk (20)*
Critical impact (3)	*Risk subject to review (3)*	*Undesirable risk (6)*	*Undesirable risk (9)*	*Unacceptable risk (12)*	*Unacceptable risk (15)*
Marginal impact (2)	*Risk subject to review (2)*	*Risk subject to review (4)*	*Undesirable risk (6)*	*Undesirable risk (8)*	*Unacceptable risk (10)*
Negligible impact (1)	*Acceptable risk (1)*	*Acceptable risk (2)*	*Acceptable risk (3)*	*Risk subject to review (4)*	*Risk subject to review (5)*
	Improbable (1)	**Remote likelihood (2)**	**Likely to occur sometime (3)**	**Probable (4)**	**Likely to occur frequently (5)**

SOURCE: Based on U.S. Government Accountability Office, 1998, p. 8.

Communicators should use media consistently, because the inconsistencies are confusing and often traceable to quantitative or qualitative mistakes. For instance, in 2008, the British executive first released publicly its national risk register in a much reduced form—effectively a plot of different scenarios on a space with two dimensions (impact and likelihood), each with a continuous scale (see Figure 3.3). Its second and third releases (2010 and 2012) plotted scenarios in an explicit risk matrix, by the same dimensions, each with an interval rather than continuous scale. The register actually shows two different matrices (one for terrorism and other malicious attacks, the other for natural and accidental risks), with quantitatively different scales. The government has never explained publicly its communication choices.

The risks in a risk matrix can be represented by dots, each placed in a cell corresponding with the risk's associated likelihood and returns, where each dot's size or color corresponds with the risk's rank. Such displays are called sometimes *oil stain plots* or *heat maps* (although I and others use *heat map* to describe another display described in the following section).

Risks can be plotted within a matrix to show how risks have changed over time. A particular risk could be plotted in the same matrix twice—at an earlier point in time and a later point in time. If the risk level has changed in that time, an arrow between the plots can represent the change. The change might be due to controls on the risk: In this case, some users have referred to the matrix as a *control effectiveness map*.

Pedagogy Box 11.7 Official Definitions of Risk Matrices

The ISO defines a risk matrix as a "tool for ranking and displaying risks by defining ranges for consequences and likelihood" (p. 8). The Canadian government refers to a plot of risks in a space defined by two dimensions as a "likelihood-consequence graph," but it refers to an almost identical plot (where each risk is represented as a two-dimensional cross rather than an oval) as a "risk event rating scatter plot" (Public Safety Canada, 2013, pp. 6, 54). The British government has referred to the same visual representations as *risk registers*—even though that term is used for mere records too.

Heat Maps

A heat map is a matrix on which we can plot risks by two actionable dimensions, usually risk owner and risk category. The level of risk can be indicated by a color (say, green, yellow, and red) or a number (say, from 1 to 3) in the cell formed where the risk's owner and category intersect. Such heat maps are useful for drawing attention to those owners or categories that hold the most risks or largest risks and thus need higher intervention, or those who hold fewer or smaller risks and thus have capacity to accept more risk.

Risk Radars

Risk radars are segmented, concentric circles that normally are used to represent time (circles further from the center represent time further into the future) and risk categories or risk owners (each segment of the pie would represent a different category or owner). Risk radars are useful for drawing attention to risks whose control is most urgent.

Moving outward from the center circle (which normally represents the present) each concentric circle would represent some interval of time further into the future (say, an interval of 1 year). Segments or arcs of the concentric circles can be delineated to differentiate risk by category or owner, depending on whether the categories or owners were most salient. Each risk's level or rank can be represented by a distinct color or number.

Risk Maps

Some risks are usefully plotted in space by their real geographical location. For instance, if we operate or are based in different areas, the risks to or security of our operations and bases can be plotted on a map of these areas. Vehicles or assets in transit move through areas with different risks. Some security and risk managers, such as coast guards and navies, use software to monitor the locations of assets as large as oil tankers in real time.

Often we are interested in plotting in space not just our potential targets but also the other actors, especially hazards and threats and our contributors. The British MOD has advocated a method ("center of gravity analysis") for analyzing actors involved in a conflict. These actors can be plotted on a map, where each actor is a represented by an icon whose color corresponds with the actor's assessed relationship with the British (see Figure 11.1). (In this illustration, the analysis is notional, but reminiscent of coalition operations in Iraq.)

Sources, causes, and events too can be plotted in space. For instance, the British MOD has plotted on a map of the world current conflicts and the areas experiencing two of more "stresses" (increased population, decreased crops, increased shortages of food and water) (see Figure 11.2).

Monitoring and Reviewing Risk Management

This section discusses the requirements for and process of monitoring and reviewing how others manage their risks.

Requirement

Risk management should be actively monitored to ensure that risk management is effective, because prevention of a failure in risk management is usually more efficient than curing a failure. Unfortunately,

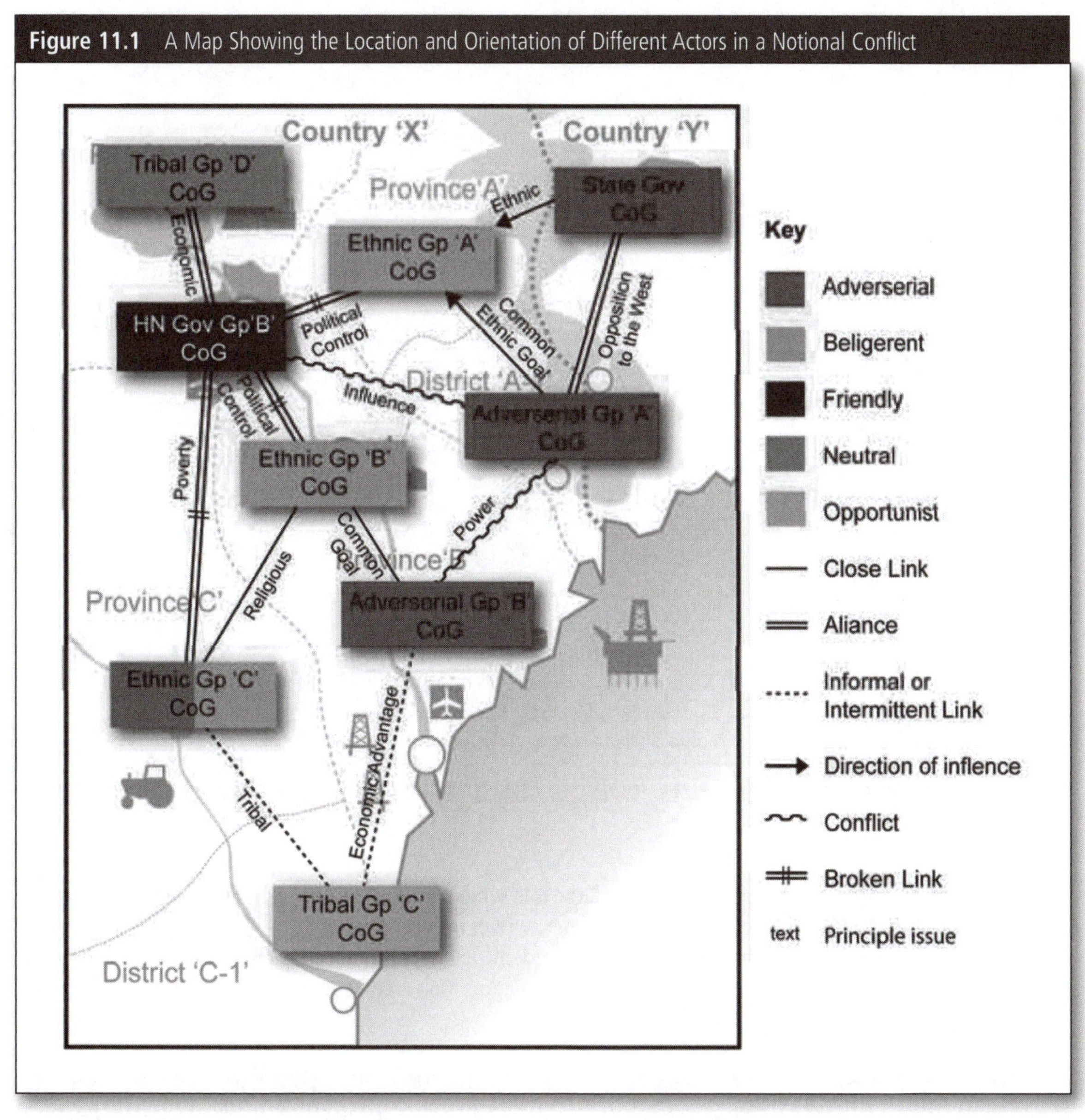

Figure 11.1 A Map Showing the Location and Orientation of Different Actors in a Notional Conflict

SOURCE: MOD, 2009, p. 148.

if performance is not monitored by a higher authority, over time, most humans cut corners and perform below standards.

Effective compliance and review is desirable at all levels. Most governments schedule a cycle of reviews of major domains, such as national security, at the highest level of responsibility, normally every few years. For political reasons, some political administrations delay such reviews (perhaps

Figure 11.2 A Map Showing the Location of Current Conflicts and Stresses in 2010

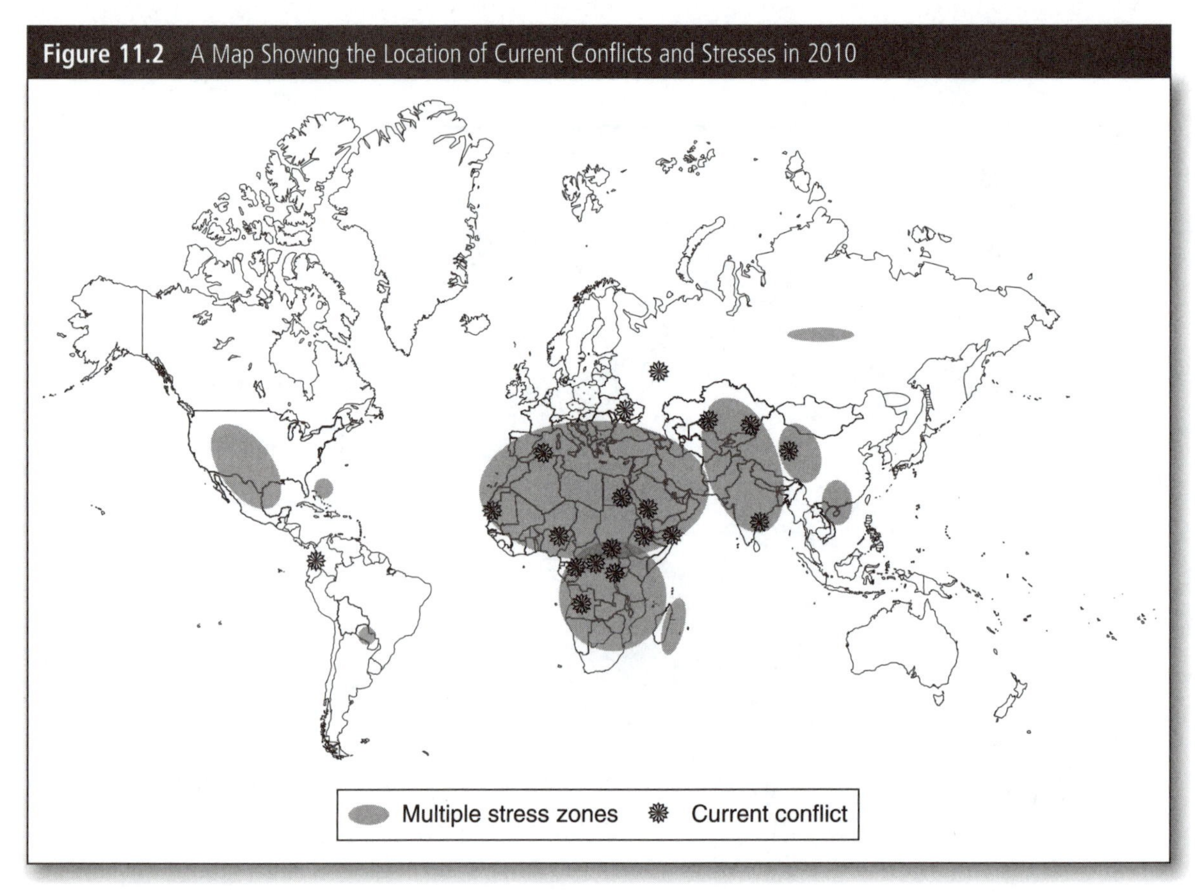

SOURCE: MOD, 2010, p. 69.

because they would prove poor policy), and the following administrations blame such delays for current issues. Since 1997, U.S. law has required a defense review every 4 years.

All of the main risk management standards identified in this book specify monitoring or reviewing as a step in their recommended processes for managing risk (see Table 8.3), although some are better at specifying what they mean.

Pedagogy Box 11.8 Other Requirements for Monitoring and Reviewing

All the standard processes of risk management identified earlier in this book (see Table 8.3) include monitoring or reviewing, but few define what they mean. The Australian/Zealand and ISO (International Organization for Standardization, 2009a, pp. 11–12) suggest that risk managers "monitor" and "review" risk management and demand "subordinate reporting":

- *monitoring* as "continual checking, supervising, critically observing or determining the status in order to identify chance from the performance level required or expected";

- *review* as an "activity undertaken to determine the suitability, adequacy and effectiveness of the subject matter to achieve established objectives"; and
- *subordinate reporting* as a "form of communication intended to inform particular internal or external stakeholders by providing information regarding the current state of risk and its management."

In Britain, the Civil Contingencies Act (2004) specified how authorities are to manage emergencies and associated risks, and also specified, under a heading titled "Monitoring by Government," any minister's authority to "require" from any of the designated contributors "to provide information about actions taken by the person or body for the purpose of complying with a duty under this Part [of the Act], or to explain why the person or body has not taken action for the purpose of complying with a duty under this Part."

Canada's Emergency Management Act of 2007 stipulates that ministers are responsible for identifying risks within their domains and for preparing to manage related emergencies. In 2011, the government published a federal cycle of assessing risks, starting in September each year (Public Safety Canada, 2013, p. 7).

The Humanitarian Practice Network (2010) has very clearly specified reviews of security management:

> A good planning process needs to be followed up with periodic reviews—as the environment changes, there is a need to adapt the plan . . . Even in a quiet and secure environment, security plans should be reviewed annually. In higher-risk environments, they should be reviewed more frequently to ensure that they reflect prevailing risks, and that the information they contain is up to date. (pp. 13–14)

According to Mike Papay, vice president and chief information officer of Northrup Grumman Corporation, information managers have focused strongly on monitoring as a critical step in information security management, probably because technologies and threats have evolved quickly in that domain:

> Understanding the security "state-of-play" for information systems is essential in today's dynamic environment. We're at a point now where annual compliance checking isn't enough. Continuous monitoring versus just spot-checking once-a-year is critical to preventing adversaries from exploiting vulnerabilities that result from a static environment. (Jackson, 2013b, p. 18)

Process

Essentially, a practical process of monitoring or reviewing involves periodic checking that subordinate security and risk managers are performing to standard. The periods should be systematized on a transparent regular schedule, while reserving the right to shorten the periods and make unannounced reviews without advance notice if necessary.

Usually, the responsibility is on the subordinate to report on schedule and to include all specified information without reminder. The report can consist of simply the current risk register. Audiences usually prefer some visual presentation summarizing what is in the current risk register (see the section above on communicating). The subordinate could be tasked with answering some exceptional questions—such questions are normally motivated by higher concerns or lower noncompliance, in which case the task amounts to an audit (see the section below on auditing).

Pedagogy Box 11.9 The Structure and Process of Official Monitoring of British Government, 2000–2011

The British government strengthened its risk management processes in the 1990s. Nonetheless, the U.K. National Audit Office (2000, p. 6) found that only 57% of British government departments (n = 237) admitted procedures for reporting risk to senior management, and 34% agreed that regular risk reports are an effective component of risk management in their department.

Each department of government has its own monitoring authority, although it might not sit full-time. For instance, the British MOD requires in advance of all programs and projects a risk assessment and a risk management plan, each compliant with the standard templates. The MOD's Investment Appraisal Board regularly requires from project managements a Risk Maturity Assessment.

On September 2, 2006, a fire broke out on a British four-engined surveillance aircraft (of a type named "Nimrod," originally delivered by Hawker Siddeley) over Afghanistan, leading to a catastrophic explosion and the loss of all 14 personnel aboard. An official inquiry into the crash, an inquest into the deaths, and a judicial review of the aircraft type each found that the fault had existed for years and been known but underassessed, in part because of weak compliance and review.

> The Nimrod Safety Case [by BAE Systems, the current design authority, monitored by Qinetiq, a defense contractor, and by the Integrated Project Team at the Ministry of Defense] was fatally undermined by a general malaise: a widespread assumption by those involved that the Nimrod was "safe anyway" (because it had flown successfully for thirty years) and the task of drawing up the Safety Case became essentially a paperwork and "tick-box" exercise. (Haddon-Cave, 2009, p. 10)

Monitoring applies not just to procurement projects but also operational and physical security. For instance, the British MOD requires its departments to submit annually "assurance reports" on their plans for business continuity. The MOD's leadership intended these reports "to ensure compliance and provide lessons for the improvement of risk management" (U.K. MOD, 2011c, Chapter 6, p. 3).

In 1998, the political administration in Britain (led by the Labour Party) published a *Strategic Defence Review*, but repeatedly deferred another review (although it did publish a "New Chapter" in 2002 and a defense white paper in 2003). After the Labour Party lost national executive power in May 2010, the following Prime Minister used the first of his traditional annual opportunities for a major speech on security to highlight his administration's quick reviews.

> We've also concluded a truly strategic review of all aspects of security and defence. This was long overdue; it has been 12 years and 4 wars since the last defence review. We started with a

detailed audit of our national security. We took a clear view of the risks we faced and set priorities including a new focus on meeting unconventional threats from terrorism and cyber attack. We then took a detailed look at the capabilities we will need to deal with tomorrow's threats. (David Cameron, prepared speech at Mansion House, City of London, November 15, 2010)

In 2011, the new political administration established a Major Projects Authority, which reports to the Cabinet Office, to monitor all projects that require approval from the Treasury. The monitoring consists mostly of a requirement for managers of major projects to submit risk management plans for approval. The Major Projects Authority can also order Assurance Reviews in response to an emergent issue. For instance, in May 2011, the British executive ordered the Major Projects Authority to investigate the National Health Service's Programme for Information Technology, which had run over time and budget since launch in 2002; the Major Projects Authority recommended termination of the program, while salvaging some of the delivered projects.

Auditing Security and Risk Management

The subsections below define a risk or security audit, describe how to prioritize targets for an audit, and suggest useful questions to ask during an audit.

Requirement

A risk or security audit is an unusual investigation into how an actor is managing risk or security. Most standard processes of risk management do not specify an audit as a separate part of the process, but at least imply that their advocacy of monitoring and reviewing includes a prescription to audit where and when necessary.

Pedagogy Box 11.10 Other Definitions of a Risk or Security Audit

The Humanitarian Practice Network (2010) defined *security auditing* as "an evaluation of the strengths and weaknesses in an organization's security management and infrastructure in order to assess its effectiveness and identify areas for improvement" (p. xviii).

Australia/New Zealand and ISO (International Organization for Standardization, 2009a) defined a *risk management audit* as a "systematic, independent, and documented process for obtaining evidence and evaluating it objectively in order to determine the extent to which the risk management framework or any selected part of it is adequate and effective" (p. 12).

The British Standards Institution (BSI) (2000) defined an audit as a "systematic examination to determine whether activities and related results conform to planned arrangements, and whether these arrangements are implemented effectively and are suitable for achieving the organization's policy and objectives" (p. 11).

Choosing Who to Audit

An easy way to decide which actors to prioritize for an audit is to search for the actors

- whose compliance with the standards of security or risk management has been most tardy, incomplete, or delinquent,
- were least responsive or cooperative with reviews or monitors,
- revealed noncompliance during reviews or monitors,
- were audited least recently,
- that hold more risks or greater total risk than the average peer,
- that have experienced more than an average number of negative events, or
- where some event has revealed the organization's poor management of security or risk.

For instance, in 2009, the United Nations High Commissioner for Refugees (UNHCR) deployed 17 staff to Pakistan, but on June 9, three staff were killed by a bombing of a hotel, after which another was abducted for 2 months. Later that year, the UN Office of Internal Oversight carried out the first audit of UNHCR's security management; it recommended personnel with better training in assessment, improved operational strategies, and more integration of security management into preparedness and response activities.

Pedagogy Box 11.11 Other Prescriptions for Targets of an Audit

The BSI (2000, p. 17) prescribed "periodic system audits" to determine compliance with policies and objectives, to review the results of previous audits, and to provide information on the results of audits to managers.

The Humanitarian Practice Network (2010, pp. 13–14) prescribed an unscheduled review

- when there are significant changes in the external context, especially as a result of the actions of the major protagonists.
- when another agency has been affected by an incident, especially in or near the same operational zone.
- when someone else is affected by an incident that in its nature or intensity appears to introduce a new element into the original risk assessment.

Another useful observation, in the context of technical risks (those relating to innovation and invention), is that

- new technologies in new markets are riskiest;
- new technologies in existing markets or existing technologies in new markets are less risky; and
- existing technologies in existing markets are least risky. (Branscomb & Auerswald, 2001, p. 3)

Audit Questions

When auditing an organization's capacity for effectively managing risks, we should ask at least the following questions:

1. Has a full and clear set of standards for the performance of risk management been assigned?
2. Do personnel value and wish to comply with the standards?
3. Are the personnel trained in the skills and knowledge of the standards?
4. Have clearly accountable authorities been assigned?
5. Are the responsibilities of managers clear and fulfilled?
6. Is a register of the risks being maintained?
7. Has a cycle of reviews been scheduled and fulfilled?
8. Does risk management affect other planning?

Pedagogy Box 11.12 Audit Questions From the Institute of Chartered Accountants in England and Wales

1. Are risks being assessed properly?
   a. Are corporate objectives clear and communicated?
   b. Are risks assessed regularly?
   c. Are the acceptable risks understood?
2. Are risks being controlled?
   a. Are correct strategies being selected?
   b. Does organizational culture support risk management?
   c. Do leaders reinforce best practices?
   d. Are the authorities clear?
   e. Are the policies communicated?
   f. Are the policies updated?
   g. Are the personnel competent?
3. Is information properly recorded and communicated?
   a. Is risk management performance being reported internally?
   b. Is risk management performance being reported externally?
   c. Are the organization's needs for information being assessed regularly?
   d. Can impropriety be reported effectively?

(Continued)

(Continued)

4. Is risk management being monitored properly?
   a. Is some higher authority monitoring the organization's compliance with standards?
   b. Are the standards adjusted in light of lessons learned?
   c. Are the desired changes verified?
   d. Is the monitor reporting regularly?
   e. Are exceptional issues reported immediately? (Turnbull, 1999, Appendix)

SUMMARY

This chapter has

- described the requirement for recording risk assessments and risk management in some sort of register or log and explained why such a register is beneficial,
- advised on the process of maintaining such a risk register and on the information that should be recorded,
- described why stakeholders are often required to communicate information on risks and risk management and why such communication is beneficial,
- described alternative visual representations of risks, such as risk scales, risk matrices, heat maps, risk radars, and risk maps,
- described the requirement for monitoring and reviewing how others manage risks and why this matters,
- described the process of monitoring and reviewing,
- explained why audits may be required,
- given advice on choosing who to audit, and
- given a list of useful questions to ask during an audit.

QUESTIONS AND EXERCISES

1. Why should you maintain some record of your assessments and management of security or risk?
2. What information should you record about a risk?
3. What information should you record about your management of the risk?
4. When should one organization communicate information from its risk records to another organization?
5. Reread the case of British official communications of risks. What trade-offs or dilemmas can you identify in how the information is being communicated?

6. What is the utility of each of the following visual representations of risks?
   a. Risk scale/ladder
   b. Risk matrix
   c. Heat map
   d. Risk radar
   e. Risk map
7. Reconsider the mathematically irregular or overlapping risk rankings within the matrix shown in Table 11.4:
   a. What component of risk does this matrix bias?
   b. When are irregular rankings justifiable?
   c. When are irregular rankings not justifiable?
8. Reconsider Figure 3.3.
   a. What is this figure communicating effectively?
   b. What about the risks is this figure not communicating?
   c. How could this figure communicate changes in risk over time?
9. For what is a heat map most useful?
10. For what is a risk radar most useful?
11. When would we need a geographical map of the risks?
12. Why should we review or monitor how our subordinates and partners manage risks?
13. What differentiates monitoring from auditing?
14. Reread Pedagogy Box 11.4 above about British official monitoring of government.
    a. The official activities are described sometimes as *reviews*, sometimes *audits*. Given the information available in the case, which term would be most appropriate?
    b. Can you identify any cases where an audit would have been preferred to a review or vice versa?
    c. The explosion of the Nimrod was blamed on a "general malaise." How could a monitoring structure or process be configured to counter such a malaise?
15. Write five questions expecting answers of either yes or no, where an affirmative answer should prompt an audit of another organization.
16. Given an example of a type of project that should be prioritized for an audit.
17. Recall five questions that should be asked during an audit.

PART

III

Managing Security in Different Domains

This (third and final) part of the book explains how to manage security and risk by the five main domains: operational and logistical security (Chapter 12); physical (site) security (Chapter 13); information, communications, and cyber security (Chapter 14); transport security (Chapter 15); and personal security (Chapter 16).

CHAPTER 12

Operational and Logistical Security

This chapter describes operational and logistical security. (Chapter 13 describes site security, Chapter 14 describes information and communications security, and Chapter 15 describes transport security—all relevant to operational and logistical security.)

The sections below describe the scope of operations and logistics, operational risks, the assessment of these risks, and the provision of operational and logistical security.

 Scope

Operations include all activities that contribute or support a common goal; in military lexicons, operations tend to be larger endeavors than missions; sometimes higher operations are described as strategic, while lower operations are described as tactical.

Logistics are activities and systems concerned with supply. Other things may be outside of the control of the operators, but nevertheless relevant to operations, such as the sites, communications, infrastructure, and transport on which logistics depends, as described in the following chapters.

Pedagogy Box 12.1 Official Definitions

Business operations are "business services, processes, and associated resources that are specific to the internal functioning of a federal government institution" (Public Safety Canada, 2012, p. 8). *Logistics* is "the range of operational activities concerned with supply, handling, transportation, and distribution of materials" or "people" (UN Department of Humanitarian Affairs [DHA], 1992). Logistics are "in management, the practice of planning, organizing, and arranging the most feasible combination of resources, areas, personnel, and time needed to carry out the established objectives, policies, and mission of an organization or system" (Public Safety Canada, 2012, p. 60).

 Operational Risks

Operations can be interrupted by commercial events (such as failures of supply or income), political events (such as government regulation), crime, terrorism, insurgency, war, natural events (such as flooding), accidents (such as fire), personnel actions (such as labor strikes), organizational failures (such as inept management), or technical failures (such as a failed transport vehicle).

Operations often offer compound risks that are easy to overlook. For instance, in unstable areas, we can expect increased rates of crimes and accidents. If we were to suffer an attack, we should expect negative returns such as casualties and compound effects such as more accident-prone, illness-prone, or nonperforming personnel. Accidents are associated with increased likelihood of illness, which in turn is associated with increased likelihood of accidents. Operations away from home tend to be more stressful. Employees who underperform or are incapacitated must be repatriated and replaced, but communications become less secure as the area becomes less stable.

Some operational areas offer peculiar or untypical risks. For instance, in underdeveloped areas, an organization from the developed world might forget that local health care is riskier. Blood transfusions might not have been reliably screened for communicable pathogens such as hepatitis virus. The communications to local hospitals may be more exposed to human threats. Local health carers may be so poorly compensated that they do not work consistently.

In unstable areas where more transactions are cash based, the procurement, transport, storage, and distribution of cash create special opportunities for thieves. If the use of cash cannot be restricted, the cash should be guarded. The practices for handling cash should be varied so that threats cannot predict where and when to find cash.

Pedagogy Box 12.2 Interruptions to Commercial Operations in China, September 2012

Operations can be interrupted for external reasons that are largely outside of the control of the operators, although operators must still assess and control the risks. For instance, on September 16, 2012, Japan announced that it was purchasing from a private owner some disputed islands, known as Diaoyu in China and Senkaku in Japan. On September 17, Chinese protesters attacked Japanese businesses in China. Mazda and Nissan stopped car production in China for 2 days. Honda suspended production at two factories in the southern city of Guangzhou and the central city of Wuhan after Honda's stores in Qingdao were damaged by arsonists. Toyota, which was also targeted in the eastern city of Qingdao, said its factories and offices were operating as normal. Panasonic shut its factory in Qingdao for a day. Canon temporarily suspended operations at three plants (at Zhuhai, Zhongshan, and Suzhou).

Operations can be interrupted for largely internal reasons. For instance, in 2010, suicides of employees at a facility in China owned by Foxconn, a manufacturer of electronics components, based in Taiwan, drove the company to install netting to catch jumpers, among other responses. Pressure from its clients—especially Apple, a supplier of popular electronic devices—led to raised wages and other improvements. The Washington-based Fair Labor Association audited Foxconn's facilities in China and initially found serious violations of labor standards. In August 2012, it reported that the manufacturer was improving working conditions ahead of schedule. Yet on September 23, about 2,000 workers rioted. Production was interrupted until September 25.

Pedagogy Box 12.3 The Crisis in the Security of Supplies to Military Forces in Afghanistan, 2008–2009

In late 2001, the United States and a few allied militaries intervened on the ground in Afghanistan. The North Atlantic Treaty Organization (NATO) authorized an allied mission, although most U.S. operations remained outside of the NATO mission.

Some of NATO's supplies arrived by train through Russia. Germany and Spain had reached bilateral agreements with Russia for their military supplies to fly in via Russia. About one-quarter of supplies were flown into two air bases (Bagram and Kandahar) in Afghanistan. (By comparison, only about 5% of military supplies were flown into Iraq during the occupation there; the rest were shipped into Kuwait, then transported by land into Iraq.) Each of these bases accepted the largest U.S. transport planes (C17s), which had capacity for current main battle tanks and standard containers, as seen on transport ships and heavy goods vehicles.

Bagram, near Kabul, in the north-east of Afghanistan, serviced mostly U.S. forces. Kandahar, in southern Afghanistan, was a stage in the air bridge to Camp Bastion, the base for all British, a minority of U.S., and most other NATO forces.

Southern Afghanistan was not secure for ground transport, so forces based in Bastion and further north in Helmand province were practically dependent on air transport. NATO forces generally transported supplies from Kandahar into Bastion by C130 aircraft (a medium-class transport aircraft). At that time, British forces alone received 250 tons of ammunition every month by air. From Bastion, supplies were transported by helicopters to further operational bases or by locally contracted trucks to closer sites. Operating bases were widely separated and generally stocked for 20 to 30 days of normal consumption.

In 2008, 70%–75% of the coalition's military supplies were shipped to Karachi in Pakistan, then transported by land into Afghanistan via five border crossings. These crossings are widely separated. Supplies travelled 400 miles through Quetta to the border crossing into southern Afghanistan on their way to Kandahar. Other supplies travelled 1,100 miles through Peshawar and the Khyber Pass on their way to Kabul.

In November 2008, the Taliban (a term used widely for insurgents in Afghanistan and Pakistan, with the implication of Jihadi motivations) dramatically increased the frequency of their attacks on or hijacks of U.S. and NATO ground convoys passing through the Khyber Pass. Truck crossings at Torkham, the main crossing site, 3 miles west of the summit of the Khyber Pass, fell from an average of 800 per day to 200 for a while. On December 2, attackers ambushed 22 trucks in Peshawar, inside Pakistan. On December 6, they attacked NATO's depot near Peshawar, leaving 145 NATO vehicles, trailers, and containers burnt out. On December 8, attackers destroyed about 50 NATO containers at a supply depot near Peshawar.

NATO and U.S. security in Pakistan was not helped by increasingly tense relations between the United States and Pakistan during a return to mostly democratic government and during increasingly frequent and deadly secret U.S. air strikes against insurgent or terrorist targets inside Pakistan.

(Continued)

(Continued)

Unable to satisfactorily secure the existing routes and nodes on the ground in Pakistan, NATO negotiated additional routes through other neighbors. The shortest route would be through Iran from the Persian Gulf into south-western Afghanistan, but Iran was not friendly or trustworthy to NATO. Supplies could be shipped through the Black Sea to Georgia, carried by railway through Georgia and Azerbaijan to Baku on the Caspian Sea, then shipped to Turkmenistan, before trucks took over for the long ground journey into northern Afghanistan. To the north of Turkmenistan, Uzbekistan was less friendly. Further north, Kazakhstan was friendlier but had no border with Afghanistan. Tajikistan shared a border with north-eastern Afghanistan but is landlocked. Russian tolerance, if not support, was critical to the cooperation of any of these neighbors.

By March 2009, NATO, the United States, and Pakistan had sweetened relations and improved the security of ground transport through Pakistan: NATO was supplying 130 to 140 containers per day through Pakistan, more than demand. In 2009, the United States opened a northern distribution network, involving Azerbaijan, Turkmenistan, Russia, and China, with a planned capacity of 100 containers per day. Meanwhile, the U.S. Army Corps of Engineers and its contractors were constructing new roads in Afghanistan (720 planned miles in 2009, 250 to 350 in 2010), including a highway north from Kabul through Baghlan and Kunduz provinces, thereby improving communications with Tajikistan and Uzbekistan.

Assessing Operational and Logistical Risks

In principal, assessing risks to operations is as simple as

1. Identifying the sources (hazards and threats, which may include the stakeholders or targets of the operations). Many threats, such as thieves, saboteurs, vandals, and corrupt officials, are easy enough to profile, but terrorists, kidnappers, blackmailers, and corrupt governments are more agile and need more specialized assessments, particularly in foreign cultures.
2. Assessing the likelihood of hazards being activated as threats,
3. Assessing the intents and capabilities of the threats, and
4. Identifying operational exposures and vulnerabilities to those intents and capabilities.

Pedagogy Box 12.4 Other Methods for Assessing Operational Risks

The British Civil Contingencies Secretariat defines a "business impact assessment" as "a method of assessing the impacts that might result from an incident and the levels of resources and time required for recovery" (Cabinet Office, February 2013).

The Canadian government advocates a "business impact analysis" as "an analysis that determines the impacts of disruptions on an organization and that identifies and prioritizes critical services and business operations" (Public Safety Canada, 2012, pp. 7–8). It offers a 3-point scale for ranking the operational impacts:

1. "an event that disrupts work to a limited extent within a primary location but does not require the relocation of an entire organization or institution";
2. "an event that compromises an entire building in such a way that an organization or institution cannot perform its functions and that a partial or total relocation to a nearby secondary location becomes necessary";
3. "an event that requires that an entire organization or institution be relocated to an alternate site outside of the national capital region." (Public Safety Canada, 2012, pp. 58–59)

Private authors have prescribed the following simple process for assessing the risks to major assets:

1. List and assess the assets
2. List and assess the threats
3. Assess the vulnerabilities
4. Assess the risks (Burns-Howell, Cordier, & Eriksson, 2003)

The Software Engineering Institute has offered another process (OCTAVE–Operationally Critical Threat, Asset, and Vulnerability Evaluation) that could be used to manage the security of any systems, not just software:

1. Build asset-based threat profiles by assessing the
   a. critical assets;
   b. threats to critical assets;
   c. security requirements for critical assets;
   d. current security practices; and
   e. current organizational vulnerabilities.
2. Identify vulnerabilities to infrastructure by assessing the
   a. key components; and
   b. current technology vulnerabilities.

Pedagogy Box 12.5 United Nations Assessment of Operational Security

In the early 1990s, UN field operations and staff proliferated, and more staff were harmed by malicious attacks. At that time, the UN's highest authority on security was the UN Security Coordinator, a senior manager.

In 1994, the UN created its first handbook on field security—effectively a policy document. A *Security Operations Manual* followed in 1995 as the more practical guidance for the actual security managers. The *Field Security Handbook* was modified in May 2001.

The terrorist attacks of September 11 encouraged the General Assembly to vote for reform: effective January 1, 2002, the Security Coordinator was elevated to an Assistant-Secretary-General; and the Ad-Hoc Inter-Agency Meeting on Security Matters (IASMN) was replaced by the Inter-Agency Security Management Network, consisting of the senior security managers from each agency, chaired by the Security Coordinator. The IASMN met only once per year to review practices; the rest of the time the Office of the Security Coordinator managed security, except that Security and Safety Services managed security at the headquarters building in New York, the Department of Peacekeeping Operations managed the security of civilian staff in peacekeeping operations, and the different national military components of peacekeeping operations each managed their own security.

Meanwhile, the General Assembly authorized an independent panel to review the UN's security management. It was about to report when the UN Assistance Mission in Iraq suffered two quick suicide bombings: on August 19, 2003, 5 days after the establishment of the office in Baghdad, when 22 staff and visitors died, including the UN Special Representative, and more than 150 were injured; and on September 22, when a UN guard and two Iraqi policemen died. The UN withdrew the mission (600 staff), until in August 2004 a smaller mission returned.

The Independent Panel on the Safety and Security of United Nations Personnel reported on October 20, 2003:

> The attacks are signals of the emergence of a new and more difficult era for the UN system. It is of the utmost importance for UN management and staff to recognize the extent to which the security environment of the UN is changing. Already, parties to hostilities in numerous conflicts are targeting civilians in order to draw military advantages, in violation of the most basic principles of international humanitarian law. In several instances, staff members of the UN and other humanitarian agencies have been victims of targeted attacks for their role in assisting these civilians. The bombings in Baghdad differ from these previous attacks not so much for having targeted the UN, but for having done so by using abhorrent tactical means and military-scale weapons. These characteristics, added to the potential links to global terror groups, are significant developments that the UN needs to factor into its security strategy.

The Panel recommended clearer and more robust responsibilities and practices, including better methods for assessing risk and security. In December 2004, the General Assembly agreed to establish an Under-Secretary-General for Safety and Security, who would lead a Department of Safety and Security in place of the Office of the Security Coordinator, the Security and Safety Services, and the Department of Peacekeeping Operation's responsibility for the security of civilian staff in the field.

In the field, the most senior UN official (either the Head of Mission or the Special Representative of the Secretary General) is the highest security officer, to whom reports the Chief Security Adviser. That person is responsible for the Security Management Team, which issues minimum operating standards, with which the mission's civilian and support components comply and the mission's military and police components are supposed to coordinate. Special attention is given to coordinating the many partner organizations (sometimes thousands per mission) (UN, 2006; UN Department of Peacekeeping Operations, 2008, pp. 79–80).

The Department of Safety and Security was established effective January 1, 2005. Its Threat and Risk Unit, which is responsible for the development of risk assessment methods and for supporting risk assessments in the field, developed a Security Risk Management process, which includes a Security Risk Assessment process, which in turn includes two main parts: situational analysis and threat analysis. The IASMN approved these processes in 2005.

The *Field Security Handbook* was revised again, effective January 2006, but this lengthy and dense document (154 pages) included no definitions of security or risk and no methods for assessing either security or risk, although it included two paragraphs that specified a "threat assessment . . . before an effective security plan can be prepared" and referred readers to the *Security Operations Manual*.

The Threat and Risk Unit published its integrated version of the "Security Risk Assessment" process on November 29, 2006. In January 2007, the Staff College and the Department of Safety and Security started training staff to train other personnel in security management.

UN Security Risk Assessment starts with *situational analysis*, which means identifying the threats and their behaviors and capabilities. The *threat analysis* develops likely scenarios for attacks by the threats. These scenarios are supposed to clarify the UN's vulnerabilities, which then would be mitigated. The scenarios are developed through several matrices (the *threat matrix method*) that actually are unnecessarily more complicated than they need to be.

The matrix begins with a list of the likely scenarios alongside descriptions of each scenario; columns are added to assess (on a scale from 1 to 5) the "simplicity" or "feasibility" of the threat's implementation of the scenario, the availability of the weapons that would be required (again on a 5-point scale), the past frequency of such a scenario (5-point scale), the anticipated casualties (standardized to a 5-point scale, from two or less staff to hundreds), and an assessment of the UN's existing controls ("mitigations") on each scenario (5-point scale, from no controls to fully controlled). The matrixes had all sorts of other columns that inconsistently explicated some of the codings.

The method was supposed to produce a single matrix ("system analysis"), listing the scenarios alongside five columns for each of the five assessments (simplicity, availability of weapons, frequency, casualties, controls). The simplest and fairest output would have been a sum of the five assessments by scenario. For no good reason, the method expected users to rank by ordinal scale the codings in each column, sum the rankings across the five columns for each scenario, and superfluously express the sum as a percentage, before ranking each scenario on an ordinal scale.

In December 2007, a UN site in Algiers was attacked. The Steering Committee of the High-Level Committee on Management constituted an Operational Working Group to review the UN Security Management System. It developed a new Security Level System to replace the security phase system by January 2011.

 Providing Operational Security

This section defines the scope of operational security, describes the process for managing operational security, introduces controls on operational exposure to threats, and introduces controls on the negative returns from potential events.

Scope

Operational security is freedom from risks to operations. Inherently, operational security improves when the sources of the risks (the hazard and threats) are removed, our exposure and vulnerability decline, or we control the negative returns from a potential threatening event.

Pedagogy Box 12.6 British Military Operations Security

"Operations security [is] the discipline which gives a military operation or exercise appropriate security, using active or passive means, to deny a target decision-maker knowledge of essential elements of friendly information" (U.K. Ministry of Defense [MOD], 2009b, p. 238).

"Operational risk refers to how the adversary can affect your operations, while operating risk is that risk you expose yourself to by choosing to conduct your operations in a certain way" (U.K. MOD, 2011b, p. 5.9).

Processes for Managing Operational Risks

A privately prescribed process for managing the risks to major assets, including the assessment of risks, as described above, is

1. List and assess the assets
2. List and assess the threats
3. Assess the vulnerabilities
4. Assess the risks
5. Determine the control options
6. Control the risks (Burns-Howell, Cordier, & Eriksson, 2003)

The Software Engineering Institute's process (OCTAVE) includes a detailed process for assessing the risks (as shown above). The part for "developing security strategy and plans" is essentially

1. Assess the risks to critical assets
2. Develop controls on the risks
3. Develop a protection strategy
4. Develop risk mitigation plans

Controlling Operational Exposure to Threats

Reducing exposure can be achieved by avoiding threats or the areas where threats operate or reducing whatever identifies us as a target to the threat. The latter program of activities is sometimes known as low-profile or low-visibility programming.

Pedagogy Box 12.7 Low-Visibility Programming

"Low-visibility programming has become an increasingly common protective tactic among aid agencies. It involves removing organizational branding from office buildings, vehicles, residences and individual staff members. It can also involve the use of private cars or taxis, particularly vehicles that blend into the local context, limiting movement and removing tell-tale pieces of equipment, such as VHF [very high frequency] radios or sat[ellite] phones and HF antennae. In certain very high-risk environments, anything that might link staff to an agency—memory sticks, agency identity documents, cell phones, computers—may be "sanitized." Staff likely to stand out from the local population may be redeployed. In Iraq, more radical steps have included staff using false names, working with no fixed operating address and not being told the identities of colleagues. Beneficiaries were purposefully not made aware of the source of their assistance.

Another tactic of a low-visibility approach is to use removable (e.g. magnetic) logos for vehicles, which can be removed in areas where visibility is discouraged. Knowing when to display a logo and when to take it off demands a very good, localized, and dynamic risk assessment. One NGO working in the Occupied Palestinian Territories and Israel, for example, instructs staff to remove logos when working in refugee camps, where the risk of kidnapping is known to be high, while displaying the agency flag prominently when going through checkpoints or in areas where there is a risk of Israeli military incursion. Bear in mind that magnetic stickers can easily be stolen and used by others to impersonate the organization.

A low-profile, low-visibility approach poses significant challenges. It can make programming more complicated, particularly in extreme cases, and can distance the organization from sources of information that might otherwise enhance its security. It might also lead to suspicions and misperceptions of what the agency is doing, undermining acceptance. It is also a difficult approach to maintain if the organization is seeking wider recognition of its work from the public or from donors. Agencies generally do not see a low-profile approach as a permanent way of operating; rather, it is viewed as exceptional and time-limited. It may also be adopted at the start of a program, then gradually moderated as operations increase" (Humanitarian Practice Network, 2010, pp. 72–73).

Controlling the Negative Returns of Potential Events

Controlling the negative returns of potential threats to our operations involves, in general, any of the synonymous strategies described in Chapter 10, of which the commonest, in the context of operations, is "business continuity."

Pedagogy Box 12.8 Official Business Continuity

For U.S. Department of Homeland Security (2009, p. 109), *business continuity* is "the ability of an organization to continue to function before, during, and after a disaster." For the U.S. DOD (2012), it is "the process of identifying the impact of potential losses on an organization's functional capabilities; formulating and implementing viable recovery strategies; and developing recovery plans, to ensure the continuity of organizational services in the event of an event, incident, or crisis."

The British Civil Contingencies Secretariat and thence the MOD defined business continuity as the "strategic and tactical capability of an organization to plan for and respond to incidents and business disruptions in order to continue business operations at an acceptable, pre-defined level" (U.K. MOD, 2011c, p. Glossary-1). The Canadian government defines business continuity as "the programs, arrangements, and/or measures that provide for the continuity of critical services in the event of disruptions or emergencies" (Public Safety Canada, 2012, p. 7).

In Britain, the Civil Contingencies Act of 2004 required designated authorities to "plan" for emergencies. The Civil Contingencies Secretariat is the highest official adviser. It defines a *business continuity plan* as a "documented collection of procedures and information developed, compiled and maintained in readiness for use in an incident to enable an organization to continue to deliver its critical functions at an acceptable predefined level" (U.K. Cabinet Office, 2013). In 2003, the British government urged private businesses to plan for business continuity as well as for the safety and security of their employees. At simplest, *business continuity management* resembles most processes for managing risk: analyze your business; assess the risks; develop your strategy; develop your plan; rehearse your plan (U.K. Business Continuity Institute, National Counterterrorism Security Office & London First, 2003). In 2004, the Civil Contingencies Secretariat developed a Business Continuity Management Toolkit with prescriptions for planning against disruption of staff, physical sites, electricity, water and sewerage, fuel, communications, transportation, and supplies. In 2007, the government issued a British standard (BS 25999) for business continuity. The MOD subsequently issued a military standard in November 2011.

The Canadian government advocates a business continuity plan as "a plan developed to provide procedures and information for the continuity and/or recovery of critical service delivery and business operations in the event of a disruption" (Public Safety Canada, 2012, pp. 7–8).

SUMMARY

This chapter has introduced

- the scope of operations and logistics,
- operational risks,
- the assessment of operational risks,
- operational security, processes for managing operational security,
- controls on operational exposure to threats, and
- controls on the negative returns of potential events.

QUESTIONS AND EXERCISES

1. What is the difference between operations and logistics?
2. What are typical threats to operations?
3. Give an example of a compound operational risk.
4. What is the difference between operations risk and operational risk?
5. What is business continuity?
6. Design a better method for assessing UN operational risks.
7. How would you explain NATO's responsibility for the changes in the risks to NATO logistics in Afghanistan and Pakistan in 2008 and 2009?

Physical (Site) Security

This chapter covers site security (also: physical security). The sections below define site security, review site risks, describe site security services, give advice on site location, describe how to control access to sites, describe passive perimeters, describe surveillance and counter-surveillance, and explain security engineering (protective materials and construction).

 Scope

Site security is the security of a defined space (the site). The North Atlantic Treaty Organization (NATO) and the U.S. Department of Defense (DOD) (2012b) define *physical security* as "physical measures designed to safeguard personnel, to prevent unauthorized access to equipment, installations, material, and documents, and to safeguard them against espionage, sabotage, damage, and theft." The U.K. Ministry of Defense (MOD) (2009b) defines physical security as "that part of National Security that relates to national assets and infrastructure" (p. 6). The Humanitarian Practice Network (2010) defines a *site* as "the real estate that the agency uses on a regular basis, notably offices, residences, and warehouses" (p. 181).

 Site Risks

Some sites are valuable in themselves or accommodate other things of value. For instance, even desolate land in a downtown area is valuable depending on allowable potential uses. Illegal occupancy or contamination of such land would lower its value or prevent the owners from exploiting the value, so owners are forced to take measures to control access to valuable land even when desolate.

Sites can be temporary, such as when operators must set up temporary camps during emergencies or humanitarian operations. These camps tend to be close to the threat that displaced the persons in the first place, so sometimes the camps are exposed to travelling threats, such as a flood or any human threats who want to harm the displaced groups. Some operations must move camp daily for a period when threats are in pursuit or the environment is intolerably hazardous due to natural hazards, unexploded ordnance, etc.

Built structures represent sunk costs and critical value to wider operations. At the same time, built structures are vulnerable to destruction by sustained vandalism or occasional arson or explosive devices. More valuable material parts, such as copper pipes, attract thieves.

Structures accommodate valuable stores or equipment, or secret or proprietary information that attract thieves or vandals. Structures accommodate operational activities and associated personnel and thus attract threats intent on interrupting operations or punishing operators.

The activities or resources at different sites may represent critical nodes on which wider systems depend. For instance, a production site likely depends on a logistics site, a power supply, the residences where personnel live away from work, the transport vehicles that carry supplies to consumers and users or carry personnel from residences to offices, and the infrastructure on which transport vehicles travel.

Site Security Services

Security services can be hired from commercial providers. For the Humanitarian Practice Network (2010, p. xvii) these services range from "soft security" (consultancy, training, and logistical support) to "hard security" (guards and close protection).

Fortunately, sites do not need to rely on private security, but can build their own capacity with official help. In recent decades public authorities have made available officials as advisers on private security, at least to major sites in or near populous areas.

For instance, the Department of Homeland Security places Private Security Advisers in local communities across the United States. Similarly, the Federal Bureau of Investigation is the main sponsor of local chapters of InfraGard, which advise local businesses on criminal threats and security. For American private operators overseas, since 1985 the U.S. Department of State has administered the Overseas Security Advisory Council (OSAC) to improve the exchange of information on security between the federal government and the private businesses operating overseas. More than 100 cities around the world have OSAC councils. Within the Bureau of Diplomatic Security (also established 1985), the Threat Investigations and Analysis Directorate (since 2008), through OSAC, supplies selected information to the private sector overseas and classified information to diplomatic sites.

In Britain, each police force (most are organized geographically) assigns police officers as architectural liaison officers to advise local business on designing their built structures to be more secure and to cooperate with each other for positive externalities. Each force shares in the Counter Terrorism Security Advisers who are provided from the National Counter Terrorism Security Office, colocated in the Security Service (MI5) but reporting to the Association of Chief Police Officers (primarily a policy-making organization, funded mainly by the Home Office and the police forces). These advisers identify critical private sites, assess the security of those sites, and visit business forums to give general advice on improving security. Each local government has an Emergency Planning Officer who can advise the private sector on making sites more resilient. The Centre for the Protection of National Infrastructure, located in the Security Service with the National Counter Terrorism Security Office, advises major private owners and operators of British infrastructure.

Site Location

Geographically or topographically, some sites face less risk or are easier to secure, such as sites higher than the flood plain, remote from urban crime, or protected by intervening authorities. On the other hand, such sites may be more valuable, so can attract challengers.

Sometimes a site is given without choice, but if possible careful choices should be made about the location. The Humanitarian Practice Network (2010, p. 181) notes that "[s]ite protection starts with site selection" and recommends sites

- With low natural risks,
- With few human hazards (such as criminals),
- With good public services or at least contractors who can provide the same,
- With positive externalities (such as nearby sites with good security capacity),
- With natural perimeters (such as a river or street), but
- Without concealed approaches (such as overgrown dry river beds or dark alleyways) and
- Without negative externalities (such as gathering places for protesters).

 Access Controls

The section describes controls on access to a site, beginning with a subsection on the scope of such controls, followed by subsections on assessing access controls, known bypasses of access controls, guards, emergency services and quick reaction forces, gates, and emergency refuges.

Scope

Access controls are attempts to manage the entry of actors or agents into some domain, for instance, by demanding identification of permitted persons before entry into a building. Most physical security and crime prevention within a site depends on preventing unauthorized access or use. Access controls also can be used to prevent unauthorized persons or items from leaving. Most thefts from sites seem to be by authorized users of the site, not unauthorized visitors. In case a visitor commits a crime while on site, a controlled exit gives an opportunity to at least record information about the time of exit that would be useful to the investigation.

Analytically, all access controls are attempts to control exposure (see Chapter 5). Perimeter barriers include walls, fences, or ditches that restrict access from the outside to the inside. The perimeter has points of controlled access, where the visitor must negotiate a human guard, lock, or identity check before access. If these access controls were to work perfectly in preventing all threats from access to the inside, nothing on the inside would be exposed to threats unless it were to leave the perimeter. Thus, given perfect access controls, only the perimeter and any assets on or outside the perimeter would need to be defended. Good access controls are more efficient than whole-of-site invulnerability.

Pedagogy Box 13.1 Official Definitions of Access Controls

The U.S. DOD (2012a, p. 42–43) defines *access control* as "any combination of barriers, gates, electronic security equipment, and/or guards that can limit entry or parking of unauthorized personnel or vehicles." "At a minimum, access control at a controlled perimeter requires the demonstrated capability to search for and detect explosives."

The British Civil Contingencies Secretariat defines a *controlled access point* as a "controlled point through which essential non-emergency service personnel may gain access through the outer cordon" (U.K. Cabinet Office, 2013).

Assessing Access Controls

In assessing our site security, we should judge exposure, vulnerability, and resilience. Exposure can be measured as the inverse of the effectiveness of controls on a threat's access to the interior, while bearing in mind that security comes at the expense of convenience. We could measure vulnerability by judging how prepared we are to defend against the threat. We should measure resilience by judging our capacity to control the negative returns of any attack and to operate despite an attack. Table 13.1 shows a published attempt to judge a site's exposure (as access) and the site's controls on the returns of any attack.

Friendly personnel can be employed to pretend to be threats in order to test the access controls. The ultimate test of the controls is a real unauthorized attempt at access, but the ultimate compliment to good access controls is that nobody attempts unauthorized access.

Bypasses of Access Controls

Unfortunately, access controls are not perfect, and they can be bypassed. Technology or human guards could fail, allowing access to the wrong people or simply not detecting who should not be allowed. Malicious actors could develop fake identifications that fool guards or electronic readers. For instance, in February 2013, Pakistani immigration authorities detained three persons who admitted that they had purchased their diplomatic passports from officials for 2 million rupees each. Pakistani investigators believe that between July 2010 and February 2013, corrupt officials illegally sold at least 2,000 diplomatic passports.

Disguises could fool guards into neglecting access controls. For instance, insurgents in Iraq and Afghanistan often have worn police or military uniforms during attacks on official sites. On September 14, 2012, a carefully prepared attack by Taliban insurgents on Camp Bastion in Afghanistan culminated with a penetration of the perimeter by attackers on foot wearing U.S. military uniforms. On June 25, 2013, four Taliban suicide bombers drove inside the perimeter of the presidential palace in Kabul with vehicles similar to those used by coalition forces, coalition uniforms, fake badges, and vehicle passes. They were able to bluff their way past two security checkpoints before they were halted by guards, where they killed themselves and three guards.

Table 13.1 A Scheme for Judging: Exposure in Terms of Access Controls, and Controls on the Returns

Score	Access to Certified Personnel to Positions Where Attack Can Be Carried Out	Screening, Surveillance, or Inspections to Detect Attacks	Engineering Controls on Attack Consequences
1 (low)	Limited	Invasive	Prevent consequences
2	Limited	Invasive	Limit consequences
3	Controlled	Semi-invasive	No controls
4	Controlled	Noninvasive	No controls
5 (high)	Free	None	No controls

SOURCE: Based on Greenberg, Chalk, Willis, Khilko, & Ortiz, 2006.

Relatives have been known to share identifications in order to fool access controls after one relative has been denied access or freedom to travel. Unfortunately, some malicious actors have abused exceptions to access controls granted on religious or cultural grounds. For instance, at least one of the attempted suicide bombers on the London underground train system on July 21, 2005, escaped from London to Birmingham in a *burqa* (a full body covering), although he was soon arrested there. Sometime in the last days of 2005, one of the murderers of a policewoman fled Britain in a *niqab* (face veil) and with his sister's passport to Somalia (although 2 years later he was extradited from there). On September 14, 2011, armed insurgents dressed in *burqa* occupied an unfinished high-rise building from where they fired on the U.S. embassy in Kabul, Afghanistan.

Guards might be too lazy or disgruntled to enforce compliance with the access controls or could be bribed by material incentives or seduced by ideological appeals. Guards who help outsiders are known as *insider threats*. For instance, from November 2009 to August 2011, a U.S. citizen with top-secret security clearance was employed as a contracted guard at the U.S. Consulate in Guangzhou, China, which had been completed only in 2011 at a cost of $1.5 billion. In August 2012, he pled guilty to conspiracy to sell access to the Consulate to Chinese officials so that they could plant surveillance devices.

Many guards have been bribed to allow items or persons past access controls for smuggling purposes and have justified their actions as harmless, but they may not realize that they could be allowing weapons or weapons that were intended for use against the site and even its guards.

Malicious actors can bypass access controls by finding less controlled routes. For instance, on November 26, 2008, armed terrorists landed in Mumbai by small boats rather than use public transport or infrastructure. They went on to murder more than 160 people, including many on public transport and roads. Similarly, private boats are regularly used to smuggle drugs and people past the strict access controls into the United States from Mexico to the California coast.

Private planes can be used to bypass the much more robust controls on access into and out of airports via commercial aircraft. Private planes have been used not just to smuggle cargo but also as a weapon that can bypass controls on weapons. For instance, on January 5, 2002, a 15-year-old boy flew a stolen light plane into a Bank of America building in Tampa, Florida, killing himself and leaving a note supporting the 9/11 attacks. On February 18, 2010, an American man flew a private plane into an Internal Revenue Service office in Austin, Texas, killing himself and one other.

Guards

Guards are the personnel tasked with controlling access. Guards, at least those working around the perimeter, are more exposed than are personnel within the perimeter, so guards need different capabilities. Consequently, the guards could be justifiably equipped with arms and armor against the threats, while the personnel on the inside would not need the same equipment so long as the access controls work perfectly.

Resources and laws often restrict the capabilities that can be acquired, carried, and used, and any acquisition implies additional training and liabilities. Portable arms include sticks or batons, irritant chemical sprays, weapons that discharge an electrical charge, and handguns. Attack dogs are common alternatives to carried weapons. Portable defensive technologies include vests and helmets made with materials resistant to kinetic attack. Cheap barrier protections against communicable diseases and toxic materials include latex or rubber gloves and facemasks. Kinetic-resistant materials would be required against sharp materials and fire-resistant materials against incendiary devices. Short sticks are useful for inspecting the contents of bags and vehicles. Extended mirrors are useful for viewing the underside and interior compartments of vehicles. Systems for inspecting other personnel include magnetic metal detectors, chemical explosive detectors, and Explosives Detection Dogs.

Good access controls do not necessarily deter malicious actors with strong intent, but at least keep the attacks on the perimeter. A successful control on access prevents exposure of the interior and its assets and persons, but other areas, assets, or persons must expose themselves to the threat in order to perform the control. So long as the guards are performing their role, the guards are more exposed but less vulnerable; the personnel on the inside are more vulnerable but less exposed. For instance, on April 16, 2010, a Republican terrorist group forced a taxi driver to drive a vehicle with an explosive device up to the gate of a British military base (Palace Barracks in Holywood, Northern Ireland), where it detonated, causing considerable destruction and few injuries, fortunately without killing anyone.

The perimeter's controllers remain exposed so long as they continue to control access (and do not run away). Consequently, many guards are harmed while preventing unauthorized access. For instance, on August 15, 2012, an unarmed guard was shot in the left forearm while apprehending an armed man attempting to enter the Family Research Council in Washington, DC, with admitted intent to kill as many staff as possible. On February 1, 2013, a suicide bomber detonated inside a built access point for staff of the U.S. Embassy in Ankara, Turkey, killing himself and a Turkish guard, but nobody inside the perimeter.

Unfortunately, absent perfect diligence during the procurement of guards and perfect leadership of guards, some guards tend to inattention or even noncompliance, sometimes for corrupt reasons. For instance, all of us have probably experienced a guard who did not pay proper attention to our credentials before permitting our access. More alarmingly, some smuggling is known to occur via airport personnel who take bribes in return for placing items in aircraft without the normal controls. The human parts of the counter-surveillance system need careful monitoring and review (see Chapter 11). Consequently, much of day-to-day physical security management can seem more like personnel management and leadership.

> Too often, however, guards are ineffective because they are untrained, poorly instructed, poorly paid, poorly equipped, and poorly managed. It is not uncommon to find a bed in the guardhouse of aid agency compounds, virtually guaranteeing that the guard will fall asleep on duty. During the day guards might be busy doing other things, and may be distracted. When hiring guards, provide clear terms of reference and make these a part of the contract. (Humanitarian Practice Network, 2010, p. 188)

Guards are hazards in the sense that they could become threats, perhaps activated with the weapons and the access provided to them for their work, perhaps colluding with external threats. In theory, properly vetted guards are trustworthy guards, but vetting is imperfect and should include periodic monitoring in case the initial conditions change. Responses to distrust of guards should include banning the guards from the interior of the perimeter, close supervision, random inspections, and covert surveillance of their activities, perhaps including their activities while off duty.

Site managers might reject local guards as untrustworthy or just for difficulties of linguistic or cultural translation. Multinational private security providers proliferated during the rapid growth in demand in the 2000s, particularly in Iraq. Providers might not have any loyalties to local threats and might boast impressive prior military experience, but they might offer new negative risks arising from insensitivity to local culture and a heavy military posture.

Emergency Services and Quick-Reaction Forces

Most sites rely on police and other public security personnel as their ultimate guards. In fact, most private actors have no guards of their own and rely entirely on public services, such as police, or good neighbors or their own resources for protection. Private actors with their own guards must make choices about when to involve public authorities. For instance, if guards repeatedly disturb actors trying to enter a perimeter without authorization, the guards could ask the police to temporarily increase the frequency of their visits to that perimeter. Unless the area is exceedingly corrupt or unstable, if external actors commit any crimes, the guards should call in judicial authorities. Consequently, site security managers should liaise with public authorities—and public authorities should cooperate in site security.

In addition to temporary increases in the number of guards, we should consider allocating personnel to respond to an emergency. In military terminology, such a force is often termed a *quick-reaction force*. (A quick reaction force is sometimes categorized as threat interdiction rather than an access control, but is usefully discussed here anyway.) In areas with functioning public governance, public security personnel act as the final force in response to any emergency that the site's own guards could not handle. In areas without reliable local security forces, the site would be forced to arrange for its own quick reaction force. For instance, an embassy, as sovereign territory, may deploy any personnel and weapons it wants within its perimeter, but most embassies reach formal agreements with local authorities for local security forces to respond to emergencies at the embassy. In case local authorities fail in their duties, other personnel are prepared to deploy to the aid of diplomatic missions or posts in need. In areas where local security forces are unreliable, diplomatic missions from different countries might reach agreements on mutual aid during an emergency.

Pedagogy Box 13.2 The U.S. Diplomatic Mission in Benghazi, 2012

Local security personnel are usually cheaper and more available than foreign personnel, but their effectiveness might not justify their cheapness. For instance, in 2012 the U.S. Mission in Benghazi, Libya, had agreed that a local militia (the 17th February Martyrs Brigade) would provide guards and a quick-reaction force.

> Although the February 17 militia had proven effective in responding to improvised explosive device (IED) attacks on the Special Mission in April and June 2012, there were some troubling indicators of its reliability in the months and weeks preceding the September attacks. At the time of Ambassador Stevens' visit, February 17 militia members had stopped accompanying Special Mission vehicle movements in protest over salary and working hours. (Accountability Review Board for Benghazi, December 18, 2012)

By further request, dated September 9, 2012, the Mission requested three members of the quick-reaction force to reinforce the guards on site. However, during the attack of September 11, the guards fled and the militia did not reinforce, and the Ambassador and three others were killed.

Gates

Gates are the switchable barriers at the access control point. Gates are active barriers in the sense that they can switch between open and closed. By default (at least during higher risk periods), gates should be closed; if a visitor is permitted entry, the gate would be opened. This seems like an obvious prescription, but consider that gates are often left open because of complaints about disruption to traffic or simple laziness on the part of the guards, rather than because the risk level justifies the gate being left open.

The subsections below consider portable, antivehicle, multiple, and containment gates.

Portable Gates

In an emergency, a gate can be formed with available portable materials such as rocks or drums or trestles that can be moved by the guards. Vehicles and human chains can be used as gates, but these are valuable assets to expose. Sometimes gates are extremely portable, such as cable or rope, which are adequate for indicating an access control, but are not substantial enough to stop a noncompliant visitor. More repellent but still portable materials include barbed wire and razor wire, mounted on sticks so that the guards can handle without harm.

Sometimes, when the risk is sufficiently elevated or guards or gate materials are short, the sites of access are closed and perhaps reinforced with more substantial materials, in which case they act effectively as passive barriers (see below).

Vehicle Gates

In prepared sites, gates normally consist of barriers that can be raised and lowered or swung out of the way on hinges or that slide on rails. More substantial barriers to vehicles could be formed by filling drums or boxes with earth, rocks, or concrete, while keeping the item light and handy enough to be removed whenever the guards permitted. As portable vehicle barriers, guards could deploy spikes: a caltrop is easily improvised with four spikes so that at least one spike presents upward however it falls; some systems consist of a belt of spikes that collapses into an easy package when not needed. One-way exits can be created with spikes that are hinged to fall away when a vehicle exits but to present if a vehicle attempts to enter. These spikes would disable most pneumatic tires, but some vehicles have solid tires, pneumatic tires with solid cores, or pneumatic tires designed to deflate gracefully, permitting the vehicle to run for some distance (more than enough distance for a suicidal driver to reach any target within a typical perimeter). More substantial vehicle gates consist of bollards or plates that are raised in front of the visiting vehicle and are retracted when permitted.

Multiple Gates

Some access control points must include several gates or gates with controls on more than one type of threat. For instance, a gate might be specified to be robust enough at a low height to stop an energetic vehicle from crashing through, but also tall enough to discourage a pedestrian from climbing over the gate. Sometimes gates are placed in series, so that the visitor must negotiate one gate successfully before the visitor is permitted entry through the next gate. The traffic is sometimes slowed by passive barriers, such as bumps in the road or fixed vertical barriers staggered across the road, which the vehicle must negotiate at slow speed—these passive barriers slow traffic in case guards need time to close a gate or take offensive action against the driver. However, such measures add costs and inconvenience, so may not be justified when the risks are low.

Containment Areas

Sometimes designers must consider developing multiple gates into a containment area within which visitors, of all types, can be contained before further access is permitted. Containment areas should be established in the areas between where people, supplies, and mail arrive and where they are accepted inside the perimeter. Supplies often arrive in large packages that could contain hidden threats; the smallest mailed packages could contain hazardous powders or sharp materials. Moreover, these items usually are transported within large vehicles that themselves could contain threats. For security reasons, delivery areas should be remote from the interior, but for commercial reasons the delivery area should be close to the point of demand. An attractive compromise is a dedicated area for deliveries, close to but outside the perimeter, so that vehicles can make their deliveries without the delays and transaction costs associated with accessing the interior. The delivery or unloading area should be a contained area in which items can be inspected for threats before allowance into another area where they would be sorted and labeled for their final destination within the perimeter. The interface between the contained delivery area and the main sorting space should be strengthened against blast or forced human entry and provided with access controls. For small, quiet sites, perhaps a single room would be sufficient for storage of deliveries at peak frequency.

Pedagogy Box 13.3 U.S. Man-Traps

"The December 6, 2004, attack on the U.S. consulate in Jeddah, Saudi Arabia, provides a specific example of how Diplomatic Security adjusts its security procedures. According to State, the attackers gained entry into the U.S. consulate by running through the vehicle access gate. While Diplomatic Security had installed a device to force vehicles to stop for inspection before entering a compound, it did not prevent the attackers from entering the compound by foot once the barrier was lowered. To correct that vulnerability, Diplomatic Security has incorporated 'man-traps' in conjunction with the vehicle barriers, vehicle entry points at most high and critical threat posts, whereby, when the barrier is lowered, the vehicle enters a holding pen, or 'man-trap,' for inspection before a second barrier in front of the vehicle opens into the compound" (U.S. Government Accountability Office [GAO], 2009, pp. 13–14).

Emergency Refuges

Within the perimeter could be constructed a further controlled area for emergency shelter from threats that breach the perimeter. Such areas are sometimes called *refuges*, *citadels*, *safe havens*, *panic rooms*, or *safe rooms*. They are differentiated by extra controls on access, with few access points that are controlled solely from within.

Some safe areas are supplied in prefabricated form, the size of a standard shipping container for quick and easy delivery to the requirer.

In theory, a safe area could be constructed anywhere with normally available construction materials to a standard that would disallow entry to anybody unless equipped with substantial military-grade explosives.

> It should be easily and quickly accessible, and preferably located in the core of the building. Alternatively, an upper floor can be converted into a safe area by installing a grill on the staircase,

> which is locked at night. Safe rooms should have a reinforced door, a telephone or other means of communication (preferably un-interruptable [from outside]) in order to call for help, and a list of key contact numbers, plus a torch or candles and matches. Consider storing a small quantity of water, food, and sanitary items in the safe room as well. The purpose of a safe room is to protect people, not assets. Putting everything in the safe room is only likely to encourage robbers to make greater efforts to break in. Leave them something to steal, if not everything. (Humanitarian Practice Network, 2010, p. 187)

Structures can be built to be proof against the largest aircraft-delivered explosives and radiological, chemical, and biological threats, but they would become very expensive and are not typical of safe areas. Consequently, most safe areas should be regarded as truly short-term emergency solutions to an invasion of the perimeter pending rescue from outside the site.

However, such structures are vulnerable to any outside restriction of supplies of air, water, or food, unless the protected area is equipped with substantial reserves of water and food and is sealed. Outside air could be filtered and conditioned by a system that also produces a slight air overpressure inside the structure. Absent such equipment, fire and smoke are easy weapons for outside threats to use against those trapped within a safe area. Even if the safe area itself is not flammable, the occupants could be suffocated or poisoned by smoke from burning materials placed against the safe area's apertures or vents. For instance, on September 11, 2012, U.S. Ambassador Chris Stevens was killed by smoke inhalation inside the safe room at the diplomatic site in Benghazi, Libya. Consequently, a system for filtering incoming air, with baffles to ingress of threats (such as granades), and for generating an overpressure of air inside the structure (in combination with hermetic seals on all apertures) now seems required. Such a system became standard in military fortifications around World War II and is not prohibitively expensive.

 Passive Perimeters

This section describes the passive perimeters between the access control points. The subsections below define passive perimeters and describe the material barriers, human patrols and surveillance, and sensors.

Scope

The perimeter is the outer boundary of a site. The perimeter is controlled more passively than the access points, usually in the sense that the more passive part implies less human interaction and more material barriers. Passive perimeters can be designed to block vehicles, persons, and animals (rogue and diseased animals are more common in unstable areas) and can be equipped with sensors that alert guards to any attempt to pass the barrier.

Pedagogy Box 13.4 U.S. Official Definition

The U.S. DOD (2012a, p. 43) defines *perimeter control* as "a physical boundary at which vehicle access is controlled with sufficient means to channel vehicles to the access control points."

Pedagogy Box 13.5 Y-12 Perimeter Failure

The Y-12 National Security Complex, near Oak Ridge National Laboratory, Tennessee, is the U.S. primary facility for processing and storing weapons-grade uranium and developing related technologies. On July 28, 2010, three peace activists, including an 82-year-old nun, cut the outer security fence and reached a building where highly enriched uranium is stored. They splashed blood on the outer walls and revealed banners denouncing nuclear weapons before guards reached them. The site was shut down for 2 weeks during a review of security, after which several officials were dismissed or reassigned.

Material Barriers

Natural barriers include dense or thorny vegetation, rivers, lakes, oceans, mud, and steep ground. Even a wide expanse of inhospitable terrain can be considered a barrier. Indeed, most international borders have no barriers other than natural barriers.

Discrete artificial barriers include ditches, fences, walls, stakes, wire, and stacked sandbags, rocks, or earth. Artificial barriers include more deliberate weapons, such as sharpened stakes, metal spikes, broken glass, hidden holes, landmines, and even toxic pollutants, biological hazards, and pathogens.

The U.S. DOD (2008, pp. 4–5.3.2.1.2) prescribes a chainlink fence of 2.75 inch diameter cables, taller than the average man, with barbed wire strands at top, as a barrier against pedestrians. As barriers against vehicles, it prescribes either

- concrete bollards (no more than 4 feet apart, each 3 feet above ground and 4 feet below ground in a concrete foundation, each consisting of 8 inches diameter of concrete poured inside a steel pipe 0.5 inch thick) or
- a continuous concrete planter (3 feet above ground, 1.5 feet below ground, 3 feet wide at base, with a trough at top for planting vegetation as disguise or beautification).

Human Patrols and Surveillance

Barriers are passive if they imply no necessary human in the system (once they have been constructed), but guards are still important to the prevention of any breach of the barrier. No barrier can perfectly prevent access, but a guard could prevent someone cutting through, climbing over, tunneling under, or otherwise passing a barrier. Thus, barriers should not be considered entirely inanimate controls and should be used with periodic human patrols and inspections.

Human patrols may vary with the risk level. For instance, the U.S. Department of State has prescribed varying perimeter patrols according to "threat level" (see Table 13.2).

Humans can guard perimeters on foot and also from towers overlooking the perimeter. Towers imply more passivity, although less exposure, on the part of the guards. Surveillance technologies can help to extend the scope of the guard's control of the perimeter, as described in the next section.

Table 13.2 The U.S. Department of State's (2006) Prescribed Changes in "Perimeter Patrol Requirements by Threat Level"

Threat Level	Perimeter Patrol Requirements
Critical	24-hour foot patrol at official facilities and residences for the ambassador, deputy chief of mission, principal officers, and Marines. Guards are to be armed unless prohibited by law.
High	24-hour foot patrol at official facilities and residences for the ambassador, deputy chief of mission, principal officers, and Marines.
Medium	12-hour foot patrol of perimeter during the day and at residences at night, where required, to supplement host country support at official facilities.
Low	No provision for foot patrol of official facilities' perimeters

Surveillance and Counter-Surveillance

This section describes the scope of surveillance, the practice of counter-surveillance at a site, surveillance technologies in general, surveillance of communications, and surveillance in poor light.

Surveillance

Surveillance is systematic observation of something. Surveillance is an activity open to both malicious actors and guards. Malicious actors often survey potential targets before choosing a target, then survey the target in order to plan an attack, and survey the target again in order to train the attackers. In turn, guards should be looking to counter such surveillance.

Pedagogy Box 13.6 U.S. Official Definition

For U.S. DOD (2012b), *surveillance* is the "systematic observation of aerospace, surface, or subsurface areas, places, persons, or things, by visual, aural, electronic, photographic, or other means."

Counter-Surveillance

Counter-surveillance is "watching whether you are being watched" (Humanitarian Practice Network, 2010, p. xvi). Energetic guards, by discouraging loitering or suspicious investigation of the site's defenses, can disrupt malicious surveillance before the attack could be planned. For instance, in March 1999, the U.S. State Department's Bureau of Diplomatic Security introduced the concept of "surveillance detection teams" at most diplomatic posts. These teams look for terrorist surveillance of diplomatic sites and operations (U.S. GAO, 2009, p. 13).

Also, surveillance can be useful to the investigation after an attack. Television cameras that record images of a site are less deterrent than guards but more useful for investigators because their images are usually more accurate than human memories and more persuasive as evidence during criminal prosecutions.

Be careful not to underestimate the audacity of threats to the most secure sites. For instance, in September 2010, British officials ordered trees to be cut down around the headquarters in Northern Ireland of the British Security Service (MI5), inside Palace Barracks, a secure military site. Four surveillance cameras had been found hidden among the tree branches. On September 26, 2012, Irish police arrested two men suspected of spying on the operational headquarters in Dublin of the Irish police (*Garda Siochana*). One of the suspects was recognized as a known member of the Real Irish Republican Army, a terrorist group, by police officers passing through the hotel opposite the headquarters. Police officers searched the suspect's hotel room, where they found parabolic microphones and digital cameras.

The Humanitarian Practice Network (2010, p. 194) describes five steps in the typical attack on a site:

1. Initial target selection
2. Preattack surveillance
3. Planning the attack
4. Rehearsing the attack
5. Executing the attack

It recommends the following five counter-surveillance activities:

1. Identify likely observation posts and point them out to staff.
2. Instruct guards to patrol the potential observation points.
3. Instruct staff to look out for behaviors that indicate external surveillance, such as loitering or frequent passes by the same vehicle or person.
4. Build relationships with neighbors and ask them to report suspicious behavior.
5. Vary routines and routes into and out of the site.

Surveillance Technologies

Surveillance technologies can be as simple as binoculars or even the optical sights on weapons (although the latter can be provocative). Remote television cameras allow guards to more efficiently and securely watch sites. Radar devices can be used to track vehicles out of visual range. Range-finders can be used to measure the ranges of targets within line of sight. (Range-finders can be as simple as hand-held prismatic or laser-based instruments.) Unmanned aerial vehicles (UAVs) can be launched to film targets further away. Earth-orbiting satellites also can take images.

Most of these technologies are available in cheap and portable forms for the poorly resourced user or for temporary sites. A small robotic camera, a remote control interface, and display screen can be packaged inside a briefcase. Radar devices can be packaged inside something the size of standard luggage, yet still offer a range over miles. Prismatic range-finders are cheap and satisfactory for most uses short of long-range gunnery; laser range-finders are more accurate. UAVs too can be small enough to be carried and launched from one hand. Commercial satellites can provide images to any private client.

Passive barriers can be made more active if equipped with sensors, such as video cameras or trip wires or lasers that detect movement, or infrared or thermal sensors that detect body heat, although all motion or heat sensors can be triggered by false positives such as harmless animals. Still a guard dog is the best combined sensor/nonlethal weapon available to the human guard on foot.

Pedagogy Box 13.7 Closed-Circuit Television (CCTV)

CCTV essentially refers to cameras that transmit images electronically to some remote monitor (the term was developed as a distinction from television that is broadcast on an open network). CCTV cameras remain attractive for material reasons, despite their limitations. Cameras are much cheaper than human employees; juries often prefer camera-captured images as evidence over human testimony and studies show that human witnesses are often mistaken when they claim to identify others as the perpetrators. However, their use can be challenged on ethical, legal, and effectiveness grounds.

Britain is often given as the country with the most CCTV units deployed, most of them deployed since the mid-1980s in response to urban crime and terrorism. By the early 2000s, Britain had more than 4 million cameras, by 2007 more than 25% of the world's CCTV cameras. Ten thousand had been installed in London alone. Certain parts of the United States boast similar densities. For instance, more than 500 had been installed in Times Square, New York City, by 2007.

Cameras deter some crime, and their images can be used as evidence of crime during investigation or prosecution of criminals. However, most cameras have narrow fields of view and poor resolution. Some cameras are dummies, some are not operable some of the time, and some recorded images are not saved up to the time when investigators realize that they are needed. Most cameras are passive, although some cameras can be controlled remotely, and a few can even react automatically to certain target behaviors (such as the erratic circular walking as the criminal ponders the target). Criminals would not be deterred if they were to know how to avoid cameras or hide their identity or realize that not all cameras are recording effectively. Even perfect images of criminals do not necessarily lead to identification of a criminal. Evidence from Britain suggests that only 20% of the crimes captured on CCTV actually lead to an arrest. In Britain, CCTV cameras are installed in almost every public space, but some evidence suggests that cameras abate crimes only inside mass car parking structures. Meanwhile, law-abiding citizens are increasingly concerned about privacy violations via cameras (Kennedy & Van Brunschot, 2009, pp. 14–19).

Surveillance of Communications

Scanning for two-way radio traffic near a site makes sense because the short-range of such traffic and the lack of a service provider implies irregular motivations. Organized actors often use two-way radio communications during surveillance and attacks: cheap and portable scanners can search likely bandwidths for traffic, although a linguist too might be required to make sense of foreign languages. However, the threats could use coded signals to defeat even a linguist.

Scanning for private telephone traffic is technically possible but is more legally restricted and implies more false positives. An organization usually faces few restrictions on tapping the e-mail systems, telephones, and radios that the organization itself provides to employees or contractors. In fact, organizations often unadmittedly intercept employee e-mails in search of noncompliant behaviors. Judicial authorities with probable cause can seek legal powers to seize any communications device.

Malicious actors can avoid such observation by avoiding the organization's communications systems. Indeed, terrorists now routinely use temporary e-mail accounts, unsent draft messages with shared access, temporary cell/mobile telephones, text messages that are deleted after one reading, coded signals, and verbal messages to avoid surveillance of their communications (see Chapter 14).

Surveillance in Poor Light

In poor light conditions (night-time, dust-storms, cloudy weather), observers can turn to artificial sources of light for illumination. Indeed, artificial light is considered a key technology in countering night-time crime in urban areas. The perimeters of sites, or at least the access points, are often artificially lit. Guards of sites should have access to electrically powered lamps at these points and carry battery-powered lamps.

Infrared filters block visible light but permit infrared radiation, which occupies a range neighboring the visible light range, so infrared lights can be used to illuminate targets without the target being aware (unless the target was equipped with infrared sights). Passive infrared sights (available since the 1950s) rely heavily on active infrared illumination (usually from electrically-powered infra-red searchlights), which in turn is easily detected by passive infrared sights. Infrared images are higher in resolution than later competitive alternatives, including thermal and intensified visible-light images, although infrared images are monochrome. Infrared systems also remain much cheaper than those later alternatives.

Like infrared sights, thermal imagers (deployed from the 1970s) detect radiation in the infrared range of the electromagnetic spectrum. Thermal imagers focus on the narrower range associated with temperature and do not rely on active illumination. As long as the target's temperature is sufficiently distinct from background temperature and is not obscured by dampening materials, it can be distinguished through a thermal imager.

However, thermal images are not as high in resolution as actively illuminated infrared images. Moreover, thermal signatures can be dampened. Intervening materials can totally obscure the thermal signature, so targets can hide from enemy thermal imagers in much the same ways they hide from illumination by visible light, i.e., behind structures, forested or urban areas, inclement weather, or the appropriate type of smoke. Since glass and transparent plastic materials permit visible light but not infrared radiation, targets can use these materials to obscure themselves from thermal imagers without obscuring visible light. Human beings give off an easily detectable infrared signature in the open; automotive engines are hotter still, but engine compartments can be dampened and will equalize with background temperatures within 30 minutes or so of turning off the engine (and parking outside of sunlight).

Thermal imagers can see through light fog and rain but are confused by thick fog (whose water droplets refract light in unpredictable ways). They can see through most types of battlefield smoke, but modern forces can lay smoke that is chemically configured to obscure infrared signatures.

The lenses of thermal imagers are expensive and easily damaged by a fingernail, dust, or sand, so they are normally covered by a protective cover when not in use, unlike a cheap, robust, and always available infrared filter. Like image intensifiers, thermal imagers are easily dazzled by laser weapons. Some cheap handheld laser pointers are sufficiently powerful to dazzle thermal imagers from a range of about one mile.

Image intensifiers (deployed from the 1980s) are vacuum-tube based devices that intensify visible light. Like thermal imagers, they are less reliant than are infrared sights on active illumination, but they are expensive (most are confined to major military platforms) and can be disabled by pulse lasers.

Security Engineering

Built structures accommodate people, stores, equipment, operational activities and thus are part of the material protective system at a site. The construction of buildings and other structures to be more secure is a technical area sometimes termed *security engineering*.

The subsections below describe how to protect materially the site by setback or stand-off construction, blast barriers, barriers to kinetic attack, and protective glass.

Setback or Standoff

The most effective way to materially improve invulnerability within the perimeter is to expand the distance between the perimeter and the site's assets, such as the buildings, although this ideal is often retarded by urban constraints, material limitations, or desires for accessibility.

The effectiveness of setback can be appreciated from the many recent attacks on sites using substantial explosive devices outside the perimeter without killing anyone inside the perimeter (such as the van bomb that detonated on the road outside the military headquarters in Damascus, Syria, on September 25, 2012), compared to similar devices that penetrated the target building in the days of lax attention to setback (on October 23, 1983, a suicide vehicle-borne explosive device exploded inside the lobby of the U.S. Marine Corps barracks in Beirut, killing 242).

The stand-off distance can be engineered simply with winding access routes or access controls along the access route. Passive barriers can be used to increase this stand-off distance. Passive barriers to vehicles can be as unobtrusive as raised planters for trees or benches, as long as they are substantial enough to defeat moving vehicles. Setback can be achieved urgently by closing roads outside the perimeter. For instance, after Egyptian protesters invaded the U.S. Embassy in Cairo on September 11, 2012, Egyptian authorities stacked large concrete blocks across the ends of the street.

The U.S. DOD (2012a) recommends at least 5.5 meters (18 feet) between structures and a controlled perimeter or any uncontrolled vehicular roadways or parking areas, or 3.6 meters (12 feet) between structures and vehicular roadways and parking within a controlled perimeter. Reinforced-concrete load-bearing walls could stand as little as 4 meters (13 feet) away from vehicles only if human occupancy of the building was relatively light and the perimeter were controlled. (An "inhabited" building is "routinely occupied by 11 or more DoD personnel and with a population density of greater than one person per 430 gross square feet—40 gross square meters".) The same walls would need to stand 20 meters (66 feet) away from the perimeter in the case of primary gathering buildings or high occupancy housing. (Primary gathering buildings are "routinely occupied by 50 or more DoD personnel and with a population density of greater than one person per 430 gross square feet"; "high occupancy" housing is "billeting in which 11 or more unaccompanied DoD personnel are routinely housed" or "family housing with 13 or more units per building".)

The DOD issues different standards for stand-off distances by building material, occupancy, and perimeter. For instance, containers and trailers that are used as primary gathering places during expeditionary operations are supposed to stand at least 71 meters (233 feet) away from a perimeter, although fabric-covered structures (which generate fewer secondary projectiles under blast) could stand 31 meters (102 feet) from the perimeter.

The DOD no longer endorses a previous standard (2007) that physical security managers might remember in an emergency, if they were unable to access the current standards: high occupancy and primary gathering buildings were supposed to stand 25 meters or no less than 10 meters (33 feet) away from vehicle parking or roadways or trash containers within the perimeter; other "inhabited" buildings were supposed to stand 25 meters away from an uncontrolled perimeter and 10 meters away from vehicles and trash containers within the perimeter; and low-occupancy buildings were allowed to be closer still.

The Department of State's standard, since 1985, for diplomatic buildings is 30 meters (100 meters) setback, although many diplomatic buildings remain substandard due to the constraints of available land and demands for higher occupancy in dense central urban areas. A full U.S. embassy requires about 15 acres of land even before setback is factored in.

Where setback is not possible, buildings need to be hardened above standard, which is very expensive, or the standards are waived. For instance, in 2009, U.S. officials sought waivers to State Department standards in order to build a consulate in Mazar-e-Sharif, in northern Afghanistan. The officials signed a 10-year lease and spent more than $80 million on a site currently occupied by a hotel. The setback distance between the buildings and the perimeter was below standard; moreover, the perimeter shared a wall with local shopkeepers and was overlooked by several tall buildings. Following a revealing departmental report in January 2012, the site was abandoned before the consulate was ever established.

Setback is specified mostly as a control on blast, but firearms can strike from further away, particularly from elevated positions. For instance, in Kabul, Afghanistan, on September 13, 2011, insurgents occupied an unfinished high-rise building overlooking the U.S. Embassy about 300 yards away. With assault rifles and rocket-propelled grenades they wounded four Afghan civilians inside the U.S. perimeter before Afghan forces cleared the building the next day.

In suburban locations, diplomatic missions typically have more space but are more remote to urban stakeholders. Sometimes diplomatic missions are established in suburban and rural locations with plenty of space, but with exceptions to the security standards given their ongoing temporary status, the constraints of surrounding private property, and diplomatic goals of accessibility to locals. For instance, the small U.S. mission in Benghazi was noncompliant with the standards at the time of the devastating attack of September 11, 2012, which killed the Ambassador and three other federal employees. In fact, it was little more than a small private villa on lease.

Blast Barriers

Blast barriers are required to baffle and reflect blast—often they are incorporated into the barriers to vehicles and humans too.

Specialized blast walls are normally precast from concrete and designed for carriage by standard construction equipment and to slot together without much pinning or bonding. They can be improvised from sandbags, temporary containers filled with earth (some flat-packed reinforced-canvas bags and boxes are supplied for this purpose), vehicles filled with earth, or simply ramps of earth. Stacked hard items of small size do not make good blast barriers because they collapse easily and provide secondary projectiles.

The readiest and best blast barriers are actually other complete buildings. Any structure will reflect or divert blast waves. Buildings have layers of load-bearing walls. The first structure to be hit by blast will absorb or deflect most of the energy that would otherwise hit the second structure in the way, so the ideal expedient is to acquire a site with buildings around the perimeter that are not needed and can be left unoccupied to shield the occupied buildings on the interior of the site. However, this ideal sounds expensive in material terms and also implies extra burdens on the guards who must ensure that malicious actors do not enter the unoccupied structures. This is why setback usually specifies an uncovered space between perimeter and accommodation. However, advantages would remain for the site security manager who acquires a site surrounded by other built sites with sufficient security to keep blast weapons on the outside of them all. Indeed, this is one principal behind placing a more valuable site in the center of an already controlled built site.

Barriers to Kinetic Attack

Typical walls, even typical load-bearing walls in the largest buildings, are not proof against projectiles fired from some portable firearms. Typical wood-framed and -paneled structures can be perforated by the bullets from any small arms. Typical masonry walls will defeat a few bullets from light assault firearms but will not resist larger caliber projectiles of the sort fired from a sniper's rifle or heavy machine gun. Indeed, damage from multiple rounds of such caliber would cause masonry walls to fail. Armor-piercing bullets, although rare outside of major militaries, would pass cleanly through typical masonry.

Reinforcing rods will dramatically increase the tensile (shear) strength of masonry and concrete—effectively holding the matrix together despite the stresses caused by blast or the damage caused by projectiles. Additionally, concrete is a harder material than clay or mud brick. A typical load-bearing wall in reinforced concrete (6 inches thick is standard in the United States) is not quite proof against typical firearms. To resist ubiquitous 7.62 mm bullets (as fired by most assault rifles since Soviet proliferation of the AK47), reinforced concrete needs to be 0.15 meters (7 inches) thick, while reinforced masonry needs to be 0.20 meters (8 inches) thick (U.S. DOD, 2008). To defeat better equipped threats or mixed threats (such as blast followed by kinetic attack), the walls should be much thicker. The standard U.S. embassy has walls 0.76 meters (2.5 feet) thick. During World War II, the standard thickness of military fortifications was 2 meters (6.5 feet) if mostly buried or 3.5 meters (11.5 feet) if fully exposed.

These standards assume that the material was constructed correctly, which would be a bad assumption in unstable areas, where contractors or laborers are less incentivized or regulated to supply the correct materials (cement and steel reinforcing rods are expensive materials), to use concrete correctly (concrete is normally allowed to cure for 28 days before further construction, although it can be considered about 80% cured after 7 days; wet-curing for 90 days would double the hardness), or to use reinforcing rods correctly (the steel should be mild, rods should join, and their matrix should be sufficiently dense without disturbance during pouring of the wet concrete). For example, the reasons that the State Department's inspector gave for condemning the U.S. consulate in Mazar-e-Sharif, Afghanistan, in January 2012 included the poor materials (sun-dried mud bricks and untreated timber) and construction techniques used for the nascent perimeter wall.

Protective Glass

Glass is a frequent material in windows and doors and surveillance systems (see above). However, it is usually the most fragile material in a built structure, so is easiest for actors to break when attempting to access. Moreover, when glass fails, it tends to shatter into many sharp projectiles, although species are available that shatter into relatively harmless pieces. Shatterproof and bulletproof species are essentially laminated plastic and glass sheets, where more sheets and stronger bonds imply less fragility.

Glass can be minimized by designing buildings with fewer and smaller apertures. Glass can be used in shatterproof or bulletproof species where human break-ins or small arms attacks are sufficiently likely. Laminated sheets of glass and plastic are useful for protecting guards who must have line of sight in exposed locations in order to perform their duties. Pieces of such material can be set up even in temporary or emergency sites, where no built structures are present.

SUMMARY

This chapter has described

- the scope of physical site security,
- site risks,
- site security services,
- site location,
- access controls, including the scope of access controls, how to assess them, how they are bypassed, guards, emergency services and quick reaction forces, gates, and emergency refuges,
- passive perimeters, including their scope, the material barriers, and human patrols and surveillance,
- surveillance, counter-surveillance, surveillance technologies, surveillance of communications, and surveillance in poor light, and
- security engineering, including construction setback from the perimeter, blast barriers, barriers to kinetic attacks, and protective glass.

QUESTIONS AND EXERCISES

1. How could you select locations that are more secure?
2. Why are controls used to control exit as well as access?
3. What is the best way to assess our access controls?
4. How can threats bypass control controls?
5. Why do guards face more risks?
6. Why would good guards need a quick reaction force?
7. Why would we want multiple gates at the point of access?
8. Why would we want a containment area at the point of access?
9. What should you specify for a refuge?
10. Give some examples of passive material barriers.
11. Why should humans be part of a perimeter?

12. Why is counter-surveillance useful at a site?
13. What are the advantages and disadvantages of setback as material protection?
14. Give some examples of improvised blast barriers.
15. Why is reinforced concrete a useful material for resisting kinetic attack?
16. What two threats are blocked by protective glass?

Information, Communications, and Cyber Security

This chapter covers the increasingly salient domains of information, communications, and cyber security. The five main sections below define information, the technologies, and cyberspace; describe the different sources of malicious activities; describe the access vectors and how they can be controlled; describe the actual malicious activities; and give advice on how to provide information and cyber security in general.

 Scope

This section defines information security, information communications technology, and cyber space.

Information

Information security includes the security of information in all its forms, of which the most important conventional categories are verbal and cognitive forms, hard forms (including paper documents and artifacts), information technology (IT), information and communications technology (ICT), and cyber space (essentially electronically networked information and ICTs).

> Information can take many forms—from data sets of confidential personal information through to records of sensitive meetings, personnel records, policy recommendations, correspondence, case files[,] and historical records . . . Therefore, information risks are not necessarily the same as IT security risks (although managing IT security is usually a critical component of any strategy to manage information risks). (U.K. National Archives, 2008, p. 2)

ICTs

Information technology normally refers to any electronic or digital means of holding or communicating information. Some authorities prefer to refer to *information and communications technology* (ICT) in order to bring more attention to communications technologies, such as radios, telephones, and e-mail.

Cyber Space

In recent decades, information and communications technology have tended to be conflated inaccurately with cyber space. Cyber space is not a tight term but best refers to digitally networked information and information technologies, normally personal computer terminals, but increasingly also mobile devices such as mobile telephones, connected to remote computers or hard drives ("servers") via a digital network (either the Internet/World Wide Web or an organizational Intranet).

Pedagogy Box 14.1 Official Descriptions and Definitions of Cyber Space

The British Ministry of Defense (MOD) (2010a, p. 138) describes the following historical growth of cyber space:

- the personal computer era from 1980 to 1990, when information proliferated on desktop computers;
- the first web era from 1990 to 2000, when information moved on to the World Wide Web;
- the second web era from 2000 to 2010, when the web became more social;
- the third web era since 2010, when the web connected knowledge (the "semantic web"); and
- some future fourth web era, when some *metaweb* would connect intelligence.

The U.S. Government Accountability Office (GAO, 2011a) described cyber space as a network of more than 12 billion digital devices and more than 2 billion users. The United States certainly has the most personal computers in use and hosts the most valuable websites, service providers, and online businesses. China, the most populous country, has the second largest national population of personal computers and the largest national population of mobile telephone subscribers. India and Russia follow with the next largest populations of mobile telephone subscribers, but much fewer people have personal computers there. Japan, Australasia, Western European countries, and Canada are densely populated with mobile telephones and personal computers. The regional leaders include Brazil in South America, Mexico in central America, and South Africa in Africa.

The U.S. Department of Defense (DOD) (2012b) dictionary definition of *cyber space* is a "global domain within the information environment consisting of interdependent network of information technology infrastructures, including the internet, telecommunications networks, computer systems, and embedded processors and controllers."

The U.S. Office of the National Counterintelligence Executive (ONCIX) (2011) defined cyber space as "the interdependent network of information technology (IT) infrastructure, and includes the internet, telecommunications networks, computer systems, and embedded processors and controllers in critical industries."

For U.S. Department of Homeland Security (DHS) (2009) a *cyber system* is "any combination of facilities, equipment, personnel, procedures, and communications integrated to provides cyber services" (p. 109).

Sources of Attacks

The sources of cyber attacks are the human sources of the attacks. These sources include official actors (such as spies), profit-oriented organized criminals, terrorists, commercial competitors, ideologically motivated hackers (including campaigners for political and Internet freedoms), inquisitive and curious people, and journalists. Another key categorization is between external and internal threats (those without or within the target organization).

Some of the categories above overlap and some are defined more by their vectors than motivations. (Vectors are described later.) Here, the subsections below describe the four main categories of source: profit-oriented criminals; insider threats; external threats; and nation-states.

Pedagogy Box 14.2 Official Categories of Cyber Attack Sources

In 2003, a survey of experts by the Federal Bureau of Investigation (FBI) and Computer Security Institute identified the likeliest sources of cyber attacks on American or U.S. targets as

- independent hackers (82% of respondents);
- disgruntled employees (77%);
- American competitors (40%);
- foreign governments (28%); and
- foreign corporations (25%).

The Industrial Control Systems Computer Emergency Response Team (ICS-CERT), a unit of the DHS since 2009, identifies five primary cyber threats:

1. National governments
2. Terrorists
3. Industrial spies and organized crime organizations
4. Hacktivists
5. Hackers

(Continued)

(Continued)

The U.S. GAO (2005b, p. 5) reviewed data from the FBI, Central Intelligence Agency (CIA), and the Software Engineering Institute before publishing the following list of sources:

- Hackers break into networks for the thrill of the challenge or for bragging rights in the hacker community. While remote cracking once required a fair amount of skill or computer knowledge, hackers can now download attack scripts and protocols from the Internet and launch them against victim sites. Thus, while attack tools have become more sophisticated, they have also become easier to use. According to the CIA, the large majority of hackers do not have the requisite expertise to threaten difficult targets such as critical U.S. networks. Nevertheless, the worldwide population of hackers poses a relatively high threat of an isolated or brief disruption causing serious damage.
- Bot-network operators are hackers; however, instead of breaking into systems for the challenge or bragging rights, they take over multiple systems in order to coordinate attacks and to distribute phishing schemes, spam, and malware attacks. The services of these networks are sometimes made available on underground markets (e.g., purchasing a denial-of-service attack, servers to relay spam or phishing attacks, etc.).
- Criminal groups seek to attack systems for monetary gain. Specifically, organized crime groups are using spam, phishing, and spyware/malware to commit identity theft and online fraud. International corporate spies and organized crime organizations also pose a threat to the United States through their ability to conduct industrial espionage and large-scale monetary theft and to hire or develop hacker talent.
- Foreign intelligence services use cyber tools as part of their information-gathering and espionage activities. In addition, several nations are aggressively working to develop information warfare doctrine, programs, and capabilities. Such capabilities enable a single entity to have a significant and serious impact by disrupting the supply, communications, and economic infrastructures that support military power—impacts that could affect the daily lives of U.S. citizens across the country.
- The disgruntled organization insider is a principal source of computer crime. Insiders may not need a great deal of knowledge about computer intrusions because their knowledge of a target system often allows them to gain unrestricted access to cause damage to the system or to steal system data. The insider threat also includes outsourcing vendors as well as employees who accidentally introduce malware into systems.
- Phishers [are] individuals, or small groups, that execute phishing schemes in an attempt to steal identities or information for monetary gain. Phishers may also use spam and spyware/malware to accomplish their objectives.
- Spammers [are] individuals or organizations that distribute unsolicited e-mail with hidden or false information in order to sell products, conduct phishing schemes, distribute spyware/malware, or attack organizations (i.e., denial of service).
- Spyware/malware authors [are] individuals or organizations with malicious intent carry out attacks against users by producing and distributing spyware and malware. Several destructive

computer viruses and worms have harmed files and hard drives, including the Melissa Macro Virus, the Explore.Zip worm, the CIH (Chernobyl) Virus, Nimda, Code Red, Slammer, and Blaster.

- Terrorists seek to destroy, incapacitate, or exploit critical infrastructures in order to threaten national security, cause mass casualties, weaken the U.S. economy, and damage public morale and confidence. Terrorists may use phishing schemes or spyware/malware in order to generate funds or gather sensitive information.

Cyber-security experts at the Sandia National Laboratories in New Mexico noted that the assessment of threats "remains immature. This is particularly true in the dynamic and nebulous domain of cyber threats—a domain that tends to resist easy measurement and, in some cases, appears to defy any measurement." They identified seven "semi-descriptive labels" of cyber threats that "reinforce preconceived notions regarding motivation and resources":

- Nation state.
- Organized criminal.
- "A cyber terrorist uses internet-based attacks in terrorist activities, including acts of deliberate, large-scale disruption of computer networks."
- Hacker.
- "A hactivist uses computers and networks as a means of protest to promote social, political, or ideological ends."
- "A script kiddie uses existing computer scripts or code to gain unauthorized access to data, but lacks the expertise to write custom tools."
- Malicious insider (Mateski et al., 2012, pp. 7, 11)

Pedagogy Box 14.3 Official Method of Threat Assessment

In 2007, the Risk and Vulnerability Assessment (RVA) program (part of the Federal Network Security program, which assists federal executive agencies in assessing cyber risks, inside DHS) and the Sandia National Laboratories cooperatively developed an Operational Threat Assessment (OTA), which includes a scheme (known as the *generic threat matrix*) for judging the relative scale of each threat on an ordinal scale "without assigning a label (with its preconceived notions) [such as "hacker"] to a specific threat." It assigns a threat level from 1 (most threatening) to 8 (least threatening) for each of seven dimensions (see Table 14.1). It also allows for consideration of three "threat multipliers": outside monetary support; assets, such as the equipment and accommodation to dedicate to the attack; and superior technology.

Table 14.1 A Suggested Scheme for Assessing Cyber Threats

	Commitment			Resources			
	Intensity	**Stealth**	**Time**	**Technical personnel**	**Cyber knowledge**	**Kinetic knowledge**	**Access**
Threat level	**"the diligence of persevering determination of a threat in the pursuit of its goal"**	**"the ability of the threat to maintain a necessary level of secrecy throughout the pursuit of its goal"**	**"the period of time that a threat is capable of dedicating to planning, developing, and deploying methods to each an objective"**	**"the number of group members that a threat is capable of dedicating to the building and deployment of the technical capability in pursuit of its goal"**	**"the theoretical and practical proficiency relating to computers, information networks, or automated systems"**	**"the theoretical and practical proficiency relating to physical systems, the motion of physical bodies, and the forces associated with that movement"**	**"the threat's ability to place a group member within a restricted system—whether through cyber or kinetic means—in pursuit of the threat's goal"**
1	High	High	Years to decades	Hundreds	High	High	High
2	High	High	Years to decades	Tens of tens	Medium	High	High
3	High	High	Months to years	Tens of tens	High	Medium	Medium
4	Medium	High	Weeks to months	Tens	High	Medium	Medium
5	High	Medium	Weeks to months	Tens	Medium	Medium	Medium
6	Medium	Medium	Weeks to months	Ones	Medium	Medium	Low
7	Medium	Medium	Months to years	Tens	Low	Low	Low
8	Low	Low	Days to weeks	Ones	Low	Low	Low

SOURCE: Mateski et al., 2012, pp. 13–16.

Profit-Oriented Criminals

Most profit-oriented criminals are phishing for information that would allow them to steal the target's identity for profit. Normally they are looking for control of financial assets. Even if the victim loses no financial asset, they would face at least opportunity costs in restoring the security of their identity. More than 1.5 million people a year suffer the theft of their identity for an annual economic loss estimated at $1 billion (UN Office of Drugs and Crime [ODC], 2010).

Profit-oriented criminals target mostly individuals, by sending emails pretending to be a friend in need, a charity, or a potential business partner, and asking for money.

Rare, more sophisticated threats have stolen from the largest banks and official departments. For instance, in July 2007 malware, nicknamed "Zeus," which had been downloaded mainly from phishing e-mails and fake websites, was identified after it had stolen information from the U.S. Department of Transportation. Zeus was designed to harvest login credentials stored on the target computer and to capture keystrokes during the user's logins. Zeus was also a backdoor malware, meaning that it could take commands from its controllers, who remotely upgraded it and changed its missions. In June 2009, Prevx (a commercial security service provider) reported that Zeus had compromised more than 74,000 File Transfer Protocol accounts across dozens of websites, including websites owned by the Bank of America and the U.S. National Aeronautics and Space Administration. Thousands of login credentials were stolen from social media offered by Facebook, Yahoo, and others. In July 2010, Trusteer (another security service provider) reported that Zeus had captured information on credit cards issued by 15 U.S. banks (Trusteer did not name the banks). On October 1, 2010, the FBI announced that it had discovered an international criminal network that had used Zeus to steal around $70 million from U.S. targets. Arrests were made in the United States, Britain, and Ukraine. Around 3.6 million computers had been infected in the United States, perhaps millions more internationally (Netwitness, 2010).

In 2007, TJX Companies admitted that 45 million credit card numbers were exposed to hackers who had accessed databases over a period of 3 years. In 2009, Heartland Payment Systems admitted that malware had penetrated the servers that processed 100 million credit card transactions per month, but did not know the actual number of credit cards compromised.

On May 9, 2013, prosecutors in New York unsealed indictments against eight men accused of being the local team of a global cyber theft. Since October 2012, hackers broke into computer networks of financial companies in the United States and India and eliminated the withdrawal limits on prepaid debit cards before withdrawing tens of millions of dollars from ATMs in more than 20 other places around the world. First, hackers breached an Indian firm that processes credit card transactions for MasterCard debit cards issued by Rakbank, an institution in the United Arab Emirates, then they withdrew $5 million in 4,500 ATM transactions. Second, hackers breached a MasterCard processor in the United States that handled transactions for prepaid debit cards issued by the Bank of Muscat in Oman, then they withdrew $40 million in 36,000 transactions over a 10-hour period.

Pedagogy Box 14.4 Official Responses to Identity Theft

The USA PATRIOT Act of October 2001 provides authority to prosecute fraud involving American credit cards even if abroad. In July 2010, U.S. President Obama's administration published a draft National Strategy for Trusted Identities in Cyberspace to improve the security of personal identities in cyber space. Its principal immediate measure was to demand only minimal necessary information to be transferred during any cyber transaction. In April 2011, the final version was released: This provided guidelines for voluntary compliance (U.S. White House, 2011).

Insider Threats

Insider threats are personnel who are employed, authorized, or granted privileges by the organization but who harm the organization in some way. For instance, Dongfan Chung, an engineer who transferred secrets to China, mostly relating to military aircraft and the Space Shuttle, had hidden 250,000 pages of paper documents with sensitive information under his home by the time he was arrested in 2006. Almost twice as much information would fit on one compact disc (ONCIX, 2011, p. 2). Similarly, in January 2010, Bradley Manning, a soldier of Private rank in the U.S. Army, then assigned as an intelligence analyst to a base in Iraq, stole the largest amount of restricted data ever leaked from one source—more than 260,000 U.S. diplomatic cables and more than 500,000 military reports about or from Iraq and Afghanistan. He downloaded all the information on to digital media, which he carried out of the secure facility. In March 2010, he started to leak documents to the website Wikileaks. He was betrayed to the FBI in May by a hacker to whom Bradley had described his activities in an online forum. His correspondence included this damning revelation of the information security: "Weak servers, weak logging, weak physical security, weak counter-intelligence, inattentive signal analysis . . . a perfect storm."

A public-private survey in the United States in 2007 found that 31% of electronic crime perpetrators in the United States were insiders: 60% of them were thieves; 40% of them intended to sabotage IT, of which very few (2% of all cases) sabotaged for financial gain, while most were seeking vengeance against an employer or colleague. Almost all of the sabotage was of IT from inside the IT industry.

Insiders could be intrinsically inspired or directed by external actors, perhaps unknowingly (the external actor could trick the internal threat into thinking that they are acting on behalf of the same employer) or knowingly (the insider could accept a bribe to traffic information). US-CERT drew attention to the increasing role of external actors in insider threats after finding that half of insider threats from 2003 to 2007 in the United States had been recruited by outsiders, including organized criminals and foreign governments. CERT found also more crimes perpetrated by the employees of business partners that had been granted privileges inside the organization. New mergers and acquisitions also increase the chance of insider threats (Cappelli, Moore, Trzeciak, & Shimeall, 2009, p. 6). Germany's Federal Office for the Protection of the Constitution (BfV) estimates that 70% of all foreign economic espionage involves insiders (U.S. ONCIX, 2011, p. B1).

Although espionage is likely to involve malicious choices, most insider threats who release sensitive information are carelessly rather than maliciously noncompliant with the access or transfer controls. Even the most senior employees can be noncompliant. For instance, on November 9, 2012, General David Petraeus resigned as U.S. Director of Central Intelligence after revelations of his affair with Paula Broadwell, a former U.S. Army intelligence officer (and his biographer). Her harassing e-mails to another woman prompted a criminal investigation that unearthed her privileged access to Petraeus' private and classified information, partly through a web-based e-mail account that they had shared in an attempt to communicate privately.

Information security experts prescribe more monitoring and training of compliance, but also suggest that about 5% of employees will not comply despite the training. Most training is formal, but most people are better at recalling than applying formally trained knowledge. More experiential training would help the employee to become more self-aware of their noncompliance, but even so, some people are not inherently compliant or attentive. In order to catch the very few people who are chronically noncompliant, the organization is forced to monitor them increasingly obtrusively, which is restricted by ethical and legal obligations and the material challenges—in a large organization, monitoring most people most of the time would be prohibitively expensive, legally risky, and would raise the employees' distrust and stress. In many jurisdictions, dismissal of employees is difficult. At the same time, the risks of an insider threat are increasingly great. By 2010, some companies had added noncompliance as a dismissible offense (after two or three breaches) to employment contracts. Nondisclosure agreements (in which the employee promises not to release sensitive information, even after separation) became commonplace in the 1990s.

Pedagogy Box 14.5 Official Definition of Insider Threat

US-CERT defines an insider threat as "a current or former employee, contractor, or business partner who has had authorized access to an organization's network, system, or data and intentionally exceeded or misused that access in a manner that negatively affected the confidentiality, integrity, or availability of the organization's information or information systems." ONCIX defines an insider threat as "a person with authorized access to U.S. Government resources, to include personnel, facilities, information, equipment, networks, and systems, uses that access to harm the security of the United States" (CERT Insider Threat Center, 2012).

Pedagogy Box 14.6 Official Advice for Managing Insider Threats

The U.S. Office of the National Counterintelligence Executive suggests the following cycle for managing insider risks:

1. Assure insider security, by for instance, checking the backgrounds of new hires and reaching nondisclosure agreements.
2. Assure information security, by for instance, imposing controls on the insider's access to and transfer of information, particularly around the time when the employee separates.
3. Control external travel or contacts with external hazards.
4. Train insiders in secure behaviors and promote awareness of their behaviors.
5. Analyze insider behaviors and respond to issues.
6. Audit and monitor insider behaviors and their management. (ONCIX, 2011, p. A4)

U.S. CERT recommended the following 16 "practices" for controlling insider risks:

1. Consider threats from insiders and business partners in enterprise-wide risk assessments.
2. Clearly document and consistently enforce policies and controls.
3. Institute periodic security awareness training for all employees.
4. Monitor and response to suspicious or disruptive behavior, beginning with the hiring process.
5. Anticipate and manage negative workplace issues.
6. Track and secure the physical environment.
7. Implement strict password and account management policies and practices.

(Continued)

(Continued)

8. Enforce separation of duties and least privilege.
9. Consider insider threats in the software development lifecycle.
10. Use extra caution with system administrators and technical or privileged users.
11. Implement system change controls.
12. Log, monitor, and audit employee online actions.
13. Use layered defense against remote attacks.
14. Deactivate computer access following termination.
15. Implement secure backup and recovery processes.
16. Develop and insider incident response plan. (Cappelli, Moore, Trzeciak, & Shimeall, 2009, pp. 27–31)

External Threats

External actors are not employed by the target organization, but the target organization may have granted them privileged access to internal information or domains. Practically, any commercial or public relationship involves some compromise of the boundary between internal and external actors. For instance, when the organization outsources services, such as Internet services, to an external actor, the external actor would be granted privileged information about the organization's network. Some competitors may pretend to be potential clients or business partners in order to gain information that is then useful for developing some competitive product or service. For instance, in the 2000s, some French, German, and Japanese companies complained that Chinese partners developed high-speed electric railways from information gathered from bids for unawarded contracts, as well as from supplied but patented technologies.

When the organization procures anything externally, the resulting supply chain is exposed to malicious actors. For instance, official procurers worry about buying computers from abroad where foreign intelligence services could plant malware on the computers to spy on official users. In theory, malicious actors could sabotage acquisitions in more traditional ways, such as by planting an explosive device inside a delivered package. (These risks—potential espionage or sabotage—are separate to traditional commercial risks, such as a supplier's nonperformance—its failure to deliver something on the schedule or with the capabilities specified.) Official procurers also worry about external ownership of their supply chain, where an external actor could steal intellectual property (in addition to the more traditional supply chain risk of simply interrupting supply).

External threats may access information or plant malware after procurement, during the deployment, configuration, and integration of some procured hardware, such as when external actors are employed to train users in their new hardware or to set up the new hardware for use. External actors could distribute malware through the software acquired for the hardware or through peripheral devices. Periodic maintenance, servicing, and upgrades are also opportunities for external malicious intervention. A final opportunity for the malicious actor in the life cycle of the hardware is during the organization's retirement or deletion of the hardware from service or use. The hardware is often sent for disposal without proper removal of the information contained therein. (Many operating systems do not entirely delete files when ordered to delete.) Insiders may contribute to this risk by selling hardware to external actors or by diverting hardware to their friends and family rather than obeying orders to destroy it.

Pedagogy Box 14.7 Chinese Gathering of French Proprietary Information Around 2011

In January 2011, a French news magazine (*Le Parisien*) published a leaked French intelligence document that describes three Chinese techniques for gathering foreign proprietary information: lamprey, mushroom factory, and reverse counterfeiting.

The *lamprey technique* advertises for commercial bids on large projects, such as infrastructure. After Western companies bid, they are urged to offer more information in order to secure a contract. After several rounds of re-bidding, the competing bidders are summarily informed that the project has been shelved, but Chinese developers would use the information to develop their own alternative. For instance, TGV of France was the leading bidder on a multi-billion dollar tender to build China's high-speed train. As part of the process, the French embassy in Beijing organized a six-month training course for Chinese engineers. A few months after the course, China revealed its own high-speed train remarkably similar to the TGV and Germany's ICE train.

The *mushroom factory* involves manipulation of a joint venture between a foreign company and a local Chinese firm. After the foreign company has transferred enough technology, the Chinese company would divest a new company, outside of the joint venture, to offer the same technology. For instance, Danone, the French dairy and drinks group, alleged that the Chinese drinks producer, Wahaha, divested their joint venture.

Reverse counterfeiting means stealing technology but accusing the victim of counterfeiting. For instance, in 1996, Schneider Electric of France patented a hook in its fuse box. Its Chinese rival Chint started building the same hook and took Schneider to court in China for copying its design, where Schneider was ordered to pay a fine worth 330 million yuan.

Nation-States

The average national state government has more capacity than the average private actor (although some private corporations are wealthier than most governments). Less than 10 of the nearly 200 sovereign governments in the world are commonly cited as having most of the capacity or intent for cyber attacks. Official capacity for cyber attacks (also known as offensive cyber warfare) is usually assigned to intelligence or military agencies. U.S. intelligence and security agents often categorize foreign intelligence services (FISs) and security services (FISSs) separately from other threats, operationally meaning any foreign official threat, short of positive identification as a particular service or agency. In recent years, U.S. officials referred to advanced persistent threats (APTs) as code for national threats in general, Chinese threats in particular.

National threats have more capacity for using information and communications technologies as vectors for their phishing. The victims are often unwilling to reveal events because of the commercial impacts (in the case of commercial victims) or the bureaucratic or political impacts (in the case of official victims), so the true frequency of these attacks is largely underestimated.

Largely anonymous and anecdotal reports suggest that APTs will research a particular organization over weeks before attacking over days, as widely and repeatedly as possible before the different attacks are recognized as threatening. The attacks are conducted in campaigns with multiple methods, cumulatively penetrating deeper into a target's defenses, despite frequent failures. Human operators are more important than the technological tools: the sources gather much of their information by phishing and social engineering through direct communications with the targets and by adapting to the defenses. The attacks themselves are usually e-mails to executives, usually tailored to the target person by pretending to be someone whom the target knows or by attaching malware disguised as something of interest to the target (such as a document about the oil industry sent to an oil industry executive).

Mandiant, a cyber security provider, describes (2013, p. 27) the following activities within the APT "attack lifecycle":

1. Initial external reconnaissance
2. Initial compromise (access) inside the target's secured domain
3. Establishing a foothold inside the domain
4. Escalating privileges
5. Internal reconnaissance
6. Movements laterally within the domain
7. Maintaining presence and perhaps returning to Step 4
8. Ending the mission

APTs are countered by

1. Preparing human targets to spot suspicious communications
2. Preparing real-time threat management software that can detect the APT's more sophisticated and stealthy malware and network traffic
3. Legally prosecuting the sources
4. Deterrence or retaliation (more likely when the APT is controlled by a national government)

Pedagogy Box 14.8 U.S. Warnings About Foreign National Threats

Unofficially, some U.S. officials have stated publicly that about 140 FISSs target the United States, of which about 50 have serious capacity to harm the United States and five or six are severe threats. The commonly identified national cyber threats are China, Russia, Israel, Iran, North Korea, and France (the sources are not necessarily official; they could be private activists, private actors with official support, or disguised official actors).

On April 12, 2011, the Director of Intelligence at U.S. Cyber Command (Rear Admiral Samuel Cox) told subordinates that "a global cyber arms race is underway" and at least six countries have offensive cyber warfare capabilities that they are using to probe U.S. military and private computer networks.

> There are a number of countries that we see attacks emanating from. And, again, they can be just individuals who are located in the country.
>
> But three that I think are of special concern would be Iran, would be Russia, and China. (Janet Napolitano, U.S. Secretary of Homeland Security, interviewed for "The Newshour," PBS, first broadcast on February 15, 2013).
>
> [Russia, China, and Iran] will remain the top threats to the United States in the coming years... Russia and China are aggressive and successful purveyors of economic espionage against the United States. Iran's intelligence operations against the United States, including cyber capabilities, have dramatically increased in recent years in depth and complexity. (Director of National Intelligence James R. Clapper Jr. written statement to U.S. Senate Armed Services Committee on February 16, 2013)

 Access Vectors

While the ultimate sources of cyber attacks are human actors, most cyber attacks are vectored by some sort of information technology or communication technology. The subsections below describe these vectors and their controls: printed documents, social interactions, malware, databases, webpages, social media, postal communications, telephone communications, e-mail, removable digital media, cloud computing, and unsecured wireless networks.

Pedagogy Box 14.9 Attack Vectors

Sandia National Laboratories identified a number of *attack vectors*, where each is "an avenue or tool that a threat uses to launch attacks, gather information, or deliver/leave a malicious item or items in those devices, systems, or networks" (Mateski et al., 2012, p. 23).

Printed Documents

Printed documents are ubiquitous; they include maps, plans, photographs, letters, notes, books, and other texts. In the 1970s and 1980s, futurists forecasted the imminent demise of anything but digital information, but still we use printed information, in part because digital information is less secure than they had hoped, in part because electronic screens still do not offer higher resolution (higher resolutions imply more information and less stress of the human eye).

In 2012, the U.S. Government Business Council asked federal officials and contractors to choose the media that represented their "biggest security concern for 2012"—they were more concerned about paper documents than digital documents:

- paper documents (91%);
- e-mail (89%);
- digital text and documents (77%);
- transitory content (68%);
- digital audio and video (53%);
- paper drawings and charts (47%);
- social media (42%);
- film (24%);
- microfiche and microfilm (24%); and
- other (6%). (Jackson, 2012b, p. 10)

The loss of information on paper is normally due to a failure to control social transfer or physical access. As an example of the risks of unsecured information on paper, consider the masses of paper (some of it containing information embarrassing to Western governments and commercial suppliers) found by rebels, activists, and journalists inside abandoned official sites in Iraq in 2003, in Libya during the revolution against Muammar Gaddafi in 2011, and in Syria since the revolution against Bashir al-Assad from March 2011. Some of these documents revealed surprising cooperation between western governments, commercial suppliers, and autocrats, contrary to official policy. Other information revealed operational and personal secrets. For instance, militants, looters, and journalists picked up paper documents, including security protocols, information about personnel, contracts with commercial providers and militia, and diplomatic messages, from the U.S. diplomatic outpost in Benghazi, Libya, after U.S. personnel and allies had abandoned the post following an armed attack overnight September 11–12, 2012.

Social Interaction

Most harmful leakage of privileged information arises from a social interaction, such as when people talk too loosely about private information or are verbally persuaded to give up information to somebody who is not what they pretend to be. Similarly, most unauthorized access to digital information is gained socially, even if the source uses digital media as their vector for the social interaction. ICTs (especially mobile telephones and Internet-based communications) have enabled more remote communications that users tend to treat casually.

A malicious social interaction could take one of four main directions:

1. The threat could contact you pretending to be someone you know, such as a client or colleague (known as *phishing* or *spear phishing*)
2. The threat could pretend to be you in order to persuade a third-party, such as your bank, to release information about you (known as *spoofing* in American English or *blagging* in British English)

3. The threat could bribe someone to release information about you
4. The threat could blackmail you or someone you know

Of these routes to information, the route that has become much easier through digital technologies is phishing. Phishing can be used as a means to any end, including sabotage, but is commonly defined and discussed as a form of espionage.

Pedagogy Box 14.10 Social Gathering by British Journalists and Private Investigators in the 2000s

"The 'suppliers' almost invariably work within the private investigation industry: private investigators, tracing agents, and their operatives, often working loosely in chains that may include several intermediaries between ultimate customer and the person who actually obtains the information.

Suppliers use two main methods to obtain the information they want: through corruption, or more usually by some form of deception, generally known as 'blagging'. Blaggers pretend to be someone they are not in order to wheedle out the information they are seeking. They are prepared to make several telephone calls to get it. Each call they make takes them a little bit further towards their goal: obtaining information illegally which they then sell for a specified price. Records seized under search warrants show that many private investigators and tracing agents are making a lucrative profit from this trade" (U.K. Information Commissioner's Office [ICO], 2006, p. 5).

Pedagogy Box 14.11 Official Definitions of Phishing

US-CERT (part of DHS) defines phishing as "an attempt by an individual or group to solicit personal information from unsuspecting users by employing social engineering techniques" (US-CERT, n.d.).

Under this definition, phishing could be achieved socially without any technology, but other authorities define phishing as a cyber activity. For instance, the U.S. GAO (2005b, p. 8) defines phishing as "the creation and use of e-mails and Web sites—designed to look like those of well-known legitimate businesses, financial institutions, and government agencies—in order to deceive Internet users into disclosing their personal data, such as bank and financial account information and passwords. The phishers then take that information and use it for criminal purposes, such as identity theft and fraud."

Malware

Malware is software that is harmful. It is sometimes created by accident or for fun, but is usually developed or exploited for malicious objectives. One expert noted "that the current trend is that there is now less of a propensity to make the user aware of the presence of malicious code on a computer, and more of a will to have the code run silent and deep so that the attacker can remotely control the target's computer to launch massive attacks or exfiltrate data from a sensitive network" (Yannakogeorges, 2011, p. 261).

Commercial software itself has become more complicated, increasing the chance of inherent flaws or of vulnerabilities to attack. In 2005, the U.S. National Institute of Standards and Technology estimated 20 flaws per thousand lines of software code; Microsoft Windows 2000 (a computer operating system) had 35 million lines (U.S. GAO, 2005b, pp. 9–10). U.S. officials once estimated that 80% of successful intrusions into federal computer systems are vectored through flawed software (Wilson, 2003, p. 6).

Pedagogy Box 14.12 Official Definitions of Malware

Malware is "software designed with malicious intent, such as a virus." A *computer virus* is a "program that infects computer files, usually executable programs, by inserting a copy of itself into the file. These copies are usually executed when the infected file is loaded into memory, allowing the virus to infect other files. Unlike the computer worm, a virus requires human involvement (usually unwitting) to propagate." A *worm* is an "independent computer program that reproduces by copying itself from one system to another across a network. Unlike computer viruses, worms do not require human involvement to propagate." A *Trojan horse* is "a computer program that conceals harmful code. A Trojan horse usually masquerades as a useful program that a user would wish to execute" (U.S. GAO, 2005b, p. 8).

Databases

Almost everybody provides sensitive information that is held on some other organization's media—sensitive information such as ethnicity, gender, sexuality, religion, politics, trade union membership, birth, death, marriage, bank account, health care, and crimes (either perpetrator or victim). The growth of bureaucratic capacity and digital communications has encouraged wider handling of such data and the handling of more data. One British authority estimated that such sensitive information about the average adult Briton is held in around 700 databases (U.K. ICO, 2006, p. 7). ICTs have made the holding of data easier but also exposed more data to cyber attack. The Privacy Rights Clearinghouse estimated that in 2011, 30.4 million sensitive records were exposed by just 535 cyber intrusions in the United States that year.

The U.S. ONCIX (2011, p. A4) gives this advice on managing data:

- Get a handle on company data—not just in databases but also in e-mail messages, on individual computers, and as data objects in web portals; categorize and classify the data, and choose the most appropriate set of controls and markings for each class of data; identify which data should be kept and for how long. Understand that it is impossible to protect everything.
- Establish compartmentalized access programs to protect unique trade secrets and proprietary information; centralize intellectual property data—which will make for better security and facilitate information sharing.
- Restrict distribution of sensitive data; establish a shared data infrastructure to reduce the quantity of data held by the organization and discourage unnecessary printing and reproduction.

Pedagogy Box 14.13 Regulation of Data Privacy

Since the 1980s, standards, regulations, and law have increased the responsibilities and liabilities of organizations for securing data and for granting freedom of access to data by those whom it concerns. In 1980, the Organization for Economic Cooperation and Development (OECD) issued its seven "Guidelines Governing the Protection of Privacy and Trans-Border Flows of Personal Data":

1. Notice: Data subjects should be given notice when their data is being collected.
2. Purpose: Data should only be used for the purpose stated and not for any other purposes.
3. Consent: Data should not be disclosed without the data subject's consent.
4. Security: Collected data should be kept secure from any potential abuses.
5. Disclosure: Data subjects should be informed as to who is collecting their data.
6. Access: Data subjects should be allowed to access their data and make corrections to any inaccurate data.
7. Accountability: Data subjects should have a method available to them to hold data collectors accountable for following the above principles.

In 1981, the Council of Europe agreed the Convention for the Protection of Individuals with regard to Automatic Processing of Personal Data. This convention obliges the signatories to enact legislation concerning the automatic processing of personal data.

In 1995, the EU adopted the Data Protection Directive (officially Directive 95/46/EC on the protection of individuals with regard to the processing of personal data and on the free movement of such data), which adopted the OECD's seven guidelines and directed member states to regulate the processing of personal data, effective 1998. Under an amendment of February 2006, EU law requires Internet and telephone service providers to retain data on the location and parties to each communication for at least 6 months and no more than 24 months, but not to record content. On January 25, 2012, the European Commission unveiled a draft European General Data Protection Regulation that will supersede the Data Protection Directive by extending the scope to all foreign companies processing data of European Union residents.

In Britain, responding to European legislation, the Data Protection Act of 1998 requires organizations that hold data about individuals to do so securely and only for specific purposes. Section 55 specifies as offenses any attempts to obtain, disclose or "procure the disclosure" of confidential personal information "knowingly or recklessly" without the consent of the organization holding the data. The Act also gives individuals the right, with certain exemptions, to see personal data that relates to them. The Freedom of Information Act of 2000 entitles people to receive information from an organization unless the organization faces high burdens in gathering the information or the information is protected on the grounds of privacy, commercial sensitivity, or national security.

(Continued)

(Continued)

The United States has not followed with a data protection act, but its criminal laws against economic espionage and its protections of intellectual property discourage theft of proprietary data, while its strong civil laws against defamation and slander help to control misuse of private information. In U.S. jurisdictions, organizations face severe legal and commercial risks for violating data privacy (although they are also incentivized by commercial advantages). For instance, in 2005, after the U.S. Federal Trade Commission accused an American consumer data broker (ChoicePoint Incorporated) of improperly securing confidential data from theft, the broker admitted that the personal financial records of more than 163,000 consumers in its database had been compromised and agreed to pay $10 million in civil penalties and $5 million in consumer redress, while millions of dollars were wiped off its stock-market value.

The International Organization for Standardization (ISO) and the International Electrotechnical Commission (IEC) have led international standards for information security including expectations for technical and organizational controls on unauthorized or unlawful processing of personal data (ISO/IEC 17799:2005 and ISO/IEC 27001:2005).

Pedagogy Box 14.14 British Journalistic and Official Abuses of Confidential Data, 2000–2012

The increasing exposure of private information and the potential abuses of such exposure were revealed most shockingly in Britain in the 2000s, where journalists routinely intercepted private communications or paid officials for information that was supposed to be private or confidential. The slow official reaction to private complaints indicates wider corruption than was ever prosecuted, despite occasional scandals and official responses.

On March 1, 2000, the Data Protection Act of 1998 came into force. In the next 6 years, some 1,000 complaints about illegal violations reached the Information Commissioner's Office (ICO; established in 1984 as the Data Protection Registrar). Most complaints originated from private individuals. Some were passed on by the police as criminal investigations; a few were passed on by official agencies that believed their data had been targeted. The ICO brought only 25 criminal prosecutions and obtained only 22 convictions, none of them resulting in a prison sentence and only a few resulting in a fine, of which the largest was £5,000.

A disproportionate number of complaints originated from celebrities who complained about journalistic invasions of privacy, such as when journalists questioned the victim about their confidential report to police of a property theft. In 2000, a few journalists started reporting the problem, mostly blaming unauthorized access to private telephone conversations and voicemails ("phone hacking"). In the six years since 2000, *The Guardian* published the most stories (545) about phone hacking; the ICO found that four of its journalists had paid for private information. The next most investigative newspapers (*The Independent* and *Independent on Sunday,* 367 stories; *The Daily Telegraph* and

Sunday Telegraph, 160 stories) had not paid for private information at all. Another two British groups had reported less on the scandal but more of its journalists had been caught paying for private information: the Mirror Group (*The Mirror*; *Sunday Mirror*; *The People*) had published 25 stories and 139 of their journalists had been caught paying for private information; the *Daily Mail* and *Mail on Sunday* had published 90 stories and 91 of their journalists had been caught. None was within News International. News International's British newspapers (*News of the World*; *The Sun*; *The Times*; *The Sunday Times*) had reported on the scandal least (22.5 reports per newspaper) and fewest of its journalists had been caught paying for private information (7.5 per newspaper). The *News of the World* was the most salacious and purchased newspaper, but the News International newspapers were better able at hiding their illegal activities or getting official protection. Since September 2002, a few newspapers (principally *The Guardian*) had named other newspapers (principally the *News of the World*) as illegal gatherers of data.

In November 2002, a regional police force invited the ICO to view evidence that Metropolitan police offices and other officials had sold information from the Police National Computer and the Driver & Vehicle Licensing Agency databases. Subsequent ICO and police investigations identified thousands of privacy violations and implicated 305 journalists, but only four officials were prosecuted.

In January 2003, the House of Commons Committee on Culture, Media, and Sport started its first investigation into journalistic abuses. The witnesses included the editor (Rebekah Brooks) and deputy editor (Andy Coulson) of Britain's most popular newspaper (*News of the World*). Brooks absent-mindedly admitted that her newspaper routinely gathered information illegally "in the public interest" and that her newspaper had paid police officers for stories, and Coulson admitted that they would do so again "in the public interest." The Committee reported its concern about journalistic activities, but no criminal or political inquiry followed, until 2012, when Brooks, Coulson, and other staff were indicted with conspiracy to unlawfully intercept communications.

In 2006, the Information Commissioner's Office presented to Parliament its first report on public complaints about violations of privacy.

> This report reveals evidence of systematic breaches in personal privacy that amount to an unlawful trade in confidential personal information... Much more illegal activity lies hidden under the surface. Investigations by the ICO and the police have uncovered evidence of a widespread and organized undercover market in confidential personal information... Among the 'buyers' are many journalists looking for a story. In one major case investigated by the ICO, the evidence included records of information supplied to 305 named journalists working for a range of newspapers. Other cases have involved finance companies and local authorities wishing to trace debtors; estranged couples seeking details of their partner's whereabouts or finances; and criminals intent on fraud or witness or juror intimidation.
>
> The personal information they are seeking may include someone's current address, details of car ownership, an ex-directory telephone number or records of calls made, bank account details

(Continued)

(Continued)

> or intimate health records. Disclosure of even apparently innocuous personal information–such as an address–can be highly damaging in some circumstances, and in virtually all cases individuals experience distress when their privacy is breached without their consent. (U.K. ICO, 2006, p. 4)

The Information Commissioner blamed principally weak criminal prosecution of trafficking in private information.

> The crime at present carries no custodial sentence. When cases involving the unlawful procurement or sale of confidential personal information come before the courts, convictions often bring no more than a derisory fine or a conditional discharge. Low penalties devalue the data protection offence in the public mind and mask the true seriousness of the crime, even within the judicial system. They likewise do little to deter those who seek to buy or supply confidential information that should rightly remain private. The remedy I am proposing is to introduce a custodial sentence of up to two years for persons convicted on indictment, and up to six months for summary convictions. The aim is not to send more people to prison but to discourage all who might be tempted to engage in this unlawful trade, whether as buyers or suppliers. (U.K. ICO, 2006, p. 3)

In January 2011, the Metropolitan Police (Met) opened a new investigation into phone hacking, but it appeared to languish, like most others before it. However, in July 2011, the Met announced a new operation to investigate payments made to police by News International (the owner of *News of the World* and several other implicated British newspapers, as well as several prominent newspapers in the United States and Australia and other countries). The Met's Commissioner (Sir Paul Stephenson) and Assistant Commissioner (John Yates) both resigned. Yates had unofficially socialized with the deputy editor and other employees of the *News of the World,* while he led dismissive investigations, since September 2009, into the allegations made against *News of the World*.

From January 2011 through October 2012, Met police made more than 90 related arrests: 17 for interception of mobile phone voicemail messages, 52 for payments to public officials, and 17 for intrusion into digital information, usually by hacking into computers or bribing operators for access. These arrests must account for a small fraction of the total population of journalists and officials who have illegally violated privacy (Leveson, 2012, pp. 8, 13, 19; U.K. House of Commons, 2011a).

Webpages

Most Internet activity involves online searches, browsing, and e-mail. Visiting the associated webpages exposes the user to malware—particularly if the user downloads or is misled into visiting a webpage resembling a login page, where the threat gathers the user's passwords and other access keys.

Users tend to underestimate the insecurity of their online activities. Unlike the typical software on an Intranet or other organizationally secured domain, web-based applications are designed to be accessible and easy to use more than secure. Some sites and browsers, by default, place information packets known as "cookies" on the user's computer: legitimately these cookies are used by the site to recognize the user; illegitimately they can upload information back to the site that the user has not authorized. Some of this information may be used for purposes that the user finds useful, such as more targeted advertising, but often it leads to unwanted advertisements or can be sold to third-party marketers, including "spammers"—people who send you information you never requested and do not want. Worse, cookies can be vectors for malware.

Social Media

Social media are normally websites on which personal users release information about themselves or subscribe to information from other users. The most used social websites are Facebook, LinkedIn, and Twitter. Some sites specialize in sharing photographs, videos, and audio files, some in romantic connections, some in professional connections, some in social games. Many alternatives exist—some official actors, such as the Iranian government, have developed alternatives in an effort to impose control on or gain information from social media.

Social media are exposed to anyone who browses the same sites. Social media encourage users to expand their social network, but unguardedly or superficially. Many social media allow anonymous discussions and postings. Generally, users tend to behave more anonymously but revealingly when online. Users of social media may believe that their information is restricted to their friends, but some social media allow anybody to view information on anybody else, store such information in insecure domains, or even sell such information. Some social media promise not to sell information or to prevent access to the posted information except to the user's "friends," but the friends, as defined by the user and the site, likely include casual acquaintances—indeed, users, in pursuit of a larger count of online "friends," often agree to "friend" anyone who asks. Social media contribute to their cumulative online presence, from which threats might gather enough information to steal the individual's identity.

Some very important persons and officials have been careless on social networks. For instance, in November 2012, a Belgian newspaper published an investigation into how many employees of the Belgian state security service listed their employer on Facebook or LinkedIn. Several French users of LinkedIn had listed their employer as France's external intelligence agency. American journalists found more than 200 users of LinkedIn listing the Central Intelligence Agency as their employer.

Users are likelier to be more revealing of personal and professional information when they are looking for another job or romantic partner. For instance, official employees, after leaving official employment or when seeking another job, have been known to distribute online, as evidence for their professional qualifications, photographs of themselves inside secured domains, of their official credentials, and of themselves with important persons.

Additionally, the privacy and accuracy of information is less protected legally when online than offline, encouraging rampant online slander, defamation, misinformation, and abuse, including online bullying. Private citizens face practically no criminal legal restrictions on online behavior. The tort system is usually a waste of time for claimants or victims; the few cases that have been heard in civil or criminal court usually fail to clarify responsibility or harm. In practice, cyber information and misinformation are controlled by users and hosts, motivated mostly by their intrinsic ethics and external commercial pressures, not the law. In the United States, the Communications Decency Act of 1996 makes clear that Internet service providers and online hosts are not responsible for the content of posts from outside parties, although the positive implication of this clarity is that hosts are free to moderate or delete content without legal liability.

Traditionally, public concern has been raised over juvenile use of social media where adults (probably pretending to be other juveniles) could groom them for abuse, such as by asking them to share intimate information or even to meet in the real world. Some social media are supposed to be reserved for juveniles, but any adult could register as a user. In any social media, juveniles routinely disclose their own identities or the identities of other juveniles, in contrast to most news media, where journalists normally follow codes of ethics that prohibit revelations of juvenile identities, even when juveniles are accused of crimes. Juveniles are capable of undermining such regimes. For instance, in February 2013, users of online forums on a website devoted to issues in Fairfax, Virginia, revealed the names of three male high school students who had been arrested for allegedly making videos of themselves having sex with several girls, during a news embargo on those same names. More worrying, juveniles are quite capable of exploiting each other and adults—by online bullying, slander, and defamation. Adults are disadvantaged against juvenile threats because juveniles are protected in ways that adults are not and are not equally accountable.

Adult users too can be exploited sexually, in similar ways (posting of intimate information or grooming for sexual exploitation). The average adult, being wealthier and in possession of more valuable information than the average juvenile, is more likely to be exploited financially or professionally. In pursuit of friends, employers, or romantic partners, individual users tend to post online information that they would not reveal offline—commonly including their sexuality, age, address, profession, and hobbies. In communicating through social media with supposed friends, they may discuss private information such as their health or romantic partners; they may also reveal plans, such as foreign travel, that encourage thieves to target their homes. They also may be persuaded to send money to strangers or agree to meet people in the real world who turn out to be robbers or worse.

Pedagogy Box 14.15 Social Media Risks Today

"Social networking has proven to be a double-edged sword, becoming an important medium for business communication and at the same time providing a rich source of data for social engineering and misinformation. It is no surprise that increasingly popular sites have become tools for phishing attacks and launching malicious code. The risks do not seem to have outweighed the perceived advantages yet, as organizations constantly look for ways to use social channels, focusing their concerns on making them more effective rather than more secure. Getting more attention that the malicious use of the sites are the privacy policies of the companies running them . . . The threat [from current events] was that 2012's high-profile events–such as the London Olympics and the U.S. Presidential election–would be used to ensnare victims with phishing attacks and search engine poisoning. Some of this did happen, but it didn't seem to be any worse than any other year" (Jackson, GCN, 2013a, p. 20).

Postal Communications

Posted mail can be intercepted; postal deliverers have been bribed to divert mail; threats can also seize the mail from the container into which it has been posted or delivered, before it is picked up by the deliverer or the recipient. Some private actors, such as unscrupulous journalists, commercial competitors, jealous romantic partners, petitioners for divorce, and stalkers, are incentivized to intercept communications. Common thieves also steal mail in pursuit of financial checks and credit cards or information that helps them to steal personal identities. Official investigators may also intercept mail in pursuit of evidence for crimes.

Nevertheless, postal mail remains ubiquitous, despite some replacement by ICTs. The increasing use of electronic means of transacting business has reduced the use of paper transactions, but increasing interception of the electronic means (by stealing credit card numbers or intercepting transactions, including wireless means of paying) suggest that electronic means are not perfect replacements. Meanwhile, official authorities have demonstrated increased capacity and willingness for intercepting or blocking private communications.

Some people, including activists, businesspersons, diplomats, profit-oriented criminals, and terrorists, have returned to verbal and postal communications since more revelations in the 2000s of the insecurity of their digital and electronic communications. For instance, al-Qaida's most senior staff switched back to traditional communications in the early 2000s, after discovering that some of their e-mails, mobile telephones, and satellite telephones had been intercepted occasionally since the 1990s, although U.S. intelligence eventually identified a courier whose movement led them to the hiding place in Pakistan of Osama bin Laden, where he was killed by U.S. special operations forces on May 2, 2011.

Similarly, official authorities continue to use couriers because of concerns about electronic and digital espionage. For instance, the U.S. Bureau of Diplomatic Security (part of the Department of State) operates a courier service for the carriage of classified materials in diplomatic pouches (which international law treats as sovereign territory) between diplomatic sites at home and abroad. In 2008, the service employed 98 couriers and delivered more than 55 million pounds of classified diplomatic materials (U.S. GAO, 2009, p. 6).

Telephone Communications

Increasing use of information and communications technology implies increasing exposure to interception of our communications. Telephones have been commercially available for more than 100 years. By 2012, more than half of the world's population possessed a mobile telephone. The Internet offers effective telephone replacement technologies, such as Voice Over Internet Protocol (VOIP), of which the most well-known carrier is Skype.

Most people underestimate their exposure; new technologies encourage more spontaneous and casual communications. The growth of e-mail tends to obscure the inherent exposure of telephones to hacking. Telephones and the cables carrying wired communications always have been easy to "tap" for anyone with physical access to the hardware. Such tapping is still rife in autocracies and is more likely where the government controls the service or the service providers or the service providers are open to corruption. In most democracies, taps are allowed only with a temporary warrant for the purposes of criminal justice or national security, but some officials have allowed unwarranted taps, while nonofficials, such as private detectives, have illegally tapped telephones or obtained data from a corrupt service provider.

A mobile or cellular telephone, like any telephone, can be tapped directly if the threat can physically access the device and place a bugging device within it. Otherwise, mobile telephones are more difficult to tap physically because their communications pass wirelessly, but the threat can use cheap technology to intercept wireless communications (if the threat knows the user's telephone number and is proximate to the target). Smartphones (telephones that run software) can be infected, through Internet downloads or an open Bluetooth portal, with malware that records or allows a remote threat to listen in on the target's conversations. Sophisticated threats can remotely turn on a target's mobile telephone and use it as a bugging device without the target even realizing that the telephone is on: the only defense is to remove the battery.

Voicemail and text messages in many ways are more exposed than is a verbal conversation. A telephone conversation is fleeting and not recorded by default, but voicemail and texts are stored until the user deletes them. Many service providers allow remote access to voicemail and texts through a third party telephone or website, perhaps after passing some control on access, such as by typing in a personal identification number (or password). Many users do not change whatever default password was issued with a particular telephone or by a particular provider, so a threat (hacker) could access private voicemail using a third-party telephone or computer and a known default password. The hacker could call the provider and pretend to be the user in order to reset the password. The hacker could configure another telephone to pretend to have the same telephone number as the target's telephone. The hacker could also bribe an employee of the service provider to reveal confidential information.

Concerned users should add access controls to their telephones, such as passwords, before the telephone can be used. They should check and delete their voicemails and text messages frequently. They could choose to prevent access to their voicemails and texts except with a passcode entered from their own phone. They could remove the battery from their mobile telephone except when they need to use it. They could also use temporary telephones that expire or can be discarded regularly. They could avoid smartphones or Bluetooth devices or at least eschew any access to the Internet from such devices. If they need to use such devices, they should procure security software and keep it up to date. They could avoid personal ownership of communications technology entirely—an extreme solution, but one that more officials are adopting.

These controls may sound severe to casual users of current communications devices, but many official organizations and some highly-targeted corporations now ban their employees from using or carrying smartphones, Bluetooth, or third-party devices, inside secure domains or for the discussion of any organizational information. In addition, many malicious actors, such as terrorists, avoid such devices after revelations of how easily counter-terrorist authorities can use them for spying.

Pedagogy Box 14.16 Official Surveillance of Telephone Communication

Under its charter, the U.S. Central Intelligence Agency is not allowed to gather intelligence on U.S. citizens at home, but from 1961 to 1971 the CIA spied on domestic anti-Vietnam War groups, communists, and leakers of official information. Both CIA and NSA intercepted private telephone communications during that time. In 1972, the CIA tracked telephone calls between Americans at home and telephones abroad.

The Foreign Intelligence Surveillance Act (FISA) of 1978 criminalizes unauthorized electronic surveillance and prescribes procedures for surveillance of foreign powers and their agents (including U.S. citizens) inside the United States. The Foreign Intelligence Surveillance Court (FISC) issues the warrants for such surveillance. The USA PATRIOT Act of October 2001 extended FISA's scope from foreign powers to terrorists. The Protect America Act of August 2007 removed the warrant requirement if the individual is "reasonably believed" to be corresponding with someone outside the United States. It expired on February 17, 2008, but the FISA Amendments Act of July 2008 extended the same amendment. On May 26, 2011, President Barack Obama signed the PATRIOT Sunsets Extension Act, which extended for 4 years the provisions for roving wiretaps and searches of business records. The FISC is known to have approved all warrant requests in 2011 and 2012. In December 2012, Congress reauthorized FISA for another 5 years.

Confidential information includes the parties to a private conversation, not just the content of the conversation. Internet and telephone service providers hold data on the location and other party in every communication made or received. Most democracies have strict legal controls on the storage and use of such data, and do not allow official access except with a court order granted to official investigators who can show probable cause of a severe crime, although such controls are easy to evade or forget in emergencies.

European law requires providers to retain such data for at least 6 months and no more than 24 months, and not to record content.

On October 4, 2001, before the PATRIOT Act was introduced, President George W. Bush secretly authorized NSA to collect domestic telephone, Internet, and e-mail records, focusing on calls with one foreign node. In 2006, the *USA Today* newspaper reported that the NSA had "been secretly collecting the phone call records of tens of millions of Americans, using data provided by AT&T, Verizon and BellSouth" and was "using the data to analyze calling patterns in an effort to detect terrorist activity." The NSA's legal authority is the "business records" provision of the PATRIOT Act. Since 2006, the FISC has approved warrants to service providers every 3 months; Congress was informed. The most recent FISC order to Verizon was published by *The Guardian* newspaper on June 5, 2013. Senator Diane Feinstein, the chair of the Senate's Intelligence Committee, confirmed the 3-monthly renewals back to 2006.

In January 2010, the Inspector General at the Department of Justice reported that, between 2002 and 2006, the FBI sent to telephone service providers more than 700 demands for telephone records by citing often nonexistent emergencies and using sometimes misleading language. Information on more than 3,500 phone numbers may have been gathered improperly, but investigators said they could not glean a full understanding because of sketchy record-keeping by the FBI.

Pedagogy Box 14.17 British Journalists' Intercepts of Private Telecommunications

In November 2005, the *News of the World* published a story about Prince William's knee injury. After a royal complaint to police, they opened an investigation into whether mobile phone voicemail messages between royal officials had been intercepted. In January 2007, the editor (Clive Goodman) of

(Continued)

(Continued)

royal affairs at the *News of the World* and one of his private investigators (Glenn Mulcaire) were convicted of conspiring to intercept communications. Mulcaire had kept a list of 4,375 names associated with telephone numbers. Police estimated that 829 were likely victims of phone hacking. Other journalists and private investigators certainly were involved, but few had kept such records, without which police struggled to gather evidence against more perpetrators.

In January 2011, the Metropolitan Police (Met) opened a new investigation into phone hacking. From January 2011 through October 2012, 17 of the 90 related arrests were for interception of mobile phone voicemail messages (Leveson, 2012, pp. 8, 13, 19; U.K. House of Commons, 2011a, pp. 47–50).

E-mail

E-mail or electronic mail is a digital communication sent via some computer network. The ease of e-mail, and the easy attachment of files to e-mail, has improved communications, but also increased the leakage of sensitive information. E-mails are prolific, users are casual in their use, and service providers tend to hold data on every e-mail ever sent, including user-deleted e-mails.

> Email systems are often less protected than databases yet contain vast quantities of stored data. Email remains one of the quickest and easiest ways for individuals to collaborate—and for intruders to enter a company's network and steal data. (U.S. ONCIX, 2011, p. A3)

E-mail is a vector for sensitive information in three main ways, as described in the subsections below: external phishing, unauthorized access to stored e-mail, and insider noncompliance with controls on the release of information.

Phishing

Network applications, such as organization-wide e-mail, are exposed to phishing attacks (see the higher section above on sources for a definition of phishing). If the threat could identify the e-mail address of a target within the network, the threat could send an e-mail that persuades the target to download malware that infects the target's computer; the infected computer could infect the whole network, perhaps by sending a similar e-mail to everyone else on the network.

Access to Stored E-mail

Hackers can hack into e-mail accounts after discovering passwords or by bribing service providers. For instance, in February 2013, a website published information received from a hacker identified only as "Guccifer," who had downloaded e-mails and attached photographs sent between former President George W. Bush and his family, including information about their e-mail addresses, home addresses, mobile telephone numbers, and photographs of his father, former President George H. W. Bush, receiving hospital treatment.

E-mailers increasingly must worry about official interception of e-mails, particularly in authoritarian countries where governments routinely search for dissidents, but also in democracies, where, since 9/11 particularly, officials and service providers have become more cooperative in their access of private e-mails. Official investigators cannot practically differentiate in advance what particular e-mail they may be looking for and service providers prefer not to search for such an e-mail—consequently, they tend to access the user's entire e-mail account. "You're asking them for emails relevant to the investigation, but as a practical matter they let you look at everything," said one anonymous former federal prosecutor. "It's harder to do [be discriminate] with e-mails, because unlike a phone, you can't just turn it off once you figure out the conversation didn't relate to what you're investigating," said a former chief (Michael DuBose) of the Department of Justice's Computer Crime and Intellectual Property Section (quoted in: Greg Miller and Ellen Nakashima, November 17, 2012, "FBI Investigation of Broadwell Reveals' Bureau's comprehensive Access to Electronic Communications," *Washington Post*).

Much of this official vigor is justified as counterterrorism, but in the process rights and freedoms are degraded. For instance, in April 2013, the judge at the U.S. military tribunal court at Guantanamo Bay, Cuba, revealed that digital files owned by defense counsels official computer networks had been inexplicably deleted and that unrelated mining of data held by prosecutors revealed that prosecutors had access to around 540,000 e-mails between defense counsels and alleged terrorist clients, which should enjoy attorney-client privileges. Defense counsels were ordered to stop using U.S. official networks and current legal proceedings were postponed.

Concerned users of e-mail could use the few e-mail service providers (such as HushMail) that promise encrypted e-mail and more access controls. They could use temporary e-mail accounts. (For instance, terrorists are known to have deployed after agreeing with their handlers a list of anonymous e-mail accounts, one for each day of deployment.) Users could agree to share a single e-mail account, in which they write up their messages as draft e-mails that the recipient would delete after reading, without either user needing to send an e-mail (sent e-mails tend to be stored on a server, even after the user has ordered deletion). Sophisticated users could convert a digital image into characters, into which they could type a message before converting it back into a digital image (terrorists are known to have achieved this method). Users could avoid e-mail in favor of text messages (text messages can be intercepted, but the content is not normally recorded on any server after the user has deleted it). Users could avoid both e-mail and text messages in favor of old-fashioned verbal messages or hand-delivered written messages, although these have separate risks.

Noncompliant Users

E-mail can be hacked maliciously, but most unauthorized access of information through e-mail is due to noncompliant releases of information by the legitimate user of that e-mail. Phishers could encourage such release, for instance by pretending to be a colleague asking for information, but insiders could e-mail sensitive information on a whim, such as when they want to share a story for amusement or complaint, without realizing that they are violating privacy.

A study by MeriTalk (October 2012) reported that the U.S. federal government sends and receives 1.89 billion e-mails per day—the average federal agency sends and receives 47.3 million e-mails each day; 48% of surveyed federal information managers reported that unauthorized information leaked by standard work e-mail, more than by any other vector, 38% by personal e-mail, and 23% by web-based work e-mail. 47% wanted better e-mail policies, 45% reported that employees did not follow these policies, and only 25% of them rated the security of their current e-mail system with an "A" grade.

E-mail can be encrypted before it leaves the internal network, but encryption can be used to hide sensitive information as it leaves through the e-mail gateway. Eighty percent of federal information security managers were concerned about the possibility of unauthorized data escaping undetected through encrypted e-mails, 58% agreed that encryption makes detection of such escapes more difficult, and 51% foresaw e-mail encryption as a more significant problem for federal agencies in the next 5 years (MeriTalk, 2012).

Removable and Mobile Devices

Removable media, such as plug-in Universal Serial Bus (USB) "flash memory" or "stick" drives and mobile telephones, can be used as vehicles for unauthorized removal of information out of a secured domain and as vectors for malware into a secured domain. In response to MeriTalk's survey of July 2012, 47% of federal information managers reported that unauthorized data left their agency on agency-issued mobile devices (almost as many who reported that it left in e-mail), 42% on USB drives, 33% on personal mobile devices. In February 2011, a survey of private sector information technology and security professionals revealed that 65% do not know what files and data leave their enterprise. According to a March 2011 press report, 57% of employees save work files to external devices on a weekly basis (U.S. ONCIX, 2011, p. A3).

Mobile devices, especially smartphones, are particularly exposed to malware downloaded within apps (application software) or automated connections.

> The migration of increasingly powerful mobile devices into the workplace was a major concern for administrators [in 2012] who had to find ways to manage and secure the devices and control access to sensitive resources. Malware for the devices continued to grow, especially for Androids, and even legitimate applications have proved to be leaky, buggy, and grabby . . . The predictions [for 2014] are not comforting. They include death by internet-connected devices and the use of emerging Near Field Communications [NFC] in smartphones for large-scale fraud and theft. The first phones using NFC already are on the market, and proof-of-concept attacks to control or disrupt internet-enabled medical devices have been publicly demonstrated. (Jackson, GCN, 2013a, p. 20)

Bluetooth technology—normally used to wirelessly connect a telephone to an ear/mouth piece or car-based speaker/microphone—can be intercepted by practically any other Bluetooth device, unless the target user switches off the device. The Bluetooth device can be used to directly listen in on the user's direct conversations, not just their telephone conversations. Bluetooth devices tend to have very short ranges (a few yards), but a threat could get within such ranges within a restaurant or other public space and these ranges can be amplified.

Spaces can be secured by disallowing entry to any digital devices. This is a common regulation for sensitive compartmentalized classified information facilities (SCIFs) and conference rooms. However, people may forget more innocuous devices on their person, such as key fobs, pens, cigarette lighters, and apparel, inside which recording or tracking devices can be hidden. Such items may be provided by agents of the threat to the target as corporate gifts or in commercial transactions.

Cloud Computing

Cloud computing involves access from remote terminals to shared software or data. In recent years, information managers have sought to reduce the financial overhead associated with distributed data centers by moving to cloud computing, where more information and applications are held on remote servers and only accessed by individual terminals when users require. Cloud computing also helps users to share information, collaborate on projects, and back up their information.

Cloud computing improves security in the sense that information and applications can be gathered more centrally and distributed only when properly demanded. However, centralization of data creates a single point of failure, and shared code implies more vulnerability to malware inside the system.

> Over the past year, cloud services have proven no more or no less secure than other platforms. Cloud computing is a hot business opportunity in government, but both providers and customers seem to be cautious enough about the security of the services that has not become a major issue. But with major cloud service providers having experienced several high-profile service outages in the past two years, reliability has emerged as more of an issue than security. Google suffered a brief outage in October, but Amazon was the worst hit (or the biggest offender) with three outages of its Web Services in 2011 and 2012. Most recently, its Northern Virginia data center in Ashburn was knocked out by severe weather in June and then again because of an equipment failure in October. Planning for outages and data backup are as important as security when moving critical operations or services to the cloud. (Jackson, 2013a, p. 20)

The U.S. DOD intends to transition from more than 1,500 data centers to one cloud that would be secure against the most sophisticated foreign state sponsored attacks. In 2011, DOD announced its Mission-oriented Resilient Clouds program, and scheduled testing of a system for 2015. The projects include redundant hosts, diverse systems within the system, and coordinated gathering of information about threats.

Wireless Networks

In theory any digital network could be tapped. Wired networks must be tapped inside the network, either by malware or a hard device on the cables between computers. A wireless network is less exposed to a hard tap but more exposed to wireless taps. Since wireless traffic is broadcast, no one has to join the network just to record the traffic, but one would need to break into the nodes in order to read the traffic. Directional antennas can collect traffic from further away.

This exposure is more likely for public networks, such as at hotels and cafes, where access controls are low so that guests can use the network temporarily using their personal computers. Malicious actors could dwell in such spaces waiting for a high-value target to use the same network. If the target's security is poor, the threat could observe the target's wireless communications and even access the target computer itself.

Private networks, such as a network that a family would set up within a household, become public when households forget to set any access controls (as simple as a password), share their password with the wrong people, or forego any password on the common assumption that nobody would be interested enough to attack a home network. Since households increasingly work online, bank online, and send private digital communications from home networks, the exposure could include professional information, personal identities, financial assets, and intimate private information. Sometimes holders assume that their wireless network is too short range or remote for anyone else to access, but a skilled threat only needs minutes of proximate access to do harm.

The exposure of private information on unsecured wireless networks is illustrated by Google's inadvertent gathering of private data (including the users' passwords, private e-mails, and websites visited) from unsecured household wireless networks while gathering data on locations for its Street View service. In 2008 and 2009, Google sent especially equipped personnel to drive around streets taking images and collecting data on locations for the database that would found Street View. Their equipment triangulated locations by tapping into unencrypted wireless signals but gathered more data than was needed. In 2011, the French Data Protection Authority fined Google $142,000 for taking the private data. In April 2012, the U.S. Federal Communications Commission found no violation of U.S. law, but fined Google $25,000 for obstructing the investigation. (Google's revenue topped $50 billion in 2012.) Most states within the United States continued to pursue Google on criminal grounds. In March 2013, Google settled with attorneys general from 38 states and the District of Columbia: Google committed to pay $7 million, destroy the personal information, and implement a 10-year program to train its own employees on privacy and to make the public more aware of wireless privacy.

 Malicious Activities

The two preceding sections respectively described the human sources of malicious activities and the vectors for malicious activities. This section describes the actual activities. The subsections below describe malicious activities by their four primary objectives or effects:

1. Misinformation
2. Control of information or censorship
3. Espionage, including the collection of information and the observation of the target
4. Sabotage, or some sort of deliberate disruption or damage of the target, and terrorism

Cyber warfare is not examined separately here but is some collection of all these activities. It is ill defined, and is normally used in the context of international conflict, but cyber warfare has been waged between governments, insurgents, and terrorists.

Pedagogy Box 14.18 Official Definitions of Malicious Cyber Activities

The International Organization for Standardization (ISO) and the International Electrotechnical Commission (IEC) issue a standard (ISO/IEC 2382-8: 1998) that defines a *cyber crime* or *computer crime* as "a crime committed with the aid of, or directly involving, a data processing system or computer network."

The U.S. DHS defines *cyber threats* as "any identified efforts directed toward accessing, exfiltrating, manipulating, or impairing the integrity, confidentiality, security, or availability of data, an application, or a federal system, without lawful authority."

For the Canadian government, a cyber attack is "the unintentional or unauthorized access to, use, manipulation, interruption, or destruction, via electronic means, of electronic information or the electronic devices or computer systems and networks used to process, transmit, or store that information" (Public Safety Canada, 2012, p. 22).

Misinformation

New technologies have eased the distribution of information, potentially helping individuals to access the facts, but also helping malicious actors to spread misinformation.

The trends are addressed in the subsections below by the democratization of information, social media, public liabilities, and private liabilities.

Democratization of Information

Traditionally, information was gathered and distributed by officials and journalists, but consumers have more access to the sources of information, are better able to gather information for themselves and to share information, are becoming more biased in their choices, and are more self-reliant. Potentially this trend creates more discerning and informed consumers and less centralized control of information, but it also allows for more varied misinformation. Certainly, the traditional sources, filters, and interpreters are diminishing. In the new year of 2013, the World Economic Forum offered a warning about "digital wildfires" due to digital interconnectivity and the erosion of the journalist's traditional role as gatekeeper. The report warned that the democratization of information, although sometimes a force for good, can also have volatile and unpredictable negative consequences.

Officials often complain about journalists or private interpreters misrepresenting them, although officials also often manipulate or collude with these other sources. In effect, we need higher ethical standards on the side of information providers and fairer discrimination on the side of the consumer.

Pedagogy Box 14.19 British Journalistic and Official Information Ethics

The British judicial enquiry into journalistic ethics found that most editors and journalists "do good work in the public interest" but too many chased sensational stories with no public interest, fictionalized stories, or gathered information illegally or unethically, such as by hacking telephones, e-mail accounts, and computers and by paying officials and commercial service providers for confidential information (Leveson, 2012, p. 11). "[T]he evidence clearly demonstrates that, over the last 30–35 years and probably much longer, the political parties of UK national Government and of UK official Opposition have had or developed too close a relationship with the press in a way which has not been in the public interest" (Leveson, 2012, p. 26).

Social Media

Social media can be used to undermine centralized control of information and to spread misinformation rapidly or convincingly, although social media can be used also to counter misinformation and to gather intelligence.

Private use of information and communications technology, through social media particularly, can challenge any person's or organization's control of information and increase their exposure and liabilities. For instance, after United Airlines denied a claim for damages to a passenger's guitar, he wrote a song ("United Breaks Guitars") about it; in July 2009, he uploaded a video of himself performing the song to YouTube, where it was viewed more than 12 million times within a year, by when United Airlines stock had dropped by about 10%, costing shareholders about $180 million. On October 18,

2012, NASDAQ halted trading on Google's shares after a leaked earnings report (coupled with weak results) triggered a $22 billion plunge in Google's market capitalization.

Sometimes sources are deliberately misinformative and disruptive. For instance, in 2012, 30,000 people fled Bangalore, India, after receiving text messages warning that they would be attacked in retaliation for communal violence in their home state (Assam). In July 2012, a Twitter user impersonated the Russian Interior Minister (Vladimir Kolokoltsev) when he tweeted that Syria's President (Bashar al-Assad) had "been killed or injured"; the news caused crude oil prices to rise before traders realized the news was false. On April 23, 2013, Syrian hackers sent a fictional Tweet through the Associated Press' Twitter account to more than 2 million users about explosions in the White House that injured the U.S. President. The stock market briefly crashed; although it recovered within minutes, the crash had been worth more than $130 billion in equity market value.

In politics, the practice of creating the false impression of grassroots consensus or campaigning is called *astroturfing*. For instance, in 2009, during a special election for a U.S. Senator from Massachusetts, fake Twitter accounts successfully spread links to a website smearing one of the candidates.

Sometimes, satirical information is mistaken for accurate information. For instance, in October 2012, Iran's official news agency repeated a story that had originated on a satirical website ("The Onion"), claiming that opinion polls showed Iran's President (Mahmoud Ahmadinejad) was more popular than the U.S. President (Barack Obama) among rural white Americans.

Misinformation can be corrected by social media. For instance, during Storm Sandy in October 2012, social media in general proved very effective for public authorities seeking to prepare the affected population in the north-east United States. Additionally, after a private tweet claimed falsely that the New York Stock Exchange was flooded, and it was reported by a televised news channel (CNN), it was discredited by other tweets (as soon as 1 hour after first tweet).

Social media can be used to track misinformation or emerging issues. For instance, in 2012, the U.S. Centers for Disease Control and Prevention developed a web application that monitors the Twitter stream for specified terms that would indicate an epidemic or other emerging public health issue. Meanwhile, the same technologies have been configured by official authorities to track political opposition (see the section below on censorship).

A combination of new consumer technologies and increased personal and social responsibility would be the least controversial solution:

> In addition to seeking ways to inculcate an ethos of responsibility among social-media users, it will be necessary for consumers of social media to become more literate in assessing the reliability and bias of sources. Technical solutions could help here. Researchers and developers are working on [software] programs and browser extensions, such as LazyTruth, Truthy, or TEASE, that aim to help people assess the credibility of information and sources circulating online. It is possible to imagine the development of more broad and sophisticated automated flags for disputed information, which could become as ubiquitous as programs that protect Internet users against spam and malware. (World Economic Forum, 2013, p. 26)

Public Liabilities

Popular information technologies challenge official control of information, yet encourage popular perceptions that governments are responsible for permitting freedom of objectionable information. The same people that challenge censorship of wanted information might challenge freedoms to distribute unwanted information. For instance, on September 30, 2005, a Danish newspaper published cartoons featuring the Prophet Mohammed; a few outraged local Muslims made threats against the newspaper and the cartoonist, but the issue became global only in January 2006 after news media in largely Islamic countries publicized the story. The news then spread rapidly, prompting protests within days in several countries, targeting varied Western diplomatic and commercial sites (few of them Danish). Clashes between protesters and local authorities, including foreign coalition troops in Afghanistan and Iraq, resulted in perhaps 200 deaths.

Similarly, violent protests started in Egypt on September 11, 2012, after a video clip from a critical film about the Prophet Mohammed appeared online dubbed into Egyptian Arabic. The film featured American actors and was produced by American residents but was known to few other Americans. Nevertheless, protesters focused on U.S. diplomatic sites: The same day, the U.S. Embassy in Cairo was invaded; that night, four U.S. personnel were killed at the mission in Benghazi, Libya; protests spread internationally and claimed around 50 lives.

Pedagogy Box 14.20 Official U.S. Statement on "Leveraging Culture and Diplomacy in the Age of Information"

"The world's cultures have become too interconnected and interdependent, socially, economically, and politically, to ignore. The digital age has forced us into ever closer intimacy. Our modes of communication are no longer constrained by geography or cultural divisions. More and more people converse, operate, trade, invest, interact, and take decisive and groundbreaking action—with social media as their central tool.

So, more people than ever are accessing and sharing information about their cultures—virtually and in real space.

We have seen the negative consequences of our digital connections, such as the violent uprisings that occurred in response to controversial Danish cartoons, the desecration of Korans, and one hateful film about Islam.

We have seen, too, how autocratic governments and terrorist organizations have concocted false cultural narratives of their own, to deceive followers or citizens, while also limiting their access to the news and truth.

It is also true that there are those who have no connection to digital media, for whom other cultures can seem alien, suspect, and who we also need to reach—person to person, face to face. And we have seen how anti-Americanism persists in many corners, giving rise to violence against our citizens, our nation, and our partners.

So whether we choose to accept it or not, the United States will always be part of the global conversation—not only through our actions as a government but through the popular culture with which we are identified.

The question isn't whether we should participate in public diplomacy—of which cultural diplomacy is a major part—but how we can harness cultural diplomacy as a force for good.

(Continued)

(Continued)

Which brings me to the opportunities. They are too important to ignore: People worldwide are hungering for freedom and opportunity and searching for examples to emulate. While the U.S. doesn't provide the only model to emulate, we know we have positive contributions to make. And we know that when we engage on a cultural level, we can open doors that might otherwise be locked."

SOURCE: Prepared speech by Tara Sonenshine, U.S. Under Secretary for Public Diplomacy and Public Affairs, at the Institute for Cultural Diplomacy, Washington, DC, January 9, 2013.

Private Liabilities

Unfortunately, we live in an increasingly digital world where severe censorship and abuses of information live side by side with largely unrestricted freedoms to slander and defame. Deliberate misinformation is difficult to prosecute as a crime because of the ease with which the perpetrators can disguise themselves through social media, the burden of proof for intent and harm, and the right to freedom of speech. New technologies have created practical and legal difficulties for the traditional actors who countered misinformation.

Consequently, some official prosecutors have focused their attention on easy targets without a clear case for the public good, while ignoring more socially damaging misinformation and the rampant defamation and slander on social media. For instance, a British court convicted a man for tweeting that he should blow up an airport in frustration at the cancellation of his flight, but in July 2012, his conviction was overturned on appeal—justly, given absence of malicious intent or harm.

False allegations can be very costly if made against someone with the capacity to pursue civil claims. For instance, in November 2012, the British Broadcasting Corporation (BBC) broadcast an allegation that a senior politician had been involved in child abuse, which transpired to have been a case of mistaken identity on the part of the victim. Although the BBC had not named the politician, he had been named in about 10,000 tweets or retweets. On top of pursuing legal action against all the people who had spread this false information on Twitter, the injured politician settled on £185,000 in damages from the BBC. The BBC's culpability emerged after revelations that BBC staff had neglected warnings, including from BBC journalists, that one of its long-standing television presenters (Jimmy Savile) had abused children, allegations that were publicized widely only after his death (October 2011).

Censorship and Controls on Freedom of Information

New technologies have democratized information and challenged official control of information. Many governments are explicitly looking for the correct balance between freedom of speech and accuracy of information. Some governments, such as those in China, Cuba, Ethiopia, Libya, Myanmar (Burma), North Korea, Iran, Syria, Tunisia, Turkmenistan, and Yemen, routinely control their residents' access to information, including certain websites. They could shut down access nationally to the Internet within minutes, thanks to centralized official control of the telecommunications hardware or the service providers.

The subsections below review global trends in national control of information then give more details on the role of the United States, China, Russia, Iran, Syria, Egypt, and Pakistan in particular.

Global Trends

In 2012, Freedom House reported, for the period January 2011 through May 2012, that restrictions on Internet freedoms had grown globally and had become more sophisticated and subtle. Freedom House collected data on only 47 countries; it claimed to lack data on other countries, which included most of central America, western South America, most of Africa, and parts of the Middle East and central Asia, which would make the world look even less free.

Twenty of the 47 countries examined experienced a negative trajectory in Internet freedom, with Bahrain, Pakistan, and Ethiopia registering the greatest declines. Four of the 20 in decline were democracies. In 19 countries examined, new laws or directives were passed that restricted online speech, violated user privacy, or punished individuals who had posted uncompliant content. In 26 of the 47 countries, including several democratic states, at least one person was arrested for content posted online or sent via text message. In 19 of the 47 countries, at least one person was tortured, disappeared, beaten, or brutally assaulted as a result of their online posts. In five countries, an activist or citizen journalist was killed in retribution for posting information that exposed human rights abuses. In 12 of the 47 countries examined, a new law or directive disproportionately enhanced surveillance or restricted user anonymity. In Saudi Arabia, Ethiopia, Uzbekistan, and China, authorities imposed new restrictions after observing the role that social media played in popular uprisings. From 2010 to 2012, paid progovernment commentators online spread to 14 of the 47 countries examined. Meanwhile, government critics faced politically motivated cyber attacks in 19 of the countries covered.

Freedom House rates Internet freedom by country by judging restrictions in three main dimensions:

- Obstacles to access: Infrastructural and economic barriers to access; governmental efforts to block specific applications or technologies; and legal, regulatory, and ownership control over Internet and mobile phone providers.
- Limits on content: Filtering and blocking of websites; other forms of censorship and self-censorship; manipulation of content; the diversity of online news media; and usage of digital media for social and political activism.
- Violations of user rights: measures legal protections and restrictions on online activity; surveillance; privacy; and repercussions for online activity, such as legal prosecution, imprisonment, physical attacks, or other forms for harassment.

Freedom House scores each country from 0–100 points and then ranks each country on a 3-level ordinal scale (free or 0–30 points; partly free or 31–60 points; and not free or 61–100 points). In 2012, 11 countries received a ranking of "not free" (in order from the least free): Iran, Cuba, China, Syria, Uzbekistan, Ethiopia, Burma, Vietnam, Saudi Arabia, Bahrain, Belarus, Pakistan, and Thailand.

In 2012, Freedom House rated 14 countries as Internet free (in order): Estonia, United States, Germany, Australia, Hungary, Italy, the Philippines, Britain, Argentina, South Africa, Brazil, Ukraine, Kenya, and Georgia. In 23 of the 47 countries assessed, freedom advocates scored at least one victory, sometimes through the courts, resulting in censorship plans being shelved, harmful legislation being overturned, or jailed activists being released. Fourteen countries registered a positive trajectory, mostly democracies; Tunisia and Burma experienced the largest improvements following dramatic partial democratization.

In March 2013, Reporters Without Borders listed (in order) Finland, Netherlands, Norway, Luxemburg, Andorra, Denmark, Lichtenstein, New Zealand, Iceland, and Sweden as the ten free-est for the world press. It listed (in order) Eritrea, North Korea, Turkmenistan, Syria, Somalia, Iran, China, Vietnam, Cuba, and Sudan as the ten least free for the world press. It identified five states (Bahrain, China, Iran, Syria, Vietnam) whose online surveillance results in serious human rights violations.

Pedagogy Box 14.21 International Governance of ICTs

In 1865, leading states agreed the International Telegraph Union to govern the international interoperability of telegraph communications and the associated commercial and economic flows. This union took on the governance of telephone and wireless radio communications too, becoming the International Telecommunication Union (ITU), based in Geneva, Switzerland. Its activities include governing the international sharing of the radio spectrum, assigning incoming telephone dialing codes to different countries, and standardizing technical performance and interoperability. In 1950, it became an agency of the United Nations, representing all member nations of the UN and concerned organizations. In 1988, the members of the ITU agreed major changes, mostly in response to new technologies, primarily those related to the Internet.

In 1988, the U.S. DOD established the Internet Assigned Numbers Authority (IANA) to assign Internet protocol (IP) addresses and related systems. In 1998, the Internet Corporation for Assigned Names and Numbers (ICANN) was established by the Department of Commerce as a nonprofit organization headquartered in Playa Vista, California, to take over IANA's responsibilities.

The U.S. continues to boast the base for ICANN and the most valuable IP addresses, websites, and Internet-based companies. Some other countries have complained about U.S. leadership. In September 2011, China, Russia, Tajikistan, and Uzbekistan wrote a letter to the UN General Assembly that called for an "international code of conduct" and "norms and rules guiding behavior" for countries overseeing the Internet. China, Russia, and several Arab countries have called for more UN control over the Internet and more controls on online misinformation and threats to privacy. On May 31, 2012, Google, Microsoft, Verizon, and Cisco jointly warned a U.S. Congressional hearing that the foreign calls threaten Internet freedoms and their business.

In December 2012, the World Conference on International Telecommunications met in Dubai to revise the treaty (1988) governing the International Telecommunications Union. The U.S. delegation (the largest) proposed a treaty that it justified mostly to preserve nonprofit, nongovernmental control of Internet content and to safeguard freedom of information. After the United States had submitted its proposal, Russia proposed intergovernmental governance of the Internet (replacing ICANN), more national control of data trafficking, and controls on unwanted advertising (spam), which it claimed would make the Internet more efficient, secure, and truthful. Russia's proposal drew support from China and some Arab states, for a total of about 10 states explicitly committed. The United States and others argued that Russia's proposed regulations could be used by individual governments to censor information or punish individuals or organizations. The delegations negotiated a proposed treaty that placed some of Russia's proposals in a nonbinding part and was about 80% agreeable to the U.S. delegation, but the United States and others opposed the remainder. The United States, Canada, most European countries, and some other states (for a total of 55) refused to sign the treaty, but 89 states supported it.

United States

Freedom House rated Estonia and the United States respectively as the first and second free-est countries for Internet freedom. U.S. courts have held that prohibitions against government regulation of speech apply to material published on the Internet. However, in almost every year from 2001 to 2012, Freedom House noted concerns about the U.S. government's surveillance powers. For instance, under Section 216 of the USA PATRIOT ACT, the FBI, without warrant, can monitor Internet traffic. At the same time, an executive order permitted the National Security Agency (NSA), without warrant, to monitor American Internet use. In early 2012, campaigns by civil society and technology companies helped to halt passage of the Stop Online Piracy Act (SOPA) and the Protect Intellectual Property Act (PIPA), which they claimed would have compromised personal privacy.

Since American companies dominate online sites and the software used online, more restrictive countries clash with American companies and the U.S. government. Google is the main private target: It provides the world's most popular search engine; Google's Gmail is the world's most popular free online e-mail service; and Google provides popular free portals of or hosts for information such as Google Maps and YouTube. Yet Google has been more aggressively investigated and punished under antitrust and data privacy legislation in Europe than in the United States, suggesting that the United States is weak on violations of privacy, even while strong on freedoms of information.

China

China is home to the world's largest population of Internet users, but also the largest system of controls, known as China's Electronic Great Wall, although these are implemented largely locally and inconsistently at the ISP level. Users know they are being watched, which results in self-censorship and evasion, including non-technical evasion, such as exploiting linguistic ambiguities to confuse the censors. Freedom House (2012) reports that in 2011 alone, Chinese authorities tightened controls on popular domestic microblogging platforms, pressured key firms to censor political content and to register their users' real names, and detained dozens of online activists for weeks before sentencing several to prison. In March 2013, Reporters Without Borders reported that China had again pushed Internet service providers to help to monitor Internet users and stepped up its counters against anonymization tools.

Russia

Russian authorities were late to censor political opposition on the Internet, having focused on using social media itself for misinformation, but in January 2011, massive distributed denial-of-service

(DDOS) attacks and smear campaigns were used to discredit online activists. In December 2011, online tools helped antigovernment protesters to organize huge assemblies, but the government signaled its intention to further tighten control over Internet communications.

Iran

After disputed elections in 2009, in which protesters had used social media to evade restrictions on freedom of assembly and on freedom of speech, Iranian authorities upgraded content filtering technology, hacked digital certificates to undermine user privacy, and handed down harsh sentences in the world for online activities, including the death penalty for three social media activists.

ViewDNS, a site that monitors servers, estimates that the Iranian government censors roughly 1 in 3 news sites and 1 in 4 of all sites on the World Wide Web. All Iranian Internet service providers must buy bandwidth from a state-owned company and comply with orders to filter out certain websites, servers, and keywords. Iranian authorities also monitor social media and prosecute noncompliant users. In April 2011, Iran announced plans for an Iranian Internet (designated Halal—an Arabic religious term for permissible), which is closed to the World Wide Web for all but official users. In January 2012, Iranian authorities announced new regulations on Internet access, declared the Halal Internet under official test (with a fully operational target of March 2013), and opened a Halal online search engine (designated to replace the Google search engine, which Iran accused of spying). Iran blocked access to Google and Gmail in May 2012 after Google Maps removed the term Persian Gulf from maps. For 1 week in September 2012, Iran blocked all Google-owned sites (Google, Gmail, YouTube, and Reader). In February 2013, Iran selectively blocked some foreign servers until, in mid-March, it blocked all VPNs, effectively including all Google sites (ViewDNS, 2012).

Syria

The Syrian government controls the licensing of or owns all telecommunications infrastructure, including the Internet, inside Syria. In 1999, the Syrian Telecommunications Establishment first invited bids for a national Internet network in Syria, including extensive filtering and surveillance, according to a document obtained by Reporters Without Borders (2013). Following revolution in March 2011, Syria has increased its domestic control to the Internet and targeted online opponents.

Egypt

In January 2011, during mass protests, the regime of President Hosni Mubarak shut down the Internet across Egypt in order to stifle the protesters' use of social media. The official effort took a few days to achieve; the result was a significant stifling of online protest and organization, but also of economic activity.

In February 2011, the Supreme Council of the Armed Forces (SCAF) took executive power after the resignation of Mubarak, but mobile phones, the Internet, and social media remained under vigorous surveillance, bandwidth speeds were throttled during specific events, SCAF-affiliated commentators manipulated online discussions, and several online activists were intimidated, beaten, shot at, or tried in military courts for "insulting the military power" or "disturbing social peace."

Pakistan

In the 2000s, mobile phones and other ICTs proliferated in Pakistan and were readily applied by citizen journalists and activists. Freedom House (2012) reports that between January 2011 and mid-2012, official actions resulted in "an alarming deterioration in Internet freedom from the previous year," including a ban on ncryption and virtual private networks (VPNs), legislation for a death sentence for transmitting allegedly blasphemous content via text message, and blocks on all mobile phone networks in Balochistan province for 1 day. After civil society advocacy campaigns, Pakistani authorities postponed several other initiatives to increase censorship, including a plan to filter text messages by keyword and a proposal to develop a nationwide Internet firewall.

Additional restrictions on Internet freedom emerged in the second half of 2012: A brief block on Twitter, a second freeze on mobile phone networks in Baluchistan, and a new directive to block 15 websites featuring content about "influential persons." In September 2012, Pakistan banned the popular video-sharing website YouTube after clips of the movie "Innocence of Muslims" sparked protests throughout Pakistan. In June 2013, Pakistan considered lifting the ban, but only if Google were to install a "proper filtration system" to remove content Muslims may find offensive. Ahead of general elections in April 2013, the government prepared sophisticated Internet surveillance technologies.

Espionage

In a world of increasing cyber espionage, espionage continues in old-fashioned ways that are easily neglected, such as surreptitiously recording or eavesdropping on private conversations. Espionage is commonly interpreted as an official activity directed against foreign targets, but as the sections above on the sources of attacks and activities suggest, official authorities continue to gain capacity and incentives for espionage on private actors too. For instance, in February 2013, a U.S. military lawyer acknowledged that microphones had been hidden inside fake smoke detectors in rooms used for meetings between defense counsels and alleged terrorists at the U.S. detention center at Guantanamo Bay, Cuba. The U.S. military said the listening system had been installed before defense lawyers started to use the rooms and was not used to eavesdrop on confidential meetings. The government subsequently said that it tore out the wiring.

As shown above, any digital media (including telephones, Bluetooth devices, computers) with a recording or imaging device can be used to surreptitiously spy. Recording devices can be hidden inside other items, such as buttons and keys.

Cyber espionage normally involves use of a computer network to access information. Some attempts to physically or digitally bypass access controls are detectable by protective software, but as the section on vectors illustrates, many vectors permit a threat to bypass such controls. Once a threat has gained the user's identification and password, it should be able to log in to a controlled space, such as a personal computer, e-mail account, or online directory, within which the threat can browse for information. *Snooping and downloading* describe such unwanted access within the controlled space (Yannakogeorges, 2011, p. 259).

Pedagogy Box 14.22 U.S. Official Definitions of Cyber Espionage

The Worldwide Threat Assessment of the U.S. Intelligence Community (March 12, 2013) defined cyber espionage as "intrusions into networks to access sensitive diplomatic, military, or economic information."

Pedagogy Box 14.23 Definitions of Spyware

Malware that is used for espionage is better known as *spyware*. "Eavesdropping and packet sniffing" are "techniques [that] refer to the capturing of data-packets en route to their destinations without altering information" (Yannakogeorges, 2011, p. 258). A *packet sniffer* is "a program that intercepts routed data and examines each packet in search of specified information, such as passwords transmitted in clear text" (U.S. GAO, 2005b, p. 8).

Key loggers record keyboard strokes on a computer. Key loggers include hardware, such as a device plugged in between a keyboard and the terminal or between a computer and its Internet connection cable, and software, such as malware placed digitally on the computer. Hardware key loggers are undetectable by the computer's software, but are detectable visually, at least by someone who knows what a typical computer's hardware should look like.

Cyber Sabotage

Cyber sabotage can disrupt private access to the Internet, damage private computers, and cause damage to infrastructure on a national scale.

As described in the subsections below, cyber sabotage is aimed mainly at denial of Internet service or sabotage of control systems.

Pedagogy Box 14.24 U.S. Official Definitions of Cyber Sabotage and Terrorism

For U.S. DOD (2012b), *sabotage* is "an act or acts with intent to injure, interfere with, or obstruct the national defense of a country by willfully injuring or destroying, or attempting to injure or destroy, any national defense or war material, premises, or utilities, to include human and natural resources."

Sabotage, disruption, or damage of a digital environment (collectively equivalent to offensive cyber warfare) can be achieved by any of the malware. Malware can be configured to damage or destroy digital systems or the other systems controlled by the infected digital networks.

Denial of Service

A denial of service (DOS) attack aims to disrupt Internet sites, principally by overloading the servers that provide the information on the site. The attacks are strengthened by using multiple sources to deliver the malicious traffic, a technique known as distributed denial of service (DDOS). Typically, malware is delivered by virus or worm, shutting down servers from the inside or taking over a network of computers (a "botnet" of "zombie" computers) so that they send requests for information that overwhelm the servers. An attacker would use a botnet in most cases, but also could recruit colleagues or volunteers.

Most DOS attacks are aimed at particular organizations but some have wider implications. In November 1988, a worm known as "Morris" brought 10% of systems connected to the Internet to a halt. In 2001, the "Code Red" worm shut down or slowed down Internet access from millions of computer users.

Denial-of-service attacks have become easier with increased availability of Internet bandwidth and technical skills. Cloud-hosting structures give attackers more processing power and more digital space in which to hide their activities.

Pedagogy Box 14.25 Definitions of Denial of Service Attacks

The U.S. GAO (2005b) defines denial of service as a "method of attack from a single source that denies system access to legitimate users by overwhelming the target computer with messages and blocking legitimate traffic. It can prevent a system from being able to exchange data with other systems or use the Internet." It defines a distributed DOS (DDOS) as a "variant of the denial-of-service attack that uses a coordinated attack from a distributed system of computers rather than from a single source. It often makes use of worms to spread to multiple computers that can then attack the target."

Collectively, these attacks have been categorized as "jamming or flooding" attacks (Yannakogeorges, 2011, p. 260).

> Denial of service is a descriptive term rather than a technical one: it describes the goal of the attack rather than the tools or techniques used. Although there are a variety of ways to carry out the attacks, they fall into two broad categories: network and application . . . A network attack . . . floods servers with high volumes of requests or packets to overwhelm the resources . . . An application attack . . . uses specially formed–or malformed–queries and requests that servers have to deal with slowly until the number of available connections or the processing capacity is exhausted. (Jackson, 2013b)

Sabotage of Control Systems

Malware, as shown above, can be used to spy, but it can be configured to damage or destroy the digital systems used to control processes (often known generically as "industrial control systems"). Most of these systems are contained within an intranet, but sometimes are open to attacks via the Internet. For instance, in March 1997, a teenager in Worcester, Massachusetts, used Internet access to disable controls systems at the local airport control tower. In the 2000s, several countries reported that their national power grids, air traffic control systems, and nuclear installations had been penetrated, although the relative roles played by malicious actors or bugs in the system are difficult to separate, particularly because officials often deny any issue for fear of alarming the public or alerting the attackers to their performance (UNODC, 2010).

Pedagogy Box 14.26 Definitions of Sabotage Malware

Viruses, worms, and Trojan Horses each could inject malicious code into other software, potentially causing the software to malfunction or to execute destructive actions, such as deleting data or shutting down the computer. A *root kit* is especially stealthy because it modifies the computer's operating system or even its kernel (core) (Yannakogeorges, 2011, p. 261). Software *tampering* or *diddling* is "making unauthorized modifications to software stored on a system, including file deletions" (Denning, 1998, pp. 33–34). A *logic bomb* is "a form of sabotage in which a programmer inserts code that causes the program to perform a destructive action when some triggering event occurs, such as terminating the programmer's employment." (U.S. GAO, 2005b, p. 8)

Providing Security

The sections above, in reviewing the sources, vectors, and activities associated with attacks on information, have provided much advice on countering these things. This (final) section presents advice for higher managers in providing information security in general and cyber and communications security in general.

Information Security

Advice on securing information has been swamped with advice on securing digital information alone, but information security must have a wider scope than digital information. Well-established advice separates information security by "three components":

1. "Protective security," meaning "passive defenses" against attempts to collect your information or information on you, defenses such as controlling access to, transfer of, communication of, and travel with information of certain classifications
2. "Detection and neutralization of intelligence threats," meaning an "active defense by eliminating the opponent's offensive intelligence threat"
3. "Deception," meaning "deceiving or confusing" the threat (Herman, 1996, pp. 166–170)

The Humanitarian Practice Network (2010, p. 154) recommends the following minimum policy on information security:

1. Define sensitive information
2. Define who is authorized to handle sensitive information
3. Define how the sensitive information is to be
   a. stored,
   b. communicated,

c. transported,
d. made unsensitive, or
e. destroyed.

A more detailed strategy for information security involves

- defense of the secure domain by
  - controlling physical access, such as by restricting the persons who are allowed to enter the physical spaces where information is stored or accessed,
  - controlling digital access, such as by restricting who may use a computer network,
  - controlling the transfer of information between domains, such as by forbidding the carriage of papers or digital media out of the secure domain, and
  - establishing *firewalls*, essentially filters or gates to information, permitting information or requesters that pass some rule-based criteria.
- redundancy, by duplicating critical parts of the operation, such as the power sources, workers, and sites (although full redundancy would be unnecessary and expensive),
- backups, in case the primary source or asset is lost, of
  - data,
  - network and processing capacity,
  - personnel,
  - processes, and
  - critical service providers and suppliers
- planning for future contingencies, and
- testing the network against modeled contingencies (Suder, 2004, pp. 196–197).

Cyber Security

This book does not have space for a full review of the technical provisions of cyber security, but many technical provisions are described above following a description of particular threats.

In general, private actors can provide minimal cyber security via the following defensive measures:

- monitoring insiders for noncompliant communication of information;
- analyzing incoming traffic for potential threats;
- consulting experts on threats, subscribing to documents issued by hacking supporters, and monitoring online forums for hackers;
- automated intrusion-detection systems;
- automated intrusion-prevention systems;
- automated logs of anomalous behaviors or penetrations and regular audits of these logs;
- firewalls (effectively: rule-based filters of traffic or gates to information, permitting information or requesters that pass some rule-based criteria);
- antivirus software;
- antispam software; and
- monitoring for security patches.

Pedagogy Box 14.27 Official Definitions of Cyber Security

The popularity of the adjective *cyber* belies the looseness of the definition, confusing even official authorities that are supposed to secure cyber space. For instance, in 2009 the U.S. military formed a Cyber Command with responsibilities in military and civilian cyber space, but for years, it has struggled with operational and technical definitions of overlapping terms and domains, including information, intelligence, communications, signals, information technology, information warfare, and cyber warfare. After a trend to conflate everything, the U.S. military and GAO (2011) properly separated IT administration, cyber defense, and offensive cyber warfare.

The DHS (2009) defines *cyber security* as "the prevention of damage to, unauthorized use of, or exploitation of, and if needed, the restoration of electronic information and communications systems and the information contained therein to ensure confidentiality, integrity, and availability. Includes protection and restoration, when needed, of information networks and wireline, wireless, satellite, public safety answering points, and 911 communications systems and control systems" (p. 109).

The U.S. DOD dictionary (2012b) does not define cyber security but includes *cyber counterintelligence* as "measures to identify, penetrate, or neutralize foreign operations that use cyber means as the primary tradecraft methodology, as well as foreign intelligence service collection efforts that use traditional methods to gauge cyber capabilities and intentions."

For the Canadian government, cyber security is "the body of technologies, processes, practices, and response and mitigation measures designed to protect networks, computers, programs, and data from attack, damage, or unauthorized access so as to ensure confidentiality, integrity, and availability" (Public Safety Canada, 2012, p. 24).

Access Controls

Access controls are the measures intended to permit access into certain domains or to certain information by the appropriate users but to deny access to anyone else. Increasingly, cyber security experts advocate the "least privilege principle"—according to which users are granted only the permissions they need to do their jobs and nothing more.

Access controls on authorized users normally consist of a system that demands an authorized user name and password. These data are much more likely to be compromised at the user-end of the system than the server-end. The servers normally hold the users' passwords in an encrypted form (a *password hash*—a number generated mathematically from the password). When the user attempts to log in, the server generates a hash of the typed password that it compares to the stored hash. If they match, the server permits access. The hash is difficult to crack, but some national threats have the capacity. Future technologies promise better encryption, but also better decryption.

> The requirement to maintain high grade cryptographic security will be imperative for commercial, defense and security requirements. Potential developments such as "quantum key distribution" will aim to guarantee secure communication between users, preventing and also detecting any information interception attempts. However, the advent of quantum information processing, before the widespread application of quantum encryption, may exponentially

> increase the speed and effectiveness of attacks on data, meta-data structures, networks and underlying infrastructures. Development of algorithms, such as Shor's, will break crypto keys with a one-way function, and make public key systems vulnerable to attack, increasing the susceptibility of coded information to be deciphered. Further challenges will arise if quantum computing can be realized before 2040; potentially stagnating other developments in either encryption or processing. (U.K. MOD, 2010a, p. 140)

Most threats are admitted to a secure space by some action on the part of the user. The user may be noncompliant with a rule (such as do not share your password) but much of the user's work activity (such as communicating by e-mail or attending conferences) implies inherent exposure to threats. Consequently, most cyber security managers, having implemented controls on access to or transfer of information, focus their attention on improving the user's compliance with secure behavior.

In theory, the advice is mostly simple (such as use only allowed software; do not download from untrusted sources; keep your security system updated), but one expert has warned that cyber security relies too heavily on users.

> Since most users lack the knowledge to discover bugs on their own, they rely on patches and updates from software manufacturers. They then have to know how to fix the problem themselves, and vigilantly keep tabs on whether or not their information systems are running software with the latest security patches installed. This focus on the user protecting his or her own information system by vigilantly patching their systems is perhaps the greatest pitfall of current cyber security systems. (Yannakogeorges, 2011, p. 261)

Consequently, as much of the controls on software use and updates should be automated so that user fallibility is removed from the risks.

User fallibility would still remain when users are granted user-controlled access, which is inherent to most work today, such as access to e-mail, data, and software. Almost all user access to such things proceeds given an authorized password, but passwords are fallible. As people use the Internet more, they use their identity across more sites, usually without varying their password. The average American holds passwords to 30–40 websites, of which he or she logs in to about 10 websites per day. Most Americans use a single password for all sites. Sixty percent of all passwords are less than five characters long. More than 80% of passwords use whole words, such as real names. Phishers could gather enough information, such as the target's favorite pet or their spouse's name, in the public domain to guess such simple passwords. Even easier to gather would be information about the target's first school or mother's maiden name, which are typical answers to questions that serve as backdoor access in case the user forgets their password. Some surprising websites have been hacked in these ways. For instance, Stratfor sells information and analysis on current international and national security issues, mostly to paid subscribers who access the information online. In December 2011, Anonymous (a hacking group) stole information on thousands of subscribers, including their credit card numbers, from Stratfor's servers, claiming that access passwords were easy to guess. Stratfor apologized to clients and promised improved security, but in February 2012, Anonymous stole some of Stratfor's e-mails with its clients.

Threats may place spyware on the target's computer in order to record the target's keystrokes, which will include their typed identities and passwords. Some malware can be designed to search for stored passwords. Users should avoid using a more exposed terminal, such as a terminal lent by a stranger or in an Internet café, but if forced to use a strange terminal, such as when away from the home or office, they could avoid using the keyboard by pasting their identity word and password after copying it from a file held on a USB drive (although USB drives are exposed to malware on the terminal).

A few online services (typically online banking websites, specialized web-based e-mail applications, and online access to organizationally controlled e-mail or data) require the user to change their password periodically, disallow whole words or common terms (such as "password"), or specify inclusion of numbers or unusual characters in the password.

Additionally, more services are requiring more than one step of identity verification. For instance, a website could ask for a password followed by an answer to one of many demographic questions. Users may be required to carry a piece of hardware that displays a periodically randomized number that only the remote serve would recognize.

Some access controls include software that looks for abnormal behavior, such as attempted log-ins from foreign countries or at untypical times of the day, or will block access completely, pending further checks, if somebody attempts more than one once to access without the correct identification.

Ultimately, any system of using and storing a typed password is personally and mathematically fallible, so digital security managers are looking for more physical checks of identity, primarily hardware that can recognize biometric signatures, such as fingerprints, irises, and skin chemistry. Some computers and peripherals already include digital readers of fingerprints and other biometric data, and some border controls include machines that read biometric data.

Defense

Systems with more bandwidth, processing power, or on-demand access to a cloud are less vulnerable to denial of service attacks. Operating systems can be configured to disable services and applications not required for their missions. Network and application firewalls can be designed to block malicious packets, preferably as close to the source as possible, perhaps by blocking all traffic from known malicious sources. Prior intelligence about the threats, their domains, and their IP addresses can help to prevent attacks.

System managers should coordinate between Internet service providers, site hosting providers, and security vendors. Contingency planning between these stakeholders before an attack can help during management of the response. Some stakeholders treat an attack as an incident triggering a business continuity plan or human-caused disaster response plan.

Deterrence

Increasingly, officials are seeking to deter as well as defend, to punish as well as to prevent, although this is usually an option that must involve a judicial authority or a government. For instance, on May 31, 2011, U.S. officials first warned publicly and officially that harmful cyber attacks could be treated as acts of war, implying military retaliation. On September 18, 2012, U.S. Cyber Command hosted a public conference at which the State Department's legal adviser (Harold Koh) stated that the United States had adopted and shared through the UN ten principles, of which the most important implications included

- international law applies in cyber space;
- cyber attacks can amount to armed attacks triggering the right of self-defense; and
- cyber attacks that result in death, injury, or significant destruction, such as a nuclear plant meltdown, a dam opened above a populated area, or a disabled air-traffic control system resulting in plane crashes, would constitute a use of force in violation of international law.

SUMMARY

This chapter has

- defined information, ICTs, and cyber space;
- introduced official categories of attackers;
- shown an official method of assessing threats;
- described the typical categories of sources:
  - profit-oriented criminals;
  - insider threats;
  - external threats; and
  - nation-states.
- described the typical access vectors and their controls:
  - printed documents;
  - social interaction;
  - malware;
  - databases;
  - webpages;
  - social media;
  - postal communications;
  - telephone communications;
  - e-mail;
  - removable digital media and mobile devices;
  - cloud computing; and
  - wireless networks.
- defined the typical malicious activities, including:
  - misinformation;
  - censorship and controls on freedom of information;
  - cyber espionage;
  - cyber sabotage.
- shown how to provide information security in general;
- shown how to provide cyber security in general and by
  - controlling access;
  - defense; and
  - deterrence.

QUESTIONS AND EXERCISES

1. Give examples of information outside of cyber space.
2. What is the difference between ICT and cyber space?
3. What was Sandia National Laboratories' warning about conventional categorization of the sources of cyber attacks?

4. What differentiates the objectives of most criminals when they acquire private information?
5. Describe the known motivations and intentions of insider threats.
6. What is the relationship between insider and external threats?
7. How could a commercial relationship become an external threat?
8. Describe the opportunities for external threats during the lifecycle of an item of ICT.
9. How can APTs be especially countered?
10. What is an access vector?
11. What is an access control?
12. What is the official difference between a computer virus, worm, and Trojan Horse?
13. By what four main social interactions could a threat obtain private information about you?
14. Consider the case of British journalists and officials accessing or transferring private data improperly. Why did this continue largely unchecked for years, despite the Data Protection Act of 1998?
15. While visiting a webpage is usually harmless, describe the harmful vector.
16. How does social media enable
    a. violations of privacy?
    b. abuse?
17. Describe the similarities and differences in risks for juveniles and adults.
18. When are people likely to be most revealing through social media of private information?
19. Why is postal communication useful to a comprehensive information security plan?
20. When are officials more likely to intercept private telephone communications?
21. How can threats intercept telephone communications?
22. How can you reduce the insecurity of your personal telephone communications?
23. How can you reduce the insecurity of your personal e-mail?
24. What are the three main ways in which e-mail is a vector for unauthorized access to information?
25. Why are mobile devices vectors?
26. What are the security advantages and disadvantages of cloud computing?
27. Under what circumstances are wireless networks likely to be less secure?
28. How can social media both contribute to and counter misinformation?
29. What is a “digital wildfire”?
30. Why are states blamed for objectionable information?

31. Why is digital misinformation difficult to prosecute in court?
32. What is the international dispute about the governance of the Internet?
33. What is the difference between a logic bomb and denial of service?
34. Why have DOS attacks become easier?
35. How can DOS attacks be countered?
36. Why should an organization define its sensitive information?
37. Give an example of a nondigital activity that would help to provide cyber security.
38. How could a threat acquire your password?
39. How could a website encourage more secure passwords?
40. Give examples of two-step access controls.

Transport Security

This chapter considers the security of transport. The three main sections below consider ground transport, aviation security, and maritime transport security (including counter-maritime piracy).

 Ground Transport Security

This section reviews ground transport security, first by scoping ground transport, second by reviewing the threats and hazards, and third by reviewing measures to improve ground transport security.

Scope

Ground transportation is mostly road and railway transportation but includes pedestrian and animal carriers, which tend to be more important in developing countries.

Maritime and aerial forms of transportation tend to be more secure because they are less coincident with malicious actors (at least between ports or stations) and have more restrictive controls on access (at least at ports and stations), but are more expensive up-front (even though they are usually cheaper to operate in the long term). Short-range aviation (primarily helicopters and small fixed wing aircraft) offers accessibility and speed, but it is much more expensive to operate and is exposed to short-range ground-to-air weapons.

Road transportation is commonplace and will remain commonplace because of private favor for the accessibility and freedom of roads, even though road transport is expensive (at least operationally, over longer distances), suffers frequent accidents, and is widely coincident with malicious actors.

Railways are more efficient and safer than roads, but some authorities cannot afford the upfront investment, in which case they invest in roads and bus services, even though these are more operationally costly and harmful in the long term. Railway lines are often more important economically and socially at local levels and in larger, less developed countries, where the railway is the only way to travel long distances or through rough terrain (short of using slow animals or expensive off-road vehicles or aircraft).

In insecure or underdeveloped areas, road transportation is often the only means of transportation, after the collapse of the infrastructure required for aviation and railway alternatives. Consequently, road transportation becomes more important in unstable or postconflict areas, even though road transport remains very exposed to threats with simple weapons and skills.

Sometimes, road transportation is the only option for routine communications, such as in the mountainous areas of Afghanistan and Pakistan, where the poor weather, thin air, and insurgent threats discourage use of even helicopters. Indeed, some of these areas are so underdeveloped as to stop automobiles altogether, leaving pedestrians and equines (primarily donkeys) as the only reliable routine means of communications between bases and the most remote official and military outposts.

Threats and Hazards

The main categories of threats and hazards to ground transport are accidents and failures, thieves, robbers, hijackers, and terrorists and insurgents.

Accidents and Failures

Rail travel is less risky than road travel—compared to car journeys, trains travel longer distances, cheaper, with fewer accidents or breakdowns. For instance, from 2008 through 2010, the European Union (EU) suffered one fatality in more than 6,400 million kilometers (4,000 million miles) travelled per passenger by train, compared to one fatality in 225 million kilometers (140 million miles) travelled per passenger by car. Railway accidents are almost as rare as airline accidents but tend to be as spectacular and memorable, helping to explain popular inflation of railway risks over road risks. For instance, on July 24, 2013, a high-speed train derailed travelling too fast on a curve near Santiago de Compostela, in Galicia, Spain, killing more than 80 passengers; Spain had suffered a rate of just six fatalities per year on its railways in previous years. In the whole of 2011 (the last year for which data are available), across the EU's 27 countries and more than 500 million residents, 1,183 people died in incidents on the railways, of which 98% were pedestrians or car drivers, not railway passengers (data from the European Railway Agency).

North America does not have nearly as intensive a passenger rail network as the EU but permits more hazardous freight on its railways. U.S. railroads carry 1 million barrels of crude oil per day but spilled just 2,268 barrels of crude oil from 2002 to 2012, much less than were spilled by pipelines or watercraft. However, increased carriage of oil may be raising the risk. For instance, on July 7, 2013, a train with 72 cars of crude oil from North Dakota ran out of control and derailed in downtown Lac-Mégantic, Quebec, Canada, causing a fire that killed 13 people (data from the U.S. Pipeline and Hazardous Materials Administration).

In the developed world, most mechanical journeys are by car, so more people are harmed in or by cars than in or by trains, aircraft, or watercraft. For various behavioral and mechanical reasons, car travel is inherently more hazardous. Road traffic accidents (RTAs) kill and injure passengers and pedestrians, disrupt traffic, damage vehicles, and sometimes damage infrastructure. Accidents are associated with increased other risks, particular in unstable areas, such as theft from disabled vehicles and passengers, insurgent or terrorist attacks on first responders, and stress and illness.

Most accidents are collisions between a single vehicle and another object, with some damage or harm but without fatality, but accidents are frequent and the rate of fatalities in cars is very high as a whole, compared to other transport risks and even criminal risks (see Table 9.2). For instance, in 2010 (the safest year on American roads to date), road traffic killed nearly 32,885 Americans (16.3 per 100,000 inhabitants), an average of 90 persons per day, and injured 2,239,000 Americans (724 per 100,000 inhabitants), an average of 6,134 persons per day. Twice as many Americans die in road traffic accidents than are murdered. The risks increase with voluntary behaviors, such as reckless driving, telephone use, or intoxication. About 30% of Americans will be involved in an alcohol-related car accident at least once during their lifetime (data from the U.S. National Highway Traffic Safety Administration).

Car travel seems less risky when the measures capture our more frequent exposure to car travel: In 2010, the United States observed one fatality per 90.9 million miles travelled per passenger by car, 12.64 fatalities per 100,000 registered motor vehicles, and 15.65 fatalities per 100,000 licensed drivers. Nevertheless, even though people take more road journeys than air journeys, road traffic is more deadly than air travel, both absolutely and as a rate per miles travelled. Road travel kills more than 600 times more Americans than air travel kills.

In developing countries, accidents run at much higher rates. Road traffic accidents kill 0.020% of low- and 0.022% of middle-income country residents per year globally (2004), 0.016% of Americans per year (2010), and 0.006% of Britons per year (2010). While the risks have fallen in the developed world, the risks are growing in the developing world as development correlates with more car use but less rapid development of the controls on accidents. In these areas risk averseness, regulations, and law enforcement tend to be weak, so simple controls are not required or enforced, such as seat belts (which reduce the chance of death in a crash by 61%), collision-triggered air bags, energy absorbing structures, and speed restrictions. Globally, the DALYs (disability-adjusted life year) lost to road traffic injuries increased by 34% from 1990 to 2010. More than 90% of road traffic deaths occur in low- and middle-income countries. In fact, in the developing world RTAs kill more people than typhoid, malaria, and AIDS/HIV combined (WHO, 2009, p. 26).

The rate of RTAs tends to increase rapidly in more unstable or conflictual environments, where public capacity and risk sensitivity dissipates further. Some risky behavior may be justified to avoid other risks (such as by speeding through an area where insurgents operate). External threats can cause accidents indirectly (such as when an insurgent attack distracts a driver who then crashes the automobile).

Thieves, Robbers, and Hijackers

Parked vehicles, stores, refueling sites, and delivery sites are exposed to opportunistic thieves and vandals. If thieves focus on the infrastructure, they can steal construction materials and equipment if left unattended, the lamps and electrical cables used in lighting or signals, and in extreme cases, may steal metals (which are easily sold for scrap) from bridges, hatches and other coverings, and cables.

Vehicles may be stopped by malicious actors who want to hijack the vehicle for its own value or to kidnap a passenger for ransom. In unstable areas, roads are easily blocked or vehicles are intercepted while in transit, sometimes by corrupt public officers in search of bribes.

Terrorists and Insurgents

Official vehicles and their cargos or passengers are normally more secure in their bases, so terrorists and insurgents are incentivized to attack official targets on the roads. They can also attack unofficial targets in pursuit of further instability or directly to harm certain out-groups. Roads are pervasive (even if those roads are materially poor by the standards of the developed world) so the network as a whole is readily exposed to terrorists and insurgents.

In recent decades, terrorists and insurgents have attacked transportation in four main ways:

1. Interrupting traffic in general by comparatively easy attacks on the infrastructure, such as blowing holes in the road surface, digging into the side of the road or railway embankment in order to cause subsidence, destroying bridges, flooding low-lying routes, causing earth or rocks to slide on to a route, or blocking the route with debris.
2. Attacking critical logistical convoys, usually on the road at a remote distance from well-protected bases.
3. Attacking bases.
4. Killing private citizens, particularly important personnel, to discourage their movements or operations. For instance, on September 17, 2012, a suicide bomber rammed a car into a minivan carrying foreign aviation workers on their way to the airport in Kabul, Afghanistan, killing ten and discouraging current foreigners from travelling inside Afghanistan and discouraging potential foreign workers from ever agreeing to operate on the roads in Afghanistan.

Pedagogy Box 15.1 Major Terrorist Attacks on Railways and Trains Since 1991

On June 15, 1991, militants attacked two trains near Ludhiana, India, with firearms, killing nearly 80 people.

On July 25, 1995, a device exploded in a commuter railway station in Paris, killing eight and injuring 80. On August 26, a device was defused on the tracks of a high-speed railway line near Lyon. On October 6, a device exploded inside a Paris underground railway station, wounding 13. On October 17, a device exploded on a commuter train in Paris, wounding 29.

On July 24, 1996, four bombs planted by the Liberation Tamil Tigers on a commuter train in Dehiwala station, Colombo, Sri Lanka, killed 64 and injured more than 400 people.

On September 10, 2002, a train from Howrah to Delhi, India, was derailed on the bridge over the Dhave River in Bihar, probably by a local Maoist group, killing more than 130. On March 13, 2003, a bomb exploded on a train as it pulled into Mulund railway station, India, killing 10 people and injuring 70.

In 2003, Lyman Farris, a naturalized U.S. citizen from Pakistan, was apprehended in New York after plotting, with al-Qaida sponsorship, to bring down the Brooklyn Bridge and derail a train. In 2004, Shahawar Matin Siraj, a Pakistani immigrant, and James Elshafay, an American with Egyptian and Irish immigrant parents, were arrested after an informer encouraged and recorded their plot to bomb a subway train station in Manhattan.

On March 11, 2004, within 3 minutes, most of a dozen improvised explosive devices detonated across four commuter trains, inside or just outside a single commuter train station in Madrid, Spain, killing 191 people and injuring more than 2,000. At least four Spanish Jihadis were involved—more than 3 weeks later, these four men blew themselves up, and killed a policeman, during a police raid on their residence. They were at least inspired by al-Qaida; they may have been assisted by other Jihadis who escaped.

On July 7, 2005, suicide bombers detonated themselves on each of three underground trains in London, within seconds of each other, killing 39 people and the three bombers. Almost 1 hour later, a fourth bomber detonated on a bus, probably after an electrical failure prevented his device from exploding on a train along with the others. He killed himself and 13 others. Two weeks later, two Somalis, one Ethiopian, and one Eritrean-borne British citizen attempted to copy the 7/7 attacks but their devices failed to explode. Like the bombers in Madrid, the British bombers were all first- or second-generation immigrants, Muslims (one was a convert), some with probable terrorist training abroad. The Spanish bombers used dynamite procured illegitimately from miners, while the British bombers used liquid explosives produced from hydrogen peroxide.

On July 28, 2005, an explosion on an express train, leaving Jaunpur, Uttar Pradesh, India, for Delhi, killed 13 and injured more than 50.

On July 11, 2006, seven bombs within 11 minutes across seven trains in Mumbai, India, planted by Lashkar-e-Taiba (an Islamist terrorist group based in Pakistan), killed 209 and injured more than 700 people.

On November 20, 2006, an explosion on a train between New Jalpaiguri and Haldibari in West Bengal, India, killed five.

On February 18, 2007, bombs detonated on the Samjhauta Express Train, soon after leaving Delhi in India for Lahore in Pakistan, killing 68 and injuring more than 50 people. The main perpetrator was probably Lashkar-e-Taiba.

In 2006, Lebanese authorities arrested Assem Hammoud on evidence gathered in cooperation with the Federal Bureau of Investigation (FBI) that he was plotting with Pakistani terrorists for suicide attacks on trains between New Jersey and New York.

In 2009, Najibullah Zazi, a childhood immigrant to the United States from Afghanistan, and two high-school friends (one another immigrant from Afghanistan, the other from Bosnia) were arrested close to implementing a long-planned al-Qaida-sponsored plot to blow themselves up on subway trains in New York.

On November 27, 2009, a high speed train was derailed by a bomb near the town of Bologoye on its way between Moscow and Saint Petersburg causing 27 deaths and about 100 injuries.

On April 22, 2013, Canadian authorities arrested a Tunisian immigrant and an ethnic Palestinian immigrant for an alleged plot, sponsored by al-Qaida, to derail a train between Toronto and New York.

Providing Ground Transport Security

Ground transport security can be improved by improving the security of the transportation infrastructure, navigation, communications, the vehicle's survivability, mobility, and escorts and guards.

Ground Transport Infrastructure Security

Ground transport infrastructure includes the roads, railways, service and support sites and systems, and the fuels and electrical power demanded. Infrastructure security includes protecting infrastructure from malicious attack, preventing accidents and injuries on the system, and preventing failures of infrastructure.

Any transport system needs a secure base, so haulers or passenger services need to secure the sites (see the chapter on site security) at which vehicles are stored, maintained, fueled, and loaded. The system benefits from some redundancy so that one insecure node, such as a fueling station, does not incapacitate the whole system. The routes need to be regularly maintained and patrolled. Local civilians should be encouraged to report malicious actors and activities. Clearing debris and vegetation from the sides of routes would help to remove the potential hiding places for thieves and attackers. Where official capacity declines, users might contract with their own maintainers and guards.

Railway systems are more critically exposed in the sense that a malicious actor could easily damage a line, thereby interrupting communications between two points, short of alternative lines between the same two points. As long as the threats can counter the repairers and whatever forces are sent to protect them, small damage would disable a system. This is not just an issue for developing countries with low capacity for repairing and defending railway systems. For instance, in the 2000s, British railway operators and transport police were forced to invest heavily in patrols, fencing, and security cameras after a surge in sabotage and theft of railway infrastructure, usually sabotage by pranksters and errant juveniles who rolled boulders onto tracks or threw stones at driver's cabs or passenger compartments, but also organized criminals who lifted trailer-loads of copper cables (used in electrical systems), timber sleepers, or steel tracks from open storage.

Pedagogy Box 15.2 U.S. Road Transport Security

In the 2000s, road traffic accidents were declining in frequency but terrorism was salient, so new government capacity focused on reducing malicious threats, such as weaponization of materials carried on the roads. These initiatives are primarily administered by the Department of Homeland Security or DHS. The Transportation Security Administration (TSA) was established in November 2001 under the Department of Transportation but moved to DHS in March 2003.

In 2011, DHS counted in America 3.9 million miles of public roads, 208 million automobiles, 15.5 million trucks (of which 42,000 are rated for carriage of hazardous materials) across 1.2 million trucking companies, and 10 million drivers licensed for commercial vehicles (including 2.7 million licenses for hazardous materials carriage). The Department of Transportation administers the Research and Special Programs Administration: this includes the Office of Hazardous Materials Safety, which issues guidance and regulations for the security of hazardous materials during carriage. In 2005, the Office of Screening Coordination and Operations (later the Screening Coordination Office), also within DHS, started checking the backgrounds of commercial drivers before granting a hazardous materials endorsement for their commercial driving licenses. In 2006, this requirement was extended to drivers crossing from Mexico and Canada. Meanwhile, the TSA started the Trucking Security Program, which included 5-year projects

- for developing plans to manage highway emergencies,
- to recruit and train drivers and officials for managing hazardous materials and emergencies, and
- to establish a Highway Information Sharing and Analysis Center.

The program allocated grants to truckers worth $4.8 million for the first 2 fiscal years (2005–2006), $11.6 million in 2007, $25.5 million in 2008, and $7 million in 2009, before termination in 2010.

Meanwhile, critics of the government's focus noted that road traffic accidents make up a much greater risk than terrorism and their long decline was stabilizing. Critics also noted that the infrastructure was aging (the greatest surge in road building was in the 1960s) with little funding for replacement. Infrastructure failures are very rare, although the risk seems to be increasing. For instance, in 2008, a bridge carrying the Interstate 35W highway across the Mississippi River in Minneapolis, Minnesota, collapsed, killing 13 and injuring around 100.

Pedagogy Box 15.3 U.S. Railway Security Since 9/11

In March 2003, the DHS announced Operation Liberty Shield to improve railway security. It asked

- state governors to allocate additional personnel from police or national guard forces at selected rail bridges,
- railroad operators to increase security at major facilities and hubs,
- AMTRAK to align its security measures with private operators.

The Department of Transportation asked private operators to increase surveillance of trains carrying hazardous materials.

The Rail Security Act (April 2004) authorized an increase in funding for the Rail Security Grant Program from $65 million to $1.1 billion and ordered DHS to assess the vulnerability of the national rail system. Together, the DHS and the Association of American Railroads identified more than 1,300 critical assets. The results were used to inform the distribution of grants and to develop 50 changes to operating procedures, such as physical access, cyber security, employee screening, and cargo tracking. A full-time Surface Transportation Information Sharing and Analysis Center (ST-ISAC) was created at the Association with clearance for top-secret intelligence. A rail police officer joined the FBI's National Joint Terrorism Task Force.

The TSA provided Explosives Detection Dog teams to the top ten passenger rail agencies under the Transit and Rail Inspection Pilot (TRIP) program. Phase I (at New Carrollton, Maryland) evaluated technologies for screening passengers and baggage before boarding the train. Phase II (Union Station, Washington, DC) evaluated the screening of checked baggage and cargo prior to loading. Phase III (aboard a Shore Line East commuter car in Connecticut) evaluated technologies to screen passengers and baggage during transit. In fiscal year 2011, the DHS launched the Freight Rail Security Program ($10 million appropriated), which invited railroad carriers of toxic inhalation hazards (TIH) to apply for funds to acquire trackers in their cars and invited owners of railroad bridges to apply for funds to install access controls and monitoring systems at such bridges.

By 2011, DHS counted 120,000 miles of mainline railways and estimated 15 million passengers on railways per day.

Navigation

Good navigation saves time in transit and thus reduces exposure to the risks in the system and reduces wear to the system. Navigation is also important to avoiding and escaping particular threats. Users of the transport system should be advised how to avoid natural hazards. In unstable or high crime areas, drivers and passengers should be trained to evade malicious roadblocks, hijackers, and other threats. The best routes of escape and the places to gather in an emergency should be researched and agreed in advance of travel.

Personnel should have access to suitable maps marked with the agreed bases, other safe areas (such as friendly embassies), escape routes, and rendezvous locations. Compasses are useful acquisitions for each person and automobile. Where the budget allows, each vehicle could be acquired with an electronic navigation system (a Global Position System triangulates locations with data sent from earth-orbiting satellites; an inertial guidance system, using motion and rotation sensors, plots movements based on the vehicle's attitude and speed), although in case this system fails the personnel should be trained to read a paper map too.

Communications

Vehicles should be equipped with radio or telephone communications so that passengers can communicate with emergency services or a base in case of any emergency while in transit. Vehicles can be equipped with tracking technology in case a vehicle is hijacked or the passengers otherwise lose communications (trackers are simple and cheap enough to be widely used to track vehicles in commercial operations). Some trackers can be configured to communicate with base if they sense that the vehicle has been involved in an accident or the driver has been away from the vehicle outside of the programmed schedule. Passengers too can be equipped with trackers—usually in their clothing or mobile phones.

Vehicle Survivability

Typically, vehicle manufacturers and users must fulfill some obligations for the safety of vehicles in terms of their reliability and the passenger's survivability during an accident. The vehicle's survivability under malicious attack is a dramatically more challenging requirement. The subsections below explain why the requirement has increased, how to improve resistance to kinetic attacks, how to improve blast resistance, how to control access to vehicles, the balance between overt survivability and stealth, and the personal aid equipment that should be carried.

Requirement

The demand for more survivable vehicles has risen dramatically in response to increased terrorism and insurgency. For instance, prior to the terrorist bombings of U.S. Embassies in Kenya and Tanzania in 1998, the U.S. diplomatic service provided around 50 armored vehicles for chiefs of mission at critical and high-threat posts. Thereafter, the service prescribed at least one armored car for every post. By 2009, the service had acquired more than 3,600 armored vehicles worldwide, including 246 vehicles for chiefs of mission (U.S. Government Accountability Office [GAO], 2009, pp. 13, 24). Meanwhile, as insurgencies in Afghanistan and Iraq grew in quantity and quality, operators there realized requirements for more survivable vehicles of all types, from the smallest liaison vehicles to large "force protection" vehicles and logistical vehicles. The period of most rapid acquisition of armored vehicles was in 2007.

The North Atlantic Treaty Organization (NATO) long ago agreed on standards of protection for military vehicles that are widely used to define the survivability of all vehicles (see Table 15.1). The standard (STANAG 4569) specifies five protection levels, where most available vehicles do not meet Level 1, most of the military armored vehicles (including wheeled and tracked armored personnel carriers) that were acquired through the Cold War do not surpass Level 1, most armored vehicles fall within Level 2, a few of the larger wheeled vehicles (normally six- or eight-wheeled) fall within Level 3, including the mine-resistant ambush protected vehicles that were widely acquired in the 2000s, light tanks and infantry fighting vehicles lie within Level 4, and only main battle tanks surpass Level 5.

No armor is proof against all threats and uncomfortable trade-offs must be made between protection, mobility, and expense.

Resistance to Kinetic Attack

Automobiles are not proof against portable firearms, despite popular culture's depiction of bullets bouncing off a car's panels and windows. Automobiles can be armored reliably against firearms, but at great cost, financially and in weight. The extra load implies that the automobile's motor and running gear should be upgraded too; survivability includes capacity to escape and evade, so the vehicle is often upgraded for more rugged off-road travel and for crashing through barriers (hence the term *ruggedized*). The limousines acquired to carry the U.S. President are supposed to cost more than $1.5 million and weigh 8 tons each.

Table 15.1 NATO's Standard Vehicle Protection Levels

	Projectile defeated						
STANAG 4569 level	**Caliber (mm)**	**Projectile**	**Range (m)**	**Muzzle velocity (m/s)**	**Blast defeated**	**Artillery shell fragments defeated**	**Estimated minimum armor steel thickness (mm)**
1	7.62	Lead core	30	833	Fragmentation grenade, landmine, or submunition	–	10
2	7.62	Steel core	30	695	Blast mine of 6 kilograms under running gear (2a) or center (2b)	–	15
3	7.62	Tungsten carbide core	30	930	Blast mine of 8 kilograms under running gear (3a) or center (3b)	–	30
4	14.5	Tungsten carbide core	200	911	Blast mine of 10 kilograms under running gear (4a) or center (4b)	155 mm caliber high-explosive shell at 30 meters	40
5	25	Discarding sabot	500	1,258	As above	As above except at 25 meters	60

The armor materials traditionally include hardened ("armor") steel plates. Hardness is best for defeating projectiles, so is best on vertical surfaces. However, tougher steel is preferred for surviving blast without cracking, so is best as floors. Hardness and toughness are normally antagonistic properties: The correct physical balance is achieved by chemically and physically producing materials that are both unusually hard and tough or by layering hard and tough materials. Other hard materials include certain species of aluminum, ceramics, and titanium that deliver superior protection for the same weight of steel. Hard materials can be layered on top of other materials so that the outer materials defeat hard projectiles while inner materials resist blast. Windows and other apertures should be minimized and filled with impact-resistant laminates of glass and plastics and provided with shutters made from a harder material.

Armor can be improvised from scrap materials, but these tend to be mild steels that give a false sense of security (they are easily punctured or broken). Armor can be improvised from sand bags: The sand should be as fine as possible, since larger pieces are more likely to become projectiles. Keeping the sand wet increases its capacity to absorb energy and also dampens the chemical explosive. Rubber mats and belts help to contain flying dirt while retaining the flexibility to survive blast without tearing. However, all these materials add weight. Ideally, sandbags should be more than one layer deep, but most vehicles lack internal capacity and load-bearing capacity for more than one layer. If the sandbags cannot be placed around all sides, they should be prioritized around crew positions and wheel wells (ground explosives are most likely to be detonated by wheels).

Liquids can be used to protect; water is physically resistant to projectiles and also dampens explosives and fuels before they can fully combust. Water inside pneumatic tires helps to dampen explosives detonated under the wheel. Less volatile fuels can be used as protection. Diesel fuel is not naturally flammable except under high pressure or temperature or when agitated; most military vehicles are diesel fueled, and some incorporate their fuel tanks into their protection against projectiles. At the same time, fuel tanks should be armored against hot fragments and separated from crew compartments.

Bar or slat armor is a particular physical defense against rocket-propelled grenades, which are normally detonated by an electrical signal running from the point of the projectile to the explosive at the base. A rocket that impacts between bars or slats, if arranged with the proper separation, will be crushed, damaging its electrical circuit before it can detonate. Bar/slat armor is attached to the outside of a vehicle's vertical surfaces, resembling an outer cage.

Blast Resistance

Vehicles can be designed and constructed to be dramatically more survivable against blast, which is typically produced by chemical explosives hidden on or in the ground. This blast resistance was the main capability offered by a class of vehicles known as "mine resistant ambush protected" vehicles or MRAPs in the U.S. military, "Heavy Protected Patrol Vehicle" in the British military, which was urgently required in Afghanistan and Iraq from the mid-2000s. From 2005 to 2009 alone, the U.S. military urgently ordered more than 16,000 MRAPs. The U.S. Army's National Ground Intelligence Center's Anti-Armor Incident Database suggests that a MRAP vehicle reduced interior deaths, compared to an armored Humvee, by between 9 times (Afghanistan) and 14 times (Iraq) (based on data for the average number of troops killed per explosive attack on each vehicle, 2005 to 2011).

However, MRAPs are more than four times more expensive than replaced vehicles, about twice as heavy, larger, slower, less mobile, and more burdensome to sustain. Their size meant that often they could not fit in confined urban areas or on narrow roads, while their weight often caused roads or bridges to collapse. Their height contributed to higher rates of roll-overs (such as when roads collapsed and a vehicle tumbled into a ravine). Often they were confined to good roads (where insurgents could more easily target them). In 2009, the U.S. military required, especially for Afghanistan, another 6,600 vehicles of a smaller more mobile class of blast resistant vehicle, designated MRAP all-terrain vehicles (M-ATVs). Also in 2009, the British required a similar class that they called Light Protected Patrol Vehicle. By mid-2012, around 27,000 MRAPs and M-ATVs had been produced to urgent orders, of which 23,000 had been deployed to Afghanistan and Iraq.

In practice, most operators and situations require all classes of vehicle: MRAPs should patrol and escort on the good roads and in the spacious urban areas, but M-ATVs are required for poorer terrain. However, MRAPs and M-ATVs each remain imperfect trade-offs; M-ATVs proved insufficiently survivable for some roles, so more than 6,000 of them were upgraded to be more resistant to blast from beneath.

Areas facing blast should be made from tougher materials and can be filled with energy-absorbing materials or constructed to collapse gracefully (although these materials tend to reduce interior space). Higher ground clearances increase the distance between ground-based blast and the vehicle's interior, although tall vehicles tend to roll easier and to be more difficult to hide. The bottom armor of the vehicle should be v-shaped so as to deflect blast to the sides and should contain the automotive parts so that they do not separate as secondary missiles. Monocoque hulls (where the same structure bears all loads and attachments) eliminate some of the potential secondary missiles associated with a conventional chassis. Wheel units should be sacrificial, meaning that they separate easily under blast without disintegrating further, taking energy away from the vehicle interior without producing further secondary missiles. The interior passenger compartments should be protected as interior compartments separate from the automotive and engine compartments. Interior passengers should be seated on energy-absorbing or collapsible materials, or suspended from the roof, to reduce the energy transmitted from below into the passenger's body. Foot rests and foot pedals also should be energy absorbing (otherwise they would transmit energy that could shatter the legs) without separating as secondary missiles.

Access Controls

Vehicles need apertures for human ingress, egress, and visibility, but apertures increase the interior's exposure to sudden ingress of projectiles, human attackers, and thieves. Vehicles should be secured from unauthorized access by specifying locks on all doors and hatches, and windows constructed from a puncture-resistant material. Door and hatch hinges should be designed and constructed to be resistant to tools. In hot environments or prolonged duties, crews will tend to leave doors and hatches open for ventilation, where they can be surprised, so an air-conditioning system should be specified. Rules on closing and locking hatches and leaving at least one guard with a vehicle should be specified and enforced.

When civilian vehicles are converted to armored versions, some minor upgrades may be forgotten. For instance, on February 15, 2011, two U.S. Immigrations and Customs Enforcement agents were shot (one was killed) inside an armored civilian vehicle in north-eastern Mexico after the driver was forced off the road by armed threats (probably robbers targeting an expensive vehicle)—unfortunately, the vehicle was configured to automatically unlock the doors when the driver put the transmission in "park" (a typical safety feature in ordinary cars), but this allowed the threats to open a door; during the struggle to close and relock the door, the window also was lowered, through which the threats fired some bullets. Once the door and window were secured, the vehicle survived all further bullets (around 90), but the harm to the two agents was already done.

Operators face a choice between complying with external requests to stop and ignoring such requests in case they have malicious intent disguised as official duties or requests for assistance. For instance, on August 24, 2012, in Mexico City, two U.S. agents (probably from the U.S. intelligence community) were wounded by some of around 30 bullets fired by Mexican federal police during a chase after the Americans refused a checkpoint, probably influenced by the event in 2011. They were driving in a ruggedized, armored vehicle, but its rear wheel and some of its apertures did not survive the bullets. A Mexican passenger was unharmed.

Stealth

Operators face a choice between armored, ruggedized vehicles and vehicles that do not attract as much attention. Some operators have very contrasting preferences in the trade-off between visible deterrence or defense and stealth, with some operators insisting on travelling everywhere alone in randomly hailed taxis, while others insist on travelling nowhere without visibly armed escorts and armored vehicles. Some operators like to hire local vehicles that resemble the average local vehicle and to remove any branding from their vehicles, while others prefer to procure more robust and armored vehicles, even though they stand out from most other vehicles. Commercial interests, home funder requirements, and local laws may force operators to display their branding and ride in specialized vehicles, whatever the cost in stealth.

Personal Aid Equipment

The automobile should be equipped as appropriate to the particular threats, but a minimal set of equipment would include first aid kits—perhaps including blood ready for transfusion, defibrillator, and oxygen, firefighting equipment, drinking water, food, fuel, and pedestrian navigation equipment.

Mobility

Survivable vehicles are normally acquired with run-flat tires, which are pneumatic tires with solid or rigid cores, which will continue to run for dozens of miles after a puncture. The pneumatic tire may be reinforced with a tear- and puncture-resistant material. Given a sudden change in threat level, pneumatic tires can be replaced with solid rubber tires, which cannot be punctured (although they can be chipped), or filled partly with water, which helps to dampen chemical blast, although their extra weight and reduced flexibility transfer more vibration and wear to the vehicle.

Armoring the vehicle and adding equipment implies an added load, which implies a need for upgraded running gear and to permit running over rougher grounds and inferior roads in case the vehicle needs to escape threats on superior roads. The U.S. President's limousines offer excellent armor protection around a voluminous passenger compartment, but they do not offer good off-road capabilities. On March 23, 2011, the President's spare limousine for his official visit to Ireland grounded on a small hump in the gateway leaving the U.S. Embassy in Dublin and was temporarily abandoned in front of crowds of spectators and journalists. Most civilian armored vehicles are based on chassis designed for off-road use, while military armored vehicles are based on more specialized platforms.

Still, procurers must trade expense and mobility against survivability, so survivable vehicles tend to be very expensive with short life cycles. For instance, as of October 2009, 914 (32%) of U.S. diplomatic armored vehicles were in Iraq, at a procurement cost of about $173,000 with a life cycle of just about 3 years due to Iraq's difficult terrain (U.S. GAO, 2009).

Increased survivability implies increased risks associated with accidents and reduced mobility. Increased armor and equipment on and in the vehicle implies reduced internal space, which implies more heat stress, biomechanical stress, and acceleration injuries. Reduced mobility implies that the vehicle is restricted to the best terrain, helping threats to target the vehicle. Increased protection also implies more separation between the passengers and locals on the ground, thereby alienating locals and interrupting opportunities for local engagement and intelligence.

Escorts and Guards

Guards can ride in vehicles, but guards can be provocative to external threats and are hazards that may be activated, perhaps by external bribes or ideologies, as insider threats.

Road convoys can be escorted by police or military vehicles or by privately contracted armed and armored vehicles that should deter attackers, but these escorts can also draw attention to convoys that would otherwise blend in to routine traffic. Operators from different companies or authorities can cooperate by choosing to travel at the same time with shared escorts. They could also choose to follow a better protected convoy, although if they failed to notify the other convoy in advance its escorts might interpret followers as threats.

Escorts may be subject to ethical standards, regulations, or laws issued by the home organization or local authorities, but in unstable areas escorts may be reckless and uncontained. In Afghanistan, Iraq, and Libya police and military forces have a reputation for a mix of absenteeism and reckless violence. Private security contractors were not subject to local or coalition military laws or to professional or industry standards of behavior, so they developed a reputation for varied performance, such as reckless driving in order to reduce exposure to attackers on the roads and shooting to death other drivers who approached too quickly (as a suicide bomber would approach). Contractors were supposed to reduce the overall costs and inflexibility of military security, but when the security situation deteriorated some refused to work unless accompanied by military escorts.

Aviation Security

This section concerns civilian aviation security. The sections below explain the scope of civilian aviation, aviation accidents, sovereign threats, aviation terrorism, and the provision of aviation security.

Pedagogy Box 15.4 International Laws on Aviation Security

- Convention on Offenses and Certain Other Acts Committed on Board Aircraft, signed in Tokyo on September 14, 1963.
- Convention for the Suppression of Unlawful Seizure of Aircraft, signed at The Hague on December 16, 1970.
- Convention for the Suppression of Unlawful Acts against the Safety of Civil Aviation, signed at Montreal on September 23, 1971.
- International Convention against the Taking of Hostages, adopted by the General Assembly of the United Nations on December 17, 1979.
- Protocol for the Suppression of Unlawful Acts of Violence at Airports Serving International Civil Aviation, supplementary to the 1971 Convention, signed at Montreal on February 24, 1988.

Scope

Civilian aviation covers commercial transportation of cargo by air, commercial carriage of passengers by air, privately owned and operated aircraft, and all associated infrastructure, such as airfields and service and support facilities.

Pedagogy Box 15.5 U.S. Civilian Aviation

About 28,000 flights take off from the United States per day, accounting for half of global commercial air traffic. In a year, commercial flights carried about 600 million people and 10 million tons of air freight within the United States or between the United States and another country.

In 2011, DHS counted as aviation infrastructure: 19,576 general airports (including heliports), 211,450 general aviation aircraft, 599 airports certified to serve commercial flights–including 459 federalized commercial airports (Guam is most remote to the continental United States).

At the 459 federalized airports, 43,000 Transportation Security Officers and 450 Explosives Detection Dogs from the U.S. TSA work at more than 700 security checkpoints and 7,000 baggage screening points.

In 2006 (the last year for which numbers are available), the TSA screened 708,400,522 passengers on domestic flights and international flights coming into the United States. This averages out to over 1.9 million passengers per day (data source: TSA).

Accidents

Air accidents make up a specialized subject across engineering, industrial psychology, and policy science, for which this book has insufficient space, but the risks of air accidents should be acknowledged here as low. Compare the section above on road traffic accidents: Air safety is rigorously regulated and inspected, whereas individual car owners and drivers effectively regulate their own safety, outside of infrequent and comparatively superficial independent inspections. Consequently, an average aircraft flight is much less likely to cause fatality than an average car journey. According to data from the U.S. Centers for Disease Control, fatalities compute at about 0.00001 per flight. Yet the fatalities of air travel seem large because an aircraft typically carries more passengers than a car carries, so a catastrophic failure in an aircraft tends to kill more people per failure.

Sovereign Threats to Civilian Aviation

Air travel is covered by many international laws, some of which guarantee rights of travel that conflict with national sovereignty, but ultimately a sovereign and materially capable state could close its airspace to anyone. This is advantageous as an option against airborne terrorism or foreign attacks, but it also allows for illegitimate interruptions to international flows of travelers and cargo, perhaps because of accidental military responses, deliberate state terrorism, or deliberate political linkage of issues.

Pedagogy 15.6 Major Incidents of Sovereign Interference With Civilian Aviation

On September 1, 1983, a Soviet fighter shot down Korean Air Lines Flight 007 en route from New York City to Seoul via Anchorage after it had strayed into Soviet airspace over the Sea of Japan, west of Sakhalin Island. All 269 passengers and crew aboard were killed.

On July 3, 1988, the United States Navy guided missile cruiser USS *Vincennes* (CG-49) shot down Iran Air Flight 655 while flying in Iranian airspace over Iran's territorial waters on its usual flight path from Bandar Abbas, Iran, to Dubai, United Arab Emirates. All 290 onboard including 66 children and 16 crew perished. The ship's crew had mistaken the flight for an attack plane.

On October 10, 2012, about 19 months into the Syrian civil war, Turkish military aircraft intercepted a Syrian airliner from Moscow to Damascus with 30 passengers on board, as it entered Turkish airspace, on suspicions that it was carrying weapons. Turkey claimed to find Russian military communications and missile parts. Hours earlier, Turkey had ordered all Turkish civilian aircraft to cease flights through Syrian airspace, apparently to prevent Syrian retaliation. Russia protested on behalf of Russian passengers. On October 14, Syria and Turkey closed airspaces to each other.

On July 2, 2013, Italy, France, and Portugal prevented the passage from Russia to Bolivia of Bolivian President Evo Morales' official plane, suspecting that an American fugitive, Edward Snowden, formerly a contractor working for the U.S. National Security Agency, was on board. It was grounded in Vienna, where Austrian authorities boarded the plane without discovering Snowden. Bolivian Vice President Alvaro Garcia Linera said the plane was "kidnapped by imperialism."

Aviation Terrorism

Passengers use ground transport more frequently, and most cargo is carried in ships, so rationally terrorism would be more cost-effective if it targeted ground or maritime transport, yet terrorists like to target passenger airliners. Attacks on passenger airliners offer catastrophic direct effects, great human harm (one airliner could carry 850 passengers), and major indirect economic effects. Additionally, airliners are mostly Western-produced, -owned, -operated, and -used. Airliners are symbols of globalization and material development, which some terrorists, particularly Jihadi terrorists, oppose.

Pedagogy Box 15.7 Major Terrorist Attacks on Aviation

- On December 21, 1988, a small explosive device, hidden in luggage, exploded on Pan Am flight 103 over Lockerbie, Scotland, on its way from Frankfurt via London to New York, killing all 259 aboard and 11 on the ground. The bomb had been loaded onto the plane probably in Frankfurt, from a connecting flight from Malta. Investigators accused two employees of Libyan Arab Airlines, whom Libya surrendered for trial in 1999; only Abdel Basset Ali al-Megrahi was convicted by a

(Continued)

(Continued)

Scottish court in 2001 (but he was freed in 2009 on compassionate grounds relating to cancer, although he did not die until May 2012); Libya reached a civil-international legal settlement in 2002 but always claimed that its officials had been acting without government orders.

- On March 9, 1994, the Irish Republican Army launched four improvised mortar shells from the back of a car parked at a hotel near the perimeter of London Heathrow airport. Some impacted on the apron between two runways. On March 12, a similar attack was launched from woods on the perimeter. On March 13, another was launched from scrub land. None of the twelve projectiles exploded, but each was filled with high explosive. After each attack, the runways were closed during the searches for the projectiles and the launch areas.
- In 1994, Ramszi Yousef and Khalid Shaikh Mohammed, both primary members of al-Qaida, then in the Philippines, planned to bomb 12 U.S. airliners in a single 48-hour period as they flew from the Far East to the United States. They also planned to fly a hijacked plane into the headquarters of the Central Intelligence Agency. (They called the collective plans the Bojinka plot.) On January 6, 1995, an explosive fire in a private apartment led to police arrests of the bomb makers.
- On September 11, 2001 (9/11), terrorist attacks caused the destruction of four airliners, the collapse of both towers of the World Trade Center in New York, and the destruction of part of the Pentagon building in Washington, District of Columbia. These events are normally considered one attack; it caused the greatest loss of life to any terrorist attack ever—just under 3,000 people. 9/11 remains the costliest terrorist attack in history: The direct material cost was about $22 billion, including insured damage to property ($10 billion), insured interruption to business ($11 billion), and insured event cancellation ($1 billion). The human deaths of 9/11 (nearly 3,000) and disabilities were unprecedented; they amounted to less than $5 billion in insured lives and workers' compensation. The human effects of 9/11 amounted to less than $10 billion in lost earnings. All in all, the insured losses from 9/11 amounted to $40 billion—about twice as much as the last costliest event for insurers (Hurricane Andrew) but much smaller than the next (Hurricane Katrina in 2005—more than $40 billion in insured losses and $100 billion in total losses and more than 1,800 dead). On top of insured losses, the federal government spent $8.8 billion in aid in response to 9/11 (it would spend $29 billion in aid in response to Katrina).
- On December 22, 2001, Richard Reid, a British-Jamaican convert to Islam, attempted to detonate a bomb hidden in his shoe on an airliner from Paris to Miami. Sajid Badat, another British-born citizen, had withdrawn from a similar attack, but was convicted on terrorism charges.
- On November 28, 2002, al-Qaida terrorists fired two SA7 surface-to-air missiles at an Israeli charter flight leaving Mombasa, Kenya, but the missiles failed to engage at such short range (also, they may have been confused by unadmitted antimissile systems on the aircraft). The same day, a suicide vehicle bomb killed 13 others at a hotel in Mombasa.
- On August 9, 2006, British police arrested 29 people in connection with a plot to bomb airlines bound for North America with explosives improvised from commercially available liquids. Eleven

of those arrested were convicted later, of which only eight were convicted in connection with the plot, and not on the most serious charges.

- In 2007, four men (three from Guyana, of which one was naturalized in the United States, and one from Trinidad and Tobago, all converts to Islam) were arrested after telling an informer that they planned to blow up fuel tanks at John F. Kennedy Airport, New York.
- In 2009, four men (three U.S. citizens, one Haitian immigrant, all converts to Islam) were arrested in New York after implementing a plot to bomb a synagogue and shoot down aircraft, all with fake weapons provided by FBI informers.
- On Christmas Day, 2009, a Nigerian man (Umar Farouk Abdulmutallab) attempted to detonate explosives hidden in his underwear while aboard a commercial flight. He had been prepared by al-Qaida in the Arabian Peninsula.
- In April 2012, U.S. and foreign intelligence learned that al-Qaeda in the Arabian Peninsula was developing an improved device. On May 7, 2012, the United States revealed that within the previous days it had taken control of the device after it had left Yemen for some other Middle Eastern country (probably Saudi Arabia).
- On June 10, 2013, seven Taliban fighters attacked the military side of Kabul International Airport, Afghanistan. Two fighters detonated suicide explosive vests, while the other five opened fire with small arms and rocket-propelled grenades from an overlooking building. All were killed. Two Afghan civilians were wounded.

Providing Aviation Security

The provision of aviation security includes the international and national legal regimes for protecting aviation, which are very mature and well enforced now, and the technical standards and regulations for ensuring the aircraft against technical or accidental failure.

Otherwise, as described in subsections below, aviation security is focused on screening the cargo, screening passenger luggage, controlling human access, preventing metallic weapons, screening footwear, liquids, clothing, and the human body for weapons, securing the aircraft during the flight against human threats aboard the aircraft, and countering antiaircraft weapons.

Cargo

The security of air cargo is addressed below via its scope, the threats, and the controls.

Scope

Global air freight is worth about $100 billion per year. Due to increased security after 9/11, air freight costs rose about 15% from 9/11 to January 2002 (according to the World Bank).

Security measures have always focused more on passenger than freight aircraft because terrorists have attacked more passenger than cargo planes, even though rationally they could more efficiently damage the economy by shutting down air freight. (See above for reasons why terrorists prefer to attack passenger aviation.)

The security of air cargo is an issue for passenger aviation too, since most passenger aircraft carry also cargo—usually smaller, faster mail, while bulk items travel in dedicated cargo planes. In the United States, about 80% of air cargo is carried by cargo-only domestic flights, 20% by passenger flights. About 3.5 million metric tons per year travels as cargo on U.S. domestic and international passenger flights.

Threats

The most frequent illegal activities relating to air cargo relate to smuggling and trafficking, including banned drugs, exotic and protected animals and plants, banned animal products, firearms, and gems. Sometimes, smuggling exposes how easily large and animated items can be carried as air cargo without discovery. For instance, in 2003, a young man sealed himself into a box that was carried as air freight from New York city via Niagara Falls and Fort Wayne, Indiana, to his parent's home in Dallas, through the hands of several commercial haulers, without discovery.

Of more concern than private stowaways are hidden explosives that could cause a catastrophe that destroys an aircraft or the storage area, kills personnel or (if an aircraft is destroyed in the air) people on the ground, and disrupts air transport, with huge economic consequences. A small device, smaller than a briefcase, would be small enough to hide inside the typical large freight containers and still threaten the aircraft catastrophically, although the blast would be mitigated by surrounding cargo. The larger containers on dedicated cargo planes are of concern for the carriage of weapons of mass destruction that would be too heavy or easily detected to be loaded as passenger luggage on a passenger flight.

In recent years, terrorists have attempted to mail devices that were designed (probably using a timed detonator) to explode in mid-air over the destination country. In October 2010, after a tip-off derived from a multinational intelligence operation directed against al-Qaeda in the Arabian Peninsula and American exile Anwar Al-Awlaki, East Midlands airport in England and Dubai airports discovered explosives hidden inside printer toner cartridges on UPS and FedEx flights respectively, both mailed from Sanaa, Yemen, to addresses in the United States, and configured to detonate over the U.S. east coast. On October 30, 2010, Britain banned all air cargo from Yemen and Somalia. On the same day, the U.S. DHS banned all air cargo from Yemen. Later (November 9), it banned all air cargo from Somalia and all "high-risk" cargo on passenger planes.

In October and November 2010, a Greek anarchist group mailed bombs to various embassies and foreign leaders, including two that were intercepted at Athens airport before being loaded as air freight.

In March 2011, Istanbul airport discovered a dummy bomb inside a wedding cake box that had arrived on a UPS flight from London. British police arrested a Turkish man on suspicion of a hoax. On June 17, 2011, the British Department for Transport banned UPS from screening air cargo at some facilities in Britain until it could meet British security requirements.

Controls

Since 9/11, all cargo is supposed to be screened before loading on to passenger aircraft within or inbound to the United States (this is the same rule as for passenger baggage). Cargo on nonpassenger aircraft faced lighter controls for several years after 9/11 so that most air cargo was practically not inspected during transport. Effective October 2003, the U.S. Customs and Border Protection agency required electronic submission of the manifest, if the plane originates abroad, at least 8 hours before an air courier boards or 12 hours before any air cargo is loaded abroad. The 9/11 Commission Act of 2007 required the TSA to screen 50% of cargo on cargo-only flights by February 2009, 100% by August 2010.

TSA screens all packages from Afghanistan, Algeria, Iraq, Lebanon, Libya, Nigeria, Pakistan, Saudi, Somalia, and Yemen.

Businesses generally oppose more security because of the costs and the delays to commercial flows. Many commodities and raw materials must travel quicker or more sensitively than routine inspections would allow. Consequently, officials have focused on acquiring technologies that allow quicker, nonintrusive inspections or intelligence that enables more targeted inspections. In 2009, the TSA piloted (at Houston) a Pulsed Fast Neutron Scanner (which can differentiate materials at the molecular level), but the unit cost $8m, and the funding covered just a few months of operating costs.

Luggage

Before 9/11, much checked luggage (luggage intended for the hold, separate to the passenger cabin) was not inspected or screened at all, although higher-risk airlines (such as the Israeli and Jordanian national airlines) screened all luggage for explosives and temporarily passed all luggage through a pressure chamber before loading on to aircraft (because some explosive devices had been improvised with detonators triggered by changes in pressure as the aircraft climbed into the air).

After 9/11, the United States ordered a rate of 100% inspection of anything loaded on to passenger aircraft, including checked luggage, involving at least x-ray screening for explosives. Initially, the promise was 100% manual inspection, but that promise fell away given the burden. Information on the true rate of manual inspection remains guarded.

Metallic screening is less important for checked luggage than for carry-on baggage, because the passenger has no access to the hold, so any metallic weapons hidden there would be an issue of trafficking rather than hijacking.

Human Access Controls

Before 9/11, controls on human access to airports were lax, since friends and families were in the habit of seeing off the passenger before the gate of the aircraft, and airports appreciated the extra business. The human access controls mainly started at the gate of the flight (baggage would be separated or screened earlier).

Human access controls became stringent after 9/11. In most cases, only ticketed passengers or airport or airline personnel can pass the controls from the "land" side to the "air" side (where passengers and aircraft are prepared). The United States maintained a database (the "no-fly list") of people forbidden from flying into or within the United States—convicted terrorists were uncontroversial targets, but many people found that they were forbidden to fly because they had similar names to someone of concern. A new redress system soon cleared up most of the complaints, but sometimes the explanation was lacking, and the false positive was fixed only after years of complaints.

Despite post-9/11 measures, some people have managed to access flights illegitimately. For instance, on June 24, 2011, a Nigerian man flew from New York to Los Angeles with a boarding pass for the same flight of the previous day, a student card, and a police report about his stolen passport. He was arrested 5 days later when he tried the same trick from Los Angeles to Atlanta. He was found to be carrying several stolen boarding passes.

Air side personnel are hazardous in that they could exploit more trusting controls on their access. For instance, from 2007 to 2010, Rajib Karim, a Bangladeshi-British male working for British Airways as a computer specialist, conspired with American exile Anwar al-Awlaki to blow up a U.S.-bound plane. On March 18, 2011, he was sentenced to 30 years in jail.

Air side personnel may unwittingly attack aviation. For instance, air side workers are known to have taken money to place items, such as illegal drugs, aboard aircraft or take them off aircraft without the proper screening. While they may be loath to place weapons aboard an aircraft for terrorist purposes, a threat could pretend to be placing contraband rather than a bomb.

Air side access controls can be exploited too. For instance, cargo and supplies are delivered to airports at delivery sites with a short space between the land side and air side. Many airports require personnel at such sites to check the credentials of deliverers and to keep the air side closed while the land side is open, but sometimes, due to carelessness or to promote air flow during hot weather, both sides are left open, and unauthorized personnel are left to walk around without being challenged.

Metallic Weapons Screening

Magnetic and x-ray scanners became routine in the 1970s, mainly to spot metallic weapons, such as knives and firearms, that could be used to hijack planes. On 9/11, terrorists evaded these controls by carrying small knives ("box-cutters") and by travelling in a sufficiently large group per plane to intimidate passengers (at the time, conventional wisdom and official advise was to avoid confronting hijackers). After 9/11, authorities banned knives of any size and even banned metallic cutlery, which traditionally airline crew had issued with meals, although cynics pointed out that the regulations permitted glass bottles, which could be smashed to produce sharp weapons, and wooden objects that could be combined and sharpened as weapons. Soon enough, metallic cutlery returned to airlines without any recorded use as a weapon.

Despite extra controls since 9/11, metallic weapons or fake weapons have been used inside the cabin for old-fashioned hijackings. For instance, on November 27, 2002, a schizophrenic Italian man used a fake bomb to hijack an Air Italia flight from Bologna to Paris. On February 17, 2007, a man used two pistols to hijack a Spanish flight from Mauritania to Canary Islands. On April 24, 2011, a Kazakhi man used a knife to attempt a hijack of an Air Italia flight from Paris to Rome but was restrained by crew.

Footwear Screening

Al-Qaida evaded the enhanced access controls by hiding explosives in the sole of a large training shoe (as worn by Richard Reid in December 2001), after which some authorities required passengers to place their shoes through x-ray screening devices. However, implementation is inconsistent, with some airports allowing some shoes to remain on the feet, while others insist on all footwear being screened.

Liquids Screening

Terrorists have planned to use liquid explosives, to be prepared on the flight using materials carried aboard without alerting the screeners. According to the plot intercepted in August 2006, the main component would have been hydrogen peroxide, hidden inside commercially available bottles, whose tops remained sealed because the terrorists had replaced the contents using syringes stuck through the plastic sides. A detonator would have been disguised as the battery inside a disposable camera. Another disposable camera could have served as the electrical ignition source. Intelligence during the planning stage led to arrests that prevented the plot of August 2006 from being finalized, but, under the regulations of the time, the materials probably would have passed the access controls.

The initial solution was to ban liquids entirely from passing through the access controls (although passengers could purchase more from the secure area of the airport). This led to long lines as baggage and persons were inspected manually, and some farcical confrontations (such as intrusive inspections of colostomy bags, breast milk, and hand creams), before screening technology was adjusted to better detect liquids, agents aligned their activities, and the public became more familiar with the new regulations. Soon the rules were adjusted to allow liquids in small containers, although cynics have pointed out that enough terrorists travelling with enough small containers could carry enough materials to make the same explosive device that had been planned in August 2006.

In 2009, the TSA procured 500 bottled-liquid scanners in a $22 million contract with a commercial supplier. It deployed more than 600 of the scanners to airports nationwide in 2011, 1,000 by 2013. These scanners are used to screen medically required liquids (data source: TSA).

Clothing Screening

Since 9/11, authorities have demanded more screening of passengers and their clothing by x-ray and evolved systems, but are opposed by passengers who prefer to remain covered, on personal, cultural, or religious grounds.

Thick or outer garments are usually passed through Explosive Detection Systems—conveyer-fed machines, often described inaccurately as x-ray machines but using evolved technology in order to differentiate explosive materials. However, they are unlikely to differentiate small amounts, as could be distributed thinly within the lining of heavy clothing, or trace amounts, as left behind when someone handles explosives. Some suppliers have offered hand-held electronic devices for detecting the chemical traces, but these are ineffective unless practically touching the person. From 2004 to June 2006, the U.S. TSA acquired 116 full-body explosives sniffers ("puffers") at 37 airports, despite poor tests of effectiveness. They were deleted because of poor detection and availability rates, after a sunk cost of more than $30 million.

Since 2009, the TSA's systems for detecting explosives have included table-top machines (Explosives Trace Detection machines) for detecting explosive residues on swabs. In February 2010, TSA announced that these machines would be deployed nationwide. These machines are used mainly for random or extra inspections of clothing worn by the passenger.

Explosives Detection Dogs are the best sensors of explosives, although they are hazardous to some people and have short periodic work cycles, so could not screen lines of people efficiently or effectively. They are used mostly for random patrols on the land side.

Body Screening

Body imagers produce an electronic image of the person's body underneath their clothes and can be configured to reveal items hidden between the body and clothing. They are quicker than a manual inspection (about 30 seconds to generate the scan and inspect the image, compared to 2 minutes for a pat-down), but are expensive and violate common expectations of privacy and health security.

Body imagers come in two main technologies: backscatter x-ray and millimeter wave. Backscatter units are less expensive but still costly (about $150,000 per unit at the time of first acquisition). They use a flat source/detector, so the target must be scanned from at least two sides (the system looks like a wrap-around booth inside of which the passenger stands facing one side). Many passengers are understandably reluctant to subject themselves to a backscatter x-ray, having been told to minimize their exposure to x-rays except for medical purposes. Additionally, health professionals have disputed official claims that the energy emitted by a scan is trivial. Meanwhile, reports have emerged that backscatter images do not adequately penetrate thick or heavy clothing; some entrepreneurs have offered clothing to shield the body from the energy, casting doubt on their effectiveness at their main mission.

Millimeter wave systems produce 360-degree images, so are quicker, and their images are more revealing, but they are more expensive, their health effects are less certain, and their revealing images are of more concern for privacy advocates. Authorities claim that software is used to obscure genitalia, but obfuscation of genitalia would obscure explosives hidden in underpants. Operators generally keep the images and the agent hidden inside a closed booth and promise not to record any images. However, these measures do not resolve all the ethical and legal issues. For instance, British officials admitted that child pornography laws prevented scans of people under 18 years of age.

Backscatter imagers have been available commercially since 1992. They have been deployed in some U.S. prisons since 2000 and in Iraq since 2003, but at no airports before 2007. The United States trialled one at Phoenix airport in February 2007, then deployed 40 at 18 airports before 2010. The United States also donated four to Nigeria in summer 2008. Britain trialled one at London Heathrow airport in 2007. By then, officials already realized preferences for millimeter wave systems. The Netherlands trialled three millimeter wave systems at Schipol airport in 2007. Canada trialled one in fiscal year 2008. Britain trialled some at Manchester from December 2009.

Body imagers of all types were deployed slowly and restrictively because of privacy, health, and cost issues. In 2009, the GAO faulted the TSA for poor cost-benefit analysis: The agency's plan to double the number of body scanners in coming years would require more personnel to run and maintain them—an expense of as much as $2.4 billion. Until 2010, all of the deployed machines were used for secondary inspections only, as a voluntary alternative to a manual inspection, which itself was occasional.

After the new controls on outer clothing and liquids, terrorists planned to hide explosives in underpants (as worn by Umar Farouk Abdulmutallab in December 2009). He passed screeners and boarded an aircraft to the United States but failed to detonate catastrophically (although he burnt himself), probably because damp had degraded the explosive.

Within days of this attack, U.S., British, and Dutch governments required scans of all U.S.-bound passengers or a manual inspection of the outer body (*pat-downs*). Within one year, more than 400 body imaging machines had been deployed at 70 of the 450 airports in the United States. Today, some of these major airports require all passengers to pass through imaging machines or opt-out in favor of a manual inspection, although cynics noted that the requirement was sometimes abandoned during heavy flows of passengers.

After years of more access controls and delays at airports, passengers rebelled most against body imagers and intrusive pat-downs. Certainly some of the inspections were farcical or troubling, such as an agent inspecting a baby's diaper or making contact with an adult's genitalia during a pat-down. In November 2010, private citizens launched "We Won't Fly," essentially an online campaign against excessive access controls, including a National Opt-Out Day on Thanksgiving, 2010, although few passengers opted out on America's busiest travel day. Polls showed that the public disliked the new procedures but also thought them necessary. Meanwhile, in November 2010 and repeatedly in subsequent months, U.S. Representative Ron Paul (Republican from Texas) introduced a bill, the American Traveler Dignity Act, to hold officials accountable for unnecessary screenings.

Although officials would not admit that procedures can change due to public pressure rather than changes in threat, in fact security is an evolving balance between commercial and popular and official requirements. Universal body imagers and pat-downs probably represented the high-tide of controls on access to passenger aviation. From January 2011, the TSA tested a new millimeter wave software for 6 months at three airports, including Reagan National, on the promise of less violations or privacy with the same detection of weapons. On July 20, 2011, the TSA announced that the new software would be installed on 241 millimeter wave units at 41 airports. Information on the full distribution, use, and effectiveness of units remains guarded.

Pedagogy Box 15.8 Intelligence Versus Defensive Technologies

The rebellion against body imagers in 2010 prompted a reconsideration of the wider approach to aviation security, with some critics identifying too much emphasis on defensive technologies at the expense of intelligence-led targeting of real threats or policy-led prevention of threats.

From foundation in late 2001 through 2010, the TSA spent roughly $14 billion in more than 20,900 transactions with dozens of contractors. Sometimes, the contracts were unambiguously regrettable, as illustrated by the "puffers" fiasco (see above). In 2009, the GAO stated that the TSA had "not conducted a risk assessment or cost-benefit analysis, or established quantifiable performance measures" on its new technologies. "As a result, TSA does not have assurance that its efforts are focused on the highest priority security needs" (p. 22).

Nevertheless, spending on technology remained high. For 2011, the TSA required $1.3 billion for airport screening technologies.

The rebellion against body imagers, which peaked in November 2010, prompted some officials to complain about the overall strategy, usually anonymously, to journalists.

> In every known recent attempt, terrorists have used a different tactic to evade the latest technology at airport checkpoints, only to be thwarted by information unearthed through intelligence work—or by alert passengers in flight. (Anne E. Kornblut and Ashley Halsey III, "Revamping of airport checkpoint system urged," *Washington Post,* 17 December 2010)

In-Flight Security

On 9/11, hijackers burst into cockpits and overpowered flight crews. After 9/11, national and commercial regulations specified that cockpit doors were to be locked during flight from the inside (previously, pilots on long flight were in the habit of allowing other staff to visit the cockpit with refreshments and of inviting select passengers to view the cockpit). Some cockpit crew were armed and trained in self-defense. Some cabin crew were trained in self-defense, although not armed.

The Federal Air Marshal Program deploys officers with concealed weapons on commercial aircraft in case of hijackings. At the time of 9/11, perhaps 33 air marshals were active, according to press reports, primarily on international flights. The number was expanded rapidly after 9/11 but remains secret—perhaps in the thousands. The TSA, which administered the Marshals since 2005, admits that only about 1% of the 28,000 daily flights have an air marshal aboard.

Passengers have proven to be most effective guardians of cabin security. Before 9/11, officials and the industry advised passengers not to confront hijackers in case they retaliated, but after 9/11, that conventional wisdom was reversed. On 9/11, the fourth plane to crash did so after passengers attempted to take control of the cockpit, having heard reports from colleagues, friends, and family on the ground that the other three hijacked planes had been flown into buildings. Passengers overpowered Richard Reid in December 2001 and Umar Farouk Abdulmutallab in December 2009 after they tried to detonate their explosives.

Countering Antiaircraft Weapons

Antiaircraft weapons could be used to shoot down aircraft in flight. These weapons are categorized as small arms, rocket-propelled grenades, cannons, and MANPADS.

Small Arms

Small arms fired from the ground could critically damage an aircraft, but their bullets are not energetic enough except when the aircraft is at very low altitude or when the discharge is from within a pressurized compartment during flight.

Rocket-Propelled Grenades

Rocket-propelled grenades are as available and portable as small arms, but have similar range and are not accurate enough to attack aircraft, although the self-destruct timers could be shortened so that the grenade would explode at a predictable altitude near the target. This altitude is below most flight paths, but could threaten any aircraft in theory as it takes off and lands. Helicopters at low altitude and slow speed are most exposed. Such threats are most profound in peacekeeping, counterinsurgency, and counterterrorism operations, which rely heavily on helicopters for logistics, transport, surveillance, and fire support. In 1993, Somali militia reconfigured their rocket-propelled grenades to explode at the low altitude used by U.S. military helicopters in support of ground operations. On one day in October 1993, they brought down two U.S. UH-60 Blackhawk helicopters that were providing support to U.S. special operations forces on the ground in Mogadishu. On August 6, 2011, a rocket-propelled grenade struck the aft rotor of a U.S. Chinook (a twin rotor transport helicopter) while it was transporting special operations west of Kabul, Afghanistan, killing all 38 people on board.

Cannons

Projectiles of less than 15 mm caliber are not energetic enough to harm aircraft at normal flying altitudes. Automatic cannons (15–40 mm) fire projectiles with sufficient energy and explosive content at an automated rate to be catastrophically destructive at altitudes up to several thousand feet, just enough to threaten light aircraft at cruising altitudes. These weapons are specialized military weapons and are not man-portable, but many have fallen into the hands of malicious actors and some can be transported by ordinary pick-up trucks.

MANPADS

Scope

Very large radar-guided surface-to-air missiles (as carried by very large trucks) have been deployed for decades, and these are severe threats to all aircraft at almost any practical altitude, but such missiles are too cumbersome and detectable to be of much use to terrorists. Man-Portable Air Defense Systems (MANPADs) are essentially shoulder-launched antiaircraft missiles. MANPADs are portable enough to be carried on the shoulder or hidden in an automobile, but have sufficient range and destructiveness to bring down any plane (although not at airliner cruising height). A MANPAD, with launcher, weighs from 28 to 55 pounds (13–25 kilograms) and measures 4 to 6.5 feet (1.2–2 meters) in length and about 3 inches (72 mm) in diameter. The missile is launched at about twice the speed of sound and reaches an altitude around 15,000 feet (4.57 kilometers). No helicopter can cruise above this altitude; airliners cruise above this altitude, but are exposed during their long approaches before landing and after taking off before reaching cruising altitude.

Past Use

More than 40 civilian aircraft have been hit by MANPAD missiles from 1970 through 2011, resulting in 28 crashes and more than 800 fatalities. All occurred in conflict zones. Almost all targets were cargo aircraft, delivering freight to peacekeepers, counter-insurgent forces, or unstable authorities. The count is an underestimate, because some smaller aircraft disappear without a full explanation and some authorities may be unwilling to admit such a loss during a counter-terrorist or counter-insurgency campaign.

In November 2002, al-Qaida's agents attempted to use two Soviet-produced SA7 MANPADs to shoot down an Israeli commercial passenger aircraft departing Kenya. This attack failed probably because the range was too short for the missiles' sensors to lock on to the target, although rumors persist that the target was equipped with an unadmitted antimissile system.

Since then, al-Qaida seems to have considered antiaircraft weapons against very important persons. According to documents captured during the U.S. operation to kill him in May 2011, Osama bin Laden ordered his network in Afghanistan to attack aircraft carrying U.S. President Obama and General David H. Petraeus (then commander of the International Security Assistance Force in Afghanistan) into Afghanistan.

Countering MANPADs

Military air forces commonly acquire counter-missile technologies, as simple as flare dispensers (flares confuse any heat sensor on the missile). The U.S. President's official planes are equipped with the technology. Israel's national airline already had acquired antimissile systems for commercial planes, although it is secretive about the capabilities and extent of the acquisition. No other national airline is believed to have acquired the same technology. Richard Clarke has advocated more widespread acquisition, arguing that such technology would cost about $1 billion to acquire across U.S. airliners, while a single downed airliner would cost the U.S. economy about $1 trillion in economic disruption (Clarke, 2008).

In fiscal year 2003, the U.S. State Department started a program to counter MANPADs, mostly activities to prevent acquisition by terrorists, insurgents, or other nonstate actors, and to reduce accidental explosions in stores. The Department engaged 30 countries, focusing on the Near East, North

Africa, and Sahel. The State Department claims that the program led to the reduction of over 33,000 MANPADs in 38 countries and the improved security of thousands more MANPADs. In fiscal year 2012, the State Department distributed $9.3 million through the program.

Proliferation

Yet hundreds, perhaps thousands, of MANPADs remain unaccounted for. In the 1980s, the U.S. Central Intelligence Agency supplied about 500 FIM-92 "Stinger" missiles to Afghanistan's mujaheddin fighters in response to the Soviet invasion. Some were expended there, some were bought back, some leaked to other countries.

Hundreds of Soviet-made MANPADs leaked from Libya during the civil war there in 2011. In November 2011, the United States launched a $40 million effort to recover the missiles. In September 2012, an anonymous U.S. official claimed that 100 to 1,000 from Libyan sources were still unaccounted for, and that Egyptian terrorists and Somali pirates had acquired some. On September 22, 2012, around one year after the end of the civil, progovernment Libyans and militiamen protesters overran an Islamist militia (Rafallah al-Sahati) base in Benghazi and discovered MANPADs.

When civil war broke out in March 2011 in Syria, rebels overran many Syrian military stores of MANPADs. In late summer 2011, videos showed Soviet-produced SA-14 MANPADs in rebel hands. By November 2012, Syrian rebels had about 40 MANPADs, according to Western and Middle Eastern intelligence. At least some were supplied by the Qatari government. (U.S. and Western European governments officially support the rebels with only nonlethal material.)

Maritime Security

This section reviews maritime security. The subsections below describe its scope, port security, cargo security, maritime terrorism, and maritime piracy.

Scope

Maritime risks include potential theft of cargo, damage to cargo, sabotage of vessels, sabotage of ports and related infrastructure, smuggling and trafficking, accidental release of hazardous materials, accidental collisions, illegal immigration, maritime terrorism, and maritime piracy.

Any of these risks have direct commercial and economic implications—potentially some of the returns include a temporary shutdown of global logistics and thence of national economies. Some of these risks have implications for society and politics at the national level, including slow-onset risks, such as potential harm to individuals and societies from illegal drugs. Others are rapid-onset risks, such as potential terrorist attacks via shipped weapons or personnel.

Pedagogy Box 15.9 International Maritime Laws and Regulations

The Convention for the Suppression of Unlawful Acts against the Safety of Maritime Navigation (SUA), agreed in Rome on March 10, 1988, defines unlawful acts against ships, such as

- the seizure of ships by force;
- acts of violence against persons on board ships; and
- the placing of devices on board a ship which are likely to harm.

The Convention obliges contracting governments either to extradite or prosecute alleged offenders. The 2005 Protocol to the SUA Convention broadens the offenses to include

- when the purpose of the act, by its nature or context, is to intimidate a population, or to compel a Government or an international organization to do or to abstain from any act;
- uses against or on a ship or discharging from a ship any explosive, radioactive material or BCN (biological, chemical, nuclear) weapon in a manner that causes or is likely to cause death or serious injury or damage;
- discharges, from a ship, oil, liquefied natural gas, or other hazardous or noxious substance, in such quantity or concentration that causes or is likely to cause death or serious injury or damage;
- uses a ship in a manner that causes death or serious injury or damage;
- transports on board a ship any explosive or radioactive material, knowing that it is intended to be used to cause, or in a threat to cause, death or serious injury or damage for the purpose of intimidating a population, or compelling a government or an international organization to do or to abstain from doing any act;
- transports on board a ship any BCN weapon, knowing it to be a BCN weapon;
- any source material, special fissionable material, or equipment or material especially designed or prepared for the processing, use or production of special fissionable material, knowing that it is intended to be used in a nuclear explosive activity or in any other nuclear activity not under safeguards pursuant to an IAEA (International Atomic Energy Agency) comprehensive safeguards agreement; or
- transports on board a ship any equipment, materials or software or related technology that significantly contributes to the design, manufacture or delivery of a BCN weapon, with the intention that it will be used for such purpose.

The Protocol for the Suppression of Unlawful Acts against the Safety of Fixed Platforms Located on the Continental Shelf, agreed in Rome on March 10, 1988, specifies the following offenses:

a) seizes or exercises control over a fixed platform by force or threat thereof or any other form of intimidation; or

b) performs an act of violence against a person on board a fixed platform if that act is likely to endanger its safety; or

c) destroys a fixed platform or causes damage to it, which is likely to endanger its safety; or

d) places or causes to be placed on a fixed platform, by any means whatsoever, a device or substance which is likely to destroy that fixed platform or likely to endanger its safety; or

(Continued)

(Continued)

e) injures or kills any person in connection with the commission or the attempted commission of any of the offences set forth in subparagraphs (a) to (d).

The 2005 amendment broadened the offenses to include

- when the purpose of the act, by its nature or context, is to intimidate a population, or to compel a Government or an international organization to do or to abstain from doing any act; or
- uses against or on a fixed platform or discharges from a fixed platform any explosive, radioactive material or BCN weapon in a manner that causes or is likely to cause death or serious injury or damage; or
- discharges from a fixed platform, oil, liquefied natural gas, or other hazardous or noxious substance, in such quantity or concentration, that it causes or is likely to cause death or serious injury or damage; or
- threatens, with or without a condition, as is provided for under national law, to commit an offence.

A new article includes the offenses of unlawfully and intentionally injuring or killing any person in connection with the commission of any of the offenses; attempting to commit an offense; participating as an accomplice; or organizing or directing others to commit an offense.

The International Maritime Organization's International Convention for the Safety of Life at Sea (SOLAS) requires all internationally voyaging passenger vessels or vessels of 300 gross tons or more to carry an Automatic Identification System (AIS), which automatically sends (by radio) information about the vessel to other ships and any interested shore-based agencies. The Class of vessel affected includes more than 40,000 vessels.

Additionally, many countries, including the United States, China, and India, and the European Union, require other classes to fit an approved AIS device for safety and national security purposes. The U.S. Coast Guard aims to complete a Nationwide AIS by 2014. In 2010, the EU ordered most commercial vessels operating on inland waterways to use an AIS Class A device. The EU also ordered fishing vessels over 15 meters length to do the same by 2014.

However, vessel crews can turn this system off. For instance, in June 2012, a Russian vessel carrying attack helicopters to Syria turned off its AIS after its insurer removed coverage while the vessel was transiting the North Sea without declaring its cargo (the insurer probably had been tipped off or pressured by the British government, which opposed arms imports by Syria).

Pedagogy Box 15.10 EU Legislation on Maritime Security

- Regulation (EC) No 725/2004 of the European Parliament and of the Council of March 31, 2004, on enhancing ship and port facility security.
- Directive 2005/65/EC of the European Parliament and of the Council of October 26, 2005, on enhancing port security.

- Report from the European Commission to the Council and the European Parliament on transport security and its financing (COM/2006/0431 final).
- European Commission Regulation (EC) No 324/2008 of April 9, 2008, laying down revised procedures for conducting Commission inspections in the field of maritime security.
- European Commission Decision of January 23, 2009, amending Regulation (EC) No 725/2004 of the European Parliament and of the Council as far as the IMO Unique Company and Registered Owner Identification Number Scheme is concerned.
- European Commission Recommendation of March 11, 2010, on measures for self-protection and the prevention of piracy and armed robbery against ships (2010/159/EU).

Port Security

Ports as small as village harbors handle commercial trade of one sort or another, at least fish or tourists, but most concern is expressed over busy commercial ports with capacity to handle standard shipping containers and to service container ships and large passenger ships.

The busiest ports are generally in the northern hemisphere, in east Asia, south-east Asia, the eastern coast of South Asia, the southern Middle East, Egypt, Greece, Italy, Spain, Germany, the eastern and western coasts of the United States, and central America.

Interruptions to these major ports could have national and international implications. A 10-day labor lockout in 2002 at the Port of Los Angeles/Long Beach cost the U.S. economy $1 billion per day (Blumenthal, 2005, p. 12). Some observers claim that a single terrorist attack on a prime container port could trigger a global recession (Flynn & Kirkpatrick, 2004).

Pedagogy Box 15.11 U.S. Maritime and Port Security

By 2011, DHS counted 12,383 miles of coastline, 25,000 miles of commercial waterways, and 361 ports. The Coast Guard (administered by DHS since January 2003) prioritized 55 ports for the Port Security Assessment Program. The TSA (under DHS since March 2003) administers grants to ports, totaling more than $235 million in 2011 for the 52 riskiest port areas.

The U.S. Coast Guard (USCG) leads maritime security activities, including ensuring the safe operation and flow of maritime traffic, rescue at sea, the protection of natural resources, protected environmental areas, and fishing, the interdiction of illicit traffic (mostly illegal drugs and immigrants), countering maritime terrorism, and keeping the marine environment open for military use. It administers the National Targeting Center, which assesses risks from incoming vessels and containers and supports risk reduction activities. Maritime Intelligence Fusion Centers are located in Norfolk (Virginia) and Alameda (California). The Coast Guard has established Area Maritime Security Committees in all U.S. ports to coordinate federal, state, and local authorities, port authorities, and

(Continued)

(Continued)

private operators. By authority of the Maritime Transportation Security Act of 2002, the Coast Guard commands Maritime Safety and Security Teams (MSST) (each about 75 persons) that can deploy rapidly by helicopter in response to a terrorist attack on a port or vessel. By 2006, two MSSTs had been created, although one (at Anchorage, Alaska) was deleted in 2011.

Under the Marine Transportation Security Act of 2002, the International Ship and Port Facility Security Code (ISPS) requires large foreign vessels and ports to manage their security in compliance with Customs and Border Protection (CBP) standards.

The International Port Security Program (IPS) facilitates the exchange of information between the USCG and foreign official partners and allows for reciprocal regulations of U.S. exports into foreign ports.

In November 2002, the Department of Commerce and the U.S. CBP launched Operation Safe Commerce to research and test technologies and methods for improving security in maritime commerce. It closed in 2004 after giving more than $200 million in grants to U.S. and foreign ports, including Los Angeles, Long Beach, Seattle/Tacoma, and New York/New Jersey.

The SAFE Port Act of October 2006 ordered DHS to ensure the security of maritime transport and ports and to create a plan for mitigating the economic consequences of a terrorist attack on a major port. In October 2007, the TSA started credentialing workers at the Port of Wilmington, Delaware, under the Transportation Workers Identify Card program. By the end of 2011, nearly 2 million workers had been enrolled at more than 165 enrollment centers, and more than 1.8 million workers had received cards.

Cargo Security

Scope

Ships carry 99.5% of transoceanic trade. States with long coastal borders tend to depend most on oceanic trade. For instance, Britain, Japan, and South Korea each import or export by ship more than 90% of their trade by value or 95% by weight.

More than 90% of global cargo moves in shipping containers. At any time, 12 million to 15 million containers are in use. In 2011, the equivalent of more than 300 million containers were handled around the world. Approximately 10.7 million containers arrived in U.S. ports that year (U.S. GAO, 2012, p. 1).

Cargos are of concern because they can be stolen, hijacked, held to ransom, used for smuggling or trafficking, and they could carry hazardous materials. In 2003, the Organization for Economic Cooperation and Development estimated worldwide cargo theft at $30 billion to $50 billion per year. Vessels and hazardous cargoes could be used as weapons or weapon delivery systems, harming directly at the local level and generating cascading economic consequences.

Maritime Cargo Security

As described by subsections below, initiatives to secure cargo and cargo shipping include certification of safe traders, manifest rules, the Container Security Initiative, the Smart Box Initiative, and new inspections at port.

Safe Traders

The U.S. Customs-Trade Partnership Against Terrorism (C-TPAT) came into existence in November 2001; it was formalized into law with the SAFE Port Act in October 2006. It is administered by the CBP agency within the DHS. It invites businesses (such as importers, carriers, brokers, port authorities) to voluntarily ensure compliance, internally and within their supply chains, with U.S. security standards, in return for which they can expect fewer inspections. The program has no regulatory authority, so responsibility by members to maintain standards is self-regulating.

In 2005 the World Customs Organization (WCO) established the Framework of Standards to Secure and Facilitate Global Trade (SAFE Framework) to effectively extend C-TPAT beyond the sphere of U.S. bound trade. In 2006 the terms and conditions of an Authorized Economic Operator (AEO) status were put into document form. For firms that are involved in international trade, AEO is the corresponding designation to C-TPAT certification. C-TPAT certification automatically affords the holder AEO status. As of 2011, more than 10,000 companies had enrolled in C-TPAT.

Manifest Rules

In October 2003, the United States first implemented the 24-Hour Advance Manifest Rule, which mandates all sea carriers (except for bulk carriers and approved break bulk cargo) to submit specified information about the cargo to the U.S. CBP through the Sea Automated Manifest System, 24 hours before loading cargo intended for a U.S. port. Risk assessments are produced from a rule-based system known as the Automated Targeting System at the National Targeting Center in Virginia. The U.S. CBP can order the carrier not to load the cargo if it is assessed as too risky ahead of a local inspection.

Foreign ships must send information about the cargo, passengers, crew, and voyage to the U.S. Coast Guard 96 hours before arrival in a U.S. port. If the Automated Targeting Center rates the vessel as high risk, the Coast Guard can be ordered to board the vessel before it enters port. The Coast Guard can also inspect vessels randomly.

The SAFE Port Act of 2006 requires that importers electronically file 10 additional data elements (manufacturer; seller; consolidator; buyer name and address; ship name and address; container stuffing location; importer record number; consignee record number; country of origin of goods; and the Commodity Harmonized Tariff Schedule number) to the CBP no less than 24 hours prior to the landing of containers at a U.S. port of exit. This requirement is known as the "10 Plus 2 Program" or just the "24-hour rule."

In 2010, the EU announced its own 24-Hour Advance Manifest Rule, effective from 2011. It demands 24-hours notice before cargo is loaded aboard any vessel that will enter the EU across deep seas, or 2 hours before short sea shipments arrive in an EU port, or 4 hours before break bulk cargo arrives in an EU port.

Container Security Initiative

In January 2002, the U.S. government announced the Container Security Initiative (CSI) to ensure containers overseas by committing overseas ports to U.S. security standards. The Initiative is administered by U.S. CBP, but foreign personnel provide most of the security abroad, sometimes with U.S. agents based at foreign ports. Local officials could identify high risk cargos for themselves; U.S. intelligence contributes to some of those assessments; additionally, U.S. officials could ask foreign officials to screen high-risk containers as assessed from the United States. Low-risk and prescreened containers gain rapid entry into the United States.

By 2003, 18 foreign ports had joined; by 2008, 58; this remained the total in 2013. These 58 ports account for 85% of all U.S.-bound containers, or around 8 million containers per year, of which about 45,500 containers are screened in the foreign port (equivalent to about two containers per port per day). About 2% of all inbound containers were screened in 2008, but the proportion dropped to 0.5 in 2011. Despite CSI, about 10% of containers are screened after arrival in the United States, almost all of them (99%) for gamma radiation. Fifteen percent of all inbound containers originate in a port outside of CSI.

The 9/11 Commission Act of 2007 ordered all inbound containers to be scanned overseas by x-rays and for gamma radiation by July 2012, but many officials soon predicted that this target was unreasonable. In May 2012, the Homeland Security Secretary (Janet Napolitano) extended by another 2 years the exemption for all foreign ports, claiming that screening of all inbound containers would cost $16 billion. Perhaps 10% of inbound containers could be screened without disrupting trade flows.

The European Union and many countries have opposed the Container Security Initiative as a nontariff barrier to trade and worry about bad U.S. intelligence or U.S. political biases causing harm to certain trade without improving security.

Smart Box Initiative

In 2003, the CSI spawned the Smart Box Initiative, which developed new containers that include an internationally approved mechanical seal that attaches to the container's hinges and records or signals any attempt to open the door after sealing. Some have signaling devices; some are able to record the container's movements using the global positioning system. The seals are commercially available to U.S. standards. Users gain privileges such as quicker routing through ports.

Inspections at Port

Cargo security authorities can inspect containers afloat or ashore randomly but mostly respond to intelligence, tip-offs, and automated inspections. Most inspections are conducted at the exit from the port. For instance, the U.S. CBP deploys large "nonintrusive" x-ray inspection systems and nuclear "radiation portal monitors," through which a truck can drive. For "intrusive" inspections, fiber-optic cameras can be pushed through apertures into the container without opening its door. Most intrusively, a container can be unloaded and opened for a full intrusive inspection with handheld detection systems, Explosives Detection Dogs, and by hand.

Inspections at port are heavily biased toward nuclear radiation. U.S. capacity to detect nuclear and radiological material at the ports of entry has improved dramatically in recent years. The GAO (2012) agreed with the DHS that "the likelihood of terrorists smuggling a WMD into the United States in cargo containers is low, [but] the nation's vulnerability to this activity and the consequences of such an attack—such as billions of losses in US revenue and halts in manufacturing production—are potentially high" (p. 1). In 2006, the DHS and Department of Energy launched the Security Freight Initiative (SFI) to counter-nuclear and radiological terrorism through shipped containers. All U.S. ports and 75 foreign ports (as of 2013) have U.S.-supplied radiation portal monitors in order to screen containers destined for U.S. shores. Honduras and Pakistan joined the SFI immediately, followed by Britain, Hong Kong, and Singapore.

Maritime Terrorism

The subsections below summarize maritime terrorism attacks and terrorist flows by sea.

Maritime Terrorism Attacks

Maritime terrorism is rare but is potentially catastrophic to the international economy and has encouraged wide-ranging and expensive international legal and material responses. A useful estimate of maritime terrorist risks to the United States is summarized in Table 15.2.

Pedagogy Box 15.12 Past Terrorist Attacks at Sea

- From October 7 to October 10, 1985, Palestinian Liberation Front terrorists hijacked an Italian cruise ship (MS *Achille Lauro*) in the Mediterranean on its way from Alexandria to Port Said. They killed a Jewish-American passenger after their demands for release of 50 Palestinians from Israeli detention and to dock in Tartus, Syria, were unmet. After 2 days of negotiations in Port Said, the hijackers agreed to leave the ship in exchange for safe conduct to Tunisia in an Egyptian commercial airliner, but U.S. fighter aircraft forced the aircraft to land at a U.S. base in Sicily. After a tense standoff between Italian and U.S. authorities, the former took the hijackers into custody and eventually convicted them, but allowed their leaders, who had met the aircraft in Egypt, to leave, against U.S. wishes.
- On January 3, 2000, al-Qaida-sponsored suicide bombers attempted to bring their explosives-laden boat alongside the USS *The Sullivans* (a guided missile destroyer) while it was visiting Aden harbor, Yemen, but their boat sank. On October 12, 2000, other bombers detonated explosives on a boat alongside the USS *Cole* (another guided missile destroyer) in Aden, killing 17 and injuring 39 U.S. sailors.
- On October 6, 2002, near Aden a suicide explosive boat struck a large French-flagged oil tanker (*Limburg*) on its way from Iran with nearly 400,000 barrels of crude oil to another pickup of crude oil. One crewman was killed and 12 crewmen were injured, a fire broke out, and around 90,000 barrels leaked, but the explosion failed to perforate the inner of the tanker's double walls, so the ship was eventually towed to safety. Al-Qaida claimed responsibility.
- On February 27, 2004, Abu Sayyaf Group planted a bomb on the Superferry-14 out of Manila, the Philippines, in an attempt to extort money from the commercial operator, but the small explosion started a fire that killed 118 people and almost sank the ship. In October 2005, the European Commission introduced a new regulation for ship and port security, including new rules (effective July 2007) for the security of domestic ferries.
- On January 29, 2010, Israel reported that improvised explosive devices in floating barrels, launched from off-shore, had drifted on the coast. They were probably launched by Palestinian Islamic Jihad and Popular Resistance Committees against Israeli patrol vessels.
- On July 28, 2010, a suicide explosive boat struck an oil tanker in the Strait of Hormuz en route to Japan from Qatar. The ship's outer structure was damaged but not perforated, and the true cause was not confirmed for 2 weeks. A new Jihadi group (Abdulla Azzam Brigades) claimed responsibility.

Table 15.2 Maritime Terrorism Risks

Maritime Terrorism Scenario	Potential Human Consequences	Potential Economic Consequences	Potential Social Consequences
Sink or disable a ship in a channel or port	Tens of injuries and deaths among the crew	Tens of millions of dollars in life and injury compensation, repair, and replacement; Hundreds of millions of dollars in lost cargo; Billions of dollars in short-term business disruption and augmented security	Loss of human capital and changes in consumer behavior
Hijack ship and use to destroy infrastructure	Injuries and deaths among the crew; several hundred civilian casualties	Tens of millions of dollars in repair and replacement; Tens of millions of dollars in damaged infrastructure; Hundreds of millions of dollars in life and injury compensation	Loss of human capital and changes in consumer behavior
Using a shipping container as a delivery device for a conventional bomb	Several hundred injuries and deaths	Millions of dollars in damaged infrastructure; Millions of dollars in destroyed property; Hundreds of millions of dollars in life and injury compensation; One billion dollars in short-term business disruptions; Billions of dollars in augmented security	Loss of human capital
Using a shipping container as a delivery device for a radiological dispersion device	Tens to hundreds of injuries and deaths	Hundreds of thousands of dollars in contaminated or damaged infrastructure; Millions of dollars in contaminated or damaged property; Hundreds of millions of dollars in life and injury compensation; Billions of dollars in augmented security; Tens of billions of dollars in long-term macroeconomic effects	Loss of human capital, changes in consumer behavior, and political consequences
Using a shipping container as a delivery device for a nuclear weapon	50,000–1,000,000 deaths	Billions of dollars in damaged or contaminated infrastructure; tens of billions of dollars in short-term business disruptions and augmented security; Hundreds of billions in life and injury compensation, contaminated or damaged property, and long-term macroeconomic effects	Loss of human capital, changes in consumer behavior, and political consequences

SOURCE: Greenberg, Chalk, Willis, Khilko, & Ortiz, 2006.

Terrorist Flows by Sea

Terrorist attacks afloat are rare, but maritime smuggling of terrorist personnel and weapons is common, particularly in and around countries with long insecure maritime borders:

- Burma, Thailand, Cambodia, Vietnam, Malaysia, the Philippines, and Indonesia in South East Asia;
- Sri Lanka and India;

- Tanzania, Kenya, Somalia, Eritrea, Sudan, Egypt, Saudi Arabia, Yemen, and Oman in east Africa and Arabia;
- West Africa from Senegal to Congo; and
- the Caribbean and the Gulf of Mexico from the southern states of the United States to Venezuela.

Most terrorist smuggling in these areas does not directly lead to a maritime terrorist attack but could smuggle weapons, persons, or money that enable other terrorist attacks.

Pedagogy Box 15.13 Past Terrorism on Land Enabled by Maritime Smuggling

- The explosives used in the bombing of the U.S. embassies in Kenya and Tanzania in 1998 probably were imported by a vessel controlled by al-Qaeda.
- On December 14, 1999, an al-Qaida terrorist (Ahmed Ressam, an Algerian living in Montreal, Canada) drove a car loaded with explosives onto a ferry from Vancouver. He was arrested at Port Angeles, Washington State, after a search by U.S. customs officials called by a suspicious border agent. Ressam probably planned to bomb Los Angeles International Airport around the new year of 1999–2000.
- Khalid Sheikh Mohammed, who was arrested in Pakistan in March 2003 before transfer to U.S. detention sites, reportedly told interrogators that he had prospected the shipping of explosives into the United States, hidden in a container of personal computers from Japan.
- In March 2004, the same week of the commuter train bombing in Madrid, a suicide attack at the Israeli port of Ashdod killed 10 Israelis: *The Jerusalem Post* reported that Palestinian operatives might have imported the weapons from Gaza in an undetected, hidden compartment of a shipping container.
- On November 26, 2008, armed terrorists from Pakistan-based Lashkar-e-Taiba landed at the port in Mumbai, India, by private boat, from where they proceeded to kill 101 people at the railway station, a synagogue, from passing cars, and at a hotel.
- Palestinian groups outside of Israel probably have smuggled items into Israel by direct landings from boats and by dropping floating containers offshore from where they would drift on shore. These containers are probably mostly portable and easily hidden, but some may be as large as barrels, similar to those dropped as sea mines in 2010.
- On September 13, 2011, armed men used a boat from Somalia to access a bungalow on Kiwayu island, Kenya, near the border with Somalia. Officials suspected that the attackers were affiliated with al-Shabaab, a Somalia-based Jihadi terrorist group, but it denied this. A British couple was vacationing at the bungalow: The attackers shot dead David Tebbutt and took his wife Judith hostage to a hideout in Somalia. On March 21, 2012, she was released after her family paid a ransom.

Maritime Piracy

Maritime piracy is much riskier than maritime terrorism, because maritime piracy is much more frequent and imposes routine costs. The subsections below describe the scope of maritime piracy, pirate operations in practice, the frequency of maritime piracy over time, the geographical distribution of piracy, the costs of piracy, and counter-piracy.

Scope

Maritime piracy is any attempt to board a vessel in order to steal or extort for profit. The UN effectively separates maritime theft from extortion:

> The term "piracy" encompasses two distinct sorts of offences: the first is robbery or hijacking, where the target of the attack is to steal a maritime vessel or its cargo; the second is kidnapping, where the vessel and crew are threatened until a ransom is paid. (UN Office of Drugs and Crime, 2010, p. 193)

The International Maritime Organization's Maritime Safety Committee Circular of 1993 categorized maritime piracy three ways:

1. Low-level armed robbery or assault
2. Medium-level armed robbery and assault
3. Major criminal hijacks

Piracy and terrorism are increasingly intertwined: Terrorists sometimes turn to piracy as one means to fund terrorism; many pirates in Nigeria, Somalia, and South East Asia have the ideological predilection to fund Jihadi terrorism or to engage in it themselves (Luft & Korin, 2004).

Pirate Operations

Pirates generally operate in full view of foreign shipping, including navies, while searching for targets. Their small boats are difficult to identify on the open ocean and are difficult to distinguish from fisherman, and are not actually committing any crime until they attack.

Pirates generally use small fast boats (*skiffs*; each carrying half a dozen men) to attack ships within 50 nautical miles of shore; they generally need a larger boat for operating further off shore. A *mother ship* normally tows a fast boat that would carry the attackers. Despite the term mother ship, it is not a large vessel, just a small boat carrying a dozen or two dozen men, often powered by small engines and sails, indistinguishable from fishing boats until the attack starts. Sometimes mother ships tow more than one fast boat or cooperate with each other. Multiple fast ships will confuse the target's crew, whose visibility and room for evasion is limited. The attackers are armed with ubiquitous Soviet-manufactured automatic firearms and rocket-propelled grenades. An attack is normally completed within 30 minutes.

Pirates are often controlled from shore. Since the 1990s, pirates have used satellite telephones to communicate from ship to shore. They also use commercially available navigation equipment that can direct them anywhere given a target coordinate and information about current position from the Global Positioning System. The coincidence of pirates with valuable vessels in more remote seas suggests that some are tipped off by employees with access to the vessel's coordinates (UN Office of Drug and Crime [ODC], 2010, p. 198).

Most successful piracy ends in theft and resale of the cargo, the crew's possessions, the vessel's portable items, or sometimes the vessel itself (in the case of small craft). West African pirates target fuel cargo for illegal sale through the developed infrastructure of Nigeria.

Off the Horn of Africa, which lacks Nigeria's infrastructure, most pirates aim at holding a large ship, cargo, and crew for ransom. Pirates target vessels that can be held ransom for large amounts of money. These tend to be large container and tanker ships; small yachts suggest wealthy owners who could be held for ransom, although they are more likely to outpace pirate mother ships, given sufficient warning. Shippers can negotiate with the hijackers via the hijacked vessel's communications systems or the pirate's satellite telephones. Ransoms are normally paid in cash and delivered physically to the hijackers by an intermediary. Sometimes the ransom is dropped by parachute from an aircraft. Rarely, the pirates will accept payment to a trusted third party. The pirates normally honor agreements to release their prizes for ransom, but they usually release a vessel, cargo, and crew only after stripping them of anything valuable and portable. The vessel and cargo may be damaged too during the attack, the subsequent thievery, or long periods under hijack without proper maintenance.

Costs

From 2003 to 2008, the global economic cost of piracy was $1 billion to $16 billion per year. From 2009 to 2012, it was somewhere between $7 billion and $12 billion per year. Most of these costs relate to controlling the risks rather than the direct costs of pirate attacks.

In controlling the risks, shippers pay additional costs, such as insurance, armed guards, antiboarding materials, defensive weapons, extra fuel costs due to higher speeds and evasive routes in riskier waters, and the extra operational costs of longer journeys to avoid riskier waters.

The cost of ransoms is difficult to calculate because shippers and pirates tend to underreport. In 2010, the reported average and median ransoms were around $4 million to $5 million, with a high of $9.5 million. By 2012, the average and median were about the same, but the high had reached $12 million. Ransoms totaled around $135 million in each of 2011 and 2012.

Delivering the ransom and recovering the vessel is costly in itself. In some cases shippers have procured a light aircraft to drop the ransom on the ship or near the pirates' base. The ship must be recovered, cleaned, and repaired. The cargo may be spoiled. In worst case, all are lost. For instance, on July 8, 2013, the Malaysian-flagged and -owned M/V ALBEDO, which in November 2010 had been pirated with 15 crewmen aboard, sank at anchor off the coast of Haradhere, Somalia.

The human costs are confined to the few crew who are unfortunately killed or detained. Fortunately, these rates have declined in recent years but are still terrible for those directly affected. In 2011, 15 crew were killed, 714 crew were taken hostage afloat on 45 vessels, and 15 were kidnapped (taken ashore). In 2012, four were killed, 484 taken hostage on 28 vessels, and 25 kidnapped. The first 6 months of 2013 gives an annualized rate of two killed, 160 taken hostage on 12 vessels, and 56 kidnapped. If the crew are lucky enough to survive their abduction, they likely will need rest, treatment, and compensation, although the flexibility of crew contracts often leaves the shipper with few obligations (data source: International Maritime Bureau).

Frequency

Piracy is an underreported problem because of the shipper's desire to hide vulnerability and costs from stakeholders. Worldwide frequency of piracy increased in the early 1990s, mostly due to increased sources from China and Indonesia. In the late 1990s, austerity, competition, and automation encouraged ship owners to reduce crews and defenses. Piracy peaked in 2000 and remained high in that decade (around 350 to 450 events per year, according to the International Maritime Organization). Official reactions to 9/11 encouraged states to divert resources away from counter-piracy to counter-terrorism. Many states declined into further instability during that decade. Pirates found their environments more permissive and also found weapons and equipment more accessible (Chalk, 2009). Global incidents peaked at 445 in 2010, a peak last seen in 2003, although still short of the peak of 469 in 2000. The frequency then declined as official and commercial focus returned. The International Maritime Bureau reported 439 vessels attacked and 45 hijacked in 2011, 297 attacked and 28 hijacked in 2012, and an annualized rate of 270 attacked and 12 hijacked given the first half of 2013.

In the 1990s, sources surged most rapidly from Indonesia—sources surged in Bangladesh, India, and Malaysia too. Piracy dropped by half in 2005, thanks to international responses in South East Asia and South Asia, but from 2008 to 2009, it surged again, mostly due to increasing piracy from Somalia, a persistent failed state. Sources surged in Nigeria too (data source: International Maritime Bureau).

Geographical Distribution

Shipping is not evenly distributed across the world's oceans. Most ships follow predictable routes due to the predictability of markets, ports, and coastlines. Thus, shipping routes offer at least 11 bottlenecks:

1. The Panama Canal in Panama is an artificial link between the Pacific and Atlantic Oceans.
2. The Strait of Magellan off Chile is the quickest ice-free natural link between the Pacific and Atlantic Oceans.
3. The only natural link between the Atlantic and Indian Oceans is south of the Cape of Good Hope, South Africa.
4. Shipping crosses between the Atlantic Ocean and Mediterranean Sea through the Strait of Gibraltar.
5. Shipping between the Mediterranean and Caspian Seas must travel through the Bosporus, Turkey.
6. The quickest route between Europe and the Indian Ocean is via the Suez Canal, Egypt. This Canal artificially links the Mediterranean and the Gulf of Aden. Transits of the Canal declined in the later 2000s due to increased piracy in the Gulf of Aden.
7. The Gulf of Aden narrows at Bab-el-Mandeb between Yemen and Djibouti. By 2006, 3.3 million barrels of oil per day transited these straits (UNODC, 2010, p. 198).
8. The Gulf of Aden remains a narrow stretch of water between Yemen and the Horn of Africa, Somalia.
9. Most oil from the Middle East is shipped out of the Persian/Arabian Gulf via the Straits of Hormuz between Iran and Qatar.
10. Most shipping between the Indian Ocean and South China Sea must travel through the Malacca Strait between Malaysia and the Philippines.
11. Shipping between South East Asia and Australasia generally travels between Indonesia and Australia.

Piracy tends to concentrate in four areas:

1. Measured over the last couple decades, the most concentrated piracy has occurred in the Gulf of Aden and off the Horn of Africa. About 10% of shipping passes through these seas, although some shippers have chosen the less risky but slower route around the Cape of Good Hope between the Indian and Atlantic Oceans. According to the International Maritime Bureau, the number of pirate attacks off the Horn of Africa doubled from 111 in 2008 to 217 in 2009 and peaked in 2010, but fell to 237 in 2011 and to 75 in 2012, thanks to sustained counter-piracy. Nevertheless, Somali pirates still held eight ships and 127 hostages at the end of 2012. Somalia is the main national source of the pirates in these seas.

2. About 10% of shipping passes the Gulf of Guinea off West Africa. Piracy there is less frequent than off the Horn of Africa, but more successful now, thanks to international attention on Somalia. In 2012, West African pirates attacked ships 62 times and threatened 966 sailors, compared to 851 in Somali waters. West African pirates hijacked 10 ships and took 207 new hostages, of which five were killed, according to the International Maritime Bureau. Nigeria is the largest and most populous state in West Africa and the main national source of pirates in the region.

3. In the early 2000s, most piracy risks were concentrated in the seas between Vietnam, Indonesia, and Malaysia—particularly the Malacca Straits between Malaysia and the Philippines, where about 50% of shipping passes. In 2012, 81 pirate attacks were reported in South-East Asia, 31 in the rest of the Far East.

4. The Caribbean Sea and the sea off Panama is a hazardous and poorly policed area rife with short-range piracy.

5. The Bay of Bengal is another poorly policed area, opening up on the Indian Ocean. Bangladesh is the main national source here.

Pedagogy Box 15.14 Somali Piracy

Pirates from one of the world's poorest countries (Somalia) are holding to ransom ships from some of the richest, despite patrols by the world's most powerful navies. Almost all piracy in the Gulf of Aden and off the Horn of Africa originates in Somalia, a failing state since the 1980s. Central government finally collapsed in 1991, leaving an independent state of Somaliland to the north, an effectively autonomous province of Puntland, and a failed state of Somalia in the south-west, where Somalia's capital and largest port (Mogadishu) is located. In 2012, international forces secured Mogadishu and drove south, but most of the nominal territory of Somalia remains insecure.

Somali pirates numbered about 1,400 as of 2009. They are concentrated in Puntland and south-central Mudug. The lowest ranked pirates are easily replaced with recruits from the majority destitute population, which includes 40,000 internally displaced Somalis. A pirate earns somewhere from

(Continued)

(Continued)

$6,000 to $10,000 for each $1 million in ransom paid. About 30% of ransoms go to the pirates, 10% to local militia, 10% to local elders and officials, and 20% to the financier. The period of hijack ranged from 6 days to 6 months with an average around 2 months; ransoms totaled somewhere between $50 million and $100 million. From 2008 to 2009, insurance premiums for vessels in these waters jumped from $20,000 to $150,000.

In 2004, the International Maritime Board warned all vessels to travel further than 50 nautical miles off the Somali coast. In 2005, it raised the specification to 100 nautical miles. By 2006, some Somali pirates were operating as far as 350 miles from Somalia, into the Red Sea and the Indian Ocean. From 2007 to 2008, piracy shifted from mainly southern Somali waters to the Gulf of Aden. By 2009, some Somali pirates were attacking ships more than 1,000 nautical miles from Somalia.

Some shippers accepted the risks of operating closer to shore in return for faster journeys, while the World Food Program continued to ship 30,000–40,000 metric tons of food aid every month into the Horn of Africa (by late 2008, 43% of Somalis were dependent on food aid, of which 95% arrived by sea). In late 2008, the World Food Program required naval escorts from European Union or Canadian forces, while some Somali pirates consented to honor humanitarian aid (such cargos would garner lower ransoms anyway) (UNODC, 2010).

Since December 2008, the European Union Naval Force Somalia (EUNAVFOR) and the North Atlantic Treaty Organization's Combined Task Force 151 have been the main international antipiracy forces off Somalia, but they patrol more than one million square miles of ocean. Somali pirates now operate in a total sea space of approximately 2.5 million square nautical miles (about the size of the continental United States). Nevertheless, relative to prior enforcement, naval impact was great: up to August 2009, they seized or destroyed 40 pirate vessels and rendered 235 suspected pirates. The Indian Navy extended its patrols from the Indian Ocean into the Gulf of Aden. Since January 2009, the Chinese Navy has maintained at least two frigates in the Gulf of Aden. By 2012, up to 30 vessels from 22 navies were patrolling the Gulf of Aden.

These naval forces operate with fewer restrictions on the use of force than their predecessors. In November 2008, an Indian warship in the Gulf of Aden destroyed a pirate mother ship. In April 2009, French marines rescued four French hostages from their yacht and detained three pirates, although one hostage was killed. On April 12, 2009, U.S. Navy personnel shot to death three pirates and freed the captain of the *Maersk Alabama* from a lifeboat under tow. In December 2009, an Indian navy helicopter with marines helped to deter hijackers from boarding a Norwegian ship. In January 2012, U.S. forces freed a Danish hostage.

Meanwhile, states have agreed international responses beyond naval force. In December 2008, the UN Security Council (Resolution 1851) established the international Contact Group on Piracy off the Coast of Somalia, chaired by the United States in 2013 and the EU in 2014.

Also in December 2008, the U.S. National Security Council issued the Partnership and Action Plan for Countering Piracy off the Horn of Africa and established the Counter-Piracy Steering Group, coled by the Departments of State and Defense, with representatives from the Departments of Justice, Homeland Security, and Treasury and the U.S. Maritime Administration and the U.S. Agency for

International Development. The U.S. Partnership and Action Plan has included a Maritime Security Sector Reform framework.

The Contact Group now boasts 62 states and 31 international organizations and maritime trade associations as participants. Working Group 1 (chaired by Britain) promotes international military coordination and the development of regional capacity for maritime security. Working Group 2 (Denmark) works on legal issues. Working Group 3 (Korea) helps to develop commercial shipping's awareness and protections. Working Group 4 (Egypt) works on public awareness and support for counter-piracy. Working Group 5 (Italy) coordinates the countering of pirate financing. The Contact Group claims a "marked reduction" in piracy: successfully pirated ships off Somalia fell from 47 in 2009 and 2010 to 25 in 2011, and five in 2012.

Local stabilization and capacity building are solutions to the root causes or enabling conditions of piracy in Somalia. On April 23, 2009, a European donor conference raised $160 million for security sector reform in Somalia. In February 2012, Britain hosted an international conference on the future of Somalia, which reiterated that force alone could not solve the problem and advocated more support of local communities. In August 2012, central authorities in Mogadishu adopted a new provisional constitution, legislature, and president, and, with international military support, started to expand their control outside the capital.

Counter-Piracy

Counter-measures include stricter laws and law enforcement, naval enforcement, defensive options for ships, and activities to counter the wider pirate networks, as explained in the subsections below.

Legal Responses

International norms and laws have proscribed maritime piracy for a long time, including the Paris Declaration of 1856, the Geneva Convention of 1958, the UN Convention on the Law of the Sea of 1982, and the Convention for the Suppression of Unlawful Acts Against the Safety of Maritime Navigation (SUA) of 1988, which allows any state to detain, extradite, and prosecute maritime terrorists and pirates; 150 countries are party to SUA.

While the norms and laws are strong on paper, they are difficult to enforce in practice. International law constrains an outside state's right to intervene. Mackubin Owens (2009) has argued that "a sovereign state has the right to strike the territory of another if that state is not able to curtail the activities of *latrunculi*" (pirates and other outlaws), but no state has exercised this right in decades.

Pirates are based in unstable or weakly governed areas where the judicial system tends to be weak. For instance, international authorities still regard Somalia as unable to try pirates properly. Outside states can prosecute pirates, but democracies, which have been most engaged in countering piracy at source, have honored human rights legislation or the detainee's claims of asylum to the extent that most pirates were released after arrest without any indictment. For instance, for many years, European naval forces were advised by home governments that rendition to states around the Indian Ocean, each of which had unreliable human rights, would violate the European Human Rights Act.

Even if the judiciary is strong, practical difficulties remain. Pirates are difficult to prosecute unless caught in the act. Witnesses are difficult to bring to court: Sailors are keen to return to work, particularly because most are not compensated for their time as hostages or in court; most sailors are from developing countries and spend most of their time at sea without a mailing address. Given the diverse nationalities of sailors and pirates, the court often requires as many translators as witnesses.

In the late 2000s, outside states started to act more responsibly. In late 2008, France started to send pirates for prosecution in France. In March 2009, Kenya agreed to try pirates in return for help from the European Union with judicial reform. In September 2010, international naval forces handed over to Kenya nine Somali citizens who had hijacked a vessel, *MV Magellan Star*, in the Gulf of Aden. In June 2013, a Kenyan Court sentenced each of them to 5 years in prison.

In April 2009, after U.S. naval forces shot to death all remaining pirates, except one, who were still holding the crew from the U.S.-flagged *Maersk Alabama*, U.S. authorities rendered to New York the surviving Somali pirate; in February 2011, he was sentenced to 33 years in prison. By March 2012, the United States had prosecuted 28 Somali pirates. The United States, like many states, maintains that the flag state should prosecute the pirate but has arranged for Somali pirates to serve out their sentences in Somalia, thanks to international military support of a new provisional constitution and government in Somalia in 2012.

During the February 2012 London Conference on Piracy and Somalia, Britain pledged more than $1 million and founding staff from the British Serious Organized Crime Agency to establish a Regional Anti-Piracy Prosecutions and Intelligence Co-ordination Centre (RAPPICC) in the Seychelles. The temporary offices opened on June 1, 2012, the permanent building in January 2013, including a fusion center for coordinating international judicial information and enforcement and a 20-person detention facility for conducting interviews. By 2013, more than 1,000 pirates were in detention in 20 countries, of which most had been or would be convicted.

Naval Enforcement

Ships are supposed to travel through national waters patrolled by national coast guards or international shipping lanes patrolled by multinational naval forces. International naval counter-piracy surged in 2009 off Somalia in response to new international forums and national commitments, but even there, the area of operation is vast and the forces are small. The Gulf of Aden is a well patrolled channel, although highly exposed to pirates in the Indian Ocean and Horn of Africa. The narrow channel through the Straits of Hormuz is easiest to patrol, although the threats there are more military and terrorist than pirate. The Straits of Malacca have a well-patrolled channel and are tightly contained by Malaysian and Indonesian land, but exposed at either end to traffic from the Indian Ocean and South China Sea. Other oceans with pirates are barely patrolled at all.

Ship Defenses

Requirements

Vessels, even in international waters, must comply with regulations and guidance intended to prevent piracy, as issued by international authorities, national authorities, trade associations, or owners. In American English, guidance tends to be termed *best management practices*.

The UN International Maritime Organization is the highest authority. It requires all vessels of 500 gross metric tons or larger to acquire a Ship Security Alert System, which allows the crew to send a covert signal to shore in case of piracy. The UN Office on Drugs and Crime is also strongly involved.

Some vessels are required to obey national regulations and guidance, certainly if they were to take the national flag or travel into national waters. The U.S. Coast Guard has issued a Maritime Security

Directive that is more rigorous than any international regulation. The U.S. Maritime Administration (MARAD, part of the Department of Transportation) issues area-specific advice. The U.S. Merchant Marine Academy trains midshipmen in counter-piracy.

The best defense for smaller vessels is to outpace the pirate vessels. The larger ships, despite their bulk, are more vulnerable: Their crews are surprisingly small and have become smaller with more automation and reliability over the last 2 decades. Ship owners are incentivized to keep their costs down and have traditionally acquired for their ships no defenses against pirates.

> Some in the shipping industry have been unwilling to make basic investments that would render their crews and cargoes less vulnerable to attack. Approximately 20 percent of all ships off the Horn of Africa are not employing best management practices or taking proper security precautions. Unsurprisingly, these 20 percent account for the overwhelming number of successfully pirated ships. We have intensified our efforts to encourage commercial vessels to adopt best management practices. (Andrew J. Shapiro, Assistant Secretary, Bureau of Political-Military Affairs, prepared remarks to the U.S. Chamber of Commerce, Washington, DC, March 13, 2012)

Defeating Boarders

Behavioral best management practices include

- seeking secure national waters or internationally designated shipping lanes;
- travelling at full speed through high-risk areas (ships otherwise operate at much less than full speed in order to save fuel and wear);
- reporting location and progress to military authorities;
- seeking a naval escort; and
- forming a convoy with other vessels.

Closed circuit television camera can be installed to monitor areas of the ship that are otherwise invisible to the aboard crew. Additional lookouts on bridge wings help to spot threats on the sides. The ship could change course rapidly to prevent pirates coming alongside or to capsize the pirate vessel, although large vessels have little agility to change course significantly within the minutes that an attack might last.

The bridge should be armored against small arms so that the crew can keep the ship under full control during the attack. Crew should be provided with body armor and helmets. Side ladders or nets should be taken up once the vessel is underway, although pirates could launch grappling hooks. Physical barriers such as razor wire or electric wire are cheap and can prevent pirates from climbing from the sides onto the deck. Locked entryways could prevent entry, although pirates could shoot off the locks, and any such defense could be considered a provocation that encourages the pirates to be trigger-happy. A "citadel" or refuge (usually the engine room) could be provided with extra access controls; it could be provided with master ship controls and emergency supplies so that the crew could continue to control the ship's movements even after pirates come aboard, although pirates still can steal from open areas.

Fighting Back

Preparations to defeat an attack are more expensive and controversial. Large vessels already carry water dischargers for cleaning or fighting fires that could be turned on pirates, although operators would be exposed to the pirate's weapons unless protected behind some sort of shield. Some water cannons have been installed closer to the sides of the ship behind protection from where they can be brought to bear on pirate ships alongside. Heated water has proved most effective at deterring pirates. Slippery foam could hinder the pirate's attempts to board. Acoustic guns are additional nonlethal options. In December 2008, the Chinese crew of *Zhenhua 4* fought off pirates with fire hoses and incendiary devices improvised from fuel containers.

Increasingly, operators are willing to hire armed guards for high-risk vessels. These personnel are best armed with high-powered, large caliber firearms and scopes with which they can out-range the typical assault rifles carried by pirates. Body armor helps to protect them while they are targeting the pirates. Usually, the visible presence of prepared armed personnel deters pirates. Otherwise, the guards could escalate by firing warning shots to demonstrate their greater capabilities at long range. Night-vision equipment helps to maintain their superior range at night, although pirates increasingly use the same equipment.

The U.S. government has effectively encouraged private operators to acquire armed guards.

> The reality is that international naval forces simply might not be there to respond. The problem of piracy is one that can't simply be solved by national governments. Therefore, we have also supported industry's use of additional measures to ensure their security—such as the employment of armed security teams. To date, not a single ship with Privately Contracted Armed Security Personnel aboard has been pirated. Not a single one . . . At the State Department, we have encouraged countries to permit commercial vessels to carry armed teams. However, we do note that this is a new area, in which some practices, procedures, and regulations are still being developed. We are working through the Contact Group and the International Maritime Organization or IMO on these issues. For instance, we have advised that armed security teams be placed under the full command of the captain of the ship. The captain then is in control of the situation and is the one to authorize the use of any force. Last September [2011], we were encouraged to see language adopted by the IMO that revised the guidance to both flag States and ship operators and owners to establish the ship's master as being in command of these teams. (Andrew J. Shapiro, Assistant Secretary, Bureau of Political-Military Affairs, prepared remarks to the U.S. Chamber of Commerce, Washington, DC, March 13, 2012)

As of 2013, no vessel with armed guards has been hijacked. However, increased use of force deters some pirates while prompting others to be vengeful or trigger-happy. On April 14, 2009, Somali pirates announced by radio: "If they have started killing us, we have decided to take revenge and kill any American or French crew of passenger members of ships we capture fishing in our seas." In 2010, Somali pirates attacked two U.S. warships. On February 22, 2011, pirates shot to death four U.S. hostages on their yacht after the U.S. Navy detained two pirate negotiators.

Countering the Wider Networks

The UN, the Contact Group, and states agree that they must reduce the enabling conditions of piracy, not just the pirates at the point-of-attack, by stabilizing the countries where they are based, building local capacity to counter piracy, and pursuing the wider network of people who control, support, benefit from, or finance piracy.

The United States has led funding for such initiatives.

Our approach to combating piracy has also taken on new dimensions. In the effort to combat piracy, we are now targeting pirate ringleaders and their networks. While expanding security and prosecuting and incarcerating pirates captured at sea is essential, we also recognize that the pirates captured at sea are often low-level operatives. Their leaders and facilitators are ashore in Somalia and elsewhere relatively unaffected. After an intensive review of our strategy, Secretary Clinton last year approved a series of recommendations which, taken together, constitute a new strategic approach. A focus on pirate networks is at the heart of our strategy. (Andrew J. Shapiro, Assistant Secretary, Bureau of Political-Military Affairs, prepared remarks to the U.S. Chamber of Commerce, Washington, DC, March 13, 2012)

The current U.S. counter-piracy strategy emphasizes

- a multilateral approach (cooperating with other governments to enforce international law and build local capacity),
- military enforcement of international law,
- making the private sector more aware of "best management practices,"
- judicial prosecution of pirates and related criminals,
- stabilizing the areas where pirates proliferate, and
- targeting the wider pirate networks. (Thomas P. Kelly, Principal Deputy Assistant Secretary, Bureau of Political-Military Affairs, prepared remarks at Combating Piracy Week, London, October 25, 2012)

SUMMARY

This chapter has:

- described the scope of ground transport security,
- described the threats and hazards to ground transport, including
    - accidents and failures,
    - thieves, robbers, and hijackers, and
    - terrorists and insurgents,
- explained how to improve the security of ground transport via
    - the infrastructure,
    - navigation,
    - communications,
    - vehicle survivability, including resistance to kinetic projectiles, resistance to blast, access controls, stealth, and personal aid equipment,
    - mobility, and
    - escorts and guards,
- described the scope of civilian air transport security,
- noted the risks of aviation accidents,

- reviewed sovereign threats to civilian aviation,
- described aviation terrorism,
- explained how to improve aviation security via
  - cargo screening,
  - passenger luggage screening,
  - human access controls,
  - metallic screening,
  - footwear screening,
  - liquids screening,
  - clothing screening,
  - body screening,
  - intelligence,
  - in-flight security, and
  - countering antiaircraft weapons,
- described the scope of maritime security,
- described port security,
- described cargo security, including
  - safe traders,
  - manifest rules,
  - container security,
  - smart boxes, and
  - inspections at ports,
- reviewed maritime terrorist attacks,
- reviewed maritime terrorist flows,
- defined maritime piracy,
- explained how piracy works in practice,
- assessed the costs of piracy,
- reviewed the frequency of piracy,
- explained the geographical distribution of piracy, and
- explained how to counter piracy, by principally
  - legal responses,
  - naval enforcement,
  - ship defenses, and
  - countering the wider networks.

QUESTIONS AND EXERCISES

1. Describe different modes of ground transportation and why they become more or less important as an area becomes less stable or developed.
2. What compound risks arise from road traffic accidents?
3. Describe the three main ways in which terrorists and insurgents target ground transportation.

4. Describe routine activities necessary to secure the ground transport infrastructure.
5. How could you prepare for ground navigation in case of an emergency?
6. Explain why a vehicle's resistance to kinetic attacks can be antagonistic to blast resistance.
7. Describe the trade-off between a vehicle's overt survivability and stealth.
8. Describe the trade-off between a vehicle's survivability and mobility.
9. Describe the positive and negative risks of vehicle escorts and guards.
10. In what ways are sovereign threats to aviation greater than terrorist threats?
11. Why are terrorists focused on civilian aviation?
12. In what ways are cargo-only flights more or less risky than passenger flights?
13. In what ways do checked luggage need different screening than carry-on luggage?
14. In what ways can air side personnel pose risks?
15. How have terrorist passengers evaded controls on explosives?
16. Why are body imagers controversial?
17. For critics of screening technology, what is the alternative?
18. How is security provided against human threats already aboard a flight?
19. Why are MANPADS of more concern than other antiaircraft weapons?
20. What is the difference between the Container Security Initiative and the Smart Box Initiative?
21. What is the difference between maritime terrorist attacks and flows?
22. Why are maritime pirates difficult to identify before they attack?
23. Why did maritime piracy increase in the 2000s?
24. Why are the Gulf of Aden and the Indian Ocean riskiest for piracy?
25. Why are the known costs of piracy underestimated?
26. Why are laws against piracy difficult to enforce?
27. Why is naval enforcement of counter-piracy practically difficult?
28. What are the dilemmas and trade-offs in preparing a ship for defense against piracy?
29. What do officials mean by countering the wider pirate network?

Personal Security

Personal security refers to the individual person's security. Personal security obviously is affected by the security of whatever operations, infrastructure (Chapter 12), sites (Chapter 13), information (Chapter 14), and transport (Chapter 15) are used by the person, but personal security is focused more on the individual level. Be aware too that sometimes persons are categorized as *assets*, which is a term also used routinely to describe individual entities within infrastructure, and sometimes sites, information, transport vehicles, etc.—essentially anything of value. The differential valuation of some persons over others is usually captured by the term *very important persons* (VIPs).

The main sections below consider criminal threats to individual persons, personal injuries and accidents, care of the person's physiological health, and care of the person's psychological health.

 Crime

Personal security is often defined as security from crimes or criminal-like behaviors, particularly violence. For instance, the U.K. Ministry of Defense (MOD) (2009) defines personal security as "that part of human security which ensures protection of an individual from persecution, intimidation, reprisals and other forms of systematic violence" (p. 6).

The sections below describe criminal threats, how to assess a particular threat, how to manage them, how to train the person to avoid them, how to train the person to deter and defend against them, and close protection for the person.

Criminal Threats

Humans are hazards to each other because they could harm each other, even accidentally. Human hazards and threats are described in more detail in Chapter 4. This section is concerned with criminal threats to a particular person. A minority of humans deserve special attention as criminal threats—humans who have criminal intent and capability. The Humanitarian Practice Network (2010) identifies several human threats to the person, as described in the subsections below: crowds; thieves; detainers, kidnappers, and hostage takers; and sexual exploiters and aggressors.

Crowds

Crowds, mobs, and looters may start out with no intent against a particular person, but groups tend to become more reckless with size and could turn on a passer-by, someone who disturbs their malicious activities, or someone who blocks their path. At the personal level, such threats are controlled by avoiding their area or preventing their access to your area.

Thieves and Robbers

Thieves are usually looking for cash or valuable items fungible for cash. Thieves should be kept out of your area, you should avoid where they operate, or should you leave your valuable items in a more secure area. In unstable areas where more transactions are cash based, the procurement, transport, storage, and distribution of cash create special opportunities for thieves. If the use of cash cannot be restricted, the cash should be guarded, and the routines of handling cash should be varied.

Detainers, Kidnappers, and Hostage Takers

Others may arrest or detain the person without legal cause, perhaps to exploit the person for profit, sex, or political purpose. Kidnapping implies detention with intent to exchange the captive for something (usually money, but perhaps political concessions) from a third party. Hostage taking may mean kidnapping, but it implies holding hostages collateral to another operation, such as a robbery or a hijacking that turns into a siege. Abduction implies taking someone against their will, without specified purpose (Humanitarian Practice Network, 2010, p. 229).

Known areas where these activities happen should be avoided. Any remote area in a poorly governed state is likelier to suffer such activities, particularly where the locality is governed with the help of local militia or highly decentralized authorities. Routine activities should be varied, particularly travel to more remote or publicly exposed areas, such as open markets, or travel at the same time or from the same origin. Residences and the transport between home and work should be as secure as is the work site. Colleagues should be watched for collusion with external actors who would reward insiders for information on the movements or residences of valuable persons.

Potential victims should be prepared to assert their rights while not violating local customs. Family, friends, and managers of missing persons should be prepared to call upon trusted authorities, such as the local embassy or a professional kidnap and ransom crisis manager (some insurance policies provide for such a service), who is prepared to manage the negotiation, take care of the family, manage the press, and coordinate with the home country and local authorities. Most governments have a specialist department for managing citizen hostage crises. For instance, the U.S. Department of State's Bureau of Counterterrorism leads interagency partners to accomplish the safe recovery of hostages, bring hostage-takers to justice, and prevent future incidents. The Hostage Policy Subgroup refines and implements official U.S. policy.

In order not to encourage kidnapping and hostage taking, organizations and home countries usually state in advance their policy of not negotiating and downplay their capacity to pay ransoms or make concessions, but in practice, organizations and home countries usually negotiate and transact in pursuit of a safe outcome, even though they tend to keep everything secret so as not to encourage opportunists from copying the crime.

Pedagogy Box 16.1 UN Definition of Hostage Taking

"For the purposes of the present procedures, hostage taking is defined as the seizure or detention with a threat to kill, injure or to continue to detain staff members or their recognized dependents (hostages) in order to compel a third party, namely a state, the organization, a natural or juridical person or group of persons, to do or to abstain from doing any act as an explicit or implicit condition for the release of the hostages" (UN, 2006, pp. 6–7).

Sexual Exploiters and Aggressors

Sexual exploiters can harm all demographics but tend to target women, the young, representatives of other groups that are perceived to have caused a grievance, and different ethnic, religious, and political groups.

Sometimes the exploitation is a commercial transaction, with some volunteerism on each side, but one side may feel situationally compelled. Sometimes sexual aggression is used to punish the family of someone who was alleged to have committed some transgression against the sexual aggressors. Sometimes sexual aggression is associated with group bonding or initiation. In larger conflicts, rape can be organized and used to terrorize, intimidate, and expel an out-group.

Unfortunately, exposure, vulnerability, and threat may be unavoidable during a separate crisis, such as evacuation from a site that is under attack, but potential victims should avoid exposure, vulnerability, or threat by staying within a secure site. If they must travel, they should avoid travelling alone, at night, or during mass celebrations, or in ways that attract attention (such as a woman travelling alone in a culture that expects women to be escorted).

Insiders could manifest as sexual threats. For instance, more U.S. military women deployed to Afghanistan and Iraq were sexually assaulted by other soldiers than were ever harmed by the enemy. The rate of sexual assault by fellow soldiers rose around 2.5 times for women deployed to either of those countries compared to deployment in the United States. For 2011, U.S. Department of Defense counted around 3,000 cases of military sexual assault, although a report commissioned by the Office of the Secretary of Defense estimated the real frequency at 19,000. In late 2012, the Department of Veterans Affairs surveyed more than 1,100 anonymous women who had served in Afghanistan and Iraq and found that almost half said they had been sexually harassed, and nearly one quarter said they had been sexually assaulted.

Assessing a Particular Threat

Most criminal threats are outside of our control, at least until they commit a crime against us, when we should have some rights to self-defense, public intervention, and recourse to civil law. Organizations and managers have more control over criminal hazards whom they employ; indeed, organizations and managers usually have legal obligations to protect other employees and the general public from insider threats, while also helping the insider to avoid ever becoming a threat. Often the insider threat chooses a target within the same organization, particularly around the time of separation from the organization, when a disgruntled employee or former employee could seek vengeance on coworkers. Coemployment often generates particular conflicts between particular people, so usually the target is not random but had a prior social or professional relationship with the perpetrator. These preconditions suggest opportunities for intervention.

A useful profile of and scheme for assessing a particular human as a criminal threat to a particular person focus on the individual's psychology and cognition, as below:

- Intent: Most people have no premeditated malicious intent against any other, but two profiles are of concern:
    - Hunter: The hunter is intent on harming the target and is likely to stick to task. For instance, a premeditated murderer may stalk the victim, identify the victim's vulnerabilities, plan the attack, and execute the plan.
    - Howler: The howler harbors resentments or grievances without acting on them. So far as they act on them, they would stick to rhetorical rather than physical threats. For instance, they may anonymously send messages containing threats to harm but would not wish to expose themselves to the challenges or consequences of actually carrying out any of those threats. Although the howlers are not physically harmful in these examples, they can still be harmful. For instance, their rhetoric may be very stressful to the victim, and their threats may encourage the potential victims or police to engage in expensive counter-measures.
- Premeditation: Most crimes are not premeditated, but rather opportunistic.
    - Intended: The intended criminal had the conscious intent before the crime. A suggested path to intended violence starts with the same grievances and imaginings (ideation) of acting vengefully as would be experienced by the howler, but the intended criminal researches the target, plans the attack, prepares the attack, and executes the attack.
    - Impromptu: The impromptu criminal had some grievance, some intent to harm and some ideas about how to harm but had not prepared the crime before encountering the opportunity. An impromptu violent criminal is a criminal who planned some nonviolent harm, such as covert theft, but encountered the opportunity to thieve more through violence or reacted violently to the defender.
- Situational inhibitors: The situational inhibitors are the situational factors that inhibit the crime.
    - For instance, someone who is happily employed, married, and parenting seems to have more to lose than someone who is recently separated from their job, spouse, or children.
- Psychology: An individual's psychology can inhibit or not the crime.
    - Empathic people are aware of another's feelings, so empathic people can be inhibited from harming another if they empathize sufficiently with the other's feelings about the crime.
    - Nonempathic people may be aware of another's feelings in an abstract or nominal sense but not care. Criminals often prepare themselves or each other for crimes by talking up their carelessness or talking down the effects on the victim. Psychopathic criminals have a clinically recognizable inability to empathize.
- Affect: Affects are moods or temporary feelings that will affect the potential perpetrator's behavior.
    - For instance, a person who is intoxicated or drugged with a similar stimulant typically loses inhibitions.
    - Similarly, someone who is already stressed or angry is more likely to react angrily to a new provocation.

  - A few people suffer brain injuries or disorders, such as posttraumatic stress disorder, that reduce their control over their affects.
- Knowledge: A potential perpetrator would be more likely to act or would be harmful if they are more knowledgeable about how to harm the target.
  - For instance, former employees are more intimate with the site of employment or the employees than would be an outsider, so they are more likely to know how to break into a site or when to attack employees at their most vulnerable moment.
  - Similarly, a recently separated spouse or parent is much more knowledgeable about how to harm their spouse or children than would be the average person. (Calhoun & Weston, 2012, Chapter 1)

Managing Criminal Hazards and Threats

A simple process for managing human hazards and threats would follow at the least the following four steps:

1. Establish the facts at current time.
2. Assess the threat at current time.
3. Recommend ways to defend the potential target (reduce exposure and vulnerability).
4. Recommend a strategy for managing the hazard or threat.

Having assessed the hazard or threat, security managers face these choices of response:

- Nonconfrontational: The manager or organization does not directly confront the hazard or threat, but nevertheless investigates and chooses one of three main responses:
  - Take no further action for now.
  - Watch the hazard and wait for change. This watch would be
    - passive (wait for the hazard to do something exceptional that would come to your attention) or
    - active (order an extra observation or investigation).
  - Third-party control or monitoring of the hazard.
  - Direct interview of the hazard, with one of three main purposes:
    - Gather information about or from the hazard.
    - Assist the hazard to change or contain themselves.
    - Warn the hazard of the consequences of certain behaviors. (This option crosses into the confrontational actions, below.)
- Confrontational: The manager or organization directly confronts the hazard or threat, by one of four main actions:
  - Take administrative action to contain the hazard.
  - Refer the hazard to mental health treatment.
  - Request a civil restraining order.
  - Recommend that police should arrest the threat. (Calhoun & Weston, 2012, pp. 16–19)

Personal Avoidance of Criminal Hazards

Avoidance of crime is the main personal control on victimization. Someone who becomes a victim of crime in a high-crime area and who does not move or change their behavior is just as likely to be a victim in the future (and past victimization may harm their capacity to avoid future crime). One study suggests that 10% of the crime map experiences 60% of crime, 10% of offenders are responsible for about 50% of offenses, and 10% of victims suffer about 40% of crimes (Kennedy & Van Brunschot, 2009, pp. 69–72).

When looking for the specific attributes that make victimization more likely, we should be careful in our demographic assumptions. We could assume that the elderly and female are physically more vulnerable to crime, but while the elderly and female tend to report more fear of crime, young men suffer more crimes, partly because they attract competition from other young males, partly because young men are more socially active and thus more socially exposed (although women suffer more sexual crimes). Most crimes against young males are committed during the victim's social exposure, particularly where coincident with behaviors that liberate behavior, for instance, when out drinking alcohol at public bars. Most abuse of children, women, and the elderly occurs in the home, not in public settings. Despite the higher frequency of male targets, men report less fear (perhaps because they are socially or culturally conditioned to report less fear), while women normatively report more fear. Indeed, male victims of crime will report less fear than female nonvictims will report (Kennedy & Van Brunshot, 2009, pp. 32, 42–43).

Unfortunately, victims of past crimes are more likely to suffer a future crime. The British Crime Survey of 1992 suggests that half of victims are repeat victims and they suffer 81% of all reported crimes, of which 4% of victims experienced four or more crimes per year or 44% of all crimes. Some people must have some collection of attributes (sometimes termed *risk heterogeneity*) that make them more vulnerable; perhaps an event (such as illness) makes the person more vulnerable (*event dependence*); perhaps a crime harms the person in such a way that makes them more vulnerable in the future; some people were always more susceptible to threats, a propensity that has been described as *increased vulnerability*. For instance, past abuse acclimates the victim to abuse, while past success at abusing emboldens the abuser (Kennedy & Van Brunschot, 2009, pp. 65–67; Van Brunschot & Kennedy, 2008, p. 9). Training in crime prevention helped an experimental group of repeat victims to feel more informed about crime prevention, but unfortunately, did not reduce their level of fear or the likelihood of victimization (Davis & Smith, 1994).

Personnel can be trained to avoid hazards. Knowledge about the hazards is easiest to teach. Indeed, many commercial providers deliver courses on "hazardous environments," focusing on the hazards, including criminals, hazardous materials, and ordnance, that tend to proliferate in all unstable areas. Traditionally, such training has focused on terrorism and organized profit-motivated crimes, such as kidnap for ransom. A useful following course should focus on the particular hazards in the particular destination.

Knowledge about the hazards helps the consumer to recognize and avoid those hazards. Particular skills in avoidance could be taught, such as readiness for evacuation and the technical skills of evading pursuers.

Journalists, humanitarian aid workers, and frequent commercial travelers are the most likely consumers of such courses, but in a decreasingly stable world the demand is widening. Governments fill in some of the gap by offering advice, train-the-trainer courses, or direct training to citizens, especially to citizens residing in insecure countries. Officials might receive such courses from private providers but are more likely to receive them from official sources.

Pedagogy Box 16.2 U.S. Official Counter-Threat Courses

In the United States, the Diplomatic Security Service (part of the Department of State) delivered the Diplomatic Security Anti-terrorism Course (DSAC) through the 2000s, supplemented by the Diplomatic Security Anti-terrorism Course for Iraq (DSAC/IRAQ) after the increased demand for diplomats there from the mid-2000s. Subsequently, these courses were replaced by the Security Overseas Seminar (for all officials and family members aged at least 12 years) and the Foreign Affairs Counter Threat course (for riskier states such as Iraq). The latter includes evasive car driving and familiarization with firearms.

Personal Deterrence and Defense

Hazardous environment courses normally train a few basic skills, such as first aid, but they do not normally train skills in countering hazards, for fear of encouraging the consumers to be too provocative, but for more self-reliant situations, such as when official law enforcement has weakened, the consumers should be taught how to deter and defend themselves against attackers.

Defensive and deterrent strategies can be organized at the community level, such as Neighborhood Watch Schemes. At the personal level, potential victims of violent crime can be taught to survey their environment for potential criminals. In some societies they may be taught biomechanical and psychological self-defense skills (associated with martial arts). This vigilance could help the potential victim to avoid some threats; it could also persuade the potential criminal that the potential victim is a difficult target.

Unfortunately, many criminals are impulsive and do not make rational calculations about the target. Ideological criminals, such as religious terrorists, might rationally realize that a target is very difficult to attack but feel compelled to attack it anyway for ideological reasons—a target such as a site representing another religion or the official authority that defends that other religion.

Pedagogy Box 16.3 Neighborhood Watch Schemes

Neighborhood watch schemes started in the United States in 1972 under the sponsorship of the National Sheriffs' Association and quickly spread worldwide. They encourage neighbors to organize at levels as micro as a city block or residential street, in liaison with local police officers, to look out for and report local crimes, sometimes by active patrolling, usually by vigilant observation. Relatedly, many police forces have allocated community police officers to engage with residents at such micro levels. By the 2000s, about 40% of Americans and 25% of Britons lived within neighborhood watch schemes. These schemes effectively reduce the likelihood of crime by deterring criminals and by improving the likelihood of prosecuting criminals, thereby reducing the likelihood of repeat offenses (Kennedy & Van Brunschot, 2009, pp. 38–40).

Close Protection

Some officials receive personal protection (*close protection*) from guards. For instance, the U.S. Secret Service protects U.S. executive personnel and visiting executives. The U.S. Diplomatic Security protects the Secretary of State, foreign dignitaries visiting the United States, senior U.S. diplomats overseas, and U.S. athletes in major competitions.

Sometimes private individuals are granted official protection against certain threats. They can hire close protection from commercial providers or can employ guards directly. Private security proliferated in the 2000s, but some providers raised new risks, such as underperformance by guards or service providers who were not as competent or loyal as promised. Close protection also can stimulate local jealousies and opposition, particularly to pushy, trigger-happy, or culturally insensitive guards. Close protection has turned increasingly expensive, due to high demand, high turnover, high casualties, and increasing legal liabilities raised by local victims or former guards who had suffered injuries or stress during service. Official authorities funded most of the growth in private security contractors in Iraq and Afghanistan in the 2000s, but they have since realized their preferences for more internally controlled security—primarily military and police personnel.

Close protection involves mostly guarding the target person, escorting the person, and guarding the person's residences, offices, and means of transportation, and sometimes the person's wider family or social network. The activities of close protection extend beyond guarding the person in the moment; they include research on the hazards and threats, surveying sites (such as residences and offices), acquiring sites and vehicles, reconnoitering routes, and liaising with local authorities, although the latter may be unwilling or untrustworthy. Close protection tends to be most complicated when the person must travel or meet with the public.

The person faces trade-offs between close protection and stealth (prominent guards may deter but also attract attention), between close protection and external access (guards keep threats away but also discourage potential contributors), and between close protection and operational performance (guards may interrupt the person's work). For instance, the U.S. Ambassador to Libya (Chris Stevens) in 2012 had developed a reputation for proactive relations with local stakeholders, but the Accountability Review Board (December 18, 2012) retrospectively criticized his protections around the time of his death on September 11, 2012.

> The Board found that Ambassador Stevens made the decision to travel to [the U.S. Mission in] Benghazi [from the U.S. Embassy in Tripoli] independently of Washington, per standard practice. Timing for his trip was driven in part by commitments in Tripoli, as well as a staffing gap between principal officers in Benghazi. Plans for the Ambassador's trip provided for minimal close protection security support and were not shared thoroughly with the Embassy's country team, who were not fully aware of planned movements off compound. The Ambassador did not see a direct threat of an attack of this nature and scale on the US Mission in the overall negative trendline of security incidents from spring to summer 2012. His status as the leading US government advocate on Libya policy, and his expertise on Benghazi in particular, caused Washington to give unusual deference to his judgments.

Injuries and Accidents

This section covers personal injuries and accidents. The subsections below review the scope, violent injuries, work-related (occupational) accidents, fire and smoke hazards, and safety from animals.

Scope

Personal accidents and injuries are caused by trips, falls, collisions, acceleration injuries, sharp cuts, crushes, burns, electrocutions, drownings, and poisonings. The causes of injuries and accidents include external malicious actors, self-harm, and accidents. Accidents can be caused by somebody else's carelessness, the victim's own carelessness, faulty systems, or the victim's unfortunate coincidence with some hazard, like an unstable pavement.

An average accident or injury, such as a sprained ankle, may be of little long-term consequence, but they are very frequent (much more likely than crimes) and they can increase other risks, including crime and disease. The cumulative interaction between ill-health, violence, and accident is illustrated by this notional cycle: An unstable region is a less controlled environment; as controls decline, crimes and reckless behavior proliferate; if a person suffers a crime, they are more likely to suffer stress; as a person suffers stress, they are more likely to have an accident; while injured, the person is more likely to become ill, suffer another accident, or become a victim of crime. As a result of any of these events, the organization suffers the costs of caring for the person or of lost work. The person's carers may be exposed to disease, stress-related violence, or other trauma, which increase the chance that the carers suffer stress, an accident, or crime. The family and friends of each of these victims also are affected. The cumulative effects of all these events can disable a mission or cause such concern among friends and family or at higher levels that the mission is terminated.

In any employment, even in war zones, people are more likely to be harmed by accident than by malicious intent. Accident rates rise in unstable areas as public regulations and enforcement decline, judicial systems collapse, governments are corrupted, people behave more recklessly, become more stressed (stress is associated with cognitive inattention and physiological weakness), and operate more dangerous equipment (including weapons). The British military has admitted that more than half of its casualties during operations in Afghanistan from 2001 to 2009 were caused by human error.

For 2008 (the last year for which the World Health Organization estimated deaths globally), the World Health Organization (WHO) estimated that less than 9% (5 million) of global deaths (57 million) were caused by external causes of injuries, such as road traffic accidents, crime, or combat. Normal industrial and urban pollutants kill far more people through noncommunicable diseases such as lung cancer than through accidents.

Some injury rates seem to be decreasing but injury severity is increasing. The Global Burden of Disease Study (2012) found that the DALYs (disability-adjusted life years) lost to injuries as a proportion of all DALYs increased from 10% in 1990 to 11% in 2010, even though the overall numbers of DALYs remained practically the same. The explanations include the increased frequency and destructiveness of human-made systems that can harm, such as weapons and road vehicles.

Violent Injuries

According to the WHO (2009, 2012a), intentionally violent injuries caused 1.6 million deaths in 2004: 51% of these were by suicide, 37% by interpersonal violence, and 11% in wars and other mass conflicts.

The chance of violent injury or fatality is much higher in war than in civilian life (the chance of psychological harm is even higher). Of U.S. military personnel deployed to Afghanistan or Iraq from 2001 to 2011, 2% were wounded and 0.25% killed (data source: DOD). These might seem like low rates, but consider that 0.01% of Americans were killed by guns in America in 2010, mostly suicides (returning soldiers are much more likely suicides than are civilians). The rate of Americans killed by others in firearm crimes within America was 0.003% in 2010 (data source: U.S. Centers for Disease Control).

Work-Related Accidents

Of accidental deaths, road traffic accidents account for most deaths—these are described in Chapter 15 (transport security). Occupational (work-related) accidents and injuries are more frequent but normally less injurious.

Globally, occupational accidents and injuries kill about 350,000 people per year and disable or reduce the life expectancy of many more but account for just 1.7% of global DALYs.

The U.S. Department of Labor received reports for 2011 of nearly 3 million nonfatal workplace injuries and illnesses from private employers alone, a rate of 3.5 cases per 100 equivalent full-time workers. More than half of cases affected the employee's duties or time on work. Almost all of the cases (95%) were nonfatal injuries, not illnesses.

Employees bear the burden of these accidents if they are not granted paid time off work or compensation. Employers bear the burden when they turnover employees due to accidents, pay compensation, or pay for insurance against the risks. Often laws and regulations or the tort system obliges employers to bear these burdens.

Fire and Smoke

Fire and smoke are inherent to certain occupations, such as waste disposal and home cooking on open fires. Fire can burn people and property, produces smoke harmful to the lungs and the natural environment, and could spread out of control. People are more likely to escape fire than smoke; smoke can drift over populations remote to the fire and can linger for days afterwards. A fire does not need to be out of control to be harmful—people who use more open fires for heating or cooking inevitably breathe in more smoke. Smoke is inherently harmful because some of its inherent components, such as carbon dioxide, are poisonous. Hard particles, primarily soot, also damage the lungs. Breathing in smoke at best is uncomfortable, causing coughing and shortness of breath. These simple effects also leave the victim more vulnerable to severe respiratory diseases, such as bronchitis. Additionally, smoke will be more hazardous where hazardous materials, such as carcinogenic plastics and asbestos, are being burned.

Unstable areas are associated with more open fires, as closed forms of heating and cooking, such as natural gas fired ovens, fuel lines, and electricity systems break down or are damaged. Additionally, people turn to open fires in order to dispose of trash and carcasses when public waste disposal services break down. Conflict is associated with more unnatural fires as kinetic weapons damage electrical systems (a source of ignition), fuel lines, and water distribution systems (which firefighting services normally would tap into in order to fight the fires).

Pedagogy Box 16.4 Burn Pits in Afghanistan and Iraq

In Afghanistan (since 2001) and Iraq (since 2003), American contractors were ordered to dispose of trash, including feces and construction material, from U.S. military and other official sites. They usually chose to set fire to huge collections of trash, contained by nothing more than a pit in the ground (*burn pit*). In 2008 and 2009, former contracted and military personnel filed more than 20 class action law suits against Kellogg, Brown, & Root (a contractor that had used around 25 repeat burn pits in Afghanistan and Iraq) for medical problems that they blamed on burn pits. In August 2010, 241 Americans sued in a case that remains unresolved. By then, U.S. military guidelines allowed burn pits only temporarily until more contained disposal systems could be set up, but military operations and delivery problems often delay such a transition. For instance, on April 25, 2013, the Special Inspector General for Afghanistan Reconstruction released a report that criticized Forward Operating Base Salerno in eastern Afghanistan for using burn pits after the acquisition in 2010 of incinerators that never worked and were too noisy for use at night in a combat zone.

Animals

Animals such as rats and mosquitoes can be vectors of disease; larger animals, such as dogs, have the capacity to be violent enough to kill. Their populations tend to rise in unstable areas, where owners have fled and public services have broken down. Uncollected trash supports rats, dogs, cats, and birds that scavenge. Standing water supports the propagation of mosquitoes and certain harmful worms and bacteria. These environmental changes support the propagation of these species, while controls on their population growth are declining, primarily public pest control services. Additionally, unstable human populations tend to lose control of their pets or to release pets to fend for themselves.

Pedagogy Box 16.5 Feral Dogs in Iraq, 2003–2010

After the U.S.-led invasion of Iraq in 2003, stray dogs in Baghdad reached a population of 1.25 million. These dogs stirred up trash, distributed hazardous materials, vectored diseases, and formed aggressive packs that sometimes attacked people. These dogs could work themselves inside the protected perimeters of military or humanitarian bases where humans would be deterred or easily observed. In the first years of the occupation, soldiers were practically the only control on such dogs, but their actions often created new risks, such as injured suffering animals and dead animals that were not removed and thus attracted other scavengers or vectored other diseases. In late 2008, the Baghdad provincial government started to cull stray dogs, with a surge in culls in 2010 after receiving more resources to support the activities.

Physiological Health Care

Managing personal and personnel health is a responsibility shared between the person and the organization, with considerable legal liabilities for the organization if the person suffers any harm in the course of employment, although organizations are often prohibited from discriminating against applicants by health.

Organizations have more choice when selecting personnel for some new assignment or deployment, when managers should

- assess the person's health in advance;
- assess the minimum health standards for the assigned tasks and mission;

- assess health care capacity at the point of assignment or deployment;
- assess the person's personal and corporate insurance coverage and if necessary adjust;
- directly control any gaps between personnel needs and local capacity, such as by providing a particular medication or service that is not provided locally, acquiring medical staff to replace dissatisfactory local medical skills, and acquiring safe blood and plasma in replacement of locally screened blood transfusions; and
- prepare for repatriation of incapacitated employees.

Psychological Health

Psychological health tends to be more difficult to assess and provide than physiological health. As described above, organizations and individuals share an interest in not exposing psychologically dysfunctional people to situations that exacerbate psychological conditions. Ideally, those with psychological ill-health should not be employed in such situations, but often regulations prevent an employer from discovering such ill-health until it manifests during employment. Stress is the main situational cause of ill-health and is subject to control. The subsections below describe stress and how to manage it.

Stress

Operational psychological health issues are likely to arise from or be exacerbated by stress during operations. Stress is useful where it helps the person to focus on a task or avoid a risk, but severe or routine stress is debilitating, in two main ways:

1. Cumulative stress is accumulated from lots of stressful events. Cumulative stress leads to exhaustion, which is associated with declining performance and increased susceptibility to other health problems.
2. Traumatic stress arises from exposure to a particularly traumatic event, such as physical or emotional loss or a life-threatening event. Such events are infrequent for most people but can become likely in unstable or conflicted areas. Even though a minority of soldiers are dedicated to combat roles, during current deployments most seem to observe at least the after-effects of life-threatening events.

Stress develops clinically in two main presentations:

- Acute stress disorders are quick to develop, within hours or days, and are often described as emotional breakdowns.
- Posttraumatic stress disorders (PTSDs) are delayed, sometimes years, often because the victim is focused on the immediate mission or on more direct risks.

The common symptoms of stress include fatigue, extreme imbalances between work and sleep, sleeping problems, negative feelings such as depression, irritability, extreme emotions, social withdrawal, and substance abuse.

The consequences of negative stress include psychological problems (extending to self-harm and suicide), physiological health problems (a stressed person is more likely to have an accident or contract a disease), social problems (such as interpersonal conflict), and professional problems (such as task nonperformance and time off work). The lifetime costs, such as extra health care, missed work, and opportunity costs, often are underestimated.

The effects extend from the employees to their families and friends. Stress, particularly PTSD, causes periodic or chronic psychological issues that can be debilitating for the victim and for society. PTSD is linked with self-harm and violence against others.

Certain people are more susceptible to stress, often because of past cumulative stress or trauma, or a psychologically vulnerable situation that preceded the operation. Certain tasks, situations, and locations are particularly stressful.

Pedagogy Box 16.6 U.S. Military PTSD Since 2003

About one-third of U.S. soldiers are diagnosed with PTSD after operational deployments. (The real rate is probably higher, at least 75% by some professional estimates: See Rosenbau, 2013.) In 2012, suicides by U.S. military personnel reached a record high (349), more than soldiers killed in combat in Afghanistan that year (229).

Pedagogy Box 16.7 Criminal Violence Due to Military PTSD

A study of British military veterans of wars in Afghanistan and Iraq suggests that combat roles, exposure to traumatic events, and posttraumatic stress disorder each increase the frequency of violent offenses after return home. The violent offenders included:

- 6.3% of those in the sample who had deployed in a combat role, compared to 2.4% in a noncombat role;
- 5.1% of those exposed to 5 to16 traumatic events, 4.1% of those exposed to 2 to 4 traumatic events, and 1.6% of those exposed to none or one traumatic event;
- 8.6% of those with posttraumatic stress disorder, compared to 3.0% of those without (MacManus et al., 2013).

Managing Stress

Managing stress is a responsibility shared between the individual, organization, and society. Generally, managing stress involves iterating the person's exposure to stress (so that the victim can recover between exposures), training awareness of stress, training relaxation and other stress relief, encouraging opportunities for social support, encouraging social cohesion, encouraging positive leadership, and intervening with medical help in extreme cases (Newsome, 2007, Chapter 4). The Humanitarian Practice Network (2010) admits "the management of stress" as "a dimension of security management. Like security more generally, managing stress is both an individual and an organizational responsibility" (p. 129).

In effect, personal security trades controls on the stressors with acceptance of the stress. Some external management of stress can be counter-productive. For instance, preparing personnel for some stressors may make them more sensitive to them. Similarly, mental health care providers who attempt to encourage personnel to externalize their stress often draw attention to stress and encourage personnel to be symptomatic. Additionally, some related predeployment activities can introduce new stresses, such as preparing a will or leaving instructions for family and friends in case of death.

Pedagogy Box 16.8 U.S. Diplomatic Personnel Stress

"When you're out on the front lines representing America today, you would be foolish to feel too secure. On the other hand, we know that's part of the package and we know that our government . . . is making a sincere effort to provide the security for personnel first and facilities second." (President of the American Foreign Service Association, Susan Johnson, in answer to a question about how secure diplomatic personnel feel overseas, posed after the death of four US personnel during the attack on the US diplomatic outpost in Benghazi, Libya, 11 September 2012, in: Joe Davidson, 24 September 2012, "Foreign Service workers know risks come with job," Washington Post).

SUMMARY

This chapter has described

- criminal threats to the person, including crowds, thieves and robbers, detainers, kidnappers, and hostage takers, and sexual exploiters and aggressors,
- how to assess a particular criminal threat to a particular target,
- how to manage a particular criminal threat,
- personal avoidance of threats,
- personal deterrence and defense,
- close protection for the person,
- the scope of injuries and accidents in general,
- violent injuries,
- work-related accidents,
- fire and smoke hazards,
- animal hazards,
- managing the physiological health of the person, and
- managing the psychological health of the person, including managing stress.

QUESTIONS AND EXERCISES

1. What are the differences between criminal threats to the person and criminal threats to sites?
2. What could motivate a criminal interest in a particular person?
3. What differentiates a threatening person from a hazard?
4. What are your options for managing a criminal hazard within your organization?
5. What are your options for managing a criminal threat within your organization?
6. What minimum knowledge and skills should you expect when being trained for a hazardous environment?
7. What are the extra negative risks associated with the acquisition of close protection?
8. When would you expect accident rates to rise?
9. Why are accident, illness, and stress rates correlated?
10. Why would you expect increased frequency of fire in an unstable area?
11. Under what circumstances does someone become more exposed to smoke?
12. What are the personal risks associated with feral animals?
13. What control on the risks from smoke would increase the risks from feral animals?
14. What should a manager assess about a person's health before allocation to a particular task or operation?
15. How can stress be managed during an operation?

References

Accountability Review Board for Benghazi. (2012, December 18). Retrieved from http://www.state.gov/documents/organization/202446.pdf

Adams, J. (1995). *Risk*. London, UK: Routledge.

Association of Insurance and Risk Managers, ALARM The National Forum for Risk Management in the Public Sector, & The Institute of Risk Management. (2002). *A risk management standard*. London, UK: Authors.

Alexander, D. E. (2000). *Confronting catastrophe: New perspectives on natural disasters*. Fairfax, VA: Terra Publishing.

Alkema, L., Kantorova, V., Menozzi, C., & Biddlecom, A. (2013). National, regional, and global rates and trends in contraceptive prevalence and unmet need for family planning between 1990 and 2015: A systematic and comprehensive analysis. *The Lancet, 381*(9878), 1642–1652. doi:10.1016/S0140-6736(12)62204-1

Anarumo, M. (2011). The practitioner's view of the terrorist threat. In L. W. Kennedy & E. F. McGarrell (Eds.), *Crime and terrorism risk: Studies in criminology and criminal justice* (pp. 56–79). New York, NY: Routledge.

Anderson, D. (2012). *The terrorism acts in 2011: Report of the independent reviewer on the operation of the Terrorism Act 2000 and Part 1 of the Terrorism Act 2006*. London, UK: The Stationery Office.

Andreas, P. (2003). *The rebordering of America: Integration and exclusion in a new security context*. New York, NY: Routledge.

Ansell, J., & Wharton, F. (1992). *Risk: Analysis, assessment, and management*. Chichester, UK: Wiley.

Australian and New Zealand Joint Technical Committee. (2009). *Risk management: Principles and guidelines* (AS/NZS ISO 31000). Sydney: Standards Australia, and Wellington: Standards New Zealand.

Bakker, E. (2012). Forecasting terrorism: The need for a more systematic approach. *Journal of Strategic Security, 5*(4), 69–84.

Bar-Or, Y. (2012). *Crazy little risk called love: Wiser decisions, better relationships*. Ellicott City, MD: TLB Publishing.

Barkawi, T., & Brighton, S. (2011). Powers of war: Fighting, knowledge, and critique. *International Political Sociology, 5*(2), 126–143.

Baylis, J., & Wirtz, J. J. (2002). Introduction. In J. Baylis, J. Wirtz, E. Cohen, & C. S. Gray (Eds.), *Strategy in the Contemporary World* (pp. 1–14). Oxford, UK: Oxford University Press.

Beck, U. (1992). *Risk society: Towards a new modernity*. (M. Ritter Trans.). London, UK: SAGE.

Beck, U. (1995). *Ecological Enlightenment: Essays on the politics of the risk society*. (M. Ritter Trans.). New York, NY: Prometheus Books.

Berwick, D. M., & Hackbarth, A. D. (2012). Eliminating waste in US health care. *Journal of the American Medical Association, 307*(14), 1513–1516.

Betts, R. K. (1997). Should strategic studies survive? *World Politics, 50*(1), 7–33.

Beyer, C. C. (2008). Understanding and explaining international terrorism: On the interrelation between human and global security. *Human Security Journal, 7*, 62–74.

Biddle, S. D. (2004). *Military power: Explaining victory and defeat in modern battle*. Princeton, NJ: Princeton University Press.

Blainey, G. (1988). *The causes of war* (3rd ed.). New York, NY: Free Press.

Blumenthal, L. (2005). *Funding appropriation for U.S. seaports: A brief analysis of the methods, factors, and consequences of the allocations of resources for port security* (Report No. 05-021). Los Angeles, CA: University of Southern California.

Borgeson, K., & Valeri, R. (2008). *Terrorism in America*. Sudbury, MA: Jones & Bartlett.

Borum, R. (2004). *Psychology of terrorism*. Tampa, FL: University of Florida.

Bracken, P., Bremmer, I., & Gordon, D. (Eds.). (2008). *Managing strategic surprise: Lessons from risk management and risk assessment*. Cambridge, UK: Cambridge University Press.

Branscomb, L. M., & Auerswald, P. E. (2001). *Taking technical risks: How innovators, executives, and investors manage high-tech risks*. Cambridge, MA: MIT Press.

Bremer III, L. P. (2002). International and domestic terrorism. In National Research Council (Ed.), *High-Impact terrorism: Proceedings of a Russian-American workshop* (pp. 53–68). Washington, DC: National Academy Press.

Bricker, J., Kennickell, A. B., Moore, K. B., & Sabelhaus, J. (2012). Changes in US family finances from 2007 to 2010: Evidence from the survey of consumer finances. *Federal Reserve Bulletin, 98*(2).

British Standards Institution, Robbins, M., & Smith, D. (2000). *Managing risk for corporate governance*. (PD 6668). London, UK: Author.

British Standards Institution. (2009). *Risk management: Principles and guidelines* (BSI ISO 31000). London, UK: Author.

Bullock, J. A., Haddow, G. D., & Coppola, D. P. (2013). *Introduction to homeland security: Principles of all-hazards risk management* (4th ed.). Waltham, MA: Butterworth-Heinemann.

Burns-Howell, T., Cordier, P., & Eriksson, T. (2003). *Security risk assessment and control*. Basingstoke, UK: Palgrave Macmillan.

Buzan, B. (1991). *People, states and fear: An agenda for international security studies in the post-cold war era* (2nd ed.). Harlow, UK: Longman.

Byman, D. (2009). US counter-terrorism options: A taxonomy. In R. Howard, R. Sawyer, & N. Bajema (Eds.), *Terrorism and counterterrorism: Understanding the new security environment* (3rd ed., pp. 460–482). New York, NY: McGraw-Hill.

Calhoun, F. S., & Weston, S. W. (2012). *Concepts and case studies in threat management*, Boca Raton, FL: CRC Press.

Canada Department of National Defense. (2002). *Peace support operations*. Ottawa: Author.

Cappelli, D., Moore, A., Trzeciak, R., & Shimeall, T. J. (2009). *Common sense guide to prevention and detection of insider threats* (3rd ed.,Version 3.1). Pittsburg, PA: Carnegi Mellon University.

Carter, B., Hancock, T., Morin, J., & Robins, N. (1996). *Introducing RISKMAN: The European project risk management methodology*. London, UK:Wiley.

Cashman, G., & Robinson, L. C. (2007). *An introduction to the causes of war: Patterns of interstate conflict from World War I to Iraq*. Lanham, MD: Rowman & Littlefield.

CERT Insider Threat Center. (2012). Retrieved from www.cert.org/insider_threat/

Chalk, P. (2009). Sunken treasures: The economic impetus behind modern piracy. *RAND Review, 33*(2), 10–13.

Chalk, P., Hoffman, B., Reville, R., & Kasupski, A. (2005). *Trends in terrorism: Threats to the United States and the future of the Terrorism Risk Reinsurance Act*. Santa Monica, CA: RAND.

Chapman, C. B., & Ward, S. C. (2002). *Managing project risk and uncertainty*. Chichester, UK: Wiley.

Clarke, R. (2008). *Your government failed you: Breaking the cycle of national security disasters*. New York, NY: Harper.

Clarke, R. V., & Newman, G. (2006). *Outsmarting the terrorists*. London, UK: Praeger Security International.

Collier, P. (2009). *Wars, guns, and votes: Democracy in dangerous places*. New York, NY: Harper.

Collier, P., & Hoeffler, A. (2004). Aid, policy and growth in post-conflict societies. *European Economic Review, 48*(5), 1125–1145.

Correlates of war. Inter-state war dataset [Version 3]. Retrieved from http://www.correlatesofwar.org/cow2%20data/WarData/InterState/Inter-State%20War%20Format%20%28V%203-0%29.htm

Cox, D., Levine, M., & Newman, S. (2009). *Politics most unusual: Violence, sovereignty and democracy in the 'war on terror'*. New York, NY: St. Martin's Press.

Dahl, R. A. (1971). *Polyarchy: Participation and opposition*. New Haven, CT: Yale University Press.

Danzig, R., Sageman, M., Leighton, T., Hough, L., Yuki, H., Kotani, R., & Hosford, Z. M. (2012). *Aum Shinrikyo: Insights into how terrorists develop biological and chemical weapons* (2nd ed.). Washington, DC: Center for a New American Security.

Davis, P. K. (2003). Uncertainty-Sensitive planning. In S. E. Johnson, M. C. Libicki, & G. F. Treverton (Eds.), *New challenges, new tools for defense decisionmaking* (pp. 131–155). Santa Monica, CA: RAND.

Davis, R. C., & Smith, B. (1994). Teaching victims crime prevention skills: Can individuals lower their risk of crime? *Criminal Justice Review, 19*(1), 56–68.

Denning, D. E. (1998). Cyberspace attacks and countermeasures. In D. E. Denning & P. J. Denning (Eds.), *Internet besieged: Countering cyberspace scofflaws* (pp. 29–55). New York, NY: ACM Press.

Dixon, L., & Kaganoff Stern, R. (2004). *Compensation for losses from the 9/11 terrorist attacks*. Santa Monica, CA: RAND.

Edwards, J., & Gomis, B. (2011). *Islamic terrorism in the UK Since 9/11: Reassessing the 'soft' response.* London, UK: Chatham House.

Ender, M. G. (2009). *American soldiers in Iraq: McSoldiers or innovative professionals?* New York, NY: Routledge.

Feldman, D. (2013). *Rules of victory for future international conflict.* Retrieved from Russian International Affairs Council website: http://russiancouncil.ru/en/inner/?id_4=1372#top

Fillmore, C. J., & Atkins, B. T. (1992). Towards a frame-based lexicon: The semantics of RISK and its neighbors. In A. Lehrer & E. Kittay (Eds.), *Frames, fields, and contrasts: New essays in semantics and lexical organization* (pp. 75–102). Hillsdale, NJ: Lawrence Erlbaum Associates.

F.M. Global. (2010). *The risk/earnings ratio: New perspectives for achieving bottom-line stability.* Windsor, UK: FM Insurance Company.

Flynn, S. E., & Kirkpatrick, J. J. (2004). *The limitations of the current cargo container* targeting. Retrieved from http://www.cfr.org/border-and-port-security/limitations-current-cargo-container-targeting/p6907

FrameNet: https://framenet.icsi.berkeley.edu

Freedom House. (2012). Freedom on the net: A global assessment of Internet and digital media. Retrieved from http://www.freedomhouse.org/sites/default/files/resources/FOTN%202012%20Summary%20of%20Findings.pdf

Friedman, B. (2010). Managing fear: The politics of homeland security. In B. H. Friedman, J. Harper, & C. A. Preble (Eds.), *Terrorizing ourselves: Why US counterterrorism policy is failing and how to fix it* (pp. 185–211). Washington, DC: Cato Institute.

Fund for Peace. (2011). *Conflict assessment indicators: The fund for peace country analysis indicators and their measures.* Washington, DC: Author.

Gaines, L. K., & Kappeler, V. E. (2012). *Homeland security*. Boston, MA: Prentice Hall/Pearson.

Gleditsch, K. S., & Ward, M. D. (1997). Double take: A reexamination of democracy and autocracy in modern politics. *Journal of Conflict Resolution, 41*(3), 361–383.

Global Burden of Disease Study. (2012). Disability-Adjusted life years (DALYs) for 291 diseases and injuries in 21 regions, 1990–2010: A systematic analysis for the global burden of disease study 2010. *The Lancet, 380*(9859), 2197–2223.

Goldstone, J. A., Bates, R. H., Epstein, D. L., Gurr, T. R., Lustik, M. B., Marshall, M. G., Julfelder, J., & Woodward, M. (2010). A global model for forecasting political instability. *American Journal of Political Science, 54*(1), 190–208.

Google Ngram: http://books.google.com/ngrams

Greenberg, M. D., Chalk, P., Willis, H. H., Khilko, I., & Ortiz, D. S. (2006). *Maritime terrorism: Risk and liability*. Santa Monica, CA: RAND.

Guilhot, N. (2008). The realist gambit: Postwar American political science and the birth of international relations theory. *International Political Sociology, 2*(4), 281–304.

Haddon-Cave, C. (2009). *The Nimrod review: An independent review into the broader issues surrounding the loss of the RAF Nimrod MR2 Aircraft XV230 in Afghanistan in 2006.* London, UK: The Stationery Office.

Harrison, M., & Wolf, N. (2011). The frequency of wars. *Economic History Review, 65*(3), 1055–1076.

Hartmann, G. C., & Myers, M. B. (2001). Technical risk, product specifications, and market risk. In L. M. Branscomb & P. E. Auerswald (Eds.), *Taking technical risks: How innovators, executives, and investors manage high-tech risks* (pp. 30–56). Cambridge, MA: MIT Press.

Heerkens, G. R. (2002). *Project management.* New York, NY: McGraw-Hill.

Herman, M. (1996). *Intelligence power in peace and war.* Cambridge, MA: Cambridge University Press.

Hessl, A. E. (2011). Pathways for climate change effects on fire: Models, data, and uncertainties. *Progress in Physical Geography, 35*(3), 393–407.

Hicks, M. H., Dardagan, H., Bagnall, P. M., Spagat, M., & Sloboda, J. A. (2011). Casualties in civilians and coalition soldiers from suicide bombings in Iraq, 2003–10: A descriptive study. *The Lancet, 378*(9794), 906–914.

Heidelberg Institute for International Conflict Research. (2011). *Conflict barometer 2011*. Heidelberg, Germany: Author.

Hillson, D. A. (2003). *Effective opportunity management for projects: Exploiting positive risk.* New York, NY: Marcel Dekker.

Hoffman, B. (1999). *Inside terrorism.* London, UK: Indigo.

Hoffman, B. (2001). Change and continuity in terrorism. *Studies in Conflict and Terrorism, 24*(5), 417–428.

Horowitz, M. C., & Tetlock, P. E. (2012). Trending upward: How the intelligence community can better see into the future. *Foreign Policy*. Retrieved from http://www.foreignpolicy.com/articles/2012/09/06/trending_upward

Humanitarian Practice Network. (2010). *Operational security management in violent environments* (Number 8, new edition). London, UK: Overseas Development Institute.

Institute for Economics and Peace. (2012). *Global peace index* 2012. Sydney, Australia: Author.

Intergovernmental Panel on Climate Change. (2007). *Climate change 2007: Synthesis report.* Contribution of Working Groups I, II, and III to the Fourth Assessment Report of the Intergovernmental Panel on Climate Change [R. K. Pachauri & A. Reisinger (Eds.)]. Geneva, Switzerland: Author. International Crisis Group (2008). *Reforming Haiti's security sector,* Latin American/Caribbean (Report No. 28). Brussels, Belgium: Author.

International Risk Governance Council. (2006). *Risk governance: Towards an integrative approach.* Geneva, Switzerland: Author.

International Risk Governance Council. (2008). *An Introduction to the IRGC Risk Governance Framework.* Geneva, Switzerland: Author.

International Organization for Standardization. (November, 2009a). *Risk Management: Vocabulary* (ISO Guide 73). Geneva, Switzerland: Author.

International Organization for Standardization (November, 2009b). *Principles and Guidelines on Implementation* (ISO 31000). Geneva, Switzerland: Author.

International Union for Conservation of Nature and Natural Resources. (2008). *The 2008 review of the IUCN red list of threatened species.* Gland, Switzerland: Author.

Jablonowski, M. (2009). *Managing high-stakes risk: toward a new economics for survival.* Houndmills, UK: Palgrave Macmillan.

Jackson, J. (2006). Introducing fear of crime to risk research. *Risk Analysis, 26*(1), 253–264.

Jackson, W. (2013a). Threat predictions for 2012: The hits and misses. *Government Computer News, 32*(1), 20–21.

Jackson, W. (2013b). Surviving your next denial-of-service disaster. *Government Computer News, 32*(2), 24–27.

Kaplan, R. S., & Mikes, A. (2012). Managing risks: A new framework. *Harvard Business Review, 90*(2), 48–59.

Keeley, J. E. (2005). Fire history of the San Francisco East Bay region and implications for landscape patterns. *International Journal of Wildland Fire, 14*, 285–296.

Kennedy, L. W., & Van Brunschot, E. (2009). *The risk in crime.* Lanham, MD: Rowman & Littlefield.

Kennedy, L. W., Marteache, N., & Gaziarifoglu, Y. (2011). Global risk assessment: The search for a common methodology. In L. W. Kennedy & E. F. McGarrell (Eds.), *Crime and terrorism risk: Studies in criminology and criminal justice* (pp. 29–53). New York, NY: Routledge.

Kent, S. (1964). Words of estimative probability. *Studies in Intelligence, 8*(4), 49–65.

Knight, F. H. (1921). *Risk, uncertainty, and profit.* Boston, MA: Houghton Mifflin.

Krueger, A. B., & Laitin, D. D. (2004). Misunderstanding terrorism. *Foreign Affairs, 83*(5), 8–13.

Kupchan, C. (2010). *How enemies become friends: The sources of stable peace.* Princeton, NJ: Princeton University Press.

Kupfer, J. M., & Bond, E. U. (2012). Patient satisfaction and patient-centered care: Necessary but not equal. *Journal of the American Medical Association, 308*(2), 139–140.

Kurzman, C. (2013). *Muslim-American terrorism: declining further.* Chapel Hill, NC: Triangle Center on Terrorism and Homeland Security.

Lacqeur, W. (1977). *Terrorism.* Boston, MA: Little, Brown.

Lee, R. (2002). *Terrorist financing: The US and international response.* Washington, DC: Congressional Research Service.

Leveson, Right Honourable Lord Justice. (2012). *An inquiry into the culture, practices, and ethics of the press* (HC779). London: The Stationery Office.

Lino, M. (2012). *Expenditures on children by families.*Washington, DC: U.S. Department of Agriculture.

Lowrance, W. W. (1976). *Of acceptable risk: Science and determination of safety.* Los Altos, CA: Kaufmann.

Luft, G., & Korin, A. (2004). Terrorism goes to sea. *Foreign Affairs, 83*(6), 61–71.

MacManus, D., Dean, K., Jones, M., Rona, R. J., Greenberg, N., Hull, L., Fahy, T., Wessely, S., & Fear, N.T. (2013). Violent offending by UK military personnel deployed to Iraq and Afghanistan: A data linkage cohort study. *The Lancet, 381*(9870), 907–917.

Mandiant. (2013). *APT1: Exposing one of China's cyber cspionage cnits.* Alexandria,VA: Author.

Marcott, S. A., Shakun, J. D., Clark, P. U., Mix, P. U. (2013). A reconstruction of regional and global temperature for the past 11,300 years. *Science, 339*(6124), 1198–1201.

Marshall, M. G., & Cole, B. R. (2011). *Global report 2011: Conflict, governance, and state fragility.* Vienna, VA: Center for Systemic Peace.

Masse, T., O'Neil, S., & Rollins, J. (2007). *The Department of Homeland Security's risk assessment methodology: Evolution, issues, and options for Congress* (Report No. RL33858). Washington, DC: Congressional Research Service.

Mateski, M., Trevino, C. M., Veitch, C. K., Michalski, J., Harris, J. M., Maruoka, S., & Frye, J. (March 2012). *Cyber threat metrics* (Report No. SAND2012-2427). Albuquerque, NM: Sandia National Laboratories.

McChrystal, S. A. (2009). COMISAF's Initial Assessment to Secretary of Defense. Retrieved from http://media.washingtonpost.com/wp-srv/politics/documents/Assessment_Redacted_092109.pdf?sid=ST2009092003140

McGurn, W. (1987). *Terrorist or freedom fighter? The cost of confusion.* London, UK: Institute for European Defense and Strategic Studies.

McNabb, D. E. (2010). *Research methods for political science: Quantitative and qualitative approaches.* Armonk, NY: M.E. Sharpe.

Meltzer, J. (2011). *After Fukushima: What's next for Japan's energy and climate change policy?* Washington, DC: Brookings Institution.

MeriTalk. (2010). The encryption enigma. Retrieved from http://www.meritalk.com/encryption-enigma.php

Miller, G., & Nakashima, E. (2012, November 17). FBI investigation of Broadwell reveals Bureau's comprehensive access to electronic communications. *Washington Post.*

Molak, V. (Ed.). (1997). *Fundamentals of risk analysis and risk management.* Boca Raton, FL: CRC.

Mowatt-Larssen, R. (2010). *Al Qaeda weapons of mass destruction threat: Hype or reality*? Cambridge, MA: Belfer Center for Science and International Affairs.

Mueller, J. (2005). Six rather unusual propositions about terrorism. *Terrorism and Political Violence, 17*(4), 487–505.

Mueller, J. (2006). Is there still a terrorist threat? The myth of the omnipresent enemy. *Foreign Affairs, 12*(1), 2–8.

Munch, G. L., & Verkuillen, J. (2002). Conceptualizing and measuring democracy. *Comparative Political Studies. 35*(1), 5–34.

Nash, R., & Featherstone, H. (2010). *Coughing up: Balancing tobacco income and costs in society.* London, UK: Policy Exchange.

Nelson, R., & Sanderson, T. M. (2011). *Confronting an uncertain threat: The future of Al-Qaida and associated movements.* Washington, DC: Center for Strategic and International Studies.

NetWitness. (2010, February).The 'Kneber' BotNet—A Zeus discovery and analysis whitepaper. Retrieved from http://krebsonsecurity.com/wp-content/uploads/2011/01/NetWitness-WP-The-Kneber-BotNet.pdf

Newsome, B. (2006). Expatriate games: Interorganizational coordination and international counterterrorism. *Studies in Conflict and Terrorism, 1*(29), 75–89.

Newsome, B. (2007). *Made, not born: Why some soldiers are better than others.* Westport, CT: Praeger Security International/ABC-CLIO.

Newsome, B., & Floros, C. (July 2008). Building counter-terrorism capacity across borders: Lessons from the defeat of "revolutionary organization November 17th." *Journal of Security Sector Management, 6*(2), 1–14.

Newsome, B., & Floros, C. (2009). When international counter-terrorism succeeds: Lessons from the defeat of 'revolutionary organization November 17th'. In C. C. Beyer & M. Bauer (Eds.), *Effectively countering terrorism* (141–152). Eastbourne, UK: Sussex Academic Press.

North Atlantic Treaty Organization. (July 2001). *Peace support operations* (Allied Joint Publication 3.4.1.). Retrieved from http://www.walterdorn.org/pdf/PSO_NATO_JointDoctrine_AJP_3-4-1_PSO_July2001.pdf

North Atlantic Treaty Organization. (2008). *Glossary of terms and definitions.* (AAP-6). Retrieved from http://www.fas.org/irp/doddir/other/nato2008.pdf

O'Brien, S. P. (2002). Anticipating the good, the bad, and the ugly: An early warning approach to conflict and instability analysis. *Journal of Conflict Resolution, 46*(6), 791–811.

Organization for Economic Cooperation and Development. (2008). *OECD Environmental Outlook to 2030.* OECD Publishing. doi: 10.1787/9789264040519-en

O'Hanlon, M. (2009). *The science of war: Defense budgeting, military technology, logistics, and combat outcomes.* Princeton, NJ: Princeton University Press.

O'Reilly, P. (1998). *Harnessing the unicorn: How to create opportunity and manage risk.* Aldershot, UK: Gower.

Owens, M. T. (2009). What to do about piracy? *FPRI E-notes.* Retrieved from http://www.fpri.org/enotes/200904.owens.piracy.html

Pape, R. (2005). *Dying to win: The strategic logic of suicide terrorism.* New York, NY: Random House.

Paul, C., Clarke, C. P., & Grill, B. (2010). *Victory has a thousand fathers: Sources of success in counterinsurgency.* Santa Monica, CA: RAND.

Pausus, J. G., & Keeley, J. E. (2009). A burning story: The role of fire in the history of life. *BioScience, 59*(7), 593–601.

Perl, R. F. (2002). The legal basis for counterterrorism activities in the United States. In National Research Council (Ed.), *High-Impact Terrorism: Proceedings of a Russian-American Workshop* (pp. 5–15). Washington, DC: National Academy Press.

Pherson, K. H., & Pherson, R. H. (2013). *Critical thinking for strategic intelligence.* Los Angeles, CA: Sage.

Poterba, J. M., Venti, S.F., & Wise, D. A. (2012). *Were they prepared for retirement? Financial status at advanced ages in the HRS and ahead cohorts* (NBER Working Paper No. 17824). Cambridge, MA: National Bureau of Economic Research.

Pressman, D. E. (2009). *Risk assessment decisions for violent political extremism.* Ottawa, Canada: Her Majesty the Queen in Right of Canada.

Przeworski, A. (2004). Democracy and economic development. In E. D. Mansfield & R. Sisson (Eds.), *The evolution of political knowledge: Democracy, autonomy, and conflict in comparative and international politics* (pp. 300–324). Columbus: Ohio State University Press.

Public Law 107–56. (2001). Retrieved from http://www.gpo.gov/fdsys/pkg/PLAW-107publ56/pdf/PLAW-107publ56.pdf

Public Safety Canada. (2011). *Federal emergency response plan.* Ottawa, Canada: Her Majesty the Queen in Right of Canada.

Public Safety Canada. (2012). *Emergency management vocabulary.* Gatineau, Quebec: Translation Bureau of the Government of Canada.

Public Safety Canada. (2013). *All hazards risk assessment methodology guidelines, 2012–2013.* Ottawa, Canada: Her Majesty the Queen in Right of Canada.

Rasler, K. A., & Thompson, W. R. (1989). *War and state making: The shaping of the global powers.* Boston, MA: Unwin Hyman.

Rasmussen, M. V. (2006). *The risk society at war: Terror, technology and strategy in the Twenty-First Century.* Cambridge, UK: Cambridge University Press.

Ratner, M., Belkin, P., Nichol, J., & Woehrel, S. (2013). *Europe's energy security: Options and challenges to natural gas supply diversification* (Report No. 7-5700). Washington, DC: Congressional Research Service.

Renn, O. (2008). White paper on risk governance. In O. Renn & K. D. Walker (Eds.), *Global risk governance: Concept and practice using the IRGC framework* (pp. 6–33). Dordecht, the Netherlands: Springer.

Reporters Without Borders. (2013). World Press Freedom Index. Retrieved from http://en.rsf.org/press-freedom-index-2013,1054.html

Reynolds, C. (1989). *The politics of war: A study of the rationality of violence in inter-state relations.* New York, NY: St. Martin's Press.

Ridge, T., & Bloom, L. (2009). *The test of our times: America under siege and how we can be safe again.* New York, NY: Thomas Dunne.

Rosenbau, E. (2013). On the front lines of military mental-health issues. *The Pennsylvania Gazette, 111*(3), 71–72.

Rowe, W. D. (1977). *An anatomy of risk.* London, UK: Wiley.

Rusnak, D. M., Kennedy, L. W., Eldivan, I. S., & Caplan, J. M. (2012). Analyzing terrorism using spatial analysis techniques: A case study of Turkish cities. In C. Lum & L. W. Kennedy (Eds.), *Evidence-based counterterrorism policy* (pp. 167–186). New York, NY: Springer.

Russett, B. (2010). Peace in the twenty-first century? *Current History, 109*(723), 11–16.

Sandler, R. L. (2009). *Character and environment: A virtue-oriented approach to environmental ethics.* New York, NY: Columbia University Press.

Silver, N. (2012). *The signal and the noise: Why so many predictions fail—but some don't.* New York, NY: Penguin.

Sky, E., & al-Qarawee, H. (2013). *Iraqi Sunnistan? Why separatism could rip the country apart—again.* Retrieved from http://www.foreignaffairs.com/articles/138777/emma-sky-and-harith-al-qarawee/iraqi-sunnistan

Smith, N. J. (Ed.). (2003). *Appraisal, risk and uncertainty* (Construction Management Series). London, UK: Thomas Telford.

Sproat, P. A. (1991). Can the state be terrorist? *Terrorism, 14*(1), 19–30.

Stefanova, B. M. (2012). European strategies for energy security in the natural gas market. *Journal of Strategic Security, 5*(3), 51–68.

Stevens, R. (1998). *American medicine and the public interest: A history of specialization.* Berkeley, CA: University of California.

Stohl, M., & Lopez, G. A. (Eds.). (1984). *The state as terrorist: The dynamics of governmental violence and repression.* London, UK: Aldwych.

Suder, G. G. S. (Ed.). (2004). *Terrorism and the international business environment: The security-business nexus.* Cheltenham, UK: Edward Elgar.

Suttmoeller, M., Chermak, S., Freilich, J. D., & Fitzgerald, S. (2011). Radicalization and risk assessment. In L. W. Kennedy & E. F. McGarrell (Eds.), *Crime and terrorism risk: Studies in criminology and criminal justice* (pp. 81–96). New York, NY: Routledge.

Svendsen, A. D. M. (2010). Re-fashioning risk: Comparing UK, US and Canadian security and intelligence efforts against terrorism. *Defense Studies, 10*(3), 307–335.

Swiss Re Group. (2012). Sigma preliminary estimates for 2012 [Press Release]. Zurich, Switzerland: Swiss Reinsurance Company Limited.

Swiss Re Group. (2013). Building a sustainable energy future: Risks and opportunities [Press Release]. Zurich, Switzerland: Swiss Reinsurance Company Limited.

Syphard, A. D., Radeloff, V. C., Hawbaker, T. J., & Stewart, S. I. (2009). Conservation threats due to human-caused increases in fire frequency in Mediterranean-Climate ecosystems. *Conservation Biology, 23*(3), 758–769.

Szeltner, M., Van Horn, C., & Zukin, C. (2013). *Diminished lives and futures: A portrait of America in the Great-Recession Era.* New Brunswick, NJ: John J. Heldrich Center for Workforce Development.

Taleb, N. N. (2007). *Black swan: The impact of the highly improbable.* New York, NY: Random House.

Tetlock, P. E. (2006). *Expert political judgment: How good is it? How can we know?* Princeton, NJ: Princeton University Press.

Tucker, J. B. (2002). Chemical terrorism: Assessing threats and responses. In National Research Council (Ed.), *High-Impact terrorism: Proceedings of a Russian-American workshop* (pp. 117–133). Washington, DC: National Academy Press.

Turnbull, N., & Internal Control Working Party. (1999). *Internal control: Guidance for directors on the combined code.* London, UK: Institute of Chartered Accountants.

U.K. Business Continuity Institute, National Counterterrorism Security Office, & London First. (2003). *Expecting the unexpected: Business continuity in an uncertain world.* London, UK: London First.

U.K. Cabinet Office. (2005). *Countries at risk of instability: Risk assessment and strategic analysis process manual.* London, UK: The Stationery Office.

U.K. Cabinet Office. (2008a). *The national security strategy of the United Kingdom: Security in an interdependent world* (Cm 7291). London, UK: The Stationery Office.

U.K. Cabinet Office. (2008b). *National risk register.* London, UK: The Stationery Office.

U.K. Cabinet Office. (2010). *A strong Britain in an age of uncertainty: The national security strategy.* London, UK: The Stationery Office. Retrieved from http://www.cabinetoffice.gov.uk/sites/default/files/resources/national-security-strategy.pdf

U.K. Cabinet Office. (2012a). *UK national risk register of civil emergencies.* London, UK: The Stationery Office.

U.K. Cabinet Office. (2012b). *Emergency preparedness.* Retrieved from http://www.cabinetoffice.gov.uk/resource-library/emergency-preparedness

U.K. Cabinet Office. (2012c). *Emergency response and recovery: Non-Statutory guidance accompanying the Civil Contingencies Act 2004* (4th ed.). Retrieved from https://www.gov.uk/government/uploads/system/uploads/attachment_data/file/61047/Emergency-Response-Recovery-24-7-12.pdf

U.K. Cabinet Office. (2013). *UK civil protection lexicon* (Version 2.1.1). Retrieved from https://www.gov.uk/government/publications/emergency-responder-interoperability-lexicon

U.K. Fire Service Inspectorate. (1998). *Fire service guide: Dynamic management of risk at operational incidents.* London, UK: The Stationery Office.

U.K. Home Office. (2006). *Countering international terrorism: The United Kingdom's strategy* (Cm 6888). London, UK: The Stationery Office.

U.K. Home Office. (2010). *The United Kingdom's strategy for countering chemical, biological, radiological, and nuclear (CBRN) terrorism.* London, UK: Office for Security and Counter-Terrorism.

U.K. House of Commons, Committee of Home Affairs. (2011a). *Unauthorized tapping into or hacking mobile communications.* London, UK: The Stationery Office.

U.K. House of Commons, Select Committee on Defense. (2011b). *The strategic defense and security review and the national security strategy.* London, UK: The Stationery Office.

U.K. House of Commons, Committee of Public Accounts. (2011c). *The cost-effective delivery of an armoured vehicle capability.* London, UK: The Stationery Office.

U.K. Information Commissioner's Office. (2006). *What price privacy? The unlawful trade in confidential private information.* London, UK: The Stationery Office.

U.K. Ministry of Defense. (2004a). *Corporate governance* (Joint Service Publication 525, 2nd ed.). Shrivenham, UK: Development, Concepts, and Doctrine Centre.

U.K. Ministry of Defense. (2004b). *The military contribution to peace support operations* (Joint Warfare Publication 3-50, 2nd ed.). Shrivenham, UK: Development, Concepts, and Doctrine Centre.

U.K. Ministry of Defense. (2009a). *Corporate governance and risk management* (Joint Service Publication 525, 3rd ed.). London, UK.

U.K. Ministry of Defense. (2009b). *Security and stabilization: The military contribution* (Joint Doctrine Publication 3-40). Shrivenham, UK: Development, Concepts, and Doctrine Centre.

U.K. Ministry of Defense. (2010a). *Global strategic trends out to 2040*. Shrivenham, UK: Development, Concepts, and Doctrine Centre. Retrieved from http://www.mod.uk/NR/rdonlyres/6AAFA4FA-C1D3-4343-B46F-05EE80314382/0/GST4_v9_Feb10.pdf

U.K. Ministry of Defense. (2010b). *Risk management* (Joint Service Publication 892, 1st edition). London: Author.

U.K. Ministry of Defense. (2011a). *Peacekeeping: An evolving role for military forces* (Joint Doctrine Note 5/11). Shrivenham, UK: Development, Concepts, and Doctrine Centre.

U.K. Ministry of Defense. (2011b). *Understanding and intelligence support to joint operations* (Joint Doctrine Publication 2-00, 3rd ed.). Shrivenham, UK: Development, Concepts, and Doctrine Centre.

U.K. Ministry of Defense. (2011c). *Business continuity management* (Joint Service Publication 503, 5th ed.). London, UK: Author.

U.K. National Archives. (2008). *Managing information risk: A guide for accounting officers, board members, and senior information risk owners*. Retrieved from http://www.nationalarchives.gov.uk/services/publications/information-risk.pdf

U.K. National Audit Office. (2000). *Supporting innovation: Managing risk in government departments*. London, UK: Author. Retrieved from http://www.nao.org.uk/publications/9900/managing_risk_in_gov_depts.aspx

U.K. National Audit Office. (2011). *Ministry of Defense: The cost-effective delivery of an armoured vehicle capability*. London, UK: The Stationery Office.

U.K. Office of Government Commerce. (2009). *An introduction to PRINCE2: Managing and directing successful projects*. London, UK: The Stationery Office.

U.K. Prime Minister's Strategy Unit. (2002). *Risk: Improving government's capacity to handle risk and uncertainty*. London, UK: Cabinet Office. Retrieved from http://www.integra.com.bo/articulos/RISK%20IMPROVING%20GOVERMENT.pdf

U.K. Prime Minister's Strategy Unit. (February 2005). *Investing in prevention: An international strategy to manage risks of instability and improve crisis response*. London, UK: Cabinet Office. Retrieved from http://webarchive.nationalarchives.gov.uk/+/http://www.cabinetoffice.gov.uk/media/cabinetoffice/strategy/assets/investing.pdf

U.K. Treasury. (2004). *The orange book: The management of risk—principles and concepts*. London,UK. Retrieved from http://www.hm-treasury.gov.uk/d/orange_book.pdf

United Nations. (2006). *Field security handbook*. New York, NY: Author.

United Nations Center for International Crime Prevention. (2000). Assessing transnational organized crime: Results of a pilot survey of forty selected organized criminal groups in sixteen countries. *Trends in Organized Crime*, 6(2), 44–92.

United Nations Department of Humanitarian Affairs. (1992). *Internationally agreed glossary of basic terms related to disaster management* (DHA/93/36). Geneva, Switzerland: Author.

United Nations Department of Peacekeeping Operations. (2008). *United Nations peacekeeping operations: Principles and guidelines*. New York, NY: Author.

United Nations Development Program. (1994). *Vulnerability and Risk assessment* (2nd ed.). New York, NY: Author.

United Nations Office for International Strategy for Disaster Reduction. (2009). *UNISDR terminology on disaster risk reduction*. New York, NY: Author.

United Nations Office for the Coordination of Humanitarian Affairs. (2003). *Glossary of humanitarian terms in relation to the protection of civilians in armed conflict*. New York, NY: Author.

United Nations Office of Drugs and Crime. (2010). *The globalization of crime: A transnational organized crime threat assessment*. New York, NY: Author.

United Nations Secretariat. (1995). *Results of the supplement to the fourth United Nations survey of crime trends and operations of criminal justice systems on transnational crime*. New York, NY: UN.

United States Army. (2008). *Operations* (Field Manual 3-0). Washington, DC: Department of the Army. Retrieved from http://downloads.army.mil/fm3-0/FM3-0.pdf

United States Computer Emergency Readiness Team. (n.d.). Report phishing sites. Retrieved from http://www.us-cert.gov/report-phishing

U.S. Department of Defense. (2008). *Unified facilities criteria: DOD security engineering facilities planning manual* (UFC 4-020-01). Retrieved from https://pdc.usace.army.mil/library/ufc/4-020-01

U.S. Department of Defense. (2012a). *Minimum antiterrorism standards for buildings* (UFC 4-010-01). Retrieved from http://www.wbdg.org/ccb/DOD/UFC/ufc_4_010_01.pdf

U.S. Department of Defense. (2012b). *Dictionary of military and associated terms* (Joint Publication 1-02). Retrieved from http://www.dtic.mil/doctrine/new_pubs/jp1_02.pdf

U.S. Department of Homeland Security. (2009). *National infrastructure protection plan: Partnering to enhance protection and resiliency*. Retrieved from http://www.dhs.gov/xlibrary/assets/NIPP_Plan.pdf

U.S. Department of Homeland Security. (2010). *Risk lexicon*. Washington, DC: Author.

U.S. Department of Homeland Security. (2011). *National preparedness goal* (1st ed.). Washington, DC: Government Printing Office.

U.S. Department of State. (2006). *Overseas Security Policy Board, Security Standards and Policy Handbook* (12 FAH-6). Washington, DC: Author.

U.S. Department of State. (2010). *Leading through civilian power: The first quadrennial diplomacy and development review*. Washington, DC: GPO. Retrieved from http://www.state.gov/s/dmr/qddr/index.htm

U.S. Food and Drug Administration. (2005). *The food defect action levels*. Retrieved from http://www.fda.gov/Food/GuidanceRegulation/GuidanceDocumentsRegulatoryInformation/SanitationTransportation/ucm056174.htm#intro

U.S. Federal Emergency Management Agency. (1992). *Federal response plan; With revisions*. Washington, DC: Author.

U.S. Federal Emergency Management Agency. (1999). *The professional in emergency management* (IS-513). Emmitsburg, MD: Emergency Management Institute.

U.S. Federal Emergency Management Agency. (2005). *Risk assessment: A how-to guide to mitigate potential terrorist attacks against buildings* (Management Series, FEMA 452). Washington, DC: Author.

U.S. Federal Emergency Management Agency. (2010). *Multi-Hazard identification and assessment (MHIRA)*. Washington, DC: Author.

U.S. Government Accountability Office. (1998). *Threat and risk assessments can help prioritize and target program investments* (GAO/NSIAD-98-74). Washington, DC: Author.

U. S. Government Accountability Office. (2005a). *Protection of chemical and water infrastructure federal requirements, actions of selected facilities, and remaining challenges* (GAO-05-327). Washington, DC: Author.

U.S. Government Accountability Office. (2005b). *Critical infrastructure protection: Department of Homeland Security faces challenges in fulfilling cybersecurity responsibilities* (GAO-05-434). Washington, DC: Author.

U.S. Government Accountability Office. (2005c). *Further refinements needed to assess risks and prioritize protective measures at ports and other critical infrastructure* (GAO-06-91). Washington, DC: Author.

U.S. Government Accountability Office. (2008a). *Homeland security: DHS risk-based grant methodology is reasonable, but current version's measure of vulnerability is limited* (GAO-08-852). Washington, DC: Author.

U.S. Government Accountability Office. (2008b). *Homeland security grant program (HSGP) risk-based distribution methods*. (Presentation to Congressional Committees, GAO-09-168R). Retrieved from http://www.gao.gov/new.items/d09168r.pdf

U.S. Government Accountability Office. (2009). *State Department: Diplomatic security's recent growth warrants strategic review* (GAO-10-156). Washington, DC: Author.

U.S. Government Accountability Office. (2011). *Defense department cyber efforts: Definitions, focal point, and methodology needed for DOD to develop full-spectrum cyberspace budget estimates* (GAO-11-695R). Washington, DC: Author.

U.S. Government Accountability Office. (2012). *Supply chain security: Container security programs have matured, but uncertainty persists over the future of 100 percent scanning*. ReportNo. GAO-12-422T. Retrieved from http://www.gao.gov/assets/590/588253.pdf

U.S. Institute of Medicine. (2002). S. L. Knobler, A. A. F. Mahmoud, & L. A. Pray. (Eds.). *Biological threats and terrorism: Assessing the science and response capabilities* (Workshop Summary). Washington, DC: National Academy Press.

U.S. Interagency Working Group on the International Crime Control Strategy. (2000). *International crime threat assessment*. Rockville, Maryland: National Institute of Justice.

U.S. Office of the National Counterintelligence Executive. (2011). *Foreign Spies stealing US economic secrets in cyberspace: Report to Congress on foreign economic collection and industrial espionage, 2009-2011*. Retrieved from http://www.ncix.gov/publications/reports/fecie_all/Foreign_economic_Collection_2011.pdf

U.S. White House. (2011). *National srategy for counterterrorism*. Washington, DC: GPO.

Valentino, B. A., Huth, P. K., & Croco, S. E. (2010). Bear any burden? How democracies minimize the costs of war. *The Journal of Politics, 72*(4), 528–544.

Van Brunschot, E. G., & Kennedy, L. W. (2008). *Risk balance and security.* Los Angeles, CA: Sage.

Veselovsky, S. (2013). *Wars of the future.* Retrieved from Russian International Affairs Council website: http://russiancouncil.ru/en/inner/?id_4=1318

ViewDNS. (2012). Current state of Internet censorship in Iran. Retrieved from http://viewdns.info/research/current-state-of-internet-censorship-in-iran/

Wardlaw, G. (1989). *Political terrorism: Theory, tactics, and counter-measures* (2nd ed.). Cambridge, UK: Cambridge University Press.

Waring, A. E., & Glendon, A. I. (1998). *Managing risk.* London, UK: Thomson Learning.

Walter, B. F. (1999). Introduction, designing transitions from civil war. B. F. Walter & J. Snyder (Eds.), *Civil wars, insecurity, and intervention* (pp. 1–12, 38–69). New York, NY: Columbia Press.

Weinberg, L., & Pedahzur, A. (2003). *Political parties and terrorist groups.* London, UK: Routledge.

Weisz, G. (2005). *Divide and conquer: A comparative history of medical specialization.* New York, NY: Oxford University Press.

Westerling, A. L., Hidlago, H. G., Cayan, D. R., & Swetman, T. W. (2006). Warming and earlier spring increase western US forest wildfire activity. *Science,* 313, 940–943.

Whitlock, C. (2012, August 27). U.S. troops tried to burn 500 copies of Koran, investigation says. *Washington Post.*

World Health Organization. (2009). *Global health risks: Mortality and burden of disease attributable to selected major risks.* Geneva, Switzerland: Author.

World Health Organization. (2012). *World health statistics 2012.* Geneva, Switzerland: Author.

World Health Organization. (2012). *Defeating malaria in Asia, the Pacific, Americas, Middle East, and Europe.* Geneva, Switzerland: Author.

Wright, Q. (1942). *A study of war* (Vols. 1–2.). Chicago, IL: University of Chicago Press.

Wilkinson, P. (1977). *Terrorism and the liberal state.* London, UK: Macmillan.

Wilkinson, P. (2010). Terrorism. In V. Mauer & M. D. Cavelty (Eds.), *The Routledge handbook of security studies.* London, UK: Routledge.

Williams, P., & Godson R. (2002). Anticipating organized and transnational crime. *Crime, Law, and Social Justice, 37*(4), 311–355.

Wilson, C. (2003). *Computer attack and cyber terrorism: Vulnerabilities and policy issues for congress* (Report RL32114). Washington, DC: Congressional Research Service.

Wisner, B., Blaikie, P., Cannon, T., & Davis, I. (2004). *At risk: Natural hazards, people's vulnerability and disasters* (2nd ed.). London, UK: Routledge.

World Economic Forum. (2013). W. L. Howell (Ed.)., *Global risks 2013.* Geneva, Switzerland: Author. Retrieved from http://www3.weforum.org/docs/WEF_GlobalRisks_Report_2013.pdf

Yannakogeorgos, P. A. (2011). Privatized cybersecurity and the challenges of securing the digital environment. In L. W. Kennedy & E. F. McGarrell (Eds.), *Crime and terrorism risk: Studies in criminology and criminal justice* (pp. 255–267). New York, NY: Routledge.

Zenko, M. (2012). There's nothing in the water: 10 things that kill more people than sharks. *Foreign Policy.* Retrieved from http://www.foreignpolicy.com/articles/2012/08/10/shark_week_10_things_more_deadly

Zhukov, Y. M. (2013, 20 March). Trouble in the eastern Mediterranean Sea: The coming dash for gas. *Foreign Affairs.* Retrieved from http://www.foreignaffairs.com/articles/139069/yuri-m-zhukov/trouble-in-the-eastern-mediterranean-sea

Index